KENNETH GRAHAME
AN INNOCENT IN THE WILD WOOD

THE AUTHOR

Alison Prince is the author of many highly acclaimed children's books, including *The Doubting Kind*, *The Ghost Within* and *The Turkey's Nest*. She is also known for her children's television programmes, particularly *Trumpton* with its popular catch-phrase 'Pugh, Pugh, Barney McGrew . . .' *Kenneth Grahame: An Innocent in the Wild Wood*, which was published by Allison & Busby in hardback in 1994, is her first biography. Since then she has written her first adult novel, *The Witching Tree*, which Allison & Busby will be launching at the same time as this paperback. She lives on the Isle of Arran with two cats and two dogs.

KENNETH GRAHAME

AN INNOCENT IN THE
WILD WOOD

Alison Prince

a&b

First published in paperback in Great Britain in 1996 by
Allison & Busby Ltd
179 King's Cross Road
London WC1X 9BZ

First published in hardcover by Allison & Busby in 1994

A catalogue record for this book is available from the British Library

ISBN 0 74900 233 6

Typeset by TW Typesetting, Plymouth, Devon
Printed and bound in Great Britain by
WBC Book Manufacturers, Bridgend, Mid Glamorgan

Contents

For Lettice Philomena David

List of Illustrations

Acknowledgements

My thanks are due to the Scottish Arts Council for financial help in the form of a Travel and Research Grant. Without this assistance, the book could not have been written.

Among the many people who have given support and encouragement, I would particularly like to mention Louis Miller for his help with photography and Argyll researches, Margaret Malpas for assistance and hospitality in Oxford, and Audrey McCrone for her untiring efforts to locate second-hand books.

Professionals in the field have been marvellously co-operative, and I was given valuable help by Colonel Clements of Dorneywood in providing hitherto unseen letters and manuscripts. The staff of the Mitchell Library, Glasgow, were constantly helpful in providing photocopies and books, and my thanks are also due to the staff of the Bodleian Library, Oxford. I am indebted also to the archivists of Edinburgh and of Christ Church, Oxford, and particularly to Murdo MacDonald, archivist of Argyll, for his locating of documents.

I am grateful to the following for permission to quote from material in which they hold the copyright: David Higham Associates Ltd, for *Kenneth Grahame* by Peter Green, John Murray, 1959; Methuen, for *Kenneth Grahame: Life, Letters and Unpublished Work*, Methuen, 1933; and to Kenneth White for 'Out of Asia 8' from *The Bird Path*, Kenneth White, 1989

I am also grateful to Malcolm S. Oxley of St Edward's School, Oxford, for supplying me with the history of the school, and to the many people who have patiently answered small queries; and, finally, I would like to thank Samantha Boorer for her skilled and perceptive secretarial work in helping to prepare this book.

Alison Prince
Isle of Arran
September 1993

1

Edinburgh and the Wild West

E dinburgh is distinguished. Even today, when most towns have sunk into a sameness of shopping precincts and supermarkets, it preserves its dramatic, haughty flavour. As if alarmed by its own theatricality, it is courteous rather than kind, and hard-bitten rather than enthusiastic. "East windy and West-Endy" was the traditional Glasgow description of it, uttered with some complacency from that western city's warmth and social cohesion, and it is true that Edinburgh tends to be, in every sense of the word, cool. And yet, to come to it by train, under the shadow of the sheer cliff on which the Castle stands, is to be aware of an ineffable grandeur. The underlying geography of the place dominates the town; for all the classical architecture and leaping bridges and the grand boulevard of Princes Street, Edinburgh cannot dismiss the impressiveness of the rock and the water and the ever-moving sky. The strident rhythms of "Caledonia stern and wild" rise from the childhood memory of anyone old enough to have grown up in a familiarity with that torrent of verse, and it is perfectly plain why this city is the capital of Scotland.

At Edinburgh's heart lies a controlled energy like the radioactivity of its granite, kept in check by the severity of the material itself. Somewhere within its very geology, there is a hard, formal magic. In the mid-nineteenth century, that intrinsic flavour must have been much stronger, undiluted by the visual blanketing of modern architecture and the universality of chain-stores, banks and building societies. For Kenneth Grahame, who was not old enough to understand the city in any conscious way when his parents removed him from it, the sense of powerful landscape, more real and dependable than any construct of human beings, remained throughout his life the most dominating influence.

Castle Street rises from the Caledonian end of Princes Street, directly opposite the craggy height of the Castle itself. Above the new shop-fronts, the tall terraces are still gracious and, in their midst, a little before the roundabout at the crossing of George Street, one particular house is outstandingly impressive.

Number 32, now the offices of a chartered surveyor, is double-fronted, with a total of six floors rising from the basement to the small servants' rooms set into the grey slate roof. Curved railings of a modest, practical kind flank the two stone steps which lead to the front door, and the windows are tall and beautifully proportioned. A plaque on the wall used to read, "Kenneth Grahame of the Golden Age was born here", though it has now been replaced by one which cites Grahame as the author of *The Wind in the Willows*. It seems odd, perhaps, that the original made no reference to the famous book; one might think that "the golden age" was a sentimental description of the time in which Grahame lived.

In a sense, this is true. For his contemporaries, it was not as a children's writer that Grahame was known, but as an essayist and rememberer of his own childhood. Long before Toad and Mole and Rat were thought of, adult Victorian readers were responding to Kenneth Grahame's revelation of the child's point of view in a book which both shocked and enchanted them. *The Golden Age*, published in 1895, is a half-fictionalised account of growing up, recalled with nostalgia and rueful humour, and with an underlying thread of anger which dispels any trace of mawkishness. It was for the authorship of this that the original plaque commemorated him, and it is odd to realise that, in the eyes of those who put it there, our own view of Grahame as the writer of a classic *children's* book would be quite unfamiliar. To his late-Victorian contemporaries, Kenneth Grahame followed a well-established literary tradition, being an essayist very close in character to Robert Louis Stevenson, who was only nine years his senior.

This, too, comes as something of a shock, for *The Wind in the Willows* has the feel of a twentieth-century book, whereas Stevenson seems not far removed from the Victorian grandeur of Sir Walter Scott. The connection was, in fact, tangibly present in the young Kenneth's life, for Sir Walter had lived for twenty-four years just across the road, at 39 North Castle Street. The house is there to this day, narrow and bow-fronted, much less grand than the Grahames' residence further down towards Princes Street, despite its owner's eminence. Although the great man left there in 1826, he was such a towering figure of his time that his presence was still felt in Castle Street after his departure, and those who read Scott in our own time might reasonably say that Edinburgh is even now imbued with his spirit.

The Grahames' house has much to say, in its silent way, about the background which made Kenneth the complex, self-guarding person he was. The architecture itself embodies contradictions. Built in the grand style, there is a touch of the arrogant aestheticism which speaks of absolute financial security, and yet the design stops short of flamboyance. The silvery granite of the north-east has none of the near-foppishness of Bath. There is a decent restraint implicit in the plain façade of this house, and, too, in the almost Roman breadth of Castle Street. The Scottish capital is the antithesis of New York, where the streets are canyons packed with human activity and self-obsession. In Edinburgh, the wind-blown sky and rocky landscape form an active part of the city and impose their own reminder that humankind is not all-powerful. It expresses the essential Scottish contradiction between creative energy and a God-fearing respect for the way things are. Whoever ran the big house in Castle Street would need to observe both elements in order to keep a proper balance between ostentation and modesty.

Kenneth Grahame's father, James Cunningham Grahame, could not keep that balance, for he was unable to find it within himself. He was an aristocrat born into the failing years of aristocratic rule, when the newly rich businessmen were taking over from the easy old power of the cultured, high-born families. On both his mother's and his father's side, Cunningham Grahame could trace his descent back through the Stuarts to Robert the Bruce, and he had inherited an aristocratic confidence which, coupled with a low boredom threshold, made him impatient with the mundane details of everyday life. Ostentation ruled him. He was a *bon viveur*, a poet, a spender of money; a popular man with a taste for good claret which brought him more friends than his unenthusiastically pursued legal career. As a king, he might have been splendid, but royal freebooting was a vanished option. The more recent generations of his family had gone into banking and law, while the earlier ones had generally settled for the Church.

Religion added its own tensions to the situation in which Cunningham found himself. His instinctive desire to be happy and idle was directly opposed to the Calvinism which had dominated his childhood. He was a man whose inner being was charged with a sense of excitement and infinite possibility, but he had been sternly taught to repress these feelings. He obediently studied law and became an advocate, and kept his writing of poetry so secret that it would never have been known at all but for a note by his cousin, Colonel John Grahame, saying that Cunningham "was a poet of no mean order, with a wonderful spirit of imagination".[1] Such creativity was more likely to be thought of by his elders as Original Sin than originality. As a result, the young man felt a guilt about his own nature which prevented him from being what he wanted to be, while he could not with enthusiasm be what he was supposed to be. His appearances in court had a certain popular following among his colleagues, but more for their entertainment value than the thoroughness of their preparation – and he drank heavily.

On 13 March 1855, when he was twenty-four years old, Cunningham married Bessie Ingles, the beautiful and extremely practical daughter of David and Mary Ingles, of Heriot Row, Edinburgh, and brought her to the house in Castle Street. He himself had lived at 118 Princes Street. Although Cunningham's father had been a lawyer, in the family tradition, Bessie came of merchant stock, and had been born in Gibraltar. World travellers are apt to have an airy confidence about them, and Bessie had certainly inherited or acquired this quality. At eighteen, she was full of gaiety and charm, and Cunningham adored her. A daughter, Helen, was born to them

3

a year after their marriage, followed in 1858 by Thomas William, always known as Willie.

The third child, Kenneth, was born in the icy morning of 8 March 1859, when the east wind, according to family legend, scoured along Princes Street and snow lay in the gutters.[2] Dr James Simpson, whose pioneering use of chloroform in childbirth had become fashionable ever since Queen Victoria availed herself of it, came to the house just before dawn, and by eight in the morning had delivered Bessie of a hefty baby. Shaking hands with the proud father on the doorstep as he went out, Simpson guessed, rightly, that the child weighed little short of nine pounds. And, he said with optimism as he pulled his sealskin coat more tightly round him, blossom-time would not be long.

"The beloved professor", as he was generally known, may have felt that the family whose house he was leaving had cause to be optimistic. Cunningham and Bessie were a handsome young couple, well supplied with life's necessities. Compared with the births he had seen in his earlier years among the insanitary closes round the Grassmarket, this was a fairy-tale land, and the boy he had just delivered seemed set to be smiled upon by all good fortune.

Fairy-tales, like pearls, depend for their existence on the speck of irritant matter at the heart of the oyster. In fiction, the device of the late-arriving evil godmother, excluded from the christening, provides the impetus for the whole story. Without that tension, the human struggle for a successful outcome would never be established. Any tale worth the telling must be set against a fate which is at least partially adverse.

A real-life story must obey the same rules. Reading of someone whose circumstances are smooth and easy arouses a perverse desire for the banana-skin; the malign element lies at the base of all humour and all recognition, for the one thing we share is fallibility. The new-born Kenneth Grahame was a princeling of Scottish royal blood, but the jealous fairy made sure that he would never be dull or self-satisfied.

The grit in the Grahame oyster was, of course, Cunningham's drinking. It is only the very rich who can afford to drink as a release from uncongenial reality, and the very rich usually do not need to. Cunningham Grahame, enmeshed in an upper-middle-class respectability which was not of his choosing, drank, as most alcoholics do, for the illusion of being in touch with his true self. Good claret was far more socially acceptable than the frequently used hashish and opium which were such a marked feature of Victorian society, and to this day there is a tolerance of aberrant and embarrassing behaviour among those "under the influence" (as the smiling description goes) which is denied to the users of other drugs. For Cunningham, drinking could, for a while, seem innocently convivial.

By the time Kenneth was born, the family was beginning to feel the strain

4

of Cunningham's "weakness", as his daughter afterwards called it.[3] The financial effects of heavy drinking are two-edged, for the drinker spends a lot while gradually becoming less able to earn. Appearances, however, had to be kept up. If Bessie were worried about the situation, she could not confide in anyone other than her closest and most intimately trusted relations, for the shame and social ignominy which resulted from a man's failure to be "in control" were dreaded. She went on presiding over dinner parties and entertaining her husband's guests with the sparkling gaiety for which she is best remembered, and tried to decide what to do.

There was no doubt that Bessie Grahame's husband adored her. He liked nothing better than to show her off to his friends, delighting in her capable running of the house, her beauty and her liveliness. Unwittingly, she may have added to the tightening of the knot, for she must have made his business life seem doubly unattractive. A romantic, sensitive man, deeply in love with his beautiful wife, does not find it easy to attend to the distasteful tedium of what is supposed to be his career. As fewer people sought Cunningham's legal advice and the whispers ran round Edinburgh, the new fear of failure gave him additional reason to seek oblivion. There must have seemed no way out of the nightmare, and no release from the discomfort of his pent-up feelings. His children were still very young, and it was not until later that he would find an outlet in quoting long stanzas of Scott and Macaulay to them as they accompanied him on walks.

There are no signs that Cunningham was consciously aware of his frustrations, but this is hardly surprising. His Calvinist upbringing had given him a fixed structure of right and wrong in which feeling was presented as an irresponsible temptation to self-indulgence, a gift, not of God, but of the Devil. His struggle was to subdue it rather than to understand it. He was not alone. Earlier in the century, the unhappy Charlotte Brontë, herself the child of a ferociously repressive clergyman, had written to a friend in an agony of guilt because her "urgent thirst to see, to know, to learn" appeared to be the product of "rebellious and absurd emotions". Having "quelled them in five minutes", she said sternly, "I hope they will not revive, for they were acutely painful."

A poetic skeleton in the family cupboard perhaps made Cunningham particularly wary of revealing his secret versifying. His grand-uncle James had produced several books of religious poetry, including one called *Sabbath Walks*, and they were sufficiently bad for Lord Byron to have taken notice of them. He was, as Kenneth remarked, "a little nasty" about Uncle James.

> Lo! the Sabbath bard,
> Sepulchral Grahame, pours his notes sublime
> In mangled prose, nor e'en aspires to rhyme,
> Breaks into blank the Gospel of St Luke

And boldly pilfers from the Pentateuch;
And undisturbed by conscientious qualms,
Perverts the Prophets and purloins the Psalms.

In a 1933 biography which was heavily influenced by Grahame's widow, Patrick Chalmers doggedly refers to Uncle James as a "pleasing poet", even though Byron had added a footnote to warn the public that "Mr Grahame has poured forth two volumes of cant, under the names of *Sabbath Walks* and *Biblical Pictures*". Kenneth claimed firmly that he had never read these works. Another relative, Mrs Francis Grahame, wrote a "temperance tale" called *The Curse of the Claverings* which was published when Kenneth was seven years old, and one must wonder whether she had Cunningham Grahame in mind for, by that time, alcohol had ruined his life.

In the months following Kenneth's birth, Bessie must have become aware that the family was heading towards a crisis. The big house, with its servants and its continuing lavish entertainment, was a costly burden, and her husband's career was foundering in his ever-worsening alcoholic habit. In the immense secrecy which such an impending disaster imposed, she laid her plans. Cunningham's family was nothing if not well connected, and his mother, who lived in Edinburgh, was a shrewd, sensible woman, well aware of the problem. Half-measures would not do. A radical change in the situation was called for, and it would have to be one which was socially acceptable, preferably disguised as a good opportunity.

The solution was a drastic one. Before Kenneth was a year old, Cunningham Grahame had applied for, and been awarded, the post of Sheriff-Substitute of Argyll, based in the distant town of Inveraray. In these days of easy communication, it is difficult to comprehend exactly how dramatic the move was. By Edinburgh standards, to go to the wild West of Scotland was tantamount to emigration.

Scottish affairs, until comparatively recently, were run on an essentially tribal basis. Argyll was Campbell country, and this makes it doubly bizarre that an East-Coast Grahame should have been appointed to a prime administrative job there. The suspicion that strings were pulled is impossible to discard, though the question of who did the pulling must remain speculative. Cunningham himself may have realised in a moment of awful sobriety that his only chance was to cut and run, but the master-minding of the move seems unlikely to have been his. Bessie and her mother-in-law could between them claim the advantages of aristocratic family ties, charm and considerable organising ability, and Cunningham, whether active in the proposal or not, was in no position to raise objections. The house was sold, and the family, together with the children's nurse, Ferguson, packed up and set out for Ardrishaig, on the West Coast.

The move almost literally jolted the infant Kenneth into a first awareness of his surroundings. He declared later that he remembered "shiny black buttons, buttons that dug into dusty, blue cloth".[4] It is an apt description of the upholstery of a first-class carriage in the train which took them westward from the old Caledonian station in Edinburgh, just round the corner from the house which they were leaving. The journey continued on one of the many paddle steamers which criss-crossed the sea-lochs and the Firth of Clyde, chugging past Bute to call at Tighnabruaich and Tarbert and, finally, Ardrishaig. And there, in the little harbour town with its fishing boats and "puffers", the family settled in rented accommodation. The house was called Annfield Lodge, and it still exists, a large granite villa on Tarbert Road, now known as Allt-na-Craig. It was then the property of Dugald MacLachlan. Among the letters filed by the County Assessor is one demanding of Cunningham Grahame 12/- of Assessed Taxes "being the duty for a dog".

Pleasant though the house was, Cunningham Grahame could spend little time there. His job obliged him to work in Inveraray, where the courts were situated and, in the pre-motorised age, the journey from Ardrishaig was too long to be undertaken on a daily basis. At the time, there was a move afoot to re-site the courts in the rising town of Lochgilphead, a proposal which was naturally opposed by the dignitaries of Inveraray, and the Grahames' living arrangements were caught up in these negotiations. In order to unite the Sheriff and his job in Inveraray, it was essential for local political reasons to make him comfortable there. A letter from Alexander Campbell of Auchindarroch to the Commissioners of Supply of Argyllshire is indignant on the new Sheriff's behalf, pointing out that "Mr Sheriff Grahame has, since his appointment, been put to the double expense of a house near Lochgilphead for the accommodation of his family, and another in Inveraray for the performance of his official duties – the latter being quite unsuitable for a family residence. That he should have submitted to this expense and inconvenience, resulting as it does in living almost entirely absent from his family, offers ample evidence of the quality of the accommodation at present offered by the town of Inveraray."[5]

The Inveraray lobby had found itself a powerful, if unwitting ally in Sheriff Grahame, a stranger with no Argyll home base. To settle him and his family in Inveraray would almost certainly prevent the loss of the courts to Lochgilphead. Cunningham was evidently aware of his importance in the negotiations and, with a lawyer's acumen, he pushed his advantage. A further letter from Alexander Campbell reveals that he "declined to build upon the feu offered to him by the Duke of Argyll". Slightly shocked, Campbell went on to remark that "it might reasonably have been supposed that the Duke had fulfilled all that he was called to do, but his Grace has very liberally consented to build a large and handsome house for the Sheriff, and it is at present in the course of construction".

This letter was dated 1 March 1862, so the Grahames had been in Argyll for two years while the battle of local interests raged over their heads. The plans for the big house were drawn up by the Duke's architect, George Devey, an Englishman who had built other houses in Argyllshire, and the site which Cunningham condescended to accept was a prime one with a commanding view across the loch.

As far as the Grahames' family life was concerned, the move must have seemed a success. In the utterly new surroundings of the west, with its glinting sea between the long blue shapes of the islands and its sudden comings and goings of rain and sun across the water, life was relaxed and undemanding. Although the newcomers were undoubtedly a source of great curiosity and speculation among the town's residents, social life did not immediately embrace them. As the occupiers of a rented house, the Grahames did not qualify for inclusion in the established, property-owning society, and the relentless entertaining which had dominated their Edinburgh life gave way to an easier pace. The children were blissfully happy, and Kenneth's extraordinarily clear memory is precise about the delights of Mrs Jenkins's shop where you could buy sticky gingerbread and "conversation lozenges", and where the cockatoo called after you down the street. Their nurse-maid was being courted by the local policeman. Whether this was Ferguson herself is doubtful; if it was, she certainly never married him. It seems more likely that a local girl had been engaged as an assistant, complete with her thriving emotional life. Either way, the romance was partially conducted during leisurely trips in a rowing boat, accompanied, to their delight, by the children. They had two Cairn terriers, Bhodach and Cailliach (Gaelic for The Old Man and The Old Woman), and Helen wrote, years later, that "I rather think we had two Bhodachs one after the other. They came from the MacNeills of Colonsay who lived at Ardlussa. Mr Malcolm MacNeill was in the 78th Highlanders with Uncle Harry Ingles – one of the Bhodachs was his ... We knew a good many Gaelic phrases from the fishermen at Ardrishaig & cd say How are you? & Very well this morning – & had saithe and lythe out of the loch for breakfast – those were happy days."[6]

She added, "I don't remember the terriers coming up to the nursery – we had a big black dog called Don, extremely intelligent, who used to go out with us ..."

There was lots of going out. A photograph of Cunningham with his children shows the two little boys sailor-hatted and jacketed, Helen looking a little like Alice in Wonderland in ribbon-bordered skirts and a cape thrown about her shoulders. Their father is a big, bearded man whose unruly hair recedes from a high forehead. He stares resolutely away from the camera, puffy-featured and untidy, a Cairn terrier at his feet. Kenneth, at two or three years old, is hardly bigger than the dog, but grave and self-possessed, his brother Willie standing behind him with something of his father's air of reluctant compliance.

In the two years spent in Ardrishaig, Kenneth developed a passionate love of the sea and all its associated activities. The fishermen befriended the two little boys who hung so constantly round the harbour, fascinated by the lapping of water under boat-hulls and by the fishergirls who were so swift and so careless of mess as they threaded lug-worm and mussel on to the endless line of hooks. Rory McGilp, bearded and brown-faced, with eyes a paler blue than his jersey, gave each of the lads a carved model boat, *The Ocean's Pride* for Willie and *The Canty Queen* for Kenneth. Poor Helen was not given one; though the eldest, she was a girl, and so had to submit to the befrilled decorum expected of her, despite her robust independence of mind.

For Kenneth there were no such inhibitions. He was intoxicated with the joys of water and boats, and forty years later he could recall this first delight, re-living it through Mole "as he leant back in his seat and surveyed the cushions, the oars, the rowlocks, and all the fascinating fittings and felt the boat sway lightly under him".[7] With the Water Rat, he assures the newcomer that "there is *nothing* – absolutely nothing – half so much worth doing as simply messing about in boats". In his own voice, he recalled the "big, black-sided fishing boats" and the hours spent on the pier, watching the steamers with their "ever recurrent throb of paddle-wheel, the rush and foam of beaten water among the piles, splash of ropes and rumble of gangways".[8] While disparaging train journeys as tedious and usually disappointing, he conceded that they could sometimes lift the heart when "over the reeking house-tops there appeared a tangled tracery of masts, while a delicate waft of tar and harbour-mud breathed of the authentic, unsuspected Paradise at hand".[9]

Cunningham Grahame, when free of his duties at the Inveraray courts, shared his small son's delight. These were the years when he would walk with his children and quote the rolling verses which stayed in Kenneth's head long after the time in Ardrishaig had ended and the big man who had held his hand was no more. The idea of fatherhood lived on in the smell of seaweed and in the orderly tangles of rope and sun-faded brown canvas and in the bold stride of Longfellow's metre.

I remember the black wharves and the slips
And the sea-tides tossing free;
And the Spanish sailors with bearded lips
And the beauty and mystery of the ships
And the magic of the sea.

Early in 1863, Dugald MacLachlan sold Annfield Lodge, but it may have been before this that the family moved along the coast to Lochgilphead, where the shallower water of the loch's end offers no harbour for sea-going

9

ships. Again, they rented a house while work continued on the construction of their eventual home. Lochgilphead lacks the maritime bustle of Ardrishaig, but it stands at the junction of the roads from Tarbert and from Oban with the main route to Glasgow, and so has a kind of centrality which may have appealed to the extrovert Bessie, who always liked to be "in the swim". For the young Kenneth, it was landscape both calmer and wilder, a dreaming place "among the gleaming lochs and sinuous firths of the Western Highlands", as he wrote later, "where, twice a week maybe, the strange visitant crept by headland and bay, a piece of the busy, mysterious outer world".[10] The words are charged with the awareness that the little inlet called Loch Gilp was no more than a backwater which ran a short distance inland from the meandering length of Loch Fyne.

The stay in Lochgilphead had been a temporary and fairly brief one, for the house in Inveraray was completed in May 1863, and the Grahames moved in to take possession of its comfortable splendour. Built of red sandstone, with steeply pitched roofs interrupted by gabled windows, the house combined grandeur with appealing domesticity. It was, in truth, "a large and handsome house", as visitors may confirm to this day, for it is now the Loch Fyne Hotel.

The Sheriff of Argyll was well and truly installed in Inveraray, and the social recognition which had awaited him moved smoothly into action. The Grahames received an invitation from the Duke and Duchess to dine at the Castle. On 2 October 1863 Bessie Grahame described the occasion in a bubblingly enthusiastic letter to her mother, saying that she had met "a lot of county people, the Malcolms, the MacNeils", together with "a nice Lady Emma, the Duke's sister".[11] In the same letter, she talked of how the Duchess had promised to send her gardener "to help with the flower beds at the new house". Bessie's liveliness and beauty had scored their usual social triumph, and it was probable that nobody at the gathering realised that pretty Mrs Grahame was four months pregnant.

Eight days after Kenneth's fifth birthday, on 16 March 1864, his younger brother, Roland, was born. The children occupied luxurious quarters, with a day-room which looked out across the lawn to the loch and a night-nursery with a view through tall pines to the sugar-loaf hill of Duniquoich. Once again the fairy-tale seemed intact – and, once again, a malign element struck. A few days after the birth, Bessie went down with a virulent attack of scarlet fever. For nearly two weeks she struggled against it, but on 4 April, she died. She never lost her gaiety; with her last breath she whispered, "It's all been so lovely."

On the day of his mother's death, Kenneth became ill with the same infection. Cunningham hardly noticed. He was crazed with grief at the loss of his beloved wife, and had no concern to spare for the new-born baby or for the other three children. If anything, they were a mocking reminder of what he had lost, and reinforced a nightmare reality. Bessie had been not only beautiful and capable, she had constituted his whole emotional life. Without her, he was lost. He turned blindly to the analgesic effects of alcohol, and it may well have been the distraught servants who prompted him to write to his old mother in Edinburgh, asking her help in the nursing of the desperately sick little boy.

Old Mrs Grahame at once made the long journey to Inveraray, and sat by the feverish child's bedside day and night, to offer him the perilously slender lifeline of her presence. Holding his hand and murmuring a constant babble of stories and reminiscences, she half-penetrated his delirium and touched his interest in the world of the living which had become so remote. With a strange circularity, the last public address which Kenneth Grahame ever gave, to a packed audience in a Thames-side village hall when he was over seventy, came back to that childhood illness and to the presence of his grandmother. He remembered, in the discursive, dreamlike way which is so essentially childlike, some of the rambling tales.

"When my grandmother was a young girl, living at home with her parents, in London I think, though I cannot be sure of that, one night a certain mild excitement was caused in the house by the arrival of the Edinburgh Mail. Now the Edinburgh Mail of those days was carried by a coach and four horses, and took some four days to get through with luck and travelling hard, so its arrival was something of an event. Well, there were the usual business letters for the father, and the long letters of gossip – Edinburgh and Glasgow gossip – crossed and re-crossed for the mother, and there was besides a dumpy package tied up with string, bearing the label of the well-known publishing firm of Ballantyne, and on this, the girl, my grandmother, fell with a shout of triumph, for she knew it could be nothing else but an early copy of the very latest Waverley Novel – I forget *which* of them it was now – a book waited for throughout the length and breadth of England with an intensity which seem strange to us now. So when the girl took her bedroom candlestick and climbed upstairs to her little room at the top of the house, she managed to carry the precious parcel with her, intending to start on the book the following day, as early as her domestic duties which came first in those days, would permit her. Arrived in her bedroom, she said to herself, 'I wonder if it would be very wrong of me if I just took a peep at the first page, merely to see how the story begins?' So she stretched herself on the hearthrug, with her candlestick on the floor beside her, and cut the string of the parcel. And the hours slipped by, and the candle burnt low, and the grey dawn began to filter in past the blind, and still the girl read on. And the candle guttered in its socket, and the dawn gave way to full light which took the place of the candle, and still the girl read on, entranced, bewitched, possessed and held spell-bound by a touch of the wand of him who was already known as the Wizard of the North."[12]

11

This passage, with its rhythmic repetitions and its use of sentences which begin with the word "and", is pure story-telling, aural rather than literary, remembered as effortlessly as nursery rhyme and reproduced without artifice, in a faithful carrying-on of a tradition which, no less than Scott, has the power to entrance, bewitch and hold spell-bound. Cunningham's mother drops only this single offering into the complex pattern which made her grandson one of the best-loved writers of all time, and yet this piece of the mosaic is an important one. The girl who read on and on was giving expression to an imaginative thread which ran strongly through the apparently dour and self-controlled family, and which was suppressed in her son but came to fruition in her grandson.

Kenneth gradually pulled round from the long illness, but he came back to a changed household. Bessie's gaiety had gone from the family and so, too, had the stability which her common sense had provided. Cunningham had shut himself away in an alcoholic stupor. As soon as Kenneth was well enough to be left to the care of the servants, old Mrs Grahame went back to Edinburgh, where she called a family conference. With remarkable speed, a decision was made about the four motherless children and their collapsed father, who quite obviously could not look after them. Bessie's mother, "Granny Ingles", who lived in the south of England, would take the children, and John Grahame, Cunningham's brother, would meet the necessary expenses. This latter arrangement tends to confirm that the family had long been aware of the impending financial crisis. Now, the arrangements were made with a stoic acceptance of duty. Mrs Mary Ingles, recently widowed, had a house big enough to accommodate the four children and their nurse, and so she was the obvious choice. The fact that, at sixty, she had only just finished bringing up six children of her own and might be daunted by the prospect of starting all over again, was immaterial. The family was in too much difficulty for such personal concerns to matter.

This crisis was not the first to hit them, for John Grahame's own wife had died, leaving him with four children. His daughter, also called Bessie, wrote afterwards in affectionate memory of "dear old Grannie" who "had also to help in *our* upbringing until my father married again. There was very little money I am sure in the family & things must have been difficult."[13] Such difficulties were never mentioned in the children's hearing – and neither was the reason for Cunningham's incapacity. It remained a dark family secret, uncommunicated even to wives and close cousins unconnected to the actual events. Had it not been for a later visit to their father, the children themselves might not have known the truth and, as it was, Helen found it difficult to touch on the subject, even in her old age. Writing about her mother's death, she admitted that it "must have been a dreadful grief to my father – he was left alone to brood over it & the failing wh. he shared with many other clever men increased & made him unfit for work.

"It made our circumstances very straitened," she went on, "our Grandmother's income was a small one & if our uncle had not helped her I don't know what would have become of us."[14]

Within a few weeks of their mother's death, the children's possessions were packed and, with Ferguson, they started on the journey south to Berkshire, in the unknown country of England.

2

All on Fire

Compared to the wild beauty of Inveraray, the landscape of the southern downlands was cosy and enclosing. Granny Ingles lived in a rambling, beautiful old house surrounded by several acres of orchards and terraced gardens, no longer kept neat since the death of her husband. It was a place where four children could do little damage, and where they could play extravagantly inventive games. The Mount, as its name suggests, had been an old shooting lodge, and it lay amid rich farmland near the village of Cookham Dene, on the edge of the Berkshire Downs. The name is evocative, stirring up associations with the bosomy, checked-and-flower-spotted paintings of Stanley Spencer, who was born in nearby Cookham in 1891. Spencer said, "When I was happy, I knew what a daisy was and what Widbrook Common meant, though what exactly the meaning was I didn't need to define".[1] The young Kenneth Grahame seems to have looked at its landscape with an equally detailed visual delight. In the unsupervised freedom of a household which was not over-anxious to concern itself with four newly arrived children, he and his brothers, and Helen too, found themselves able to explore meadows and cow-parsley-scented lanes and the meandering, willow-bordered river. It was a setting which offered boundless scope for play, both of the physical kind and in that annexe to reality which can be built of the imagination.

This was the time which Grahame commemorated in his two nostalgically titled books, *The Golden Age* and *Dream Days*. When they were published towards the end of the century, there was some indignation about his assumption that children are happiest in the absence of adult care, and about his portrayal of grown-ups as "the Olympians" who, far from being important and sensible, are seen as living in a state of self-made absurdity.

"We . . ." Grahame claims, "could have told them what real life was. We had just left it outside, and were all on fire to get back to it."[2] He goes on to demolish the idea of adult superiority.

On the whole, the existence of these Olympians seemed to be entirely void of interests, even as their movements were confined and slow, and their habits stereotyped and senseless. To anything but appearances they were blind. For them the orchard (a place elf-haunted, wonderful!) simply produced so many apples and cherries; or it didn't – when

14

the failures of Nature were not infrequently ascribed to us. They never set foot within fir-wood or hazel-copse, nor dreamt of the marvels hid therein. The mysterious sources, sources as of old Nile, that fed the duck-pond had no magic for them. They were unaware of Indians, nor recked they anything of bisons or of pirates (with pistols!), though the whole place swarmed with such portents. They cared not to explore for robbers' caves, nor dig for hidden treasure. Perhaps, indeed, it was one of their best qualities that they spent the greater part of their time stuffily indoors.

Peter Green, in his 1959 biography, provides a vivid picture of The Mount as it was when he went to see it.

Round the house stand magnificent copper beeches, and the garden descends in terraced levels, decorated with flagged lily-ponds, low Italian walls, and ponderous stone flower-pots. The orchard is wild enough to contain any number of buffalo or pirates, while the house itself might have been specially made for children. The leaded windows, the old Dutch tiles, the heavy beams made out of ships' timbers, the twisting staircase leading up to a dusty, vaulted attic under the eaves – all must have been a paradise through which the young Grahames roamed in a private dream, only occasionally bothered by the claims of their latest governess or tutor.

Victorian respectability accounted to some extent for the gulf which existed between the children and the adult world, with all its formalities of dress and behaviour, but the young Grahames were particularly devoid of the adult company and influence which is nowadays thought to be so essential to children's development. Toys, too, were few, for although Uncle John's provision ensured life's necessities, he was not a philanthropic man, and had no intention of spending money on what he considered to be frivolities.

According to Grahame's own estimation, it was this gulf itself which provided the basis of the children's wildly active imagination, and, if this is true, it must lead us to the disturbing idea that our present-day inclusion of children in all the day-to-day business of adult life may be acting as a deprivation of mental stimulus rather than the benefit which we assume it to be. Certainly the young Kenneth regarded enforced participation in adult affairs as an unwelcome imposition, when he and his siblings were "captured, washed, and forced into clean collars: silently submitting, as was our wont, with more contempt than anger". Something of the same resistance remained with him throughout his life, and in his early thirties he reflected sombrely on the loss of his youth. "Somehow the sun does not seem to shine so brightly as it used; the trackless meadows of old time have shrunk and dwindled away to a few poor acres. A saddening doubt, a dull suspicion, creeps over me. *Et in Arcadia ego* − I certainly did once inhabit Arcady. Can it be that I also have become an Olympian?"[2]

There is an irony in the words which Grahame did not suspect. The original Latin tag was an inscription on a tombstone, and is spoken by Death, who is present even in Arcady. As a scholar, Kenneth was always inclined to bend learning to his own purposes rather than immerse himself in it with academic devotion. The basic conviction, however, remained unaltered by the faulty understanding. Like Wordsworth, Grahame believed that the human soul is intact and perfect at birth, and that the compromises which are forced on it by experience of the world serve only to harden it, like an ill-used heart, into eventual non-functioning.

At The Mount, the children were adequately fed, clothed and educated, but the four of them had to depend on each other for comfort and company. Granny Ingles, black-clad and tight-buttoned, was the severe "Aunt Eliza" of Kenneth's fictionalised rememberings. She was, Helen said afterwards in fairness, "Not strict, except about our table manners" − and added that she was "A fine-looking old lady, very sociable and a good talker".[3] It was virtually only at the table that the adults and the children met. For the rest of the time, the care of the four little Grahames was given over to Ferguson and the servants, whom Kenneth regarded as friends rather than Olympians. The god-like world of adult relatives had proved itself utterly unreliable. His laughing, capable mother had not been capable enough to withstand death, and his father, with his long stride and his endless memory for poetry, had disappeared as well, for reasons which nobody would explain. It was not even safe to get too fond of any particular cook or kitchenmaid, for they, too, came and went, giving no clue as to the causes.

The only person who earned himself real popularity with the children was their mother's twin brother, David. He was a curate, a graduate of Edinburgh Academy and Trinity College, Cambridge, where he had in 1860 (the year after Kenneth's birth) acquired a rowing Blue. His first curacy had been at Stoke-on-Trent, but he managed to get an appointment to Cookham Dene in the same year that the young Grahames arrived from Scotland, and lived with them in his mother's household at The Mount. Helen said simply, "He was curate at Cookham Dene which was why we went there . . ."[4] He evidently felt a real concern for his dead sister's children. He crops up in various guises several times in Kenneth's early writing, but he is never referred to by the dreadful title of "Uncle". He often apears as "the curate", and he would, Kenneth said, "receive, unblenching, the information that the meadow beyond the orchard was a prairie studded with herds of buffalo, which it was our delight, moccasined and tomahawked, to ride down with those whoops that announced the scenting of blood. He neither laughed nor sneered, as the Olympians would have done; but,

16

possessed of a serious idiosyncrasy, he would contribute such lots of valuable suggestions as to the pursuit of this particular sort of big game that, as it seemed to us, his mature age and eminent position would scarce have been attained without a practical knowledge of the creature and its native lair. Then, too, he was always ready to constitute himself a hostile army or a band of marauding Indians on the shortest possible notice: in brief, a distinctly able man, with talents, so far as we could judge, immensely above the majority. I trust he is a bishop by this time. He had all the necessary qualifications, as we knew."[5]

In a different incarnation, this time as an artist met by the wayside, David's personality causes the writer to say, "I began to like this man. He answered your questions briefly and to the point, and never tried to be funny. I felt I could be confidential with him."[6] Grahame therefore confides that in his ideal city "there wouldn't be any relations at all, unless they promised they'd be pleasant; and if they weren't they'd have to go". But, he adds, "I'd have Martha to cook and wash up and do things. You'd like Martha. She's ever so much nicer than Aunt Eliza. She's my idea of a real lady."

David and Martha apart, the most consistent reliable influence on Kenneth's life was Nature itself. When humans seemed baffling and irrational, the natural world laid out its own intrinsic logic with perfect simplicity. It was the source of all delight.

> Colt-like, I ran through the meadows, frisking happy heels in the face of Nature laughing responsive. Above, the sky was bluest of the blue; wide pools left by the winter's floods flashed the colour back, true and brilliant; and the soft air thrilled with the germinating touch that seems to kindle something in my own small person as well as in the rash primrose already lurking in sheltered haunts.[7]

His sudden use of the present tense in "seems" is revealing. In mid-sentence, he has returned mentally to that time and is re-experiencing it. Years later, when he went back to Cookham Dene with his own small son, he was in search of the same boyhood awareness. He was not disappointed.

"I can remember everything I felt then, the part of my brain I used from four till about seven can never have altered," he told Constance Smedley, but added a bleak coda. "After that time, I don't remember anything particularly."[8] His forgetting was, perhaps, half-deliberate. In a story called *The White Poppy*, he made it clear that memory was, for him, a painful business:

> Let black, then, rather stand for hideous memory; white for blessed blank oblivion, happiest gift of the gods! For who, indeed, can say that the record of his life is not crowded with failure and mistake, stained

with its petty cruelties of youth, its meannesses and follies of later years, all which storm and clamour incessantly at the gates of memory, refusing to be shut out? Leave us alone, O gods, to remember our felicities, our successes: only aid us, ye who recall no gifts, aptly and discreetly to forget.

In *The Wind in the Willows*, too, oblivion is the ultimate gift bestowed by the great god Pan in the strange dawn meeting which is the crisis of the whole book. The only thing which can be remembered without pain, Grahame suggests, is the tangible magic of the natural world. The Mole, emerging as if new-born from the dark tunnel of his underground home, is, like the young Kenneth himself, enchanted by the first sight of flowing water.

> Never in his life had he seen a river before – this sleek, sinuous, full-bodied animal, chasing and chuckling, gripping things with a gurgle and leaving them with a laugh, to fling itself on fresh playmates that shook themselves free, and were caught and held again. All was a-shake and a-shiver – glints and gleams and sparkles, rustle and swirl, chatter and bubble. The Mole was bewitched, entranced, fascinated. By the side of the river he trotted as one trots, when very small, by the side of a man, who holds one spellbound by exciting stories . . .

One senses that it was the loss of Cunningham, rather than Bessie, which was most deeply traumatic to the small boy. His mother had been removed, not by her own choice, but by death, whereas his father continued to live somewhere, complete with his power to bewitch, entrance and fascinate. In all Grahame's work, the lost father is insubstantially present, cropping up as the wise older man (or animal), culminating in the bearded, powerful figure of Pan himself. The paternal spirit is on the one hand as gruff and domestic as Badger, comfortably slippered and pipe-smoking, and on the other as wild as the god of nature, an awe-inspiring presence to be both feared and revered. To Kenneth, these romantic extremes were the essence of maleness, whereas the more mundane middle ground of plain reality was a female affair which any competent woman could manage. His mother had brought her own beauty and gaiety to her role as household manager, but her sphere had been strictly practical. Within these limitations, kindly servants could and did to some extent replace her function as a provider of domestic comfort; it was not until later, at the beginning of adult life, that the absence of a loving, communicative mother began to have a damaging effect which Grahame, like many men of his generation, never realised. At a time when women were regarded as possessions rather than fully functioning people, lack of female influence on growing sons was in no way abnormal. To be motherless, whether actually or in effect, merely demanded an earlier acquisition of strength and self-reliance, but to be fatherless was a disaster, for it robbed a boy of a semi-magical concept of what he might become.

The Mount, run by the formidable Granny Ingles and a staff of mostly female servants, provided a setting of down-to-earth practicality against which the magical quality of men stood out in sharp relief, making them appear either as heroes or villains. David was a hero, and so was Uncle Jack Ingles, "wildly welcome" on his occasional visits from Portsmouth, where he commanded HMS *Hercules*. Anything to do with the sea and ships – or even the river and small boats – constituted instant enchantment, whereas landlubbers were by definition a dull lot. Farmer Larkin, who appears in Maxfield Parrish's marvellous illustrations to *The Golden Age* as a sky-tall cudgel-waving giant, his straddled legs knee-deep in standing hay, is the arch-enemy, but reluctantly admired. His threats of what he will do if he catches the young varmints chasing his calves again cast him as Captain Hook to the children's Peter Pan. He belongs, at least partially, to their Never-Never Land.

If, as Carlyle insisted, human beings need heroes, then the young Grahames found them in their own imagination for the most part, and real people could only obtain heroic status if they could be incorporated into the world of inspired pretending. Most of them, of course, could not. They remained outside, disapproving, humourless, and all-powerful. Worst of all, in Grahame's view, were the "hopeless and pig-headed" uncles, and he wrote a savagely funny piece called *Justifiable Homicide* in which he dwelt with pleasure on the thought of a nephew's revenge.

I had a friend who disposed of a relative every spring. Uncles were his special line – (he had suffered much from their tribe, having been early left an orphan) – though he had dabbled in aunts, and in his hot youth, when he was getting his hand in, he had even dallied with a grand-parent or two. But it was in uncles he excelled.

Grahame himself admits that "to children with a proper equipment of parents these things would have worn a different aspect". The aunts and uncles "treated us, indeed, with kindness enough as to the needs of the flesh, but after that with indifference (an indifference, as I recognise, the result of a certain stupidity), and therewith the commonplace conviction that your child is merely an animal".[9]

This "commonplace conviction" underlay the Victorian attitude to children, making it quite logical that they should be "seen and not heard", much as puppies are admired for their sweet looks but not for their barking. The emotional deprivation which the young Grahames suffered was not unusual, for upper-class families tended in any case to hand over their young to the care of servants, and saw them only when they were washed and presentable. It is a coincidence that the second half of the nineteenth century saw an extraordinary flowering of literature? Grahame, in recalling his own childhood, speaks to some extent for his generation. He and his siblings were not alone in their isolation from adults; many other children turned, as they did, to the natural world for solace and for the communication of truth. A sense of connectedness to nature shines through Victorian writing and gives it a touch of wildness which is quite absent from the enclosed social dramas of Jane Austen. That "indoors" tradition continued in Thackeray and Trollope, but it co-existed with such wild men as Richard Jefferies, George Borrow, Robert Louis Stevenson, and Walt Whitman. Hardy's work is charged with a powerful sense of landscape, as is George Eliot's, while Elizabeth Gaskell and the Brontë sisters convey in every word the quality of northern moors. In all these very different writers, as in Dickens himself, there is a sense of looking in some surprise at the behaviour of human beings. There is an externality which perhaps arises when children feel themselves separate from adults. For Grahame, "the futility of imparting our ideas had long been demonstrated".[10] As a result, he became convinced that he belonged to the world in general rather than specifically to the human race. There was much to encourage that view.

At The Mount, a small boy could experience a multitude of delights. "The sun was hot, the season merry June, and never (I thought) had there been such wealth and riot of buttercups throughout the lush grass. Green-and-gold was the dominant key that day. Instead of active 'pretence' with its shouts and its perspiration, how much better – I held – to lie at ease and pretend to one's self, in green and golden fancies, slipping the husk and passing, a careless lounger, through a sleepy imaginary world all gold and green!" But then again, "To us, who had never known any other condition of things, it seemed entirely right and fitting that the wind sang and sobbed in the poplar tops, and, in the lulls of it, sudden spirts of rain spattered the already dusty roads, in that blusterous March day . . ."[11]

The house itself was not without its odd pleasures. The fictionalised older brother, Edward, recalls, " 'Do you remember we were playing with a dead mouse once on the piano, and the mouse was Robinson Crusoe, and the piano was the island, and somehow Crusoe slipped down inside the island, into its works, and we couldn't get him out, though we tried rakes and all sorts of things, till the tuner came . . .' ".[12] There is a touch of authorial artifice here, but the sense of a separate world remains intact.

The combined effect of *The Golden Age* and *Dream Days* is to convey a sense of eternal childhood, but in fact the idyll lasted only two years. Kenneth was five when they moved south after his mother's death and, by the time he was seven, it was all over. Unknown to the children, the old house had long been a source of concern to their Uncle John, the powerful figure who was, at least in Grahame's eyes, the ogre who lurked at the centre of the hated tribe of uncles. In taking on the responsibility for his brother's children, John had also stepped into quasi-landlord status regarding the house they lived in. Although The Mount had offered a ready-made solution to the problem of what to do with the family of four parentless children, the upkeep of its crumbling fabric was an increasing worry. Mrs Ingles had been left with virtually no income, the house having been her husband's only asset, so she was defenceless against John's assumed power to act as he thought best. For some time, he had been suggesting a move to somewhere smaller and more easily kept, but she had resisted. She loved her house, and doubtless felt it a double injustice that she should be deprived of it when she had already suffered the inconvenience of taking on four grandchildren. The ample space at The Mount and its surroundings not only gave the children freedom, but allowed her a certain amount of privacy, and the prospect of a smaller, closer-packed household must have been dismaying.

John bided his time and, at last, circumstances played into his hands. In a gale just before the Christmas of 1865, one of The Mount's chimneys came crashing down. Mrs Ingles was terrified that the remaining chimneys were unsafe, and it was quite obvious, even to a Victorian woman who was probably given little insight into the male world of money, that extensive rebuilding work at The Mount would be very costly. John had only to purse his lips and shake his head, and Mrs Ingles was left with the awful knowledge that she stayed in the damaged house, unrepaired, at her own risk. Fresh from the experience of howling wind and crashing masonry, she had no choice. She agreed that she and her fostered brood would move to Fern Hill Cottage, in Cranbourne. The cottage belonged to Mr Algernon Gilliatt, who, according to Helen, "was a cousin of Uncle David's first wife".[13] She must have been wrong about this, for it was John Grahame, not David Ingles, who married again after his first wife's death. David lived with his mother until his marriage in 1866. It was certainly Mr Gilliatt, however, who persuaded Mrs Ingles to move, riding across to The Mount to see her, and he afterwards became a close family friend. There are signs, though, that the change was not a happy one. The children lost the great garden which had been their make-believe world, and Mrs Ingles lost her beloved house. The new cottage was rented rather than bought, so she retained the proceeds of the sale, but it must have been a scant and bitter comfort.

For Kenneth, the move to Cranbourne in the spring of 1866 coincided with the onset of his inability to "remember anything particularly". There is no reference to the cottage in any of his writing except for episodes of escape such as his meeting with a charming and other-worldly clergyman in *A Harvesting*. This, in fact, was Mr Lockwood, who succeeded David Ingles as curate of Cranbourne, to whom, according to Helen, "Kenneth went for lessons in Latin before going to St Edward's School. He never had lessons at Cranbourne."[14] Certainly, this vicar prompts one of the few wistful references to human affection which Grahame ever permitted himself. Observing how a tramp "oozing malice and filth" nevertheless stops on the road to relieve his wife of her bundle and take her arm, the clergyman remarks on "how this strange thing, this love of ours, lives and shines out in the unlikeliest of places". Wandering through his Greek quotations, he concludes that "the fairy filaments" of this world of love are in lowly places, and that "one must stoop to see it, old fellow, one must stoop".[15]

It was a bleak time. Kenneth could not stop mourning his lost Eden. "Certain spots," he wrote long afterwards, "always had their insensible attraction for certain moods. In love, one sought the orchard. Weary of discipline, sick of convention, impassioned for the road . . . one made for the big meadow. Mutinous, sulky, charged with plots and conspiracies, one always got behind the shelter of the raspberry canes."[16] There is a note of defensive self-mockery, but the loss is plain.

There are hints that Mrs Ingles was equally discontented. From this time onward, the rest of the family began to be involved in a burden-sharing exercise which suggests that the cottage was, as she had feared, too small to accommodate herself, the staff and the children in reasonable comfort. Deprived of the space and freedom of The Mount, it would not be surprising to find that Kenneth became "mutinous and sulky"; at any rate, he and his elder brother, Willie, were with increasing frequency asked to spend holidays with the sailor-uncle Jack or with John himself at his London house in Sussex Gardens.

Ripples of resentment spread even to Cunningham Grahame, alone in his great house by the loch in Inveraray. There is no correspondence to suggest that he was urged to take up his fatherly duties, but within a few months of the move he wrote to Mrs Ingles and offered to have his children back. For Kenneth, it raised wild hopes. Half-forgotten memories surged up in excitement as preparations for the journey were begun, and his general oblivion was penetrated by the long train-trip and "the brown leaping streams and purple heather, and the clear, sharp northern air [which] streamed in through the windows".[17]

What happened in Inveraray is pushed away under the cloud of unknowing. "Return, indeed, was bitter,"[18] Kenneth said, and left it at that. Cunningham's last effort to draw together some shreds of self-respect failed abysmally, and the children saw, in helpless bewilderment, that their father was lost in dissolution. "We went back to Inveraray for a year in 66 & were there when he went to France,"[19] Helen wrote. The scant words conjure up a nightmare. Cunningham had in fact resigned his post and fled from the growing scandal of his incapacity, abandoning house, children and country. He spent the rest of his life in a cheap boarding house in Le Havre. It was only three years since he and Bessie had moved so triumphantly into their new home.

Kenneth came back from Scotland a changed boy. As if to take over his father's abandoned role, he went on long solitary walks while chanting such epics as *The Lays of Ancient Rome*. Helen, who wrote poetry herself but adopted her father's tactic of keeping it strictly private, was disapproving. "Oh, we don't go in for Kenneth, you know," she said to friends, dissociating herself from his oddness.[20] Later, the same dryness marks her account of his behaviour, "It was at Cranbourne that Kenneth began to spout poetry, first Shakespeare, then Macaulay's *Lays*, then Tennyson."[21] She makes it sound like the progress of a disease and, if grief is an affliction of the mind and heart, then she was not wrong. Her brother had entered into a conviction that the world of adult human beings was a treacherous and unpleasant place, and he never quite recovered from it.

3

Schooling and Learning

Grahame's early essays never allude to the move away from The Mount. Events of the following year or two are set in the continuing background of the old house and its comfortable, jungly gardens, as if he simply would not recognise, either at the time or later, that the unthinkable had happened. At the age of nine, he was sent away to boarding school, and he recalls the first hints of this intention with characteristic exasperation, regarding it as one more manifestation of the ridiculous adult world. *Lusisti Satis*, which, roughly translated, means an end to playing, begins with weary contempt.

> Among the many fatuous ideas that possessed the Olympian noddle, this one was pre-eminent; that, being Olympians, they could talk quite freely in our presence on subjects of the closest import to us, so long as names, dates and other landmarks were ignored. We were supposed to be denied the faculty for putting two and two together, and like monkeys, who very sensibly refrain from speech lest they should be set to earn their livings, we were careful to conceal our capabilities for simple syllogism. Thus we were rarely taken by surprise, and so were considered by our disappointed elders to be apathetic and to lack the divine capacity for wonder.

The nursery news-service was fast and efficient, based on an investigative style which MI5 might applaud. Alerted by "the use of nods and pronouns, with significant haituses and interpolations in the French tongue . . . by a studious pretence of inattention we were not long in plucking out the heart of the mystery". Accordingly, "we descended suddenly and together on Martha; proceeding, however, not by simple enquiry as to facts − that would never have done; but by informing her that the air was full of school and that we knew all about it, and then challenging denial. Martha was a trusty soul, but a bad witness for the defence, and we soon had it all out of her. The word had gone forth, the school had been selected; the necessary sheets were hemming even now, and Edward was the designated and appointed victim."

This fictional Edward is, at first sight, a mystery. The stories in *The Golden Age* and *Dream Days* are so nostalgic and personal that it is impossible to dismiss them as pure invention, and yet Grahame's own family does not match the children of whom he wrote. He himself had an older sister and brother, Helen and Willie, and a younger brother, Roland, but the fictional family consists of five children, with the anonymous narrator placed between the two pairs of siblings, the older Edward and Selina and the younger Charlotte and Harold. A possible explanation is that Kenneth as narrator has been given an honorary position in the Grahame family, thus doubling as partcipating child and recording adult, but a simpler interpretation presents itself. Uncle John had four children who related to their cousin Kenneth exactly as the fictional family does. The younger pair were called Agnes and Walter, and there was an older sister called Bessie (later Bessie Luard), with a senior brother whose name was in fact Edward.

We should not make too much of this coincidence; all writers use experience as the raw material which is put through the mincer of the writing process, and it could equally have been the name of the school which Kenneth attended – St Edward's – which he took for a fictional elder brother. More interesting is the question of how the narrator places himself in remembered events, seeing the boy he was both from within and without. Compassion for the child one was is difficult to express without mawkishness or self-pity, and a degree of externalisation is essential if that child is to be drawn clearly. The balance is a subtle one, and Grahame maintains it with a skill which seems so artless that one is hardly aware of it.

In his biography, Peter Green assumed that *Lusisti Satis* recorded Kenneth's own departure for school, even though the event is seen through the eyes of the younger brother who stays at home. This seems a perverse interpretation when it is recalled that Kenneth's brother Willie was a year older, and is known to have attended St Edward's. He, surely, must have been the Edward who was the "appointed victim".

The account is an elegaic one, forming the last episode of *The Golden Age*. "We all trooped down to the station, of course; it is only in later years that the farce of 'seeing people off' is seen in its true colours. Edward was the life and soul of the party; and if his gaiety struck one at times as being a trifle overdone, it was not a moment to be critical . . . Then suddenly, when we were about half-way down, one of the girls fell a-snivelling." For a perilous instant, the façade of sophistication is threatened as Edward "turned his head aside, feigning an interest in the landscape. It was but for a moment; then he recollected the hat he was wearing – a hard bowler, the first of that sort he had ever owned. He took it off, examined it, and felt it over. Something about it seemed to give him strength, and he was a man once more." Remembering that the hard-hatted boy was only nine years old, there is a terrible poignancy about this self-control, as there is about the bereft little group which "straggled back from the station". The narrator outlines a bleak future. "Edward might come back to us, but it would not be the Edward of yore, nor could things ever be the same again." School would change their brother into a new Edward, "ragged of attire and lawless of tongue, a scorner of tradition and an adept in strange new physical tortures, one who would in the same half-hour dismember a doll and shatter a hallowed belief". More than a century later, many families see the same change overtake their children after the first few weeks of secondary education.

Of his own experience at St Edward's, Grahame says very little. Throughout his writing, a gentle humour modifies all pain and puts an embargo on grumbling or self-pity. He never agonised, and would have found any hint of it deeply embarrassing. Like all upper-middle-class boys of his generation, the "stiff upper lip" constituted a protective armour of self-control. If emotion is to be conveyed, it insisted, then it must be conveyed lightly and obliquely; as a result, his writing is charged with what he would not say. Often it is overlaid with joviality and burdened with classical allusion, indicative, perhaps of the smoke-screen of declared confidence below which a raw sensitivity tingled. In Grahame's case, it was not until many years later, when he was invited back as a now-eminent person to address the boys at a Speech Day, that he uncovered his early school experience, and gave an account of it which was not, perhaps, quite what his fellow worthies on the platform had expected.

He recalled how pupils used to sit in rank order according to their degree of attainment, and how he, as a new boy, "was modestly occupying that position, at the very bottom, which seemed to me natural enough, when the then Headmaster entered – a man who had somehow formed an erroneous idea of my possibilities. Catching sight of me, he asked sternly, 'What's that thing doing down there?' The master in charge could only reply that whether it was crass ignorance or invincible stupidity, he wotted not, but there it was. The Headmaster, who was, I was persuaded, a most illogical man ... merely remarked that if that thing – meaning me – was not up there or near it, pointing to the head of the form, before the close of work, it was to be severely caned; and left the room.

"Well, you can imagine my feelings. I was a very little chap – not yet ten. I was not accustomed to be caned – that is, beaten. I had never been beaten. I had been doing my best, and at home had not been considered an absolute fool. And there I was, up against it in the fullest sense of the word! It was not surprising, perhaps, that I shed some bitter tears. But what happened? No one of my colleagues started forth as I half expected to champion the cause of youth and innocence. Instead, they all proceeded to display an ignorance and a stupidity, on even the simplest matters, which seemed unnatural, even for them. The consequence was, that I presently found myself, automatically it really seemed, soaring, soaring – till I stood, dazed and giddy, at the top of the form itself, and was kept there till my friendly colleagues thought the peril was safely past, when I was allowed to descend from that bad eminence to which merit had certainly not raised me."[1]

It is a revealing anecdote, not least because Grahame chose to recall the incident, not for the benefit of the masters or to impress readers, but simply to amuse a new generation of schoolboys. The conspiracy of the class to send the hapless little Kenneth to the top by seeming to be stupid themselves had been in itself the first and most important of human lessons to learn. It rubbed in the ethos of all groups – that the earning of status within the group is more important to members than whatever it is that the group is supposed to do. Attempts by teachers to "divide and rule" usually fail, because they are perceived as an attack on the group. If they succeed, they achieve an amoeba-like split into two groups, one of which will declare itself as a band of outlaws. Every schoolchild is initiated into this understanding by some personal attack on the part of an over-zealous disciplinarian, and Grahame was no exception. Returning to St Edward's as an adult, he felt impelled to demonstrate that he had kept faith with the group, and that the recognition he had achieved did not place him in "that bad eminence" at the top of the form. His Scottish soul may have been shocked to discover that the English value popularity above academic distinction, but he was too canny to ignore the lesson his fellows were teaching him.

It was, perhaps, the hardest lesson of his life. Despite the supportive behaviour of his class-mates on that first occasion, school society is very different from the puppyish warmth of the family, where squabbles, however fierce, do not seriously interrupt the sharing of experience and the participating in jointly created fantasies. School groups, as a microcosm of the larger society which awaits, impose their own subtle tests and taboos. Members may be eccentric as long as their eccentricity can be regarded as amusing, but they must not be overtly critical or contemptuous of the group – hence the traditional anxiety not to be thought a "swot". If excellence is achieved, it should appear to be accidental. The natural childhood desire to be a hero must give way to a modest self-deprecation, and the greatest virtue is the passive one of endurance. It was not for nothing that Edward came home with a knowledge of "strange new physical tortures", for passivity can only be tested by active means.

St Edward's was, in fact, grotesquely appalling. Although it is now one of Oxford's most highly respected independent schools, its early years, according to its own centenary publication, were such that the place should have been closed down at once, and very nearly was. The background to its foundation is curious, and explains much about Grahame's life-long leaning towards Catholicism – a tendency which otherwise seems so at variance with his upbringing.

In the early nineteenth century, Oxford was swept by a new move towards an intellectual Catholicism. It was a revolutionary stance whch caused revulsion in the established church and thus in the university, but its adherents were fervent. One such was Thomas Chamberlain, born in 1810 of a clergyman father. He went to Westminster School and then to Christ Church, where he took a third in Literae Humaniores. As an undergraduate, he heard John Keble preach at St Mary's, and became convinced of his true vocation. He was ordained a priest in 1835, and accepted a living in the parish of St Thomas the Martyr, which lay at the very gates of Christ Church but was desperately poor. The people, though largely illiterate, were convinced that their new vicar was heretically popish, and flung stones at him when they saw him about the parish, but Chamberlain persevered, and won respect through his selfless devotion to sufferers in the devastating cholera outbreaks of 1848 and 1854.

Feeling a little more assured of public support, he turned his formidable energies towards educating the young in the Catholic faith. He established several parish schools, then became more ambitious, setting up a girls' school, St Anne's, an Industrial Home "for children taken from evil surroundings", a School of St Scholastica "for the training of school mistresses", and a High School for boys called Osney House School, which went bankrupt within three years.

Undeterred, Chamberlain entered into negotiations with Brasenose College for the lease of a run-down, rambling house at 29 New Inn Hall Street, on a corner opposite the present site of the Wesley Memorial Chapel. One can hardly imagine a more marked religious contrast. This passionately Catholic institution in its crumbling house opened with two pupils in April 1863 and, by the time Kenneth Grahame arrived in 1868, there were about forty boys. Chamberlain, having secured the £95 p.a. lease from Brasenose, installed F. W. Fryer as headmaster and left the rest to him, with disastrous results.

Fryer was twenty-five years old, a curate with a BA from St Edmund Hall and a firm devotion to the Oxford Movement. This seems to have been Chamberlain's only criterion for appointing him. The rest of the staff consisted of a fluctuating number of undergraduates, none of whom had any qualifications or experience. The teaching was thus virtually non-existent, and the domestic arrangements were dreadful. The building was rotten and dilapidated, and rats "swarmed under the floors, in the walls and over the rotten rafters", according to the school's own account. It continues, "The sanitary arrangements were primitive in the extreme, and later the drains themselves became defective, precipitating a real crisis". It is also recorded that some of the masters "slept in cupboards". The food was appalling, consisting largely of porridge, bread, fat meat and beer, and personal hygiene was limited to a once-weekly splash in a tin bath in the boot-room. In the summer months, the water was not heated.

The school's academic activities were limited to Latin and Greek and Holy Scripture, with a lot of singing "to weird Gregorian tunes", as an ex-pupil recalled,[2] and a smattering of other subjects. Literature was not touched on. The cane was used constantly.

It seems extraordinary that parents were prepared to send, and go on sending, their sons to such an institution, but St Edward's had one immense advantage which outweighed all else. It was cheap. Fees at that time were set at £25 per annum, because Chamberlain's declared intention had been to "place within the reach of parents of moderate means a school where their children could be brought up in the true principles of the Church, and have at the same time all the advantages of a Public School".[3] Like many men of rigid beliefs, he was unswayed by the practical results of his theory. He merely observed that the school did not pay, and until it did, he would not spend money on improvements. As R. D. Hill put it in his account of the school, in Chamberlain's view, "Anything was good enough for school boys. They were no worse off than he was at Westminster".

For some, it was intolerable. A new boy drowned himself in the Cherwell in the Christmas Term of 1869. His surviving twin brother was perhaps shocked into an unguarded revealing of the horrors of St Edward's, and Chamberlain was forced into taking some action. He sacked the hapless headmaster, Fryer, who had struggled on for so many years in a crumbling building, with unqualified, poverty-stricken staff (even the second master received only £100 p.a., and some earned as little as £15 per term), and appointed Algernon Barrington Simeon, who had a Pass BA from Christ Church.

Simeon had been drawn to Chamberlain for religious reasons. He was a member of an eclectic University society called the Brotherhood of the Holy Trinity, and wrote in reminiscence about a Holy Week spent in "constant prayer to be kept up by one of us all night and most of the day, with the result that we became very hysterical and I was obliged to go to a Doctor". He was, however, enthusiastic about the headship of St Edward's, though somewhat astonished to be offered such a post at the age of twenty-two, and set about improving things where he could, renting a house two doors down the street to help with the overcrowded conditions in which the boys lived. He admitted that the school had a bad name and was "at a very low ebb".

Simeon could do little about the fabric of the school itself, which was rapidly disintegrating. The floor of the dining-room had fallen in and the banisters were off the stairs, and, in the winter of 1870–71, a large area of the outside wall collapsed into the street. It must have seemed to Kenneth Grahame, then twelve years old, that there was little security to be found in bricks and mortar. The forces of nature had overwhelmed The Mount, and now, though less regrettably, they were destroying 29 New Inn Hall Street. Chamberlain tried to get Brasenose, as landlords, to repair the house, which had been declared structurally unsafe, but the College had other plans for such a prime site, and regarded the disintegration of the existing house as a step in the desired direction. The school would have to move elsewhere.

By now, Simeon had bought St Edward's as a going concern outright from Chamberlain, for £300. He had raised the fees to a realistic level, paid off the bank debt and instituted a vigorous fund-raising operation. His searches for a suitable ready-made building were fruitless, and he turned to a hunt for a building site. He found it in the then-empty land between St Margaret's Road and Summertown, which he described as a "miserable dirty little village". In the spring of 1872, he and a well-wishing spinster called Miss Skene cut the first sod for the new building in the middle of a five-acre turnip field adjacent to Woodstock Road.

The new school was supposed to be ready by 1 August 1873, but when the boys came back on 22 August, it was to a state of chaos. The weather had been appalling and the workmen had staged a strike, and the building was far from ready. Simeon recalled how he "swept out dormitories, throwing chips and lime out of the windows", and how the boiler would not work, and a boy fell into a well, and two others ran away, and the father of two new boys tripped over a bucket of whitewash and nearly removed his sons on the spot. Two days later, however, an official opening ceremony took place, with the choir, complete with crucifix and banner, proceeding from room to room, singing psalms, and concluding with the *Missa de Angelis* in the temporary chapel.

The Oxford dignitaries were scandalised by the High flavour of St Edward's, and rumours were circulated that the place was a Popish monastery. The Public Worship Regulation Act had just been passed, making the use of ritual a civil offence and, had it not been for the support of the Bishop, Simeon might well have been forced to modify the school's religious observances.

A school photograph of Kenneth Grahame as a very small boy shows him in a formal pose, his arm resting obediently on the back of a chair (it was a stance adopted by each one of the subjects), his hair neatly cropped and brushed, his face white and enduring, already showing the wariness which was to become so characteristic. For all the rough-and-tumble of his family life, he had spent much of his time alone in his wanderings through the lanes and meadows of Berkshire, and was used to the interaction between the natural world and his solitary self. St Edward's was, to all intents and purposes, in the country, but the strangeness of it all was very stark in the small boy's mind, and it would be a long time before he could develop any intimacy with the new landscape. Later, he wrote of "a small school-boy, new kicked out of his nest into the draughty, uncomfortable outer world, his unfledged skin still craving the feathers whereinto he was wont to nestle. The barrack-like school, the arid, cheerless class-rooms, drove him to Nature for redress; and, under an alien sky, he would go forth and wander along the iron road by impassive fields, so like yet so unlike those hitherto a part of him."[4] The natural world could sometimes make itself felt in less than poetic ways. Cows grazed on Port Meadow where the boys played cricket, with no boundaries, but with the occasional hazard of a well-placed cowpat. "It was better," Kenneth remarked later, "to feign a twisted ankle or a sudden faintness, and allow some keener enthusiast to recover the ball from where it lay."[5]

After the move to Woodstock Road in 1873, Kenneth was able to enjoy the proximity of the city centre with its towers and archways, its ancient colleges of creamy Cotswold stone and its seductive glimpses of quadrangle and lawn. There were fewer academic joys as well. School supervision of the pupils' free time was surprisingly lenient, and Grahame was able to escape quite often from the "big, beefy, hefty, hairy men called masters who never explain, never retract, never apologise".[6] In his wanderings round the city's cobbled streets, the first thing which attracted him was "the market, always a joy to visit. It seemed to have everything the heart of man could desire, from livestock at one end to radiant flowers in pots at the other.".[7]

Very clearly, Grahame learned as much outside school as in it. Reminiscing later about "Teddy's", he said, "The two influences which most soaked into me there, and have remained with me ever since, were the good grey Gothic on the one hand and, on the other, the cool secluded reaches of the Thames – the 'Stripling Thames', remote and dragon-fly haunted, before it attains to the noise, ribbons and flannels of Folly Bridge. The education, in my time, was of the fine old crusted order, with all the classics in the top bin – I did Greek verse in those days, so help me! But the elements, the classics, the Gothic, the primeval Thames, fostered in me, perhaps, the pagan germ that would have mightily shocked the author of *The Sabbath*."[8] The reference is to Kenneth's great-grand-uncle, James Grahame, the poet about whom Lord Byron had been so scathing.

The attack had left the family with a strong feeling that writing was a risky business, even though James had never been rash enough to take it up as a profession. Like Kenneth's father, he had been an Edinburgh advocate and had failed at it, though not from an excess of bonhomie – quite the reverse. He was a man of gloomy disposition, and abandoned the Bar to enter Holy Orders, eventually settling in Durham as a devout but deeply melancholy curate. His presence in the family background was not an encouragement to a young man who was already showing a literary bent – and neither, Kenneth found, were the masters at St Edward's. It was expected that most of the boys would enter the Church or the Army, and to announce an intention of becoming a writer would have been as unthinkable as an ambition to run away and join a circus. Kenneth prudently kept his plans to himself, admitting only to a hoe that he would do well enough in his exams to gain an Oxford University place. Odd as it may seem now, English was not then recognised as an academic discipline in its own right, and the would-be novelist had to study some other subject, usually Law or Classics.

St Edward's itself seems to have been startled by Kenneth Grahame's eventual success, and a member of staff, writing in 1913, said of his erstwhile pupil that his first work, published in the school magazine, showed "no promise of the exquisite prose that was to be in later years the delight of thousands". It was hardly surprising. Kenneth had learnt to be cautious and to stay out of trouble. He wrote in a pedantic, uncontroversial style, and his essay, entitled *The Good and Bad Effects of Rivalry*, is calculated to win approval, exploiting the Christian ethic of the school quite shamelessly.

It certainly is a very difficult thing in practice to feel kindly towards a rival, and to anyone but to one who always bears in mind one of the chief duties of a Christian, to love one another, and keeps a good control over himself, it is a very difficult thing.

The carelessly repeated last phrase betrays the boredom which the essay barely transcends. The hypocrisy is blatant, and yet it worked. The piece was accepted and printed, even though it contains no honestly held opinion and does not touch on the fourteen-year-old author's real feelings. His later reminiscences are frank about the tedium of enforced church attendance, and the Paganism which formed the basis of his later thinking gives the lie to his pious utterances about Christian duty.

By early adolescence, Grahame was functioning on two levels. The private world which he had shared with his sister and brothers, and with the spirit of nature, had been tucked away in his mind, safe from the abrasion of the reality in which he found himself. At school, his real identity had to be kept hidden. In its place, he was required to deploy new skills as a performer. He had to behave in a way which was acceptable to his fellow pupils and to staff, even though such behaviour was contradictory to all his inclinations. His worth was evaluated, not in terms of what he felt and thought, but only as a result of what his performance had achieved. He learned that one's own being is of very little interest in a society which uses status as its sole yardstick. For many children, the old self-awareness dies quickly and without protest – if, indeed, it ever had a real existence – but for some, the duality between the competent performer and the secret inner self becomes established during these painful years, setting up a tension which may never be resolved. In Grahame's case, the two levels were very widely separated. Having received so little acceptable adult guidance, he had developed a particularly rich inner life of acute awareness and lively imaginings, on which was clamped the heavily inhibiting effect of respectable Victorian behaviour. These opposites sound like a recipe for disaster, and they certainly gave rise to much personal pain – and yet, in a larger sense, they can act like the opposing chemical elements in a battery, causing a constant potential current which demands to be used. This certainly happened in Grahame's case.

From the time he went to school, Kenneth became aware of his own identity in a new way. As a young child, he had simply been what he was, reacting to circumstances with grief or delight, but essentially contained within his own being. The requirement to be something else precipitated him into a new stance, from which he could look at his own being as an outsider. Robert Louis Stevenson, whose work was the biggest single influence on Grahame's own writing, contends that this externalising is an inevitable process of growing up. As he says in an essay called *Child's Play*, a "change takes place in the sphere of intellect, by which all things are transformed and seen through theories and associations as through coloured windows".[9] A child, he insists, must participate absolutely in his own imaginings, using a chair for a dragon or pretending that a plate of porridge is an island in a sea of milk. This is play-acting rather than true imagining, for the child "is at the experimental stage; he is not sure how one would feel in certain circumstances; to make sure, he must come as near trying it as his means permit". Adults, on the other hand, do know how they would feel, for they have had wide experience. They can imagine and know that they are imagining. "It is the grown people who make the nursery stories; all the children do, is jealously to preserve the text."

If, as Stevenson suggests, the formative part of growing up lies in the acquiring of experience, then schools assist that process by supplying experience, even (or perhaps particularly) if it is of a kind which the child would not voluntarily have chosen. If this is true, then St Edward's, in the eccentric style of its early existence, provided Grahame with some valuable material. The first headmaster, Fryer, according to a *Chronicle* piece by another ex-pupil, "would hide pence and halfpence and turn us all out in the dark to look for them. Ledges in the brick wall were always a favourite hiding place, and lighted touchwood was used as a lantern. Pits were dug and filled with mud and water, and over them, and into them, the unsuspecting ones were lured." Boys slept five or six to a bedroom in the crumbling Queen Anne building, and the only sympathetic person was the matron, Mrs Reece, who took a motherly interest in the smaller boys and would sometimes take a homesick lad into her kitchen for a nocturnal feast of bread and treacle. She was even prepared to hide her stowaways under a heap of dirty towels if she heard a master approaching. For the rest, the school seems to have been run with the mild sadism so typical of its day. In the absence of a sports field, most of the garden had been converted into a playground and in this limited space, the boys exercised in whatever ways could be devised, playing a game they called "Prisoner's Base" or, if all else failed, rolling a heavy log about the tarmac. The Revd J. C. Michel recalled that "Some of the fellows dug out pits in which they buried boxes labelled 'Gold', and we tried to imagine the feelings of the finders in after years".[10]

Grahame, of course, lamented the lost garden, which he had never seen. "Perhaps there were trees in it then," he says wistfully, and added that "there still remained, in the receding 'waist' of the house, under the dining room window, some scanty flower-beds, where the horticulturally minded were allowed, and even encouraged, to employ their grovelling instincts."[11] St Edward's, whatever its faults, was not institutional. Its architecture was absolutely domestic, with school desks pushed into ornamented, high-ceilinged rooms which had never been designed for educational purposes, and its academic discipline was balanced by an anarchic lack of interest in what the boys did with their spare time. "Some sort of stable, or garden, gateway gave issue on the street northwards;" Grahame recalls, "but this was never used, and I only happen to remember it because on my first Guy Fawkes Day we boys attempted a private bonfire, thinking in our artless way, that in Oxford bonfires were the rule rather than the exception. The authorities, however, thought otherwise, and firemen and police battered at the stable gate aforesaid till explanations ensued . . ."[12] After the move to Woodstock Road, things were far more orthodox, although the older boys enjoyed a considerable independence. As Grahame put it, "we were free to wander where we liked; but there were 'bounds', mystic but definite, and these we must never overstep − first, because it was so easy for us to be spotted in our school caps, and secondly, because we didn't want to. These bounds chiefly excluded districts like St Ebbes, St Thomas's (except for church) the cattle market, Jericho, and their like . . ."[13] Otherwise, boys could wander unsupervised round the city.

It seems that "Teddy's" was aiming for an inexpensive version of the public-school ethic, with the mixture of brutalism, anarchy and mystic tra-dition, bound together in the name of Christianity, which gave it such appeal to parents and promised their sons the cachet of belonging to a caste of favoured initiates. Thomas Hughes had written with rapture about his own experiences at Dr Arnold's Rugby in *Tom Brown's Schooldays*, and the book's influence was considerable. Many a Victorian father warmed to Squire Brown's advice to his son as the pair of them waited for the mail coach which would take the boy away to a new life.

If schools are what they were in my time, you'll see a great many cruel blackguard things done, and hear a deal of foul bad talk. But never fear. You tell the truth, keep a brave and kind heart, and never listen to or say anything you wouldn't have your mother and sister hear, and you'll never feel ashamed to come home, or we to see you.

This little homily makes no allusion whatever to learning, and, perhaps for that very reason, was embraced with enthusiasm by the upper-class English fathers of the time. St Edward's, however, could not achieve the magnificent carelessness of the old public-school system. It catered for just such men as John Grahame, who regarded education as a necessary business deal rather than a vital social achievement. Its boys were not the swaggering young gentlemen of Hughes's narrative who would for their amusement loosen the lynch-pins of a farmer's cart or pepper the Irish navvies working on the road with pea-shooters from the safety of their coach, afterwards buying themselves out of the resulting trouble. The Jubilee number of the *St Edward's Chronicle* claimed of its Old Boys that "the so-called 'gentlemen-at-large' – a dangerous sort of wild beast – is a negligible quantity in the total of our results. The O.S.Es are almost without exception workers." It is an interesting declaration of policy, and utterly at variance with the public-school tradition of the time, when the sons of gentlemen were expected to inherit land, and confidence was considered more important than knowledge. It was against such a background of personal freedom and power that Squire Brown could say that "a man is to be valued wholly and solely for that which he is in himself, for that which stands up in the four fleshly walls of him, apart from clothes, rank, fortune and all externals whatsoever", but St Edward's could not entertain any such breezy socialist ideas. Its strong religious bias inculcated humility and its grand gestures were circumscribed by expediency and its confidence limited by class-consciousness. As a result, its boys were somewhere between privilege and cap-doffing – able to claim that they had received a classical education, but not to join the public-school élite.

In such a mid-way position (which in our time has become virtually universal) every participant is fixed in a sliding scale of competition. Far from being "valued wholly and solely for that which he is in himself", he is required to justify himself through conscious action. Grahame recognised at once that this new environment did not concern itself with his real being, and began the process of self-protection. "Whenever a child is set down in a situation that is distasteful," he wrote, "out of harmony, jarring – and he is very easily jarred – that very moment he begins, without conscious effort, to throw out and to build up an environment really suitable to his soul, and to transport himself thereto."[14]

Always obliquely, as if unable to transcend the caution which school had bred in him, Grahame was to allude again and again to the crushing effect which an imposed system has on the imagination, that mysterious quality which, as he said, "begins to work at the point where vision ceases". He was a passionate defender of the inner sense of potential, that "primal quicksilver" which lives in all children, claiming that it is so often mistaken for "Original Sin; a term wherewith they brand whatever frisks and butts with rude goatish horns against accepted maxims and trim theories of education".[15]

Perhaps schools often manage to inculcate principles which are very different from the ones which they are hoping to drum into the pupils; certainly, in Grahame's case, St Edward's confirmed in him a lasting hatred for theorising. Books, however, could and did provide much-needed friendship and advice. Marcus Aurelius, in particular, became a wise companion, and his *Meditations* offered a consoling word in the ear which the fatherless boy found irresistible. "Generally those amongst us who are called Patricians are rather deficient in paternal affection," the old Roman told him, and Kenneth, descended from the kings of Scotland, must have taken some comfort in regarding the shortcomings of his upbringing as a normal Patrician quirk. That his new friend was nearly two thousand years older than Grahame himself was quite immaterial. He was a companion who might almost have come from the same Calvinist background, a Stoic of great humour, but who understood that survival depended largely on one's capacity to put up with things. "A man ought to be seen by the gods neither dissatisfied with anything nor complaining," he insisted, and Grahame quotes the remark in *The Romance of the Road*, commenting that it does not sound "an excessive demand to make of humanity". Throughout his life, he was suspicious of reformers, not through any lack of human feeling, but because he could not bring himself to believe that grand theories were more to be trusted than the immediate presence of life itself. It was a faith constantly tested by suffering, but Grahame very probably came across Aristotle's dictum that "The beauty of the soul shines out when a man bears with composure one heavy mischance after another, not because he does not feel them, but because he is a man of high and heroic temper".

Heroism was an easy concept to a boy whose childhood had been spent in romantic forays into the persona of Sir Galahad or Ulysses or Nelson. The wild inner capacity for magic was a most precious part of the inner life which he referred to as the "original Waft from the Garden". One could be a hero at will, regardless of current limitations. Even gender was of no account, and he has the fictional sister, Selina, deeply involved in Trafalgar Day, having "taken spiritual part in every notable engagement of the British navy". Planning a commemoration, she "paced the turf restlessly with a short quarter-deck walk".[16] He writes, too, of "the little girl footing it after the gypsy's van, oblivious of lessons . . . hearing naught save the faint, far bugle-summons to the prehistoric little savage that thrills and answers in the tingling blood of her".[17]

In all Grahame's copious reminiscence, there is nothing on the day-to-day work which he did at school. His later rememberings are only of such scant attention as he could give to his inner self through reading and through the free-time wanderings in Oxford. All his experience of the adult world, both at home and at school, had convinced him that it was hell-bent on suppressing the secret excitement of knowing that one is alive. In his view, all children are charged with the wild potential of this self-awareness. Looking back, he said, "The Mid-Victorian young were dangerous animals, only existing on sufferance, and kept as far as possible behind bars, where one need not be always sending to see what baby is doing and tell him not to".[18]

With the advent of school, the "bars" became much more real. Naturally, the possibility of escape was discussed. Edward, during a period of depression about the coming experience, is advised by the first-person narrator that "You can always run away, you know". Both boys are slightly irritated by the literality with which Charlotte takes this possibility. Abandoning all romanticism, she "melted into tears before her vision of a brother with blistered feet and an empty belly, passing nights of frost 'neath the lee of windy haystacks". It is subtly conveyed that the boys meant something less actual in their picture of "running away".[19] For them, the possibility of finding freedom remained a consolation only as long as it was not put to the terrible test of practicality. The real escape lay in the belief that it was possible in a thousand different ways, all of them imaginary.

Kenneth's father, through the significance of his absence, was probably an important influence at this time. An all-boys school is, inescapably, a paternal institution, based on the relationship between boys and older men, and in the late nineteenth century, when the influence of women was at a low ebb, the example set by the father was of prime importance. Victorian men were impressively dressed, wearing top hats which increased their height, black coats, high collars, flamboyant facial hair – all adopted in the interests of increasing the respect with which they were regarded. Cunningham Grahame had no doubt looked a fine and impressive figure of a man when thus dressed for his duties, and it was hard for his son to differentiate between this grandeur and his father's other attributes. The boy must have retained a confused sense of respect, not only for his father's orthodox status, but also for the mysterious power which enabled him to remove himself from the whole scene when he chose to. As Humphrey Carpenter rightly points out in *Secret Gardens*, Cunningham was the ultimate escaper. When things became impossible, he simply abandoned them and went away to a place called Abroad. To his admiring small son, he could do no wrong. After the débâcle of the 1866 Inveraray visit, Kenneth clung obstinately to his father's poetry and long walks, even though robbed of the man's physical presence, and he also clung to the conviction that a man should have the power to remove himself from an intolerable situation if he so chose.

It was a consolation which Grahame never abandoned. The theme of escape recurs constantly in his writing. Again and again his heroes abandon all commitment and make a bolt for freedom, always in response to that wild thrill in the blood which causes Mole to throw down his whitewash brush in the opening paragraph of *The Wind in the Willows*. Perhaps, however unintentionally, St Edward's acted like the wired cork in a champagne bottle, building up a pressure of ferment. In the hands of the unskilled, it is a risky process, fraught with dangers of explosion – it has the same crudity as the burning-pigsty means of producing roast pork which Lamb describes in his famous essay – and yet, occasionally, it will succeed. Grahame learned to "play the system". He worked hard at school, spurred on by the thought of the University place which might be within his grasp, and he played the team games which were instituted once a proper playing-field became available after the school's move to new premises.

He learned the lessons of diplomacy well. He became Head Boy and captain of the Rugby XV, won the Sixth Form Prize, the Divinity Prize and the Prize for Latin Prose, but he also obeyed the advice of Marcus Aurelius to "retire into this little territory of thy own, and above all do not distract or strain thyself, but be free". A kind of security began to be established. His ancient friend encouraged him in it. "A man cannot lose either the past or the future," he said; "for what a man has not, how can any one take this from him?"

The old Roman had not, perhaps, allowed for the vulnerability of the present. During Kenneth's last year at St Edward's, he and his elder brother Willie, whose ill-health had invalided him out of the school three years previously, spent Christmas with their uncle Jack Ingles, who lived in Portsmouth and commanded HMS *Hercules*. Jack was a hugely admired figure to the boys, because of the glamour of visiting him aboard the ship, but this visit was to prove tragic. Willie fell ill with his recurrent bronchitis and, this time, it turned to pneumonia. He died on New Year's Eve, the last day of 1871.

Kenneth was fifteen. He could express no reaction to his brother's death. The funeral was at Highgate Cemetery, where many Grahames lie buried, and, a little over two years later, he went back to visit the grave. Even then, there was nothing he could say. "Close by," he noted in his diary on that spring day of 22 April 1874, "is the grave of Rossetti's father, mother and wife." Somehow, it evokes the ghost of Edward, turning his new hat in his hands in a moment of struggle with boyish tears.

4

Dreams Demolished

Kenneth passed his final exams at St Edward's more than well enough to qualify for the Oxford entrance exam, but the malign influence which always seemed to negate any success made itself felt once again. This time, it spoke through Uncle John, who flatly refused to pay for any further education, announcing instead that his nephew, now the eldest son of the family, would enter the Bank of England. Willie's death two years previously had not made John Grahame any more sympathetic to the emotional needs of his brother's children. It is possible that he genuinely could not afford to see his nephew through a university course, but he was too proud to plead poverty. He knew that Kenneth, unaware of the true facts, regarded him as a skinflint, but he would not ingratiate himself, even though he was grieved by knowing that the boy never forgave him. Bessie wrote afterwards of her father, "I know he was very proud of Kenneth – but for some reason there was not much understanding between them . . . this I know was a sadness to my father".[1]

It was, ironically, Bessie's twin brother, David, the amiable curate of whom Kenneth wrote with such affection, who had unwittingly forged the Bank of England connection. At an unstated time following the move to Cranbourne, the children's old nurse, Ferguson, left the family. Uncle John would not have considered her a justifiable expense now that Roland, the youngest boy, was approaching the double figures which signified the end of childhood. Fern Hill Cottage was much smaller than The Mount, and there is a sense of constriction about the family at that time. Before Willie's death, he and Kenneth had been spending their holidays with other relatives, notably Uncle John and Commander Jack Ingles. David, who had still been living in his mother's house, got married at this period and went to take up a curacy in Halstead, Essex, in 1874. It was before this date, when Kenneth was about thirteen, that Ferguson left.

David evidently understood that this was a traumatic loss for the children, for their nurse had been the only person who had cared for them consistently since babyhood. He suggested that they should keep in touch with Ferguson, and organised a first visit to the nearby Ascot Place, where she had a new post, looking after the children of a couple called Lidderdale. Mrs Lidderdale's mother, Mrs Busk, was, as Helen Grahame recalled, "an old friend of Granny's"[2] – and Mr William Lidderdale was a high-ranking

39

official at the Bank of England, later to become Governor. The friendship between the two families was a genuine one, and Helen wrote that "we were always at Ascot Place". She remembered that there was "a large sheet of ornamental water upon which Alice Busk used to row us about & we skated there in the winter". She mentioned "gorgeous teas", and also adds that "It was through Mrs Busk that Grannie knew Mr Lidderdale. She was staying with the Busks when he proposed to Mary Busk."

William Lidderdale offered the young Kenneth a place as "gentleman clerk" which would become vacant in two year's time. Meanwhile, the boy could help out at Uncle John's office. Nobody seems to have realised how bitter the disappointment was for Kenneth. Bessie wrote innocently, "I can remember how pleased everyone was when Kenneth & afterwards Roland got into the Bank of England".[3] This follows straight on from her lament that the family had very little money, and one senses that it was a very real relief to them that Cunningham's sons were securely established in a career which would make tham financially independent.

Kenneth, however, could not believe that his dreams were to be so cruelly shattered; the betrayal filled him with an anger which never fully left him. There was a long acrimonious interview with Uncle John in which Kenneth begged and pleaded for a change of mind, promising to study hard and take a good degree which would lead to a well-paid academic career, but John Grahame was adamant. He clearly felt that his nephew was heading for a thoroughly undesirable state of existence, and that the time had come for him to put his foot down. Like many adults confronted with the erratic behaviour of an adolescent, he was both irritated and alarmed. Kenneth's habit of going for long, poetry-declaiming walks was uncomfortably reminiscent of his disastrous father, and in John's eyes the whole area of dilettante intellectualism was a dangerous one.

There are hints that Kenneth had reacted badly to the move away from his beloved private world in the rambling gardens and spacious house at The Mount. Helen's assertion that he never had lessons at Fern Hill Cottage perhaps indicates that the boy was in a state of rebellion, and in the months following the abortive trip to Inveraray, when the truth about Cunningham Grahame's dissolute state had become so painfully obvious, it may well have been that Kenneth did not bother to conceal his disillusion with the adult world. His wanderings and self-absorbed poetry-quoting were dealt with by the expedient of packing him off to school, but one feels that Uncle John, who footed the bills, watched his nephew with a suspicious eye.

Kenneth had always assumed that his uncle was simply tight-fisted, and complained afterwards that uncles in general could never see the value of "those luxuries so much more necessary than necessities".[4] It may have been that John could, in fact, have sent his nephew to Oxford, but there was another factor, of which Kenneth was acutely aware. John Grahame was a Scottish Calvinist, and equated self-indulgence of any kind with sin. Excess must be avoided. One could be comfortable, but not flamboyant. The Calvinists had heed to St Paul's words, "Having food and raiment, let us therewith be content. For the love of money is the root of all evil." Even if John had been moderately well off, nothing would induce him to behave as if he were rich.

Against this background, Kenneth's beseeching had no chance of success. He was asking, in John's view, for a gesture of careless munificence which would be deeply distasteful, if not actually sinful. There was, too, a fundamental difference between uncle and nephew in the way they regarded the value of university education. For Kenneth, brought up in the south, it was a vital key to joining the influential élite of society, but John had no patience with such nuances of English class distinction. He, descended from the kings of Scotland as he was, nevertheless had the Scottish democratic instinct, and felt that hard work and a shrewd mind could bring a man into whatever station in life he deserved. His nephew, on the other hand, seemed hell-bent on acquiring English snobberies.

Kenneth in fact remained deeply Scottish throughout his life, but St Edward's had stripped him of his native accent while it taught him its unspoken lessons of social distinction. The impasse between him and his uncle could not be resolved. He would move to London and begin work with the family firm of Grahame, Currie and Spens, Parliamentary Agents.

The dream of Oxford died only slowly. It had sustained him throughout the bleak years at St Edward's, and it was hard to relinquish. Whether John Grahame had made his nephew a firm promise of support for an Oxford place is impossible to substantiate, but he had certainly allowed the boy to think of it as a possibility. For Kenneth, the city and its colleges had become a substitute for the comforting landscape of his earlier childhood. In the high-flown style of his early, school-influenced writing, he made some notes entitled, "What one took away; the Spell of Oxford". The pencil-scribbled page, inked over at a later date, is consciously poetic.

In that gracious grey old city of our abiding, well-watered, of pleasant approach by bridge that bestrode the brimfull river or causeway through standing water lily-starred, grey straying side-streets looped or nestled all along the four noble thoroughfares rich in tower and steeple – the home of restless jackdaws forth-issuing day-long; the organmouth of bell-music vocal through daylight most passionately appealing at the quiet close of evening . . .

The schoolboy Kenneth had been intimately familiar with the cobbled streets and alleys, with the delights of St Giles's Fair and with the occasional academic jamboree to celebrate the installing of a new Chancellor or the awarding of an honorary degree. To judge by his own writings on the subject, he was very much aware of the University, and delighted in the sense of innovative, sometimes extraordinary activity which came from it. In the spring of 1874, Ruskin, who was Slade Professor of Art, proposed to his Magdalen undergraduates that they should combine physical exercise with something useful and creative, rather than indulging in the time-honoured cricket or the "fruitless slashing of the river". He took them out to construct a flower-bordered road in Ferry Hinksey, where there had previously been only a swampy lane, and among the most enthusiastic of the digging gang which rose early in the morning and then went back to Ruskin's house for breakfast was the unlikely figure of Oscar Wilde.

Grahame had expected to become part of this kaleidoscope of learning and pageantry and eccentricity, and the news of his exclusion from it was as painful as a physical assault. It was not until after his death that his feelings about it were revealed, in an article called "Oxford Through a Boy's Eyes" which appeared in *Country Life*.[5] He speaks of "the barred windows, the massive, bolted and enormous gates, which every college had, which were never used or opened, and which gave these otherwise hospitable residences the air of houses of correction". He returns almost obsessively to the theme of exclusion.

> But those great and lofty double gates, sternly barred and never open invitingly, what could they portend? I wondered. It was only slowly and much later that I began to understand that they were strictly emblematical and intended to convey a lesson. Among the blend of qualities that go to make up the charm of collegiate life, there was then more than a touch of (shall I say?) exclusiveness and arrogance. No one thought the worse of it on that account: still its presence was felt, and the gates stood to typify it. Of course, one would not dream of suggesting that the arrogance may still be there. But the gates remain.

Despite his practised stoicism, Grahame could not come to any understanding of his uncle's reasons for debarring him from the academic world. The decision seemed designed to humiliate and, in his eyes, it confirmed the narrow-minded stupidity which characterised his elders. "At a very early age," he wrote in *The Olympians*, "I remember realising in a quite impersonal and kindly way the existence of that stupidity, and its tremendous influence on the world."

There was no point in arguing further. A twentieth-century boy might have rebelled, but Kenneth had not been brought up to argue or to have confidence in his own judgement. He was acutely conscious that Uncle John had met all the expenses of rearing and educating his brother's children, and that gratitude could quite legitimately be demanded. He had no money of his own, and no means of earning any, for the classical curriculum of St Edward's did not consider such mundane matters as the means of making a living, even though the school assumed that its boys would work. In 1876, Kenneth moved to Draycott Lodge in Fulham, the house belonging to another of Cunningham's brothers Robert Grahame, and began work at the family firm.

Robert was a more easy-going man than John. He was a merchant with a free-wheeling taste for world travel, and had lived for many years in Manila, returning home in 1871. He and his wife Georgina rented a villa in Tuscany "for about eighteen years", according to their daughter, Annie,[6] and Kenneth was to spend his first holiday abroad there, accompanied by his sister, Helen. Annie wrote afterwards with affection about Draycott Lodge, "an old-fashioned house . . . which later was occupied by Holman Hunt and then pulled down to make room for a board school so that no trace of it now remains".

Annie was a lively girl with whom Grahame struck up an immediate friendship. Green suggests that she was the first and only true love of his life, but there seems little evidence of this in her letters, for she is casual about Kenneth, almost uninterested.

> I didn't really get to know him till I met him at my cousins and his – the John Grahames, – who kindly asked me to stay with them one summer to autumn in September I think at Pitlochry where they had taken a house for the holidays – I don't remember the date but it was probably 1877 or 81 . . .

Either date would have meant that Kenneth was already resident in Robert Grahame's house, so it may be that she was being deliberately vague, for these letters were written to Grahame's beady-eyed widow. Annie does say, however, "We were very sorry for him as his work at the Bank was evidently so uncongenial and so unsuitable for him with his very decided taste for literature. – I think at the time he hoped to get a job as Inspector of Schools but whenever he applied for anything he was turned down through not fault of his but because he had never been to College and taken his degree." She sounds a happy, self-confident girl, and it may well be that Kenneth was enchanted by her.

Whether or not this was true, things began to improve a little, though the work at Grahame, Currie and Spens offered no satisfaction. According to John's daughter Agnes, who saw Kenneth every other Sunday, when he had a standing invitation to dinner at Sussex Gardens, his position with the firm was ill-defined. She gives the impression that he had been taken on simply in order to fill the two years before his entry into the Bank of England, but goes on to add that he made the best of it. One of her letters recalls that "it was a pleasure to see him come into the room, he looked so happy and pleasant. He was neither too talkative nor too reserved." Even her father had to admit that the boy showed "pluck and steadiness". On the face of it, John's firm hand had produced good results.

Kenneth, in fact, had retreated into the "little territory" of the private mind. He behaved impeccably but, as Agnes observed, it was a self-controlled performance. "I have never heard him talk about himself," she said. The suppressed feelings had not disappeared, however. Kenneth was studying shorthand during some of the ample free time which Grahame, Currie and Spens afforded him, and there is some evidence that he was thinking of political journalism as an alternative career, though he was discreet enough not to mention it. Uncle John read the signs accurately and took counteraction at once, declaring firmly that his nephew was not getting enough exercise and healthy company. He suggested in his authoritative way that Kenneth should join the Volunteers, the then equivalent of the Territorial Army.

There is something faintly comic about this mustard-plaster application of Army discipline to put down an attack of decadent literary leanings, and Kenneth may well have chalked up yet another Olympian idiocy to his list, but he made no objection. He joined the London Scottish, and gave every appearance of enjoying it. He grew a moustache to go with the grey kilt, the high-buttoned tunic and the bonnet with the jaunty cockade. A photograph of him at that time shows a certain bravado in the way he sits with hands gripping the swagger-stick across spread knees, and yet there is an evasiveness about the slightly protuberant eyes which makes him seem as wary as a hare. What he called "the encaged observer within" looks at the outside world with astonishment and a trace of horror.

Together with his younger brother, Roland, Kenneth went often to the Lidderdales' London house by the Thames, keeping up their contact with Ferguson, who retained her affection for the boys. A letter from Evelyn Lidderdale says, "My memories of him go back a long way, to the days when I was a very little girl walking beside the perambulator in Hyde Park with the younger children, & watching him & Roland drilling with the London Scottish".[7] Writing in 1933, Chalmers expanded this incident into something much more dramatic.

Kenneth had become a sergeant and presently, recognizing his admirers, ordered a complimentary charge to be made upon the perambulator. His platoon, flourishing its muskets, therefore advanced with leaps, bounds and loud cheers. The two objectives in the perambulator were enchanted. Not so their guardian, who thought that her Master Kenneth had "gone gyte". "Mighty me," she muttered, "I must save the young leddies." And she upset the perambulator, upset the whole "rickmatick", over the low railing. However, her particular soldiers picked up its contents who were more enchanted than ever.

Green reproduced this story without question in his 1959 book, but there is an element of Chinese whispers about its origin. Had it been credited to Ferguson, it would have seemed more likely, but Evelyn Lidderdale would hardly have ignored such a colourful event in her more sober recollection. The sad fact is that Kenneth Grahame's widow had a fertile and enthusiastic imagination, and her influence on the first biography has set up a mythology which tends, even now, to fog the truth.

Whether factual or not, the story is intuitively right in its perception. The charge on the perambulator is exactly the sort of thing Kenneth would have liked to do, even though his care about the way he presented himself would probably have ruled out such behaviour. He never lost touch with his childhood self, and remained convinced, rightly or wrongly, that the world of one's early years is never abandoned, but merely tucked away to protect it from the ravages of adult life. Every child, he asserted, has a kingdom of his or her own which is both precious and essentially private. "Even with each other," he observed, "children do not usually share their kingdoms. To be sure, a fellow-feeling in kingdoms is a rare fine thing – the only thing, perhaps, really worthy the name of sympathy; and kingdoms blossom and expand so splendidly under a judicious dual control."[8] The London Scottish charge would have been a spontaneous blossoming of exactly this kind; but such wonderful ideas are seldom put into practice, for, as Kenneth pointed out, "the risk is too great – the risk of jeers, rebuffs, sheer incapacity to understand – to make such confidences common".

At this time of final farewell to his own physical childhood, Grahame retained an extraordinary understanding of the imaginative world which can be so real to children. The child, he asserted, "steps deliberately out of the present tangibility into his property over the border; and again, when his time is up, steps just as deliberately back. In continuity, in ordered procession of facts, the thing goes on with just the same regularity as that other routine of baths, bread-and-butter, lessons and bed; and is about as near a thing to a fourth dimension as can be found in actual working order."

He is accurate in his definition of this fourth dimension as an alternative reality, and points out that boredom triggers an immediate jump into it. "A duty-walk with an uninteresting person is simply a return ticket to cloudland. As bed-time arrives you promptly book for the same terminus; hence it comes that you never properly fall asleep in this tangible world, but pass through the stage of your own peculiar country to that droll continent which mixes up your two existences for you with a humour you could never achieve unaided."

Grahame saw imagination as the subverter of the solemnly organised adult world. He also felt that over-organisation acts as an automatic stimulus to a child's imaginings, citing the case of the tedious church services which were a fixed part of every Victorian Sunday. "The mother who notes with delight the rapt, absorbed air of her little son, during the course of a sermon that is stirring her own very vitals, and builds high hopes thereon, is probably egregiously mistaken. Ten to one he is a thousand miles away, safe in his own kingdom; and what is more, he has shut the door behind him. *She* is left outside, with the parson and the clerk."

He is emphatic that a child who is absent-minded at meals, or "who fails to catch the salient points of an arithmetic or geography lesson . . . is not necessarily a fool, nor half-baked as to mental equipment". He asks, "who shall say he is not educating himself all the time? In his own way, of course, not yours." It might be A. S. Neill speaking.

Grahame goes on to lay bare the source of his own self-protection. A sensible child, he claims, will simply escape into a make-believe world of his own devising, and "there he will stay, of a certainty, until you choose to make things pleasanter. Life is so rough to him, so full of pricks and jogs and smartings, that without this blessed faculty of projecting a water-tight skin – nay, an armour-plating – his little vessel's seams would gape and its timbers crack too early."

He cautions well-meaning adults against "desiring to walk in the child's garden as very God . . .", pointing out that this "Bird of Paradise that he carries encaged within him, this Host that he guards within his robes through the jostling mart of shouting commonplaces, may be both germ and nutriment of an individuality which shall at least never suffer him to be a tame replica". All these quotations come from "Saturnia Regna", a piece he wrote for the *New Review* in 1896.

Much of this self-consoling was a defence against the impact of London, which pitched the seventeen-year-old Kenneth into a see-sawing balance of involvement and withdrawal. His private kingdom, created of field and hedgerow memories mingled with the wild open coast of West Scotland, was utterly different from the "shouting commonplaces" of London. Although Fulham was then a village, standing among market gardens which the present-day Drayton Gardens commemorates, Robert Grahame's house was only a place to go back to in the evenings. The office was in Westminster, and Kenneth spent his days in the city centre. Then as now, there were beggars on the streets, but the difference between the classes was even more marked than it is today. Victorian dress was formal, immaculate and expensive, or else it was the ragged remains of it. Food markets were in the middle of the city's maze of cobbled streets and alleyways, and people lived in the foully overcrowded slums which were close then to the grand new buildings of the banks and insurance companies; the poor and the rich were thrust together in sharp contrast. Agriculture had given way to a vast rise in business, and a flood of erstwhile land workers had poured into the towns in search of the largely illusory well-paid work which the new enterprises promised. Kenneth had come from the sleepy rural nursery of Berkshire to a cram-full city where fortunes were being made amid the poverty which jostled him daily. For the first time, he knew from personal experience that thousands of people were dirty and foul-smelling, and that they could not afford the scrupulous morals and formal behaviour which, until now, had made the world seem relatively safe.

Paid work, he saw, supplied the only motive for remaining in such a place. The need for money was a treadmill which kept on turning, and he himself was subject to the same necessity. We are, he said in an essay called "Aboard the Galley", "galley-slaves of the basest sort, fettered to the oar ... A common misery links us all, like the chain that runs the length of the thwarts." The piece goes on to toy with the idea of rebellion, wondering "why do we never once combine – seize on the ship, fling our masters into the sea ...". His answer is interesting. He does not blame despotism, or powerlessness, but recognises bleakly that the slaves will never combine because they are divided among themselves. The same awareness of status which divides the rich from the poor divides the not-so-poor from the poorer. "A little modesty," he begs, "a short sinking of private differences; and then we should all be free and equal gentlemen of fortune, and I would be your Captain." The final phrase is knowingly provocative, and he goes straight on to the inevitable retort. " 'Who? you? you would make a pretty Captain!' " His own response is not in inverted commas, but speaks with a self-mocking editorial voice. "Better than you, you scurvy, skulking, little galley-slave!" The ship of state and commerce sails on despite all groans from below decks, because her fettered oarsmen seek to identify the differences between them rather than the similarities. "And they know this well, the gods our masters, pliers of the whip."

The shrug is ironic rather than resentful. If the Olympian adult world insisted on measuring importance by the relative standards of money and social status, then its stupidity could not be penetrated. For Grahame, inheritor of the great line of poetic anarchists which goes back to Socrates and beyond, existence itself was an ongoing astonishment, and there could be no significant difference between one man and another when each was aware of "this Host that he guards within his robe".[9] To rebel, no less than to conform, was a recognition of the status-system and implied a willingness to evaluate the self in its terms. Grahame came to understand the system very well, but although he never accepted it in the inner reality of his own mind, he would not rebel – not because he condoned it, but because to do so was not a true dissent. He stood outside it and, when he participated in it, watched himself doing so.

In these first London years, he investigated his new surroundings with the same minute care he had lavished on the "familiar fields and farms, of which we knew every blade and stick". Like most country-dwellers who find themselves confined within towns, his eye sought discontentedly for beauty and found it in unexpected things. He recalled some of them later, in a piece called "Pastels".

A welcome magician, one of the first real suns of the year, is transforming with a touch of alchemy our grimy streets, as they emerge from under the pall of another soot-stained winter; and the eye, weary for colour, bathes itself with renewed delight in the moving glint and flutter and splash of hue. The buses whirl up, and recede in vivid spots of red and blue and green, tawdry house-fronts are transmuted into mellowest shades of blue-grey and tawny; or, freshly painted, throw up broad masses of dazzling white.

The need to be in touch with nature was always dominant.

Do but give a glance up, and you are whirled away from the roaring city as though it had never been. From turquoise at the rim to the hue of the hedge-sparrow's egg, it melts through all gradations, the wonderful crystalline blue. In the liquid spaces pigeons flash and circle, joyous as if they sped their morris over some remote little farmstead, lapped round by quiet hills; and as they stoop and tumble, the sunlight falls off their wings in glancing drops of opal sheen.

But Grahame was not entirely escapist. He could find some pleasure in what he saw, even when all signs of the natural world had been obscured. "The darkness closes round with completeness; and the dainty broughams, whirling dinner-wards, flash back the successive lamplights from their polished sides. Hansoms, speeding all one way, dot the gloom with specks of red from the little hole at the back of each lamp."[10]

Even to the most devoted country-dweller, the London of the late nineteenth century had its charms. Helen Thorp wrote, with nostalgia,

London was much gayer, much prettier in those days. Piccadilly was charming, all the houses had flowers in window box and awnings over the balconies. There were simple railings round Buckingham Palace, & lovely Standard lilac trees & grass, why oh why change it to such awfulness?[11]

Inevitably, Grahame's explorations led him to Soho. He was enchanted. In the days before cheap travel and aeroplanes, "the Continent" was remote and exotic, tinged with exciting wickedness along with the utterly un-British scent of garlic. Kenneth fell in love with his first red-checked tablecloth and Italian menu, and things Mediterranean came to represent the whole restless, romantic side of his nature. He was beginning to enjoy a new confidence as a man about Old Compton Street. London, it seemed, could offer some compensations for the dreariness of his occupation at Uncle John's office as a "pale-faced quill-driver". His younger cousin, Reginald Ingles, recalled breathlessly that "Kenneth took me to dine at a small Italian restaurant in Soho and we had about ten courses for 1s. 6d. and drank Chianti out of a basket bottle and, afterwards, he took me to the Lyceum to see Faust. It *was* decent of him."

Reginald Ingles was the son of the nautical Uncle Jack, another of Bessie Grahame's brothers, and he had always liked Kenneth since the days when the Grahame boys used to come for holidays. "He was the nice one," he wrote, "who was always kind and whom we were always delighted to see and to go out with. He never ticked us off and was always ready to help us in little things." He and Kenneth had experienced the first of many delectable meals together when Commander Jack Ingles had taken them aboard the Hercules, to have a breakfast of omelettes and devilled kidneys in the ward-room. Reginald in his turn had gone to St Edward's, in 1877, starting just after Kenneth had left, and was delighted when his big cousin came to visit him.

You know how pleased a boy is when some relation comes to see him at school – and very few ever came to see me? I *was* delighted to see K. and I thought him such a nice, kind sort to come and such a nice-looking chap. He played in a cricket match for a bit. I remember it quite well. He stood at the wicket with his bat up in the air – not on the ground (some cricketers *did* in those days) – and put up a good innings and hit some fine slogs. He was mostly *awfully* nice to me.[12]

It may have been partially loneliness which drove Kenneth to seek the company of a cousin seven years younger than himself, genuine though the liking was. The first years in London began in complete friendlessness, apart from the quiet support (and perhaps affection) of his cousin Annie, but Kenneth's taste for the Continental and the Bohemian brought its own reward. One night, dining alone in Soho, he found himself unable to avoid overhearing the conversation of a cheerfully noisy party nearby. The group was dominated by a man whom Green describes as "a huge, grey-bearded, heavily-muscled lion of about fifty", and Kenneth chuckled at one of his particularly Rabelaisian anecdotes. The stranger glanced across at him and invited him to join the party. The evening was a jovial one, and cards were exchanged at the end of it. Kenneth found that he had met Frederick James Furnivall.

Furnivall was one of the most flamboyant Bohemian figures of the age, a man of recklessly wide abilities, contemptuous of the British conviction that it is somehow unsound to do more than one thing well. He had read mathematics at Cambridge and was later called to the Bar, but he had abandoned both careers in order to serve his passion for literature. By the time Grahame met him, he was editing the *New English Dictionary* (which was later to become the *Oxford English Dictionary*) for the Philological Society, and was lecturing on English poetry. A close friend of Ruskin's, he was a dedicated and eccentric Socialist, striding round London in a red shirt and escorting groups of ragged children from the slums round Kew Gardens. He was a compulsive organiser and founder of learned societies, beginning with the Early English Text Society in 1864, then moving on to the Chaucer Society, the Ballad Society and the New Shakespeare Society, which attempted to date the bard's texts by study of their metre, and which came in for a good deal of ridicule in academic circles.

Grahame was fascinated. The big, shaggy man belonged in the legendary world of Tennyson, Swinburne and Rossetti, and yet he was not an Olympian. He was fully committed to the joys of direct experience, bellowing with laughter at the folly of status-seekers and full of the delighted astonishment of a still-lively childhood. For Kenneth, he represented all the qualities he had hoped to find at Oxford. The half-day escapes from St Edward's had put him in touch with the Pre-Raphaelite flavour of the university, where William Morris had turned down the Chair of Poetry and Ruskin had taught the building of roads. Grahame had absorbed the idea that the dignity of creative labour could represent a Utopian ideal in which the galley-slaves were freed from the tyranny of money-earning, and St Edward's had unwittingly reinforced the same ethic. With the Victorian double standard which kept respectability intact, the school strove to conceal the fact that it appealed to parents because it was cheaper than Eton. Money was not talked about, and the general air of gentlemanly high-mindedness implied a contempt for commerce. Most of the boys went into the Church or the Army. Kenneth (as Uncle John had realised with some irritation) had been tacitly encouraged to regard such careers as the desirable ones. Work for the prime purpose of earning a good salary was a little distasteful, an interruption of the academic and spiritual processes.

Furnivall breezed into Kenneth's life with a confident assumption that St Edward's and John Ruskin were perfectly right in their respective attitudes. Life was too fascinating and important to be frittered away on the mere earning of money. His Socialism was of the idealistic kind which attempts to share with all people the notion that commercial values can be transcended – a very different thing from the class struggle which Kenneth found so repellant. The beautiful society envisaged by the Pre-Raphaelite ideal, however, soared above the "private differences" of the galley-slaves and represented a co-operative, creative entity which was very close to the dream kingdom of childhood. The two aspects of Socialism were, and remain, deeply incompatible, for aesthetic Utopianism does not recognise the simple need of the under-privileged to secure a larger share of the available money.

Kenneth avoided all political in-fighting. His liking for Furnivall was instinctive and personal, cemented by the discovery that his new friend shared his passion for boats. Furnivall was, in fact, a champion sculler, and had designed a new racing boat and, on finding that young Grahame was a good oarsman, the pair of them went out on the river for the first of many enjoyable jaunts.

Within the year, Furnivall had conscripted Grahame and his cousin Annie into the New Shakespeare Society, and had even talked Kenneth into becoming the Society's Honorary Secretary. It must have been a somewhat alarming post, for the group was a turbulent one, given to heated debate which had a habit of spilling over into public quarrelling. Furnivall loathed Swinburne for both literary and personal reasons, and began to refer to him in print as "Pigsbrook". Members complained to Robert Browning, the Society's vice-president, about the founder's "course and impertinent language", but Furnivall shook off such criticisms like a horse brushing away flies. Eventually, however, the literary scandal became so outrageous that members began to resign in protest, and the Society collapsed.

Secretary or not, Kenneth never once made any contribution to the stormy arguments during the Friday evening meetings at University College.[13] His instinct for self-preservation was well established, but it contributed to his popularity as a modest, sensitive young man, refreshingly lacking in bombast. Chalmers asserted unquestioningly that Mary Richardson, who was friendly with Kenneth's sister, Helen, remembered Grahame as "so much younger than all the big-wigs gathered round the table", and that she "was surprised to see the assistance he gave Dr Furnivall in the management of the meeting" – but in fact this information came, like so much that was attributed to other sources, from Kenneth's widow, Elspeth.[14] It was, perhaps, Grahame's very lack of assertiveness which made him popular with the young men and women who would become his fellow contributors to *The Yellow Book* and to the other literary periodicals of the time.

In these early days, however, Kenneth's writing was still a furtive affair, restricted to private notebooks and kept well hidden from Uncle John. There is some evidence, though, that he was trying his hand at the publication of anonymous pieces. His old school's magazine, *St Edward's Chronicle*, carried a series of essays that year by a contributor who signed himself Old Boy, but they had exactly the blend of naïve enthusiasm and slightly pompous parading of political gossip which a clever seventeen-year-old working in a parliamentary office would display. Kenneth kept quiet about these efforts, and it was not until a couple of years later that he plucked up the courage to show Furnivall some of his writing, although he was increasingly caught up in his friend's eccentric enterprises. In the early summer of his second year in London, he even allowed himself to be involved in a staging of Shelley's *The Cenci*.

It is difficult now to see what a scandalous undertaking this was. Shelley had been dead for nearly sixty years, and yet he remained outrageous in the conventional Victorian view. No one had forgotten his pamphlet on *The Necessity of Atheism* which had caused him to be sent down from Oxford, or his elopement with Mary Godwin, whose mother, Mary Wollstonecraft, had written *A Vindication of the Rights of Woman*. His death itself, followed by the notorious funeral pyre on the beach at Viareggio, was considered shocking, and the sad ghost of his first young wife, the eighteen-year-old Harriet Westbrook, who committed suicide when he left her for the equally young Mary, cast a further shadow over his reputation. Grahame, with his essential innocence, was probably simply admiring of the man and his work. Shelley's polemical essays are interesting for the intellectualism of their defence of poetry as a real human need, and a young, dismayed banker of the late nineteenth century might well have been impressed by some of his statements.

> The cultivation of poetry is never more to be desitred than at periods when, from an excess of the selfish and calculating principle, the accumulation of the materials of external life exceed the quantity of the power of assimilating them to the internal laws of human nature. The body has then become too unwieldy for that which animates it.[15]

Not all Grahame's contemporaries took such a studious view of Shelley's output. *The Cenci* itself was a violent piece on the incestuous activities of a sixteenth-century Italian family, and prurient public interest had sold out the first edition very quickly. It was, however, banned from the stage, "on a plea of being too horrible", as Shelley wrote in pained surprise. To Thomas Love Peacock he complained that "magazines blaspheme me at a great rate".[15]

In defiance of the Lord Chamberlain's prohibition, Furnivall used the legal loophole of a "club production". He went about it with a crusading conviction which was hard to refuse, and Kenneth found himself treading the boards of the Grand Theatre, Islington, as Giacomo. Furnivall gave his housemaid a ticket for the show, and, oblivious to the Gothic plot, she commented only that "Mr Grahame did look so handsome walking up and down the stage in his best clothes".[16] The critics were not so easily impressed, and the production raised a howl of disgust from the *Pall Mall Gazette*. The Shelley Society sprang into a notoriety which was much enjoyed by Furnivall, but Grahame was acutely embarrassed. He never appeared on a stage again.

He was rescued from the furore by Uncle Robert, who, with his daughter, Annie and his wife, Georgina, took Kenneth and Helen off to their villa in Tuscany for the summer holidays. There, his growing love of the South blossomed into a mature passion. He was stunned by the beauty of Italy. Georgina was a talented gardener, and from the stone archway leading out from the villa's paved courtyard, she had planted a profusion of roses, and jonquils and tall white madonna lilies. The air was scented with lemon and verbena, and in the distance one could see, as she wrote, "the Vallombrosa hills, and lying down below, veiled in the misty light of the hot June sun, were the domes and spires of Florence, with the blue Apennines rising, beyond, to the far south . . .". She published her writing about Italy in a book called *In a Tuscan Garden*.

This visit was in May 1886, and on the second Sunday, Kenneth and Annie went for a long walk across the hills to the Festival of the Madonna del Sarso. They had arranged, Annie said, for her mother and Helen to come down with the carriage and meet them, but were told, quite wrongly, by local Italians, that the couple had already left. Helen and Georgina accordingly went away again and, when Kenneth and Annie emerged from the inn where they had gone for some refreshment, they were faced by another very long walk home. "We got back about 7 p.m.," Annie said, "none the worse for the long day, which Kenneth beguiled with delightful fairy tales."[17] It sounds an innocent way for a young man to spend so much time with his pretty cousin but, at seventeen, Grahame was indeed an innocent. He had the good judgement, however, to buy a blue-and-white majolica plaque, a reproduction of a della Robbia Madonna and Child by Cantazala, although he had, as yet, no house on which to display it.

In Grahame's writing, the South is presented as a recurring compulsion, almost like the onset of a disease. The practical Water Rat, packer of picnic baskets and nifty oarsman, has no defence against it, and his friend the Mole, "looking into his eyes, saw that they were glazed and set and turned a streaked and shifting grey". And yet, with his acute awareness of the inner self, Kenneth discriminates accurately between the enchantment of the idea of travel and the reality of actually doing it. Without meaning to do so, he again identifies the nature of imagination. In a lecture given towards the end of his life before the Keats–Shelley Society in Rome, he mused on the quantum change of state which occurs between anticipation and the event itself.

Which of us, even today, when about to visit some new far-distant city or country, does not form, sometimes deliberately but usually almost unconsciously, a picture of it, more or less vivid, beforehand? . . . I suppose that all of us here can remember our coming to Rome for the first time in our lives, and the preconception of the place that we brought along with us. Do we not all remember, when we reached Rome at last, the same two things – the absence of that strangeness which I have called the fantastic element and which somehow we cannot keep out of our imaginings, and secondly, the slight touch of disappointment that even the beauty of Rome was not just that particular beauty that we had caught a glimpse of through the magic casement of our idealism?

Despite his distaste for theorising, Grahame may have picked up Ruskin's dictum that imagination "is the power of perceiving, or conceiving with the mind, things which cannot be perceived with the senses". He continued to write in secret, but after July 1878, no further "Old Boy" articles appeared in his school magazine, the editor having replaced them with contributions of a more liberal flavour. If, as seems likely, they had been a ploy designed to make Uncle John change his mind, the gambit had failed. It had been a shrewd enough idea; political journalism might well have appealed to a dour parliamentary agent more than flights of fancy. The trouble was, they had not been done well enough. Boys in their late teens, no matter how precocious, are not likely to have a mature judgement on matters of commerce and government, and if Uncle John saw the pieces, he was not impressed. Even if he had been impressed, the prospect of a literary career, with all its associated insecurity and Bohemianism, would still have appalled him. The arrangement stood firm. Kenneth would enter the Bank of England on the first day of January 1879. England, he may have reflected, had no respect for the fine old Scottish festival of Hogmanay and its sore-headed aftermath.

5

The Solitude of the Roaring Street

In preparation for his apprenticeship to the Old Lady of Threadneedle Street, Grahame left his Uncle Robert's house and found lodgings much nearer to the Bank, in a flat in Bloomsbury Street. He had been in the habit of walking to work, both as an economy measure and because he enjoyed it, but to walk from Fulham to the City was impossible. Besides, he was now nineteen years old, and knew his way round London reasonably well. It was time to have a home base of his own.

New Year's Day 1879 dawned in thick fog. The city was blanketed in its choking yellowness, giving horses a morning's rest in their stables, for no wheeled traffic moved in the streets. Pedestrians groped their way along if they were rash enough to venture out at all, feeling with toe-tip for the edge of the pavement before crossing the muffled, empty roads to their invisible further side. The new young clerk reckoned that he had better allow an hour and a half to find his way from Bloomsbury to the Bank, and set out from his flat at half-past eight. He arrived at the agreed gentlemanly hour of ten o'clock, fog-dewed and red-eyed − and found himself the only employee in the place. Fog, it seemed, constituted a well-established banking reason for a morning off. In his 1933 biography, Chalmers recorded the event with the superiority of one who had spent most of his own life as a banker. "An hour later, he was to learn from a youthful colleague, in a frock-coat and flourishing whiskers, the first principle of Finance. Which is that a London Particular excuses all things dilatory in a banker and especially is it indulgence, extenuation and ample justification for an extra hour in bed and a leisurely breakfast."

The Bank came as something of a shock to Kenneth. After two years of waiting to enter an establishment which his elders regarded with deep respect, he had assumed that it would be grave and august, a formal, well-mannered citadel of finance. Nothing had prepared him for the Hogarthian rowdiness of the place. The Bank's conservatism, he was to discover, had nothing to do with the careful self-regulation of Uncle John's office, where excess was regarded as sinful. The Old Lady thrived on excess of every kind. For all her majesty, she was a bawd with a disreputable ancestry, born in the coffee houses of the City where the bartering goldsmiths had extended their craft into loans against security. She had grown up in the eighteenth century, and clung with romantic obstinacy to that period of her glorious youth. She remained theatrical and anarchic, intoxicated with her power, and those who worked for her fell under the same spell, just as actors utterly accept the magic of the play.

Mrs Jane Courtney, whose maiden name, suitably enough, was Hogarth, was one of the first women employed by the Bank, and in her book, *Recollected in Tranquillity*, she dwells with some pleasure on its pantomine qualities.

> The Bank was full of eighteenth century, and even earlier, survivals, the dress of its gate porters, the "nightly watch" going round with Guy Fawkes lanterns (I once asked them when I met them at four o'clock on a summer Saturday afternoon, why they did this and they seemed hardly to know, except that it was an immemorial custom); the company of Guards coming in at sunset, their sentinels stationed in the courtyard . . .; the Bank cats which a parsimonious Governor put down by docking their "allowance"; the great bars of gold and silver in the fortress-like bullion vaults, brought in from Lothbury under guard through an archway which looked as if it ought to have a portcullis; the almost human gold-weighing machines, which spat out light sovereigns sideways and let the rest fall in a steady stream into copper vessels like coal pans – all the significant evidence of Britain's wealth and British solidarity, so picturesque, so historic, so reassuring, and, in the long run, so unbearably tedious.

Even more evocative are the memoirs of Allan Fea, who joined the Bank two years after Grahame and worked at first in the Drawing Office.

> In 1881 the Bank was very different from the orderly place it is now, and the above-mentioned department was one of the rowdiest of the lot. The pandemonium was a little startling to a novice – jokes shouted from one end of the office to the other, the singing of a line from some popular song winding up with "Amen" in a solemn cadence of about a hundred voices. If you were not good at dodging you were liable at any time to have your hat knocked off your head by a flying Pass-book . . .[1]

Little did the unsuspecting customers guess what went on. Fea describes the drunkenness which was prevalent. It was, he said, "by no means uncommon in the eighties to see fellows in the washing-places trying to sober themselves with douses of cold water, or lying prone upon a table for a while, ere they dare return to their desks".

The clerks were an oddly selected lot, for the most part quite lacking Grahame's sense of privilege in having been allowed to work in London's grandest financial institution. Many of them were small farmers who came wearing their unwashed country clothes, bringing with them a strong aroma of the farmyard. They also brought their fighting dogs, chaining them by the desk until the day's work (such as it was) had been completed, and they could get down to the serious business of an after-hours dog-fight in the lavatories. These same lavatories were also used for a bit of impromptu butchery, for the clerks would buy meat in bulk at the nearby wholesale market and lug it into the office. Fea observed that "it was a very ordinary thing for the householders in an office to carve up half a sheep downstairs in the washing department".

Many of the clerks were men of private means, and were not, unlike Grahame, dependent on the Bank for the salary it paid them. This information came from the Bank's then Secretary, a Mr A. W. Dascombe, speaking in the 1950s. They came in, he said, "for purely vocational reasons". One cannot help but ponder on the nature of these reasons, and on their profitability. Grahame had been led to believe that a clerkship could only be obtained as a result of humble supplication and a certain amount of string-pulling, and it must have startled him to find that, until recently, the Bank had maintained a robust tradition of advertising vacancies by means of a notice hung on the railing outside. Legend had it that a butcher left his meat with the Bank porter while he came in to apply for a job, and collected it five minutes later, a full-blown clerk.

The nineteen-year-old Grahame was half-amused, half-appalled by the goings-on. He had expected to join an Olympian society of impeccable manners, and instead found himself a member of an unrepentantly rowdy rabble, dealing in the country's commerce with all the gusto of horse-traders. He hovered between disgust and fascination, revolted by the hoggish table-manners and by such things as the fellow-clerk who continually hawked and spat as he sat at his desk, yet astounded by the sheer aplomb of the place. The head of department, he noted with astonishment, made no move to reprimand the spitter, but merely ordered a daily issue of sawdust to be strewn round his desk.

There were compensations. The Bank supplied some wonderfully colourful characters, both among the staff and customers, the latter seeming for the most part to have been a touchingly innocent lot. Green mentions an old lady, Amelia Macabe, who dressed like a little girl in muslins and a strawberry-trimmed hat, and distributed little booklets of her own poems to the clerks. There was, too, a lady who would turn up on dividend day with a touching request that the cashier would "make it as much as he could". In the lean period before pay-day, over-spent clerks would make a bit of money by raffling a possession; regrettably, there is no record of what was raised by a lot consisting of an uncle's cremated bones.

Grahame watched and learned, laying down experience which would pile up into a valuable store of material for eventual writing. Chastened by the failure of his bid to escape the Bank and become a political journalist, he kept a cautious silence about his writing ambitions, although he purloined a Bank ledger for his own use, in which he noted down scraps of poetry (both other people's and his own), together with ideas for stories and essays. The theme of escape continued to move restlessly in his mind, and he was intrigued to find that he was not alone in his yearnings. There were countless tales among the clerks of legendary figures who had in one way or another fled to their freedom, and Grahame augmented these by digging about in the official Bank records, sometimes turning up an unexpected gem. The ledger-diary, which disappeared shortly after Grahame's death and has never been rediscovered, contained an entry which Green records;

A certain old clerk in one of the pay departments of the Bank of England used to spend his yearly holiday in relieving some turnpike-man of his post and performing all the duties pertaining thereto till recalled to Threadneedle Street. This was vulgarly supposed to be an instance of slavery to one's accustomed work − of "pay and receive" − and spoken of pityingly. But that man doubtless know what he wanted, knew one way of seeking Life. And what better way? And if all he was good for was to pay and take payments at least he recognised the fact, accepted it, boldly built thereon and went for it in its best shape.

This straightforward bit of reflection re-appeared much later in an essay called "The Eternal Whither", published in the *National Observer* when Grahame was thirty-three, re-written with no specific reference to the Bank, and in far more flamboyant prose. The last sentence, however, is deleted. Instead, we read:

And yet that clerk had discovered for himself an unique method of seeing Life at its best, the flowing, hurrying, travelling, marketing Life of the Highway; the life of bagman and cart, of tinker and pig-dealer, and all cheery creatures that drink and chaffer together in the sun. He belonged, above all, to the scanty class of clear-seeing people who know both what they are good for and what they really want.

The split between the wished-for existence and the real one had continued and strenghtened in Grahame's mind, and he knew it. He adds a wistful sentence which makes this abundantly clear:

To know what you would like to do is one thing; to go out boldly and do it is another − and a rarer; and the sterile fields about Hell-Gate are strewn with the corpses of those who would an if they could.

At nineteen, however, this bleak awareness had not yet matured. He was still able to enjoy the quirky and sometimes macabre eccentricities of the

Bank at their own level, with no regretful comparisons. "The Eternal Whither" is a story based on a laconic entry in the attendance book which the clerks were required to sign each day. One particular clerk's name "ceases abruptly from appearing; he signs, indeed, no more. Instead of signature you find, a little later, writ in careful commerical hand, this entry: 'Mr . . . did not attend at his office today, having been hanged at eight o'clock in the morning for horse-stealing' ".

Almost reluctantly, one senses, Grahame began to find life at the Bank enjoyable. The pace of the work was leisured and much of the business was done simply by sending a messenger across the city with a note to be delivered or a payment to be made or collected. These errands could involve some pleasant dawdling through alleyways and markets, or might even provide a legitimate excuse for a trip on the steamer from the Old Swan pier down to Shadwell and Wapping and all the tarry, exotic life of the docks, or up to the grandeur of Westminster. Lunchtimes could provide a civilised escape from the Bank in one of the city chop-houses where succulent meat was served on pewter plates with a mug of ale. It was true that the crowdedness and artificiality of city life, together with the absence of things natural, remained as a nagging pain, familiar to anyone who has looked with sudden sadness at the clear blue sky between buildings, or become aware of the un-growing earth imprisoned under stone and tar macadam, but Grahame had become a Londoner in that partial way which is so typical of Londoners. Despite his deepest desires to escape and bury his head, like the small boy he inwardly remained, in the comforting bosom of nature, he was caught up in the bustling hurly-burly of the city, and was vastly entertained by it.

The friendship with Frederick Furnivall continued and, a few months after he began work at the Bank, Grahame plucked up the courage to show the "lion of a man" the accumulated jottings which he had entered in the purloined ledger. It was, he knew, a risky step. Furnivall was an impatient man who did not suffer fools gladly, and he was used to dealing with the work of fully professional writers. Grahame had heard his contemptuous dismissal of Swinburne as an empty windbag, and must have feared a similar blast of scorn; it is a mark of his desperation to know the truth about his abilities that he was willing to lay himself open to Furnivall's judgement.

The verdict, was, for Furnivall, a gentle one. He dismissed the poetry as unpromising, but was encouraging about the prose, considering that some of the pieces might be worth offering to an editor. Chalmers, perhaps again influenced by the dubious literary taste of Grahame's widow, questions the worth of this decision, lamenting that "a beautiful poet of the lighter sort, an Austin Dobson maybe, was strangled at birth". Sixty years later, we may be glad of this euthanasia. Dobson's *Vignettes in Rhyme* and *Proverbs in Porcelain* are peculiarly awful, as a random sample goes to show:

Rose kissed me to-day.
Will she kiss me tomorrow?
Let it be as it may,
Rose kissed me today,
But the pleasure gives way
To a saviour of sorrows; –
Rose kissed me to-day, –
Will she kiss me tomorrow?

Grahame, who could put infinite musicality into prose, was uneasy within the constriction of rhyme and metre, and tended to retreat into academic bombast in order to solve the problems. Only occasionally, when dealing with a strong, simple childhood emotion, did he transcend his self-conscious cleverness. His early lament for a puppy, called "TO ROLLO, Untimely taken", is one such.

Puppy, yours a pleasant grave,
Where the seeding grasses wave!
Now on frolic morns the kitten
Over you, once scratched and bitten –
Still forgiving! – plays alone.
You, who planted many a bone,
Planted now yourself, repose
Tranquil tail, incurious nose!
Chased no more, the indifferent bee
Drones a sun-steeped elegy.
  Puppy, where long grasses wave,
  Surely yours a pleasant grave!

"Whom the gods love" – was this why,
Rollo, you must early die?
Cheerless lay the realms of night –
Now your small unconquered sprite
(Still familiar, as with us)
Bites the ears of Cerberus:
Chases Pluto, Lord of Hell,
Round the fields of Asphodel:
Sinks to sleep at last, supine
On the lap of Proserpine!
  While your earthly part shall pass,
  Puppy, into flowers and grass![2]

One must remember that the classical personages were very real to a boy who had grown up with the characters of Greek mythology. There are infelicities of rhyme and phrasing, but the piece is free from affectation.

Grahame was immensely encouraged by Furnivall's advice. He began to send articles and stories out to every likely publication he could think of. Inevitably, "five out of six of my little meteorites" came back with rejection slips. What happened to the sixth is unknown. At this stage, Kenneth was almost certainly writing anonymously or under a pseudonym, as he did even for his old school magazine. The cautious, diplomatic side of his nature warned him against any rash actions which would be disapproved of by the Bank, for he was now financially self-supporting (if only just), and shrank from the prospect of ever again being dependent on the dreaded tribe of uncles. Caution paralysed him, and tied his prose into knots of self-consciousness. From the time he entered the Bank at nineteen, it would be ten years before his first signed piece appeared.

Meanwhile, Furnivall, a tireless reformer and socialist, had capitalised on Grahame's admiration by prodding him into socially benevolent activity. Furnivall was deeply involved in a campaign to provide education for the working-classes, and was constantly on the look-out for likely helpers. He had been a founder of the Working Men's College, in the days before the 1870 Act provided even minimal primary schooling for all children, and had made himself unpopular by attacking the rigid class divisions which, for instance, debarred artisans from membership of sporting clubs. He managed to persuade Kenneth to help out at Toynbee Hall, which had been founded by Canon Barnett, rector of St Jude's in Whitechapel, and was named after Barnett's recently dead friend and fellow pioneer, Arnold Toynbee. It was a settlement in Stepney where Oxford and Cambridge undergraduates spent their vacations with Canon Barnett in learning for themselves about the appalling social conditions and discovering what could be done to alleviate them. It was not simply a charitable enterprise. The idea was "to bring the generosity and learning of the young and the universities into effective relation with the industrial population so that both communities might come in time to serve ideals of citizenship and neighbourliness". With money collected mainly in Oxford, Barnett bought and converted the property adjacent to St Jude's, and the hostels thus provided were used right up until the 1914 war by students who came there to work and learn. The Whitechapel Art Gallery in East London is the last surviving relic of Barnett's grand scheme.

It was difficult for Grahame to refuse Furnivall's request. Not only did he value the older man's friendship; the enterprise itself had overtones of Oxford involvement which gave it some appeal to a young man still smarting from his deprivation of a University place. He could not, and did not, argue with its ethical stance. At heart, however, he had a deep distrust of the push towards democracy. On a personal level, he reserved the right to enjoy the company of people of every social class, and one remembers his assertion that Martha, the kitchen maid, was "a real lady". It was the divisions themselves which he hated, and he could find no enthusiasm for any political movement based on class warfare. He allowed himself to be involved in the work of Toynbee Hall, but only in down-to-earth and practical ways, avoiding any part in its proselytising.

It is a persistent and unfounded myth that Grahame was an arch Tory who hated the working-class. His fear and hatred were in fact directed against the schisms which set person against person, and this is a very different thing. At Toynbee Hall, he helped in the most modest and unpretentious of ways, fencing and boxing and playing billiards with the East Londoners, just as he did at the London Scottish which, with true Scottish egalitarianism, accepted young men from every class. His name does not appear on the list of those invited to lecture, though he did chair the occasional sing-song and even contributed a sentimental ballad himself from time to time. He only once let himself be cajoled into giving a talk on English literature, and was hugely embarrassed by the result. He was to talk to a group of cheerfully rowdy East End girls, but one look at his flustered, rather handsome young face undid any scant effort at decorum. They mobbed him with cuddles and kisses, or so the contemporary accounts aver. Grahame was quickly rescued before any serious indignity occurred, and he did not attempt to address an audience again until much later in his life, when he had earned a reputation which ensured respectful attention.

It may have been the Whitechapel Art Gallery, rather than Toynbee Hall itself, which appealed to Grahame. A Bank colleague, Sidney Ward, wrote,

I used to act as a sort of visiting superintendent at Canon Barnett's early Whitechapel exhibitions of modern art, where all the best Watts's, Burne Jones's, Millais' and Alma Tademas were shown – Kenneth used to go there too, & it was also there that I met Tom Greg.[3]

Tom Greg was a barrister with whom Kenneth was later to share a house; clearly, the Whitechapel "helpers" formed a close social set of their own. Sidney Ward himself became a good companion, though junior to Grahame and at first a little in awe of him.

The connection with Furnivall seems to have weakened from this time onward, although Grahame retained an affection for him, mingled with great respect for his eccentricity and the integrity of his beliefs. It is tempting to see the presence of Furnivall in one of Grahame's first stories, "A Bohemian in Exile", in which a man he calls Fothergill (the names could not be much closer) achieves a triumphant escape from the bounds of convention.

The beginning of the tale owes much to an observant eye during visits to Toynbee Hall.

> This is how Fothergill changed his life and died to Bloomsbury. One morning he made his way to the Whitechapel Road, and there he bought a barrow. The Whitechapel barrows are of all sizes, from the barrow wheeled by a boy with half a dozen heads of cabbages to barrows drawn by a tall pony, such as on Sundays take the members of a club to Epping Forest. They are all precisely the same in plan and construction, only in the larger sizes the handles develop or evolve into shafts; and they are equally suitable, according to size, for the vending of whelks for a hot-potato can, a piano organ, or for the conveyance of a cheery and numerous party to the Derby. Fothergill bought a medium sized "developed" one, and also a donkey to fit; he had it painted white, picked out with green – the barrow, not the donkey – and when his arrangements were complete, stabled the whole for the night in Bloomsbury. The following morning, before the early red had quite faded from the sky, the exodus took place, those of us who were left being assembled to drink a parting whisky-and-milk in sad and solemn silence. Fothergill turned down Oxford Street, sitting on the shaft with a short clay in his mouth, and disappeared from our sight, heading west at a leisurely pace. So he passed out of our lives by way of the Bayswater Road.

Three years later, the author meets Fothergill (and donkey, and cart) on the Berkshire Downs, and hears the story of his travels.

> The spell of the free untrammelled life came over me as I listened, till I was fain to accept of his hospitality and a horse blanket for the night, oblivious of civilised comforts down at the Bull. On the downs where Alfred fought we lay and smoked, gazing up at the quiet stars that had shone on many a Dane lying stark and still a thousand years ago; and in the silence of the lone tract that enfolded us we seemed nearer to those old times than to these I had left that afternoon, in the now hushed and sleeping valley of the Thames.

Furnivall, the passionate reformer, was on the face of it very different from Fothergill the escaper, and yet they join in a single persona of a man who "chose wisely to enjoy life his own way, and to gather from the fleeting days what bliss they had to give, or spend them in toiling for a harvest to be reaped when he was dust". The syntax here may be strange, but the meaning is plain.

Even in this early work, the recurrent themes are well established; escape and self-discovery are linked in an almost mystic love of the natural world. For Grahame, the particular always transcended the general. Like all great writers, he wrote from what he knew rather than what he thought. Experience was his raw material and, as a young man, he was acutely open to experience of every kind, even though his sensitivity often gave rise to pain. For all his Stoic efforts to be uncomplaining, he was tormented during these early London years by recurring dreams of Oxford, even though he studiously avoided contact with the place. "I constantly at night ran down to a fairy Oxford – the real thing, yet transformed, and better, because the Gothic was better – a maze of lovely cloisters and chapels and courts. I used to spend a long day there and come back next morning."[4]

Dreams had always been very real to him. He remembered how, as a boy, his sleeping mind had tried, not quite successfully, to escape into lovely imaginings. There had been "cities, faintly heard of – Damascus, Brighton (Aunt Eliza's ideal), Athens, and Glasgow, whose glories the gardener sang; but there was a certain sameness in my conception of all of them: that Wesleyan chapel would keep cropping up everywhere. It was easier to go a-building among those dream-cities where no limitations were imposed, and one was sole architect, with a free hand."[5]

London, for all its entertainments, was no dream-city. "I could not remember a day," Grahame admitted, "since those rare white ones at school when it was a whole holiday, and summer was boon and young, when I had faced the problem of getting up with anything but a full sense of disgust."[6] Books continued to provide an escape. He wrote lyrically of the gaslit bookshop windows and of "some lad – sometimes even a girl – book in hand, heedless of cold and wet, of aching limbs and straining eyes, careless of jostling passers-by, of rattle and turmoil behind them and about, their happy spirits far in an enchanted world: till the ruthless shopman turned out the gas and brought them rudely back to the bitter reality of cramped legs and numbed fingers. 'My brother!' or 'My sister!' I would cry inwardly, feeling the link that bound us together. They possessed . . . the true solitude of the roaring street." He was not, however, a devotee of libraries, perhaps discerning in them the Wesleyan reforming spirit which rationalised wild imagination into Dewey Decimal and uniform maroon bindings. "The stillness and heavy air, the feeling of restriction and surveillance, the mute presence of these other readers, 'all silent and damned'," he wrote, "combine to set up a nervous irritation fatal to quiet study. Had I to choose, I would prefer the windy street."[7]

Every instinct prompted Grahame toward that poetic anarchy which has been the fundamental viewpoint of creative people since the world began. In the piece already quoted from, called "Cheap Knowledge", he makes it clear that it is not the *provision* of free reading matter he objects to, but the *authorisation* of it. He makes the dry observation that "it is the restrictions placed on vice by our social code which makes its pursuit so peculiarly agreeable".

In marked contrast to his work at the Bank, where gradual promotion was bringing about an increasingly ordered and responsible daily routine, Grahame found pleasure in small instances of untidiness and lack of organisation, as if these offered a faint breath of nature's wilderness. He wrote with regret of the extension and re-arrangement of the National Gallery which was taking place at the time, lamenting the loss of the old overcrowded rooms. There was, he recalled, a little "St Catherine" by Pinturicchio which hung just above floor level "so that those who would worship must grovel". It was the oddness of its placing, as much as the picture itself, which appealed to him.

> Whenever I found myself near Trafalgar Square with five minutes to spare I used to turn in and sit on the floor before the object of my love, till gently but firmly replaced on my legs by the attendant. She hangs on the line now, in the grand new room; but I never go to see her. Somehow she is not my "St Catherine" of old.[8]

Like Herrick, Grahame had a taste for "sweet disorder", and this is perhaps a very deep element in English conservatism, explaining why, in the face of much needed reform, amiably disposed people will dig in their heels quite unreasonably; they are resisting any further attempts to organise and tidy up that which should remain richly untidy. We like things the way they are, or preferably, the way they recently were. Grahame approved of the novel as opposed to the non-fiction book because, he said, it "never frenzies the reader to go out and put the world right".

For a young man who knew at first hand what it was to be penniless and dependent on others, and who had worked at Toynbee Hall and seen the evidence of poverty and deprivation, this seems a strange outlook, particularly when so many of his contemporary novelists were quite specifically hoping to spur their readers into protest. Mrs Gaskell had left a powerful indictment, in *Mary Barton* and *North and South*, of the conditions in which Manchester weavers lived and worked, and Dickens was thundering about the dehumanising effects which the coveting of wealth was having an once-virtuous men. Grahame was born into a time when the great concern was about the likely results in ethical terms of the rush towards commerce and profit-making. It was a melting-pot of new religious and political thinking, of high ambition and uneasy conscience, and yet the young clerk with an unquenchable desire to write could share none of these concerns. It is difficult to see how he could have been indifferent to them.

Several factors contribute to an explanation. In the first place, Grahame was not at all sure of his own standing, or where his allegiance lay. By breeding, he was descended from the aristocracy, and may have retained an instinctive contempt for the second-rate and the meretricious, and yet his upbringing had impressed on him the unpalatable lesson that convention was the ruler of all human behaviour. Despite this knowledge, his childhood friends and confidants had been servants, and he understood their humanity better than that of his older relatives. He was thus suspended somewhere between the classes. In social terms, he was the cat that walked by himself, and he could not be sure that the basic premise of politics – that economic improvement leads to a better life – was true. He had lived at close quarters with rich and successful uncles, and remained unconvinced that they were happy men. For himself, happiness lay in escape from the whole competitive busi-ness of "getting and spending". While his work at the Bank involved him in that institution's huge investment in railways, he could still write with despair of the effects on his beloved countryside.

> Yes: today the iron horse has searched the country through – east and west, north and south – bringing with it Commercialism, whose god is Jerry, and who studs the hills with stucco and garrotes [sic] the streams with the girder. Bringing, too, into every nook and corner fashion and chatter, the tailor-made gown and the eye-glass. Happily a great part is still spared – how great these others fortunately do not know – in which the rural Pan and his following may hide their heads for yet a little longer, until the growing tyranny has invaded the last common, spinney, and sheep-down, and driven the kindly god, the well-wisher to man – whither?[8]

There is no alliance here with any particular group of people, but a distrust of the whole of humanity because of its effect on the natural state of things. Grahame was, instinctively, what we would now call a Green.

It is difficult for people brought up in the rigid structures of late twentieth-century politics to realise how fluid was the philosophy which underlay the socialist movement a hundred years ago. For Grahame, as for many leading politicians of his time, there was no contradiction between the ideas of working-class advancement and of individual, essentially gentlemanly self-fulfilment. He was caught up in a movement which was summed up a decade later by Joseph Chamberlain, who had graduated from Nettlefold's Screw Factory to become Mayor of Birmingham, and was later leader of the Liberal Unionists. Chamberlain, lamenting the rise of the commercial class which had begun in the sixteenth century, pointed out how "workmen were deprived of their artistic self-control and independence, of the absolute direction of their own creative handicrafts", thus becoming "mechanical and commonplace, sumptuous and vulgar".[9]

This William Morris socialism, with its high ideals and its belief in the creative capacity of working people, was perfectly consistent with Grahame's outlook. Chamberlain insisted that "common workmen" had built such wonders as the Parthenon, the choir at Westminster and the Cathedral at Rouen, and that they "not only made their wondrous poetry, but these common, unhistoric working men developed the progressive, copious language in which, by their special independent genius, it was elaborated . . .". He pointed out that Ben Jonson had been a brick-layer, Socrates a carver, Spinoza a lens-grinder, Rousseau a music-copier, Burns a ploughman, and that Dickens, like many other great writers, was quite without any formal literary training. It is odd to reflect that a man of such radical views should have been the father of Neville Chamberlain, the Prime Minister known primarily for his policy of appeasement in 1939.

Grahame, despite his position in the Bank, would have agreed utterly with the Utopian socialist outlook. His earlier writing makes it clear that he endorsed Joseph Chamberlain's words, spoken in Birmingham on 5 January 1891. "It is the sordid principle of making pay exclusively the object, when it should be specially regarded as the fair result of work, that keeps so many workers of all classes in a morally inferior state."

In the last hundred years, the relationship between politics and morals has become increasingly uneasy but, even in Grahame's time, it was becoming evident that there was no political party which would agree with Chamberlain's dictum that, "on this moral elevation hangs the future fate of England". To Grahame, that was self-evident; but it was then, as it is now, a view which lays the holder open to charges of priggishness and naïvety, and results in some caution about expressing it.

Grahame was, in any case, wary of trying to identify with other human beings. He had grown up with a conviction that "Olympians" could not be understood, and the poverty which he witnessed in Whitechapel, though pitiable, did nothing to dispel this opinion. Other young men and women who worked at Toynbee Hall could find a refreshing novelty in discovering the sterling qualities of working-class people, as did Ella D'Arcy, who wrote in the first volume of *The Yellow Book* about Esther Stables of Whitechapel "who was natural, simple-minded, and entirely free from that repellantly protective atmosphere with which a woman of the 'classes' so carefully surrounds herself". Grahame could make no such superficial value-judgements. On the rare occasions when he ventures into an insight into someone else's feelings, it is strictly individual and always cloaked in the innocence of a child's limited perception. In a notable story called "Dies Irae", the ostensible subject is the fictionalised young narrator's impatience with a weeping servant who is too distraught about her brother's death to procure a new bootlace as requested; but the sub-plot is allowed to reveal itself only through a brief glimpse, almost as furtive as the quick flash of stolen property before a potential buyer's eyes.

Martha's sorrow hit home a little, but only because the actual sight and sound of it gave me a dull, bad sort of pain low down inside – a pain not to be actually located. Moreover, I was still wanting my bootlace.

The hasty retreat to the safety of the mask says much about Grahame's terror of venturing into an interpretation of the adult world, but it also reveals the depth of his understanding of the child which he had continued to be. Robert Louis Stevenson, who had in so many ways prepared the ground for Grahame, even coining the original description of adults as inhabitants of Olympus, could claim no such penetration, as witness his piece called "Child's Play".

> Once, when I was groaning aloud with physical pain, a young gentleman came into the room and nonchalantly inquired if I had seen his bow and arrow. He made no account of my groans, which he accepted, as he had to accept so much else, as a piece of the inexplicable conduct of his elders; and like a wise young gentleman, he would waste no wonder on the subject.

This Stevenson unperceptively described as "an arrogance of disregard that is truly staggering".

From childhood onward, without a break, and certainly without any definitive change to a more mature attitude, Grahame gazed at what was happening around him and sensed the resonance of such events, just as he sensed the resonance of things and places, but he could not and would not stand outside them and draw abstract conclusions from what he or anyone else considered to be the sum total of them. This, more than anything else, was the reason why he could not ally himself to any movement designed to change and improve society. When reality itself seems mysterious and magical, to withdraw from it into the dry realm of abstract thinking is a betrayal of all that seems most valuable.

The flat in Bloomsbury consisted of a bedroom and a sitting-room, and it cost twenty-five shillings a week, which was, for the time, a lot of money. The prices of London accommodation have always been an accurate indicator of the social value of the district, and it is significant that Grahame chose to live in the most select area within walking distance of the Bank. He could never be indifferent to his surroundings; his acute visual awareness made him vulnerable to the impact of everything he saw, and the witnessing of ugliness was an actively painful experience. Conversely, he loved anything which delighted the eye, and spent many a happy Saturday afternoon exploring London's more exotic entertainments, regardless of how tinselled and theatrical they might be. The decorative and fantastic had an immense appeal for him. He was fascinated by the Crystal Palace and adored circuses and bazaars, arcades and markets, the Zoo and Westminster Aquarium, "which so soon degenerated into an incongruous exhibition of stewing crocodiles, fasting men and boxing kangaroos"; and the same voracious visual appetite found expression in his home surroundings. Having passed virtually the whole of his life in other people's houses, he had a passionate desire to build himself the ideal nest, a private retreat of cosy comfort, furnished with modest, well-chosen objects. He began to achieve this aim in the Bloomsbury flat, but within a year or two, his younger brother, Roland, having left St Edward's at an earlier age than Kenneth, also joined the Bank – and came to share the flat. It may have seemed a sensible arrangement in financial terms, for the twenty-five shillings a week was more easily found by two than by one, but from this time on, a sense of stress makes itself felt. Once again, Kenneth was bereft of his own space. Roland slept in the sitting-room, and the small flat, however "nice", began to seem overcrowded.

Stoicism continued to rule, and Kenneth behaved with his customary restraint and courtesy. It was at about this time that Uncle Jack Ingles's son, Reginald, began to visit the brothers, for Jack was on a long course at Greenwich, and had moved his family to Blackheath. Reginald recalled later how Kenneth "always treated me just as an equal, though I know now that I was rather young and foolish". At sixteen, he had been a gauche boy and, even as a mature man, his letters retained an appealingly artless quality. Writing after Grahame's death, his affection for this older cousin shines through the words.

> I remember their sitting-room well. Kenneth was always so kind when I went there. After dinner they smoked Honey Dew tobacco and nice briar pipes. And Kenneth made coffee. He was particular about coffee and he used to grind the beans and put the coffee in a brown earthenware coffee-pot with an earthenware strainer. It *was* good coffee that Kenneth made. Both he and Roland were very moderate drinkers, but sometimes we had a glass of hot whisky-and-water before I went home ... I remember Kenneth lending me a long churchwarden clay pipe with red sealing wax on the stem. It was one of his treasures – that churchwarden. But I unfortunately broke the bowl off by tapping it on the fire grate to knock the ash out. Kenneth, though he looked just slightly annoyed, was awfully nice about it and said that it did not matter a bit. But he was always like that.[10]

Being "always like that" took its toll. Kenneth began to dream repeatedly of a refuge of his own, and the recurring image was so strong that he recalled it some fifteen years later, in a correspondence with Helen Dunham, whom he did not meet until after the publication of *The Golden Age* in 1895, and detailed it in a piece called "The Iniquity of Oblivion".

> First, there would be a sense of snugness, of cushioned comfort, of home-coming. Next, a gradual awakening to consciousness in a certain little room, very dear and familiar, sequestered in some corner of the more populous and roaring part of London: solitary, the world walled out, but full of a brooding sense of peace and of possession. At times I would make my way there, unerringly, through wet and windy streets, climb the well-known staircase, open the ever-welcoming door. More often I was there already, ensconced in the most comfortable chair in the world, the lamp lit, the fire glowing ruddily. But always the same feeling of a home-coming, of the world shut out, of the idea of encasement. On the shelves were a few books – a very few – but just the editions I had sighed for, the editions which refused to turn up, or which poverty glowers at on alien shelves. On the walls were a print or two, a woodcut, an etching – not many. Old loves, all of them, apparitions that had flashed across the field of view in sales-rooms and vanished again in a blaze of three figures; but never possessed – until now. All was modest – O, so very modest! But all was my own, and, what was more, everything in the room was exactly right.

The theme of homecoming occurs as repeatedly in Grahame's work as his other favourite topic – that of escape. At first sight, they appear to be opposites, but in fact the escape is often away from something alien and unhomely to the welcome cosiness of a private nest. The mid-winter return to Mole's house is strikingly similar to the dream room, right down to Ratty's enquiry, "Now, wherever did you pick up those prints? Make the place look so home-like, they do".

Psychology was an infant science in Grahame's day. There was no hint in his mind that the private place of which he dreamed, with "the world walled out", so often found by traversing a staircase or penetrating an underground tunnel or discovering a secret door, could represent the lost security of the womb. Such an interpretation would have shocked him deeply. As it was, he worried at the problem of the recurring dream, trying to work out why it should seem so real, and even toyed with the idea that he might be experiencing two states of existence which were equally present, though not simultaneously. "After three or four visits, the uncanniness of the repetition set me thinking. Could it possibly be, that this was no dream at all? Had this chamber, perhaps, a real existence, and I was all the time leading, somewhere, another life – a life within a life – a life that I constantly forgot, within the life that I happened to remember."

He was not alone in these speculations. In 1886, when Grahame was twenty-seven and had still not published anything, Robert Louis Stevenson caused an immense stir with *The Strange Case of Dr Jekyll and Mr Hyde*, a book which explored exactly the double life which the young bank clerk thought a possibility. So persuaded was Grahame that the dream state might be an actual one, he set about trying "to bring the thing to absolute proof". He even toyed with the idea of checking his accounts to see if the dream room had been paid for in real money, but characteristically, took refuge from what threatened to be a serious involvement with the adult world by declaring that he "did not keep any accounts – never had kept any accounts – never intended to keep any beastly accounts". For a banker, it is an enchanting sentiment, but the neatly tied bundles of meticulous accounts tell their own story. The escape is, once again, into the responsibility-free world of childhood and a disclaimer of any possible charge of pretension.

One explanation for the compulsive dreaming is that Grahame was at that time in fact actively house hunting. Although there is no record of any overt rift between him and Roland at this period, the absence of any particular mention of this younger brother seems to indicate a lack of sympathy between them. It is the fictionalised Edward who, as the eldest of the family, was the admired figure – at least, until the advent of school changed him irrevocably – and the real-life older brother, Willie, who lay behind the Edward figure, had not lived to enter the adult world. Roland had, and if he, lacking Kenneth's intense originality, had settled down to become a proper Olympian, his presence in the Bloomsbury flat must have been intolerable.

Kenneth hunted, in all seriousness, for the actual room of his dreams, convinced that it must exist. He confided his belief to Helen Dunham, who obviously shared it. "I'm not surprised at all", he wrote, "that you too have a room. Scientific people deny the repetition, and say that the one dream has along with it, and as part of it, a confused sense of many previous ones – that it is a mirage, in fact. But we know better." He searched through Bloomsbury and Chelsea, convinced that the place waited to be found.

It waits, that sequestered chamber, it waits for the serene moment when the brain is in just the apt condition, and ready to switch on the other memory even as one switches on the electric light with a turn of the wrist. [Did Victorian electricians use those twist-type porcelain switches which one can still find in France?] Fantasy? well – perhaps. But the worst of it is, one can never feel quite sure. Only a dream, of course. And yet – the enchanting possibility![11]

Eventually, Grahame settled for a tiny top-floor flat off the Chelsea Bridge Road, at 65 Chelsea Gardens. Perhaps it was not the dream room itself, but it came near to it, a secret crow's-nest of a place at the top of the house, reached by a dark and narrow entry. He stayed there for twelve years, enjoying the proximity to the river which allowed him to go to work by taking the steamer from Chelsea Pier. With his taste for the outrageous, he must have liked it too for the Bohemian flavour of the neighbourhood. Just round the corner, in Cheyne Walk, Dante Gabriel Rossetti presided over his extraordinary ménage of animals and birds, listed by Timothy Hilton in his study of the Pre-Raphaelites as "owls, rabbits, dormice, wombats, wood-chucks, kangaroos, wallabies, a raccoon, parrots, peacocks, lizards, salaman-ders, a laughing jackass and a Brahmin bull whose eyes reminded Rossetti of Jane Morris". Meredith shared this household for a while, but left after Swinburne threw a poached egg at him for speaking lightly of Victor Hugo.

A letter from Mary Richardson recalls the occasion when she and Ken-neth's sister Helen went to take tea with him almost at the end of his time in Chelsea Gardens, and she provides the most detailed picture of the flat from among several accounts.

It was like climbing the stairs of a lighthouse, there was no lift and the dirty stone staircase swept up in endless spirals. When we got to the top we were out of breath and I remember that we stood and fanned ourselves with the Royal Academy catalogue (we had come from Bur-lington House) before we rang the bell ... [Of Kenneth, she says] he was altogether too big for his little flat! He made tea and poured it out for us himself and we all sat at a tea-table in the window. It was a beautiful afternoon and the view over Kenneth's beloved Thames, with the green of Battersea Park beyond, was a lovely one ... He collected those hollow glass rolling pins that sailors brought home to their sweethearts – or else smuggled brandy in. He showed some of these to us, holding them lovingly. He had a Chippendale bureau of which he was very proud. He had bought it as a bargain and it had, he said, belonged to the great Duke of Wellington. I said, "What fun if you found a secret drawer in it containing dispositions and dis-patches!" He beamed like a regular boy. "What a jolly idea!" he said, and then his face fell and he added, "Alas, if one may believe gossip, the drawer would be more likely to contain *billets-doux* and love-let-ters." "But, Mr Grahame," said I, "possibly love-letters might be more interesting than dispatches?" "Very likely," said he, "but neither I, nor, I hope, anyone else, would think it *right* to read them."

The Chippendale bureau was to feature in a story of its own called "The Secret Drawer", but the embargo on anything connected with love held firm. Kenneth's cautious literary explorings of female attractiveness were strictly limited to the child's-eye view, and at the time of his move into the Chelsea flat, even these had not appeared. His cousin Annie Grahame remembered that her mother helped him to furnish his new rooms. "He had very good taste," she said, "and a great appreciation of beautiful things."[12]

At least twice during these years, Grahame was seriously ill with gastritis. In those days, long convalescence was accepted as a necessary part of the treatment of such maladies, and Kenneth took full advantage of the blessed weeks away from the Bank, when he could with a sigh of relief revert to the lifestyle most natural to him, enjoying "solitude and the breezy downs". The rigid Victorian division between things physical and spiritual prevented any recognition of the fact that stress and the yearning of the soul for its real needs can produce a sickness of the body. Throughout his career at the Bank, Grahame was prey to long illnesses, despite his fine physique. It seems obvious now that they were a vital safety-valve, allowing him an excuse to return to his beloved countryside. "Up here," he wrote later, "all vestiges of a sordid humanity disappear. The Loafer is alone with the south-west wind and the blue sky. Only a carolling of larks and a tinkling from distant flocks break the brooding noonday stillness; above, the wind-hover hangs motionless, a black dot on the blue."[13]

At this time, Grahame had not found access to such fluent, lyrical expression. On the contrary, the harder he tried to impress the editors, the less attractive his prose became. He settled into an uneasy acceptance of the Bank routine, broken by minor escapes, which seemed set to last for ever.

Seen in retrospect, the escapes were more important than the routine, for it was during these releases from dutiful compulsion that Kenneth was able to pursue his true inclinations. When he was ill, it was his sister Helen who came to his rescue, both at this time and later. She had gone into nursing, with considerable success, and was one of the first nursing sisters at the Charing Cross Hospital, in London. The relationship with her brother was not an easy one, for Helen's version of their Calvinist inheritance made her disapprove of what she saw as his escapist romanticism, and in later life there was a long estrangement between them. Nevertheless, she was always there to nurse him when needed, and in her quiet, practical way, she loved him. To the present-day reader, the letters she wrote after his death come as quite a shock in the unguardedness of their grief, a rabbit-scream from a hitherto silent animal. In 1884, after one of his illnesses, Helen took Kenneth with her to Cornwall, where they stayed with her friend Mary Richardson – the same young woman who wrote with such vivid recollection of taking tea at the Chelsea flat.

Mary had a cottage at the Lizard, and the Grahame brother and sister were bowled over by the charm of the place. Helen evidently decided there and then that the Lizard was to be her eventual home, for she retired there at the end of her nursing career. Kenneth, always susceptible to a seductive landscape, fell in love with Cornwall and instantly relaxed into a life of fishing and pottering about, dressed in a rough blue jersey and cotton cap like the professional fishermen. Deep-sea fishing was new to him, and he took to it with joy, claiming like any schoolboy that "the fun with a twenty-five-pound conger only really began after you got it into the boat". His passion for the sea never left him, and one remembers the long, intensely lyrical passage in *Wayfarers All*, where Rat falls under the spell of the traveller with the sea-grey eyes.

> Of deep-sea fishings he heard tell, and mighty silver gatherings of the mile-long net; of sudden perils, noise of breakers on a moonless night, or the tall bows of the great liner taking shape overhead through the fog; of the merry home-coming, the headland rounded, the harbour lights opened out; the groups seen dimly on the quay, the cheery hail, the splash of the hawser; the trudge up the steep little street towards the comforting glow of red-curtained windows.

Just as the Scottish fishermen had befriended him in childhood, the taciturn Cornishmen took to Kenneth. There is a delightful letter from a Mrs M. E. Squibb, remembering the enthusiastic young visitor.

> I know he was very fond of my father and was always very nice to us & my family. He used to love going out fishing all night with father. They used to set a boulter (that is a long strong rope with big Hooks at intervals of about 3 yards about 100 hooks on a rope which had a cork buoy at each end) & they would catch very big fish Congers Codfish & ling which people used to salt and dry for the winter they dont seem to do that now. Father named his boat the *Mary Ellen* after me.[14]

Mrs Squibb's father, Tom Roberts, though seventy-four, was coxswain of the local lifeboat, and her husband its signalman. Kenneth went out with this boat to a wrecked ship, an incident which Helen remembered clearly, for she wrote an exasperated note after the publication of the Chalmers biography, insisting that the fleeces which floated in the water were not the main cargo, but covered the frozen meat stored in the holds. The ship, she said, was not from Morocco as reported. She was the White Star liner *Sue Vic*, from "Australia or New Zealand".[15]

For Kenneth, Cornwall picked up the frayed edges of a childhood memory of boats and the sea, and he found himself at home there. He developed a taste for Cornish cream, specially when zigzagged with black treacle as "thunder and lightening" on fresh new bread, and for the "star-gazy" pies in which a pilchard looked out from its pastry wrapping, and could not resist the little bric-à-brac shops. It was in the Lizard that he started collecting the glass rolling pins which Mary Richardson alluded to; nearly forty of them went into an auction many years later.

Most delightful of all was a mistake which he treasured gleefully for the rest of his life. A visitor (who happened to be Dr Boyd, the Principal of Hertford College, Oxford) took Kenneth for a local fisherman and asked him in the patronising tone which he thought suitable for an uneducated sea-dog whether he had had luck with the fish. "The best, sir," said Kenneth, touching his cap respectfully. The Cornish burr sounded, to Boyd's ear at least, utterly authentic. It was only later that the grinning locals explained the joke. Boyd, hotly embarrassed, hurried to apologise, but Kenneth was enchanted by the whole episode. "I have never been more flattered in my life," he said.[16]

He returned to Cornwall several times during the next few years, laying up a store of richness to last him through the long London winters of lamplit streets and fog, and mulled over his treasured memories as they ripened slowly into a kind of faith that somewhere, far beyond the city's artificiality, there reigned an unpretentious gloriously flavoured reality.

A few weeks before his twenty-eighth birthday, on the afternoon of Sunday, 27 February 1887, he took a long walk from Chelsea along Fulham Road and over Putney Bridge, across Barnes Common to Hammersmith. Unhurriedly, he walked back along the towpath and called on a friend in Putney who persuaded him to stay to tea. It was late by the time he got home, and the telegram which lay on the mat had been there for some hours. It was from Mr Currie, Uncle John's partner in the family firm, sent from the Le Havre office to say that Kenneth's father had suffered an apoplectic stroke. As Kenneth stood, reading the printed strips of letters on the form which brought this news, a second telegram arrived to say that Cunningham had died during the afternoon.

Three torn-out sheets of Kenneth's diary have been preserved, perhaps because they were considered to record an important family event, but the account of Cunningham's funeral is laconic and the facts themselves are pitifully stark.

Kenneth went down to Southampton on the Monday morning following his receipt of the news, and took the night boat to Le Havre, where Cunningham Grahame had lived since the final ignominy of resigning his post in Inveraray and leaving the country.

Mr Currie met me and we drove straight to my father's room, where I was able to see his face before the coffin was finally closed. He seems to have died instantaneously, no signs of life having ever shown themselves after those who heard the noise of his fall had reached his room and raised him . . . At three o'clock we drove to 32 rue Bougainvillea where for want of room inside, the coffin was placed in the little turfed garden or yard outside the house, and Mr Whelpton read passages and prayers, chiefly those included in the Church of England burial service. [Mr Whelpton was the resident Methodist minister.] We then drove to the little cemetery of Sainte Adresse on the heights overlooking the sea, near the lighthouses. With us were some clerks from Mr C's office who had known my father . . . and the old landlady Madame Bazille, with her son and daughter-in-law. At the grave, Mr Whelpton completed the service — I bade adieu to the other mourners at the gate of the cemetery. After speaking to Madame Bazille I put a £5 note into her hand. This had been approved of by Mr Currie, who spoke warmly of her affectionate care for eighteen years.

Five pounds, by modern standards, sounds a small token of appreciation for such long service, but it was, of course, quite a lot of money when related to the salary of a bank clerk of the time. The choice of Sainte Adresse was not without a careful regard for expenses. Grahame confessed later that the cemetery "was chosen by Mr Currie both because it was altogether more desirable than the great crowded town cemetery, and because the cost of ground for a grave *in perpetuity* was, in the latter, as much as 600 fcs — at Ste Adresse, only 100".

The rest of the day passed in a thorough search of Cunningham's room, conducted with Mme Bazille's son. If Kenneth hoped to find some message of a personal nature from his father, he was disappointed. The papers and books had already been taken to Mr Currie's office, and there was nothing of interest. Even the books gave no clue as to what Cunningham had thought and felt in the twenty years since Kenneth had last seen him. They were mostly schoolbooks and dictionaries. Kenneth took a few of them, as an inadequate keep-safe: "I made over the clothes to the Bazilles, and also the money in his purse — only 15 frs — Mme Bazille showed me a small photo of himself which he had given her, and which she wished me to take if I had not got one. I begged her to keep it."

There was nothing more to be done. Kenneth came back to London the next day. From that time on, as if released from a hidden presence which had caused him continual pain, he began to write with more confidence, discarding the wheedling, schoolboyish artifice which had previously clung about all the pieces he had offered for publication. With new courage, he wrote of his own feelings.

We, who for our sins are town dwellers, when the summer sun lights up gloomy squares and dusty streets, chafe at every sunlit day that passes as worse than wasted.

The piece was called "By a Northern Furrow", and it was accepted by the *St James's Gazette*. It was over a year before they used it but, on Boxing Day 1888, Kenneth Grahame found himself a published author.

6

Long John Silver and the Great God Pan

Shortly after the publication of his first story, Grahame was promoted to the Chief Cashier's Office. He was fascinated by the sight of gold bullion, "thought so little of that it was dealt about in shovels", but seems to have shown little aptitude for finance. He was within a few months moved to the Secretary's Office, where he handled words rather than figures. It is perhaps over-neat to assume that the transfer was due to the lively quality of the reports he occasionally had to write, for the Bank was not noted for its literary appreciation. Grahame had been the only clerk in its whole history to score full marks for the essay which fomed a part of the qualifying test, but this composition was discarded and, when *The Golden Age* was published, the Bank's chairman bought it under the mistaken impression that the book was about bi-metallism.

Grahame's first job in his new department was to catalogue the books in the Director's Library. His friend Gordon Nairne, who was to become Chief Cashier when Grahame himself had risen to be the Bank's Secretary, worried about the tedium of working among the "dry-as-dust" books, feeling perhaps that such a job was something of an indignity.[1] He need not have been concerned. Grahame, with his utter indifference to the nuances of status, was quite content. There were plenty of other things to think about.

A second story, "A Bohemian in Exile" (about the runaway Fothergill), had been published by the *St James's Gazette*, and the new writer had attracted some favourable notice. In the late 1800s, the field of published work was far smaller than it is today, and publishers had not conceived the idea that they could aim at a vast bulk of semi-literate perusers who were more profitable than serious readers. Publishing liked to think of itself as upper-middle profession, even though publishers at that date were not addressed as "Esquire", as most private individuals were, but had to be content with plain "Mr". Their activities were of interest to a fairly small minority of the population, but it was a well-defined and influential minority, keenly interested to know who was writing what. To get into print was in a very real sense an arrival in the world of letters.

Grahame came on the literary scene at a fortunate time. A wealthy Scottish businessman called Fitzroy Bell had decided to back an Edinburgh-based weekly, the *Scots Observer*. Aiming high, Bell employed as his editor one of the most charismatic personalities of the time, W. E. Henley. Given a free hand to commission his contributors, Henley wasted no time in scooping up the bright young man who had written two pieces for the *St James's Gazette*. Grahame found himself befriended for the second time by an energetic, eccentric man of immense influence. Anyone taken up by Henley was immediately rather special. "Henley's young men", as they were known, had a definite collective identity; they were the cossetted rising stars of literature, run like a stable of cherished race-horses by their massively self-confident manager.

"Bill" Henley was the real-life origin of Long John Silver. He had lost a leg thanks to childhood tuberculosis, and it was while being treated by Lister in an Edinburgh hospital that he met Robert Louis Stevenson, himself ill with pulmonary tuberculosis. The Scottish connection was a strange underlying force, which reached out to touch Grahame in unexpected ways. Stevenson, for instance, had while in Edinburgh become friendly with Walter Simpson, the son of the obstetrician who had attended Grahame's birth at 32 Castle Street. Henley and Stevenson had collaborated on the writing of four unsuccessful plays and, although they parted company after a furious quarrel, Stevenson wrote of his erstwhile friend that he was "a man of a great presence; he commands a larger atmosphere, gives the impression of a grosser mass of character than most men. It has been said of him that his presence could be felt in a room you entered blindfold." He was, Stevenson added, "boisterous and piratic . . . He will roar you down, he will bury his face in his hands, he will undergo passions of revolt and agony; and meanwhile his attitude of mind is really both conciliatory and receptive . . ."[2]

It was difficult for a writer of rising reputation *not* to quarrel with Henley, sooner or later. Although his real attitude was one of protective encouragement, the limping, irascible man had rigid ideas about how his young writers should write, and had no inhibitions about editing their work so radically that they sometimes hardly recognised it. He left some ugly marks on Grahame's early prose, for a fatal fault-line in his literary taste made him dissatisfied with simplicity, and he would put in grandiose metaphors of his own making which sat uneasily in the original text. Kenneth did not argue. Henley, he said, "was the first editor who gave me a full and a free and a frank show, who took all I had and asked me for more; I should be a pig if I ever forgot him".[3]

Others were less convinced. W. B. Yeats was secretly worried and distressed by Henley's "improvements" to his poetry, but only admitted later how the editor had "often revised my lyrics, crossing out a line or a stanza and writing in one of his own". With endearing modesty, Yeats explained why he made no protest. "I was ashamed of being rewritten," he said, "and thought that others were not."[4] The same inhibition acted to prevent the offended contributors from pooling their indignation; each one of them nursed the wounds inflicted by Henley in the silence of his own insecurity.

Grahame, with the wordy classical influence of St Edward's only a little below the surface, was ready to accept Henley's opinion. If he perceived that the editor's taste for Ancient Greece was a sentimental one based on sham heroics, he kept his opinion to himself. Fatherly advice was a rare thing in his life, and he was not prepared to quibble over the interpolation of odd scraps of flamboyant pomposity. His essay called "Loafing" is for the most part limpid and evocative, describing with gentle amusement the energetic boaters "staggering under hampers, bundles of waterproofs, and so forth . . ." who are watched by the Loafer "through the open door of his cottage, where in his shirt-sleeves he is dallying with his bacon, as a gentleman should". And yet, a page earlier, we have a very different style. "Here, *tanquam in speculo*, the Loafer as he lounges may, by attorney as it were, touch gently every stop in the great organ of the emotions of mortality."

Henley himself was a poet of prodigious output, none of which is now remembered except for the phrase, "bloody but unbowed" and for the quatrain which ends, "I am the master of my fate: I am the captain of my soul". Perhaps the fact that these snippets were true of their author contributed a kind of honesty which made them memorable.

Despite all the arrogance and bombast, Grahame found himself genuinely attracted to Henley. The older man had an immense kindness and generosity – and flamboyance was a quality which had always appealed to Grahame. Henley was never dull. He loathed dullness, and loathed even more the formalising of it into regimentation. He was known for his vitriolic attacks on Puritanism, and here Grahame could agree with him wholeheartedly. The *Scots Observer*, with its stable of writers who included Kipling and, briefly, Shaw, who soon fell out with Henley over socialism, was described by Beerbohm as "rowdy, venomous, and insincere. There was libel in every line of it. It roared with the lambs and bleated with the lions. It was a disgrace to journalism and a glory to literature."

Within two years, Henley had insisted that the *Scots Observer* should move its offices to London and change its name to the *National Observer*. This bid for wider recognition was directly opposed to Fitzroy Bell's original desire to establish a leading publication which was essentially Scottish, and it is a mark of Henley's sheer forcefulness of character that he managed to persuade Bell to go on backing the new venture. He was losing £4,000 a year on it, but he was prepared to go on doing so. In 1890 the shift to London and the change of title took place. The paper lasted for four years, and throughout its life was stamped with Henley's pugnacious views on everything he regarded as oppressive, stupid or dull – which encompassed quite a lot. It failed finally because the progressives who should have supported it found themselves attacked by Henley for being doctrinaire, while the Tories who were its chief butt would have nothing to do with it, preferring to find their humour in *Punch* and their feature writing and news in *The*

Times. The *Illustrated London News* was also in the market as the orthodox counterpart of the *National Observer*, catering for the sheep of society rather than the goats, and the sheer numbers of the faithful flock won in the end. Henley, "bloody but unbowed", to use his own phrase went on to edit the *New Review*.

It was a time of passionately held opinions, when opposing rigidities of political intention clashed ferociously, and Grahame found himself in the middle of a highly charged society in which it was difficult to define the neutral ground which he instinctively occupied. Ruskin had thundered that "there is no wealth but life", and Kenneth absolutely understood what he meant, but both the Tories and the reformers disagreed, locked as they were in a battle for economic power. The middle-classes, Grahame perceived, offered no mid-way neutrality; he would have agreed with Marx that "the *bourgeoisie*, wherever it got the upper hand, put an end to all feudal, patriarchal, idyllic relations, pitilessly tore asunder the motley feudal ties that bound man to his 'natural superiors', and left remaining no other bond between man and man than naked self-interest and callous cash payment." The words come from the Communist Manifesto, and it is extraordinary to think that they were written a full decade before Grahame was born, in 1848.

Marx died in 1884, and three years later, Queen Victoria celebrated her Golden Jubilee. Kenneth, with the London Scottish, was involved in the occasion, and described it as "full of music, marching, and much true affectionate loyalty and patriotism"[5] – and yet, in the same year, the Trafalgar Square riots took place, and Bloody Sunday left protesters dead on the streets. A few months previously, there had been the Pall Mall riots, and a mob had looted shops in Piccadilly. While the Fabians got under way with their demands for reform, so did the utterly non-political Arts and Crafts movement, in the high-flown hope that the spiritual creativity of humankind could transcend "callous cash payment" to find greater satisfaction in the making of beautiful things. Grahame together with most of "Henley's young men", embraced the small refuge offered by the idea of work for its own creative pleasure. As R. H. Tawney puts it, "unless industry is to be paralysed by recurrent revolts on the part of outraged human nature, it must satisfy criteria which are not purely economic".[6]

Henley accepted this premise completely, and lashed out at those on both sides of the political spectrum whose blindness to the needs of the human spirit was, as he saw it, bringing about a constriction in the joyously anarchic, open potential which should be present in life itself. Socialists like Shaw retorted that there had been precious little freedom or potential for the eighty per cent of the population who laboured with their hands, and lived in conditions of bestial deprivation, but Henley's eyes were on the intellectual and aesthetic horizon. He had no brief for the rapacious landlord or the cruel employer, and said so, but he could not see any need to become so entrammelled in legislation designed to benefit the essentially dull masses that imagination itself would be circumscribed by the dead hand of authority. G. M. Trevelyan, now unpopular as a historian because of his supposedly illiberal views, states in his *Social History* of 1944 an outlook with which Henley would have agreed completely.

> To millions the divorce from nature was absolute, and so, too, was the divorce from all dignity and beauty and significance in the wilderness of mean streets in which they were bred, whether in the well-to-do suburb or the slum.

Trevelyan's indifference to social background was shared by Henley and Grahame, but so, too, was the fear which he articulates.

> The race bred under such conditions might retain many sturdy qualities of physique, might develop sharp wits and a brave, cheery, humorous attitude to life, but its imaginative powers must necessarily decline, and the stage is set for the gradual standardisation of human personality.

This underlying dread constituted a strong bond between the young men and women who circled round Henley. The sense of defending beleaguered values gave them an almost soldierly comradeship, and Henley fostered this with a skill which may not have been quite deliberate. He was a generous, hospitable man, and held a dinner for contributors to the *Scots Observer* and its successor, the *National Observer*, every Friday night at Verney's Restaurant. Not content with this, he held a regular Sunday "At Home" in his own house, and the effect was to bond the young contributors together in a mutually stimulating camaraderie. Yeats, who, as he said, "disagreed with Henley about everything, but admired him beyond words", recalled these occasions affectionately. "We gathered . . . in two rooms, with folding doors between, and hung, I think, with photographs from Dutch masters, and in one room there was always, I think, a table with cold meat . . ." His visual impressions are vague, but he is in no doubt about the quality of the man who was his host, for "he made us feel always our importance, and no man among us could do good work, or show the promise of it, and lack his praise".[7]

Among the guests was C. L. Hinds, whose book, *Authors and I* contributes a perceptive portrait of Grahame. He remembers him as

> a tall, well-knit, blonde [*sic*] man, [in fact, he was dark, but began to grey quite early] who moved slowly and with dignity, and who pre-

served, amid the violent discussions and altercations that enlivened the meetings of the group, a calm, comprehending demeanour accompanied by a ready smile that women would call "sweet". And yet this blonde [*sic*], temperate, kindly-looking man had also a startled air, as a fawn might show who suddenly found himself on Boston Common, quite prepared to go through with the adventure, as a well-bred fawn should under any circumstances, but unable to escape wholly from the memory of the glades and woods whence he had come. He seemed to be a man who had not yet become quite accustomed to the discovery that he was no longer a child, but grown-up and prosperous. Success did not atone for the loss of the child outlook. Every one of us has his adjective. His adjective was – startled.

Hinds wrote his book in 1921, so he was familiar with Grahame's *The Wind in the Willows*, and this makes the accuracy of his observation about Kenneth's retained childhood rather less striking, but the impression of him as a creature somehow cut off from his natural setting in a more animal world is one which other writers also recorded. Graham Robertson picked up the same sense of estranged wildness, though he used a different image to describe it:

He was living in London where he looked all *wrong* – that is to say, as wrong as so magnificent a man could look anywhere. As he strode along the pavements one felt to him as towards a huge St Bernard or Newfoundland dog, a longing to take him away into open country where he could be let off the lead and allowed to range at will. He appeared to be happy enough and made the best of everything, as do the dogs, but he was too big for London and it hardly seemed kind of Fate to keep him there.

Robertson was writing even later, in his 1931 book *Time Was*, but he knew Grahame far better than Hinds did. The two men were close friends for many years, and Robertson, who was an artist and playwright as well as a believer in fairies and a keeper of a house full of dogs, designed the original frontispiece for *The Wind in the Willows*. Even he, however, took Kenneth to be a taller man than he really was. Grahame's passport records his height as 5'11", but nobody seemed to believe it. Mary Richardson, who knew him well both in London and through his visits to Cornwall, is equally emphatic about his height.

He was a tall (over six foot) fine-looking young man, a splendid head, broad and well-proportioned – carried himself well – a good healthy complexion, large widely opened rather light grey eyes, always with a

kindly expression in them. Not exactly handsome but distinctly strik-
ing-looking – sensitive hands and mouth, rather short and clever nose
. . . Distinctly reserved until he trusted you – he seemed to me at times
as if in his younger days he had been teased, and his boyish aspirations
trodden on . . .[9]

This perceptiveness was perhaps due to confidences about the young
Grahames' childhood imparted by Helen rather than any miracle of intuition, but Mary's liking for Kenneth is obvious – and not exceptional. He
conveyed an honest vulnerability very much like that of a willing, amiable
retriever which is secretly afraid that it may be banished at any moment,
for incomprehensible human reasons, to its kennel.

The sophisticated, fast-talking group which centred round Henley seems
to have cherished Grahame with the slightly amused affection felt by soldiers for the regimental goat. He, without realising it for an instant, had in
his essential being exactly the quality which the others sought. At heart, he
was as innocent as any wild creature which does its simple best to survive
and give no offence to those stronger or more guileful. As the 1890s approached and the effects of mechanised power began to cause concern
among the aesthetes and the intellectuals, there was a striving to recapture
the lost dignity and simplicity in which, it was now felt, plain men and
women used to labour. Innocence had become a rare and highly prized
quality, as elusive as mercury, disintegrating and running away under the
slightest pressure. The mood was backward-looking and wistful – and frightened. The old order was disintegrating fast, and glimpses into what lay
ahead showed a nightmare rather than a dream. The countryside was dis-
appearing under a mass of cheaply built, ugly housing, and there was every
sign that the slum-dwellers who had been such an easily identifiable (and
avoidable) class were bursting out of their unsavoury hovels to present
themselves as real, but uneducated and uncultured human beings. Among
the middle and upper classes, there was a desperate desire to escape this
nemesis, and the most obvious route lay in a retreat to the past, to what
seemed now an idyll of simplicity. Yeats yearned for a return to Innisfree
and his nine bean rows, and Hardy wrote of sweet Tess, caught in the
machinations of a power-seeking world which destroyed her. Above all, the
Pre-Raphaelites had gone for the re-created dream of a new past which
could somehow be dragged in an ever-thinning film across the gawky and
obstinate present. As early as 1868, William Morris had written, in his
Prologue to *The Earthly Paradise*:

Forget six counties overhung with smoke,
Forget the snorting steam and piston stroke,
Forget the spreading of the hideous town;

> Think rather of the pack-horse on the down,
> And dream of London, small, and white and clean,
> The clear Thames bordered by its gardens green . . .

He thought he was looking ahead to a new Utopia, but in fact it was a backward gaze, inspired by the same passion which had driven William Blake, a century earlier, to evoke his vision of the New Jerusalem.

Kenneth Grahame, oblivious to all Utopianism, genuinely belonged in his own mind with the "pack horse on the down", and his open, grey-eyed gaze conveyed it to everyone who knew him. He, however, did not at first trust this truth, and thought he should try harder to be a "man of the world" who could turn out a clever commentary on events. He continued to send would-be contributions to a wide variety of magazines, mostly without success. He kept a rejection slip from James Payn at the *Cornhill*, perhaps because of its encouraging tone.

> Your little paper is too short and slight for the *Cornhill*, but the humour
> it exhibits has struck me as being exceptional and leads me to hope
> that I may again hear from you.

Evidently, the idea of political journalism had not died entirely, for Grahame scored an odd success with a satirical piece about Parnell, whose divorce was linked in the public mind with a farcical episode of escape through a bedroom window from the house of Mrs O'Shea. Grahame retailed this event in the form of a conversation (overheard by the cat) between a waterspout and a verandah, both of them a little battered as a result of Parnell's flight of the previous night. As the waterspout remarked reflectively, "I've had a burglar down me, and a schoolboy or two, but never the idol of a nation's hopes and aspirations". This is the best line in the whole piece; the rest of it is, by current standards, ponderous, with much punning on he and Shea, and a reference to Gladstone as Grand Waterspout. Apart from that single allusion, there is no attempt to enter into the political implications of the affair. It is seen, with Grahame's inevitable innocence, as a comic episode involving grown-up men escaping down drainpipes.

The unsigned piece survives only because Sidney Ward kept it in a file of unpublished reminiscences, together with his personal reason for retrieving it. In conversation with Kenneth himself, Ward remarked, ' "I say, Grahame, did you see that gorgeous conversation between a balcony and a waterspout in the *St James's* last night?' 'Yes,' said K.G., 'I wrote it!' " The piece was clipped from the issue dated 19 November 1890, two years after Grahame's first signed stories were accepted, and it is very likely that there were many more mildly scurrilous pieces of the same kind. An obituary by Alan Pryce-Jones in the *London Mercury* commented on Grahame's use of quotations from Rabelais in his early work, but Green claimed, probably correctly, that this material was "firmly suppressed" by Grahame's widow when the first biography was written a year after her husband's death, and there is now no trace of anything in the least salacious. The waterspout piece, however, is marked with crosses, and did not appear in Chalmers's book.

Of all literary forms, humour is the most vulnerable to the passing fashion, and Grahame's efforts in this direction now seem elephantine, with an archness (to judge by the waterspout piece) which is direly unfunny, but Henley seems to have been impressed by his protégé's versatility. It must have seemed to him that he had discovered a new talent of enormous capacity. Kenneth Grahame could, it seemed, turn his hand to anything from low comedy to poetic prose. What's more, he was impressionable, eager to learn, impeccably good-mannered and full of admiration for his mentor. He showed every sign of being a hot literary property. The only trouble was, he seemed absurdly disinclined to leave the Bank and get down to professional writing. Henley used all his persuasive powers to try and part Grahame from The Old Lady, but without success. Despite the young man's earlier ambitions to evade the banking fate which had been planned for him, he now clung to it with infuriating obstinacy. His outlook had changed, and he turned down Henley's proposal with surprising firmness. He was, he said, "a spring and not a pump".[10]

A clue to the underlying reasons for his obstinacy can be found in a shrewd observation by C. L. Hinds after he had attended one of Henley's At Homes in September 1891. It was easy, he said, to distinguish the amateur writers from the professionals. "They looked more comfortable; they ate their food in a more leisurely way; they were readier to praise than to blame, because literature was to them a delightful relaxation, not an arduous business."[11]

In our own time, the status of the amateur has been down-graded to that of the dabbler whom nobody takes seriously. The first hurdle faced by the would-be author is to "kick the day-job" and demonstrate that writing (or music, or painting, or acting) is to be a full-time profession. Our measure of success has become the crude one of how much money one's professional activities can earn, and the longed-for "break-through" cannot be dissociated from profitability. For a banker, Grahame was curiously indifferent to any such considerations – and this was not because he received a handsome salary. It was not until well after the Second World War that bank salaries rose to anything approaching a professional level, and that they did so at all may have reflected a desire to cut down private speculation by bank officers rather than an altruistic desire to improve living standards. Grahame himself saw Frank May, the Chief Cashier in whose department he had worked, forced to resign from the Bank after a number of unauthorised dealings had come to light.

Kenneth's dreams of the "so modest" ideal room show that he could not regard his work at the Bank as a source of personal wealth, and Henley, who had no inhibitions about regarding writing as a saleable product, must have found his preference for the amateur status hard to understand. He liked Grahame's more sophisticated offerings, and his editorial amendments may have been based on a shrewd understanding of the ponderous humour of the time rather than plain self-aggrandisement. The first Grahame piece published in the *Scots Observer* is the essay called "Of Smoking", and it is charged with a slightly desperate determination to be debonair.

> There be always good fellows, with good cigars for their friends. Nay, too, the boxes of these lie open; and the good cigar belongs rather to him that can appreciate it aright than to the capitalist who, owing to a false social system, happens to be its temporary guardian and trustee. Again there is a saying – bred first, I think, among the schoolmen at Oxford – that it is the duty of a son to live up to his father's income.

The passage bristles with chips on the shoulder. Insecurities about social standing, about University status and about having a solid and reliable father jostle for space in just a couple of paragraphs. Elsewhere in the same piece there is an appeal to be considered "one of the lads" in his claim that

> for most of us who are labourers in the vineyard, toilers and swinkers, the morning pipe is smoked in hurry and fear and a sense of alarums and excursions and fleeting trains . . .

The uneasiness may in itself have had some appeal to a readership which was endlessly fascinated by the nuances of its own social standing. George Grossmith, then a police court reporter for *The Times*, realised this, and, together with his artist brother, produced *The Diary of a Nobody* in 1892. It was, and still is, a classic study of pretension, and nobody loved it more than the pretenders themselves. Similarly, F. Anstey, who was on the staff of the ultra-conservative *Punch*, had produced in 1882 an extraordinarily hard-hitting satire in *Vice Versa*, the tale of an identity-exchange between a schoolboy and his hypocritical, skinflint father in which the putting of money before humanity comes under blistering attack. It was boldly sub-titled *A Lesson to Fathers*, and remains good reading to this day. Appearing as it did, six years before Grahame's first published story, it is impossible to ignore the influence it had on a young man already consciously on the side of the child against a hostile adult world. Anstey, whose name in private life was

Thomas Anstey Guthrie, would later become well known to Grahame, but in the early '90s he was established as a tough, disillusioned journalist, contributing regular articles to *Punch* which faithfully echoed that periodical's almost hysterical loathing for the working class. These pieces were later published in book form as *Voces Populi*, and as far as Guthrie was concerned, the voices of the people could not be other than brutalistically ignorant. His soap-box orator is ridiculed for the Cockney accent which all working people were assumed to have.

"It's *hus* that reppresents the hintelleck, the henergy, the hability, the morality of a nation." (General chorus of " 'Ear, 'ear!")

Guthrie's support for humanity was evidently exclusively middle-class. Grahame, while refraining from any social partisanship, flourished in this climate of social and political hyper-awareness. The time was one of rapid change in which all things, whether welcome or not, seemed possible. From 1890 for the next six years, Kenneth entered into a period of intense creativity, producing story after story. They began as orthodox mildly humorous essays of the kind Henley liked; "The Romance of the Road", "Cheap Knowledge" (in which, as we have seen, he expresses his doubts about public libraries), followed by an equally un-egalitarian piece on the buying of books, "Non Libri Sed Liberi". He followed the Henley–Guthrie line, writing for a middle- and upper-class readership. The use of Latin tags and titles was in itself an excluding mechanism, meaning nothing to those not familiar with the legendary exclamation of a slave-buyer when confronted by a row of beautiful young Britons, "Non angli sunt, sed angeli". Not Angles but angels. Not books, but free people (who would, so the implication went, buy books if they chose to).

One of Grahame's oddest forays into writing for grown-ups was a long piece called "The Headswoman", which he began writing early in his career, while he was still dallying with the idea of Anstey-type satire. He worked on it intermittently for four years, during the time when he had hit the vein of pure gold which was making him a reputation as a writer of rare insight, and it represents the opposite extreme. All his uneasy striving for effect is concentrated into this tale, set in sixteenth-century France and centred round the notion that a woman is appointed to be the public executioner. Some have suggested that Grahame was persuaded by the suffragette cause to argue that there was no job from which a woman should be debarred but, if so, his heart was not in it, for the piece is full of a striving for joviality which is, to modern tastes, quite embarrassing. "Jeanne", the successful applicant, is a cardboard character, a Jeanne d'Arc stripped of holy fire and left only with aggression and a certain blunt, logical force of argument. Despite the awful gallows humour about the charms of a lady executioner ("the fellows as is told off for execution come skipping along in the morning, like a lot of lambs in May-time . . .") the whole essay now seems deeply distasteful. It is worth noting that the Bank had at this time taken the revolutionary step of employing women for clerical work, to the horror of its more conservative officers.

Times change, and it may well be that Victorian readers were more receptive to this kind of humour. It was the era of Gilbert and Sullivan, *The Mikado* having been staged for the first time in 1885, and the theatre-going public was vastly tickled by the "chippy-chippy chopper and the big, black block". Grahame's struggles to understand what people liked and how to please them were always fruitless. It was only when he began to write about his own inner perception of the world that he found himself admired as a writer of rare integrity and craftsmanship.

The process of self-discovery is, by its very nature, a slow one. Few people have the courage – or the perception – to write with truth and honesty from the start. Grahame, like so many other young men, was a confused entity of received wisdoms and inner promptings, not only unsure of how to present himself, but unsure at a much deeper level of what that self really was. In an age of rigid social convention, the urge to return to a more natural state must have seemed more irresponsible than it does now. There was no understanding of the many levels at which a human being functions, even though the avid thirst for fiction could be said to satisfy a need for attention to the suppressed emotional life. Charlotte Brontë had taken it for granted in *Shirley* that distress and a sense of life's uselessness could be the cause of fatal illness, and modern research tends increasingly to prove her right – but it was only the wise, the brave or the naïve who could break out of the strait-jacket of conventional cleverness to a more lambent and self-exposing form of expression.

Wisdom came slowly to Kenneth Grahame, but he had courage, and he was blessed with immense naïvety. When he began to investigate this quality, very delicately for fear of the self-hurt he might cause, the result was instantly rewarding. The turning point came in 1890, when he went to Venice for the first time. Naturally, he was enchanted by it, and abandoned himself to its pleasures with characteristically child-like enthusiasm. Canal-trips in gondola or *vaporetto* were not enough – he took off his shoes, rolled up his trousers and got down to the true joys of paddling through the sand-ribbed shallows of the Lido. It was late September, and the tourists had gone.

The bathing ladders were drawn up, the tramway was under repair; but the slant sun was still hot on the crinkled sand, and it was not so much a case of paddling suggesting itself as of finding oneself barefoot and paddling without any conscious process of thought.

It was there that Kenneth met a man who opened a new door of under-standing for him.

> He was barelegged also, this elderly man of sixty of thereabouts; and he had just found a *cavallo del mare*, and exhibited it with all the delight of a boy; and as we wandered together, cool-footed, eastwards, I learnt by degrees how such a man as this, with the mark of Cheapside still evident on him, came to be pacing the sands of the Lido that evening with me.[12]

The man (or at least, Grahame's interpretation of him) had been Secretary "to some venerable Company or Corporation that dated from Henry the Seventh" and spent his time "ticking off names with a feverish blue pencil". One night, going home on the Undergound Railway, he met the figure of Death, ticking off a list of names which, the man saw, ended with his own. He leapt out of the train at St James's Park "though it was not his right station", and fled. On the bridge over the water

> he halted, mopped his brow, and gradually recovered his peace of mind . . . Beneath his feet a whole family of ducks circled aimlessly, with content written on every feature, or else, reversing themselves in a position denoting supreme contempt for all humanity above the surface, exploring a new cool underworld a few inches below. It was then (he said) that a true sense of his situation began to steal over him; and it was then that he awoke to the fact of another life open to him should he choose to grasp it.

The ducks settled into Grahame's mind as a symbol of cocking a snook at the establishment, and reappeared years later in *The Wind in the Willows*, celebrated by Rat in his "Ducks' Ditty" with its chorus of "Up tails all!", but the wider implications had also become a conscious part of Grahame's thinking. For the first time, he took a steady look at his situation, having admitted to himself that his new acquaintance was "one of the sanest crea-tures I had ever yet happened upon". Why, then, could he not follow the beachcomber's example and abandon the days of "ticking off names"? His answer goes some way towards a self-defence against Henley's urging to take the plunge into full-time freelance writing.

> The most of us prefer to fight on – mainly, perhaps, from cowardice, and the dread of a plunge into a new element, new conditions, new surroundings – a fiery trial for any humble, mistrustful creature of use-and-wont. And yet it is not all merely a matter of funk. For a grim love grows up for the sword-play itself, for the push and the hurtle of

battle, for the grips and the give-and-take − in fine, for the fight itself, whatever the cause. In this exaltation, far from ignoble, we push and worry along until a certain day of a mist and a choke, and we are ticked off and done with.

This is the better way; and the history of our race is ready to justify us. With the tooth-and-claw business we began, and we mastered it thoroughly ere we learnt any other trade. Since that time we may have achieved a thing or two besides − evolved an art, even, here and there, though the most of us bungled it. But from first to last fighting was the art we were always handiest at; and we are generally safe if we stick to it, whatever the foe, whatever the weapons − most of all, whatever the cause.[13]

Here, in a couple of paragraphs, is Grahame's personal manifesto of the time. He did not write it down until five years after his meeting with the man on the Lido but, from that chance encounter onward, he gave up expecting that his day-to-day life would be anything other than a struggle with the outside world. The nature of that struggle was immaterial; twice, he emphasises the irrelevance of the cause. What enabled him to relax into an acceptance of it was the realisation that the struggle was contained in a water-tight capsule of city life, and need not spill over into his private awareness. That personal world of memory and imagination and selected visual impressions was open to encompass acceptable experience, but closed to the images of battle. From that time on, there is no further reference to characters from the Bank's past history and, with the single exception of his continuing obsession with *The Headswoman*, a lessening in his efforts to placate the unknown, alarming public with the cleverness he assumed it wanted. 1891 saw a change towards a newly confident, more personal style.

It was a cautious innovation, made with an eye on Henley's requirements. *The Rural Pan* introduces for the first time the figure of nature personified who was to achieve full power in *The Piper at the Gates of Dawn*, but Grahame's simple clarity of expression is still trammelled with pompous wordiness. On the one hand, he can write,

In the hushed recesses of Hurley backwater, where the canoe may be paddled almost under the tumbling comb of the weir, he is to be looked for; there the god pipes with freest abandonment.

but on the next page, we have another of those suspicious shifts in style:

Albeit shy of the company of his more showy brother deities, he loveth the more unpretentious humankind, especially them that are *adscripti glebae*, addicted to the kindly soil and the working thereof . . .

This is either Henley's hand or a Henley-prompted jab of literary conscience. And yet, the new spirit of simple, clear conviction is still determined to break through. When it succeeds in doing so, it brings hints of what is yet to come.

> Out of the hearing of all the clamour, the rural Pan may be found stretched on Ranmore Common, loitering under Abinger pines, or prone by the secluded stream of the sinuous Mole, abounding in friendly greetings for his foster-brothers the dabchick and water-rat.

There is no conscious cleverness here. This concept of the Great God comes from an early awareness, perhaps compounded by a touch of Keats, for whom autumn could be found

> . . . sitting careless on a granary floor,
> Thy hair soft-lifted by the winnowing wind;
> Or on a half-reap'd furrow sound asleep,
> Drows'd with the fume of poppies . . .

And yet, Grahame had no taste for anthropomorphism. He saw nothing self-evident in the idea that humankind is superior to the animal kingdom, and his Pan is very definitely half-goat, "linked to us by little but his love of melody; but for which saving grace, the hair would soon creep up from thigh to horn of him". This, from *The Lost Centaur*, in *Pagan Papers*, is an early, but already very clear picture of the Pan who would emerge in *The Wind in the Willows*.

Poetry experienced in childhood has a way of entwining itself in the threads of one's being and, for a child like Kenneth, whose father had seemed to be poetry and a wild sky and a warm hand, rather than a real man, no tedious adult explanations had ever been interposed between the words and the magic evocations which they brought about. Perhaps Blake, too, had crept in there with his

> Piping down the valleys wild,
> Piping songs of pleasant glee . . .

There was a warm, accepting beauty in such words, suggesting that somewhere, beyond all scoldings and tiresome duties, there was a place where one could wander without time limit, without hunger or discomfort or naggings of conscience and, most of all, *alone* with the beings who peopled it. Once such a world begins to be created, it is never dismantled. It lives on, parallel to the conventional one but utterly separate from it. It is, perhaps, the "little territory" which Marcus Aurelius recommended as the most permanent and reliable refuge – and like the more public world shared with relatives and fellow workers, it needs its own system of values and ethics, grown within its own delicate capsule. Any attempt to drag these in from the ordinary world will rupture the membrane which divides the private territory from the public one. When this happens, the dream and the reality become vulnerable to each other, with fatal damage to both.

Grahame had learned to respect the division. Pan belonged in his dream-world, which Kenneth wrote about with all the fascination of a traveller returned from an exotic place. He may have thought that Pan's values of freedom and irreverence, kindness, ruthlessness and wild poetry would make a better job of the world than orthodox Christianity did – but he would not say so. He was not a Morris, filled with burning conviction that the dream could be made real. He knew that it was only real if it was left intact.

There were some half-mystic figures who could shuttle with ease, in Grahame's view, between the two worlds.

When the pelting storm drives the wayfarers to the sheltering inn, among the little group on bench and settle Pan has been known to appear at times, in homely guise of hedger-and-ditcher or weather-beaten shepherd from the downs.[14]

The harmless country-dwellers of his childhood had never been Olympians, and so they could safely be admitted to the private territory – but Grahame never risked any close investigation into the real nature of these rustic figures. Innocence is the first casualty of knowledge.

That a man who was steadily and conscientiously working his way towards a senior post in the Bank of England should also be a pantheist would seem unusual even in our own time, used though we are to television programmes about self-declared members of witch-covens who are also local government officers or solicitors; but in the rigid conventionality of a hundred years ago, it is doubly bizarre. There are occasional reports of Grahame's attendance at a church service for particular occasions, and as a member of the London Scottish he undoubtedly had to present himself for church parades, with the loyalty to God and the Queen which was implicit in such events; his conventional Christianity seems, on the face of it, to be intact. The truth, again, seems to lie in a division between the inner world and the outer one.

As a child, the Christian God had been presented to the young Kenneth as the ultimate authority, the totem of the Olympians, a superior being who was entirely on their side. The Lord belonged with good manners and starched table-napkins and the smell of mint-sauce on Sundays; He was present in the drawing-room where the heavy curtains were always half-drawn and where ladies sat, straight-backed in their high-buttoned, long-sleeved dresses, and tea was sipped from dangerously thin cups. His approval was tacitly present in the wing-collars and side-whiskers of the men, in *The Times* and in the speaking of French *devant les enfants* to conceal adult secrets. He did not belong to children because, it was implied, they were not yet worthy of such honour, and so He could not be taken into the secret world of "unholy joy" (the phrase is revealing) which children find in the grubbinesses and conjurings-up of enchantment belonging to the fragrant, sappy, muddy outside world regarded by adults as so distasteful. That world had its own god, "and the red earth in him is strong," Grahame said.[15]

But there was more to it than that. In the London of the 1890s, Pan had become a symbol of the desire to escape from the commercial, mechanised future which lay ahead like a grinning monster. A shudder of distaste had caused an averting of the eyes from the political battle which raged on the subject of "progress", and there was a frantic seeking of spiritual safety in the pretend-lands of other times and other places. The Celtic revival seemed to offer a potential patch of security against the time when Philistinism would flood the country, and Yeats, with his blue eyes and unkempt black hair, owed much of his standing to the immense cachet of being a genuine Irishman; but the movement had spread far beyond Ireland. Ernest Renan, who died in 1892, had written *Les Poésies des Races Celtiques* five years before Grahame was born and, to Henley's young men, his gloomy prediction seemed all to palpably to be coming true. Grahame quoted him in *Deus Terminus*.

Le monde marche vers une sorte d'américanisme . . . Peut-être la vulgarité générale sera-t-elle un jour la condition du bonheur des élus.

Things Celtic, it was felt, might be a little dotty, but at least they were not vulgar. Matthew Arnold, who had relinquished the Oxford Chair of Poetry in 1877, was giving a series of lectures on the Celtic revival, and the extraordinary William Sharp, who had been born in Paisley four years before Grahame's birth in Edinburgh, single-handedly produced the *Pagan Review*, which survived for only one issue. Sharp had no sense of humour whatever, and could not see why anyone should be amused by his story about a young man in deerstalker hat and Norfolk jacket chasing a naked nymph across a grouse moor. He later retreated into the persona of Fiona MacLeod (thus giving a new forename to the English language), and took that, too, with immense seriousness.

Meanwhile, the Aesthetic movement which had begun in France had made itself felt in Britain, with its belief that a morality could be found within art itself. This inward-turning spiral of investigation arrived, inevitably, at the conclusion that pure sensation was enough. The impact of the moment, long recognised by the arts and philosophies of the East, was realised again as a source of strength, but there was a profound disinclination to follow the hard disciplines which are implicit within such a stance. The superficial appeal of a belief in instant sensation was only seductive if the deeper involvement were ignored, and so the catch-phrase "Art for Art's sake" was born, and sensation-seeking was given a quasi-philosophical rationale, which, although bogus, was very attractive. The use of narcotics and alcohol has always been a prime resort for those seeking escape from unpleasant reality, but in the 1890s it acquired a new modishness, based on the suggestion that the drinkers and smokers and laudanum-users were not simply weak, frightened people in flight from truth, but aesthetes in touch with a refined, exclusive world of delectable hyper-reality.

Grahame found this group deeply distasteful, and was horrified by the self-destruction which went on among his contemporaries, and yet he was fascinated. His taste for the exotic and the bohemian never left him, just as he retained his love of the circus, and for side-shows and freaks and fairgrounds and all that was tinselled and magical. The enjoyment of these things belonged in his child-world, to be privately treasured as rare examples of what the mysterious adults could do if they chose. To understand such manifestations would be to lose touch with their strangeness, and he never made this mistake. He would get a little drunk on occasion, but there is no hint that he ever entered the group of hashish and laudanum users, or resorted to the devastating influence of absinthe. His private world was too innocent for that, and too clean. He could rhapsodise over the joys of a pint in a country pub after a long day's walking and, like his father, he could appreciate a good glass or two of wine, but his personal escape was to the freshness of wind and sun, and he would do nothing to compromise it.

Green, writing as late as 1959, exonerated Grahame from existentialist excesses – but only just. He speaks of

a nightmare picture – and perhaps a not entirely false one – of writers and artists doping themselves silly on liquor and tobacco, walking themselves into a muscle-bound stupor every week-end, turning Nature into a kind of personalized God: and why? To produce bigger and better compensation-fantasies for the disgusting deadness of urban life; to blunt their senses enough to make existence bearable; to stimulate their imaginations into producing an inner lotus-land to which they could retreat at necessity.

As if alarmed by this revealing of prejudice, Green is at pains to stress that Grahame is "shrewd and realistic". As a result, there has been little understanding of just how committed Grahame was to the idea that there is an inherent sanctity in the intelligence of the natural world itself. He would have agreed with James Joyce, whose Stephen Dedalus watched the birds flying, and found in his mind

> shapeless thoughts from Swedenborg on the correspondence of birds to things of the intellect and of how the creatures of the air have their knowledge and know their times and seasons because they, unlike man, are in the order of their life and have not perverted that order by reason.[16]

Grahame's concept of Pan was a quintessence of all things natural and lovely, but for many of his contemporaries, the Great God represented a personal anarchy of a more malignant kind. To accept the basic premise that he was the antithesis of respectability implied that he must therefore be the champion of all disreputable behaviour. As Richard Le Gallienne put it,

> He is often found lacking in "refinement", as understood in drawing-rooms and seminaries. His exquisite products are usually brought about by processes quite coarse and shocking to refined individuals.[17]

To Grahame's perplexity, he found himself a member of a group which, while nominally sharing his own beliefs, in fact had a very different concept of the god-figure. Pantheism was prey to the same schisms which have divided the Christian church for centuries, but its lack of formal doctrine prevented these from becoming anything more than an area of reserve between fellow-believers. Grahame, the least aggressive of men, kept his opinions to himself, though he must have been slightly shocked by the licentious behaviour which a worship of the goatfoot was assumed to condone. He could not see Pan as rampantly sexual, both as a musk-reeking pursuer of maidens and as the common counterpart, homosexual and decadent, daffodil in hand. Effeminacy had become a marked characteristic of the 1890s, perhaps as a gesture of supreme contempt for the stuffy, male-dominated conventional society against which the aesthetic young had revolted, and it had the satisfactory result of pricking the public into a howl of outrage. Gilbert's "greenery-yallery" young man was anathema to the solid middle class, and the very fact of their condemnation helped to give the group a clear and enjoyable identity. Grahame, pipe-smoking and week-end-tweeded, had no intention of seeing himself in any such light, and yet the sense of boyishness naughtiness in being associated with the fashionably wicked set was delicious.

The public perception of the Pan-worshippers was predictably hysterical. W. F. Barry, in a thirty-page piece on "Neo-Paganism" for the *Quarterly Review*, traced its ancestry from pre-Christianity through Goethe, Gautier, Baudelaire and Walter Pater (among others) to its current manifestation.

Like most of his contemporaries, Barry could not see that Paganism might constitute a reasoned religious belief. As a convinced Christian, he took the view that a Pagan was, by definition, an infidel who, having no faith in Christianity, therefore had no faith in anything else. "And so it is," he said, "with our aesthetic, scientific, curled, and scented Paganism, which cannot endure the harsh Christian limitations on experience, or its antiquated warning about the law of sin in our members." Swinburne, of course, was an easy target, with his approval of "monstrous passions", but Barry goes further, pointing out that

the effeminacy, which is now identified with Paganism (in spite of Epictetus and the Stoics), though it has neither nerve nor brain, is not without danger. The moral tone of society tends to sink when peace, combined with an increase of riches like that which has gone on during the last sixty years, wraps the idle and the educated round as with a velvet cloak and suffers them to dream at their ease. Luxury and scepticism have flourished together, especially in France, where the art of enjoyment has long been cultivated. The risk of infection, however, is greatest, not, as might be supposed, when pleasure, with the light Epicurean foam upon it, fills the cup, but as soon as it is drained to the lees. For if self-indulgence slays its thousands, despair slays its tens of thousands.

Barry belonged to the purple-faced school of High Tories who, like Kenneth's Uncle John, felt that the human spirit was a dangerous thing unless well disciplined by the Church and the Army, and he had no hesitation in declaring that Paganism had "gruesome and forbidding associations" with the Devil.

The basis of Barry's argument was flawed, because he failed to recognise that Pantheism was capable of containing its own spiritual and intellectual discipline in a tradition which went back far beyond Christianity to the complex theology of Eastern religions – but some, at least, of his ammunition was unwittingly supplied by the self-styled Pantheists of his own time, a number of whom had pursued decadence to the point of self-destruction. Seekers of freedom always end by having to find new rules of their own, and the Decadents were no exception. Some of them failed, and were overwhelmed by the absinthe and opium with which they had tried to extend the limits of sensation. They were, J. W. Lambert said in his history of The Bodley Head,

a symptom of a sick civilisation: not least those who, abjuring French fumes, conjured up an ideal Britain, all meadowsweet and roses and lush green pastures, into which the ghost of the great god Pan, not to mention Cuchulain and the leprechaun, had been wistfully translated.

Even Lambert, however, exonerated Grahame from any trace of unpleasant decadence, and admitted that Pan in this writer's context represented "the source of that elusive 'purity of soul' for which Grahame describes himself as praying to the feral spirit . . .".

It was no wonder that Kenneth appeared to his friends to be "startled". Their idea of the goat-footed god was strangely contorted and overlaid with self-indulgent symbolism. For him, the genesis of Pan was altogether simpler and more innocent, well known to any decently educated boy who had learned his Latin and Greek and was familiar with the pantheon of gods and goddesses. Poetry was full of references to Bacchus and Triton, Ceres and Phoebus and Psyche, and had been for all the intervening centuries. Underlying the intellectual nonconformities of Goethe and Voltaire were the lyrical verses of men like John Fletcher, born in 1579, three hundred years before Grahame himself. His "Hymn to Pan" is a very deliberate celebration of the qualities of chastity and freedom, the bucolic metre far from accidental, for this is the sophisticated Fletcher who was the son of a bishop, and who collaborated with Francis Beaumont in the writing of such satirical plays as *The Knight of the Burning Pestle*.

> Sing his praises that doth keep
>   Our flocks from harm,
> Pan, the father of our sheep;
>   And arm in arm
> Tread we softly in a round,
> Whilst the hollow neighbouring ground
> Fills the music with her sound.
>
> Pan, O great god Pan, to thee
>   Thus do we sing!
> Thou who keep'st us chaste and free
>   As the young spring:
> Ever be thy honour spoke
> From that place the morn is broke
> To that place day doth unyoke!

Much closer to Grahame's own time, Elizabeth Barrett Browning wrote a thoughtful poem about Pan as the gentle magic-maker whose pipes were so sweet that

> The sun on the hill forgot to die,
> And the lilies revived, and the dragon-fly
>   Came back to dream on the river.

She takes a step away from the romantic acceptance of the god as a heroic figure, setting him in his place as a symbol of power and of male game-playing.

> Yet half a beast is the great god Pan,
> To laugh as he sits by the river,
>   Making a poet out of a man:
> The true gods sigh for the cost and the pain –
> For the reed which grows never more again
>   As a reed with the reeds of the river.

The preceding six stanzas have dwelt in detail on Pan's fashioning of reed-pipes, and the poem's title is "A Musical Instrument", but the underlying point is an unwittingly Taoist one, that man's sublimest and most spiritual ideas are but a passing reflection of the self, expressed through whatever means come to hand. The continuum perseveres, regardless.

If Grahame picked up the debunking element in the poem, he is unlikely to have understood it, for women, as we will see, were a frightening mystery to him. In the privacy of his mind, he was still a boy, and perhaps thought, rightly or wrongly, that his fellow pantheists, too, retained the secret land of their childhood where the shaggy god piped for ever. Emboldened, he began at last to explore this personal treasure through his writing, and in September of 1891 he produced *The Olympians*. As if half-afraid of what he had revealed, it was published in the *National Observer* without his signature.

7

Golden Days

Grahame's confidence was always a little perilously balanced but, from the publication of *The Olympians* onwards, he entered into a cautious conviction that he really could write. The story had been rapturously received by both public and critics, and the new ground which it had broken was astonishingly fertile.

The Olympians was the first account of Kenneth's childhood perception of the baffling world of grown-ups and in it he had retreated behind a fictional boy-narrator, set within the matrix of Edward and Selina, Charlotte and Harold. The children, though sketched in with the lightest of touches, were utterly convincing, and so was the amiable curate, set in sharp contrast to the solid figures of the drawing-room, who seemed as stiffly stuffed as the horsehair sofas on which they sat. The story remains to this day a passionate plea for the recognition of the child's view of things, and in 1891, it unlocked the private feelings of hundreds of people. Generously, Grahame begins with a self-excusing preamble:

> Looking back to those days of old, ere the gate shut to behind me, I can see now that to children with a proper equipment of parents these things would have worn a different aspect, but to those whose nearest were aunts and uncles, a special attitude of mind may be allowed.

Special or not, it was an attitude recognised by grown-up children all over Britain, though a few Olympians were shocked by the idea that the pink-and-white, nightgowned little creatures they saw for half an hour each evening might hold disillusioned opinions about adult persons. Kenneth's cousin Jeanie Grahame, according to Annie, "sent a copy of 'The Golden Age' to an old lady friend who returned it, saying that she could not have believed that any member of our family would write a book like this one, holding up to ridicule everything that she had been taught to respect, and including Aunts and Uncles".[1]

The story is virtually free of the labyrinthine syntax which had marked Grahame's earlier work, and Green attributes this step forward to a flash of insight on Henley's part, leading him to publish the text in its original, unadorned state because he saw that the public would prefer it that way. It seems unlikely, however, that Henley would change his spots so radically without a more specific cause. Grahame, on the other hand, had everything to fight for in this piece. With immense courage, he had laid bare his own precious inner world, and to have it chopped about and decorated by Henley might well have been intolerable.

His previous pieces had all been dispassionately written essays on an objective theme, faithfully following the example set by Robert Louis Stevenson, who had preceded him with very similar offerings – so similar, in fact, that a critic had referred disparagingly to Grahame's "Stevensonettes".[2] The very titles show how closely Kenneth had modelled himself on the example of Henley's first and most favoured protégé. *An Apology For Idlers, Walking Tours, A Plea for Gas Lamps* – these set down the conservative, country-loving material which Stevenson's younger follower exploited, albeit with a lively personal twist of his own. Stevenson had written *Pan's Pipes* in 1881, seven years before Grahame had published anything at all, but he was an extrovert who lived with relish in the real world, and he wrote with the courage of a man who, despite a constant struggle with tuberculosis, had gone wandering through the Cévennes with nothing more than a hand-made sleeping-sack and an unco-operative donkey called Modestine.

Grahame may well have been needled by the older writer's contempt, expressed in *Pan's Pipes*, for the skulkers behind desks who would not answer the call of the goat-foot; there is no doubt that he read it.

Highly respectable citizens who flee life's pleasures and responsibilities and keep, with upright hat, upon the midway of custom, avoiding the right hand and the left, the ecstasies and the agonies, how surprised they would be if they could hear their attitude mythologically expressed, and knew themselves as tooth-chattering ones, who flee from Nature because they fear the hand of Nature's god! Shrilly sound Pan's pipes; and behold the banker instantly concealed in the bank parlour![3]

That on its own had been enough to bring Grahame into line as a card-carrying pantheist. He hardly needed Stevenson's final thrust that "to distrust one's impulses is to be recreant to Pan".

Stevenson was only nine years older than Grahame, but he was infinitely senior as a writer, and it was hard for the younger man to rid himself of a sense of following in the master's footsteps. Fortunately for him, Stevenson left England in 1888, forced by his illness to seek the sun. He settled in Samoa, to die there six years later, and Grahame was left to work his way through the influence of the *Virginibus Puerisque* essays, thereafter to go it alone. *The Rural Pan* was his last "Stevensonette", and it was followed by five months of silence. Then came *The Olympians*.

It was a breakthrough which must have come as an immense relief, for starting afresh without Stevenson had been like starting from scratch. Buoyed up by the good reviews, and, perhaps, by having at last found the courage to stand up to Henley, Grahame wrote a letter to the publisher John Lane of The Bodley Head. It is dated 19 January 1893, and the tone, despite his new-found confidence, is awkward and boyish.

> I wonder whether you would care to publish a quite small selection of articles that I have had in the *National Observer* and *St James's Gazette* during the past few years?
>
> They are, I think, just sufficiently individual and original to stand it.
>
> Mr Henley suggested to me once, that a 'blend' of these short articles with verse would perhaps make a 'feature' that might take. But that is a detail I have no particular feeling about, one way or the other.
>
> The two journals mentioned would, I think, give friendly reviews.
>
> I can, of course, leave the things with you anyway, to look over.
>
> Your attractive 'format' – which you maintain so well – has mainly prompted my suggestion.

It reads like a letter which the writer had hardly been able to bring himself to pen. Somebody – probably Henley – had advised him in a debonair way to throw in a bit of flattery and promise a good review or two but this gaucheness from a man in his mid-thirties is curiously charming. John Lane was intrigued, and the book was published in October of the same year, under the title of *Pagan Papers*.

Together with other essays, the original edition contained *The Olympians*, plus five further stories about Edward and Selina and the continuing childhood saga. This was curious, for at the time of Grahame's letter to John Lane, only *The Olympians* had been written. The publisher must have spotted the outstanding quality of this new story, and given his writer some forceful advice. The effect was galvanising. Grahame turned out the additional five stories in time for them to be incorporated in *Pagan Papers* ten months later. Even allowing for the much greater speed of book production which used, mysteriously enough, to be attainable in the days of hand-setting, he must have worked fast.

Lane shrewdly withdrew the childhood stories from the second and subsequent editions of the book, and made them the basis for a separate volume, *The Golden Age*, which appeared two years later, but meanwhile *Pagan Papers* was doing nicely. This must have come as a relief to Lane, who had backed his hunch with an unusually generous royalty agreement. Grahame had proved to be a surprisingly tough negotiator, and would settle for nothing less than ten per cent for the first 200 copies on a limited edition of 450, and twenty per cent thereafter. It is enough to make a present-day author (specially of a first-time book of essays) weep with envy. Chalmers, with access to now-vanished papers, quoted a laconic note by Grahame: "I don't call this a grasping proposal – especially from a Scotchman". Self-mocking or not, he had driven a hard bargain.

The achievement is more extraordinary when contrasted with the experience of other authors. Even Lambert's celebratory account of the house's history admits that Lane was parsimonious, and Laurence Housman (brother of the poet A.E. and better known for his *Little Plays of St. Francis*), in his book *The Unexpected Years*, enlarges on a minor triumph far less impressive than Grahame's, even if it is more amusing. After several unfulfilled promises from Lane to pay the money that was owed, Housman hit on an idea.

I wrote to ask if he would, as a friend, lend me the five pounds which my publisher had promised faithfully to send me a week ago. This brought me a cheque by return . . .

Evelyn Sharp mentions the incident in her extraordinarily interesting book, *Unfinished Adventure*, and records that Lane was so tickled by Housman's cheek that he went round London telling the joke against himself – but changing the amount to £50 instead of five. A publisher who kept his contributors waiting for a fiver would not have sounded quite so funny.

Evelyn herself had personal experience of Lane's meanness, as a letter written from the New Victoria Club shows.

Thursday 21st December 1899
Dear Mr Lane
My dressmaker comes and sits on the doormat here every morning and expects to be paid; and it is no use referring her to you, for, although French, she seems to know all there is to know about English publishers, and she says it would do no good. I am inclined to agree with her, but I am writing to you, notwithstanding, in the hope that you will let me have that cheque we occasionally mention when we meet in the street, so that the doormat may be unoccupied again. It's so inconvenient this muddy weather, and the members are beginning to complain . . .

Frederick Rolfe, the self-styled "Baron Corvo", hated Lane so deeply that he wrote *Nicholas Crabbe* as a detailed and only lightly fictionalised account of his struggles to get money out of him. The book was so abusive that it was not published until 1958, and in it, Lane (disguised as "Slim Schelm") is depicted with the utmost venom.

Now that was a beery insect for you, a snivelling little swindler if you gave him a chance . . . a carroty dwarf, with a magenta face and puce pendulous lips and a vermilion necktie . . .

Not content with that, he also called him "a tubby little pot-bellied bantam, scrupulously attired and looked as though he had been suckled on bad beer".

Grahame, however, managed to find a liking for Lane, even while ruthlessly pinning him down to a decent offer. The publisher's trace of a Devon accent may have helped, for Kenneth always had a soft spot for a West Country man. He wrote in friendly advice much later, during one of Lane's frequent financial crises:

> You will find it will assist matters more immediately if you will re-acquire and retain, a strong Devonshire accent. The public like anything that smacks of the soil.

He added a salacious afterthought which, though written in the last decade of his life, indicates something of his attitude to women. "By the way, that would be a good title for your next young lady's effusion: 'Smacks of the Soil' ".[4]

Even Grahame, however, could become irritated with Lane. Royalty payments could be anything up to two years late, and the publisher's carelessly proprietorial attitude to his writers was infuriatingly off-hand. Grahame wrote: "You seem to imply that there is imposed on me some sort of restraint or qualified serfdom – not upon you, on me only, which entirely and for all time prevents me even doing freely what I may think best for myself".[5]

And yet, for all his faults, John Lane created "a nest of singing birds" as Lambert put it, which sings to this day. He had a generosity of spirit which more than compensated for his hopeless management of money, and his vision of glorious, lively books expressed itself through a hospitality which was open-handed and weirdly creative. He seemed instinctively to put his finger soothingly on the sore nerve which Yeats revealed when he wrote, "I am growing jealous of other poets and we will all grow jealous of one another unless we know each other and so feel a share in each other's triumphs".[6]

Grahame, like Yeats, had a need to feel that he belonged within a supportive group, of the kind he had already found through Furnivall and Henley. Despite his inner solitude – or perhaps because of it – he was reassured by the camaraderie of other writers, and by the fact that a publisher had confidence in him.

Pagan Papers was a success. The title of the book was deliberately provocative, placing it centrally within The Bodley Head's irreverent aestheticism, even though the contents were hardly pagan at all. The *Scotsman*, it is true, muttered dourly that the essays "do not manifestly appear to be the work of a Christian", but could find no particular point to object to, conceding that "anyone who likes showy pictorial writing may read *Pagan Papers* with pleasure". The *Literary Echo* feared that the title might deter families with growing children from reading the book. "This we should specially regret," it added. A publication called *Great Thoughts* also complained that the title was "quite grotesquely ill-fitting" but, in a long review, exorcised the ghost of Stevenson's contempt for the life-shunning banker with a great cloud of laudatory incense.

A lover of all the varied delights of life, Mr. Grahame shows, even while he is most palpably young, that he has lived his years to the utmost. Joy in the fields and in books, in boating and in old authors, in tramps over the open downs, and in poets, is his, and one gets from his diverse subjects a sense of the greatest gusto, and a feeling that here one is in touch with a writer complete and virile to his finger-tips.

The *Queen*, less enthusiastically, said that "these smart newspaper sketches" proved Grahame (of whom the reviewer had never heard) to be "one of Mr Henley's *very* clever young men".

The first edition of *Pagan Papers* carried a frontispiece drawn by Aubrey Beardsley. The original drawing is now in the V & A, and it shows two fauns, one of whom is rather strangely clothed in a Bohemian shirt and floppy tie. Like all Beardsley's work, there is a slightly reptilian quality about the thin, carefully calculated line, but in this case there is also something sardonic about the two figures, one belonging to Blake's "valleys wild" and the other halfway to a Fleet Street hack. Neither represents the shaggy father-figure of Grahame's dream. Whether Grahame liked it is not recorded, but Beardsley was the up-and-coming artist of his day, and the drawing undoubtedly helped sell the book. It did not, of course, marry up in any way with the childhood stories, but it touched a strangely accurate finger on the two essays which concluded the book, called "The Lost Centaur" and "Orion". In the first of them, Grahame expresses something close to a real dissociation from humanity. As Pan asks, "May you not have taken a wrong turn somewhere, in your long race after your so-called progress, after the perfection of this be-lauded species of yours?"

Kenneth makes it clear that his concept of the goatfoot has nothing in common with the spirit of decadent human self-indulgence, for

in the main his sympathies are first for the beast: to which his horns are never horrific, but, with his hairy pelt, ever natural and familiar, and his voice (with its talk of help and healing) not harsh nor dissonant, but voice of very brother as well as very god.

'Orion' contains the most passionate plea for the unfettered human soul that Grahame ever wrote. It begins, "The moonless night has a touch of frost, and is steely-clear". Orion, the Hunter, lies low on the horizon, "watchful, seemingly, and expectant: with some hint of menace . . .". He looks at the human progress which is "clearing forest and draining fen; policing the valleys with barbed-wire and Sunday schools . . .". It is in this story that Grahame identifies the spirit of freedom as the thing known to "pulpiteers and parents" as Original Sin. He pulls together the two themes which run through the book in his claim that this quality is strongest in children.

> In later years it is stifled and gagged – buried deep, a green turf at the head of it, and on its heart a stone; but it lives, it breathes, it lurks, it will up and out when 'tis looked for least.

He goes on to tell the story of another escapee, a stockbroker who owned "a villa and a steam launch at Surbiton" who went missing. After many weeks

> they found him in a wild nook of Hampshire. Ragged, sunburnt, the nocturnal haystack calling aloud from his frayed and weather-stained duds, his trousers tucked, he was tickling trout with godless native urchins . . .

Despite such oddities, Grahame almost despairs of the world. Orion's lovely wildness seems doomed as "the desolate suburbs creep ever farther into the retreating fields". The only hope is a bleak one.

> After some Armageddon of cataclysmal ruin, all levelling, whelming the County Councillor with Music-hall artiste, obliterating the very furrows of the Plough, shall the skin-clad nomad string his bow once more, and once more loose the whistling shaft? Wildly incredible it seems. And yet – look up! Look up and behold him confident, erect, majestic – there on the threshold of the sky!

It was stirring stuff, and the Victorian readers, almost every one of whom nursed a secret conviction that he or she had a greatness of soul which could not be contained by convention, responded enthusiastically, claiming this new writer who had touched their deepest feelings. Grahame had arrived on the cultural map. Whatever he chose to do next, it would not go unnoticed.

Grahame, in fact, very seldom made choices. The large decisions in his life had so far been made by other people, and, as his letter to John Lane so clearly showed, he was diffident about taking the initiative, even though he could be forceful and effective once the way had become plain. He was by nature an accepter rather than a decider, partly through the Calvinist and Stoic influences of his childhood, and partly through that wisdom which comes from a closeness to the natural world. People, to him, could not be anything more than small and insignificant creatures dwelling on the earth as best they could, and the pushing of one's own importance seemed not only rather vulgar but fundamentally absurd. This conviction came to a head in the depiction of Toad in *The Wind in the Willows*, but it was also manifest throughout his life as a modesty (one of his favourite words) which made him wait for opportunity to arise rather than go looking for it.

After the publication of *Pagan Papers*, he did not have to wait long for opportunities to present themselves. He went for an Alpine holiday in the summer of 1893, and, on return, found an enthusiastic demand for his work. For the rest of that year continued to turn out stories which filled in the complete picture of his childhood, each one published as soon as it was written in Henley's *National Observer*.

Early in 1894, on a wet winter afternoon, a meeting of literary people, including Aubrey Beardsley, took place at 144 Cromwell Road, in a flat belonging to Henry Harland, an expatriate American novelist. Harland's talents were entrepreneurial rather than literary. He had the same restless energy which marked Furnivall and Henley, and the same disinclination for the steady self-scrutiny which is essential in a writer, but, fortunately, his instincts were good. He had been in London barely four years, and had lost no time in getting himself established at the centre of the literary élite. Quite how he achieved this is something of a mystery, for his previous history had been quirky rather than distinguished.

Born in New York in 1861 – which made him two years younger than Grahame – Henry Harland had dallied briefly with a degree course at the Harvard Divinity School and then veered to the opposite extreme. Taking the pseudonym of Sidney Luska and a sham Jewish identity, he wrote several would-be realistic novels about Jewish immigrants in New York, under such titles as *The Yoke of the Thorah* and *A Jewish Musician's Story*. Whether his cover was "blown" at this point cannot be proved, but the year after the publication of *My Uncle Florimund* in 1888, he left America and went to Russia for a while, then settled in Paris, quietly shedding Sidney Luska en route. There, he plunged with equal whole-heartedness into Parisian life, rapidly producing a book of short stories called *A Latin Quarter Courtship*, and following it at even more break-neck speed by no fewer than four novels, all within less than two years. By 1890 he had moved to London, before the last of the French novels had appeared in print, and was now looking for something to do.

Frederick Rolfe made Harland into a leading figure in his splenetic book, giving him the hardly disguised name of Sidney Thorah. Rolfe's description, though characteristically venomous, is evocative, both of the name and his setting.

Crabbe waited a couple of minutes in a large and very dainty drawing-room. There were a couch and a piano and lots of weird and comfy chairs, and a feminine atmosphere. Sidney Thorah suddenly fell in, with a clatter and a rush; and began to talk-on-a-trot. He was a lank round-shouldered bony unhealthy personage, much given to crossing his legs when seated and to twisting nervously in his chair. He had insincere eyes, and long arms which dangled while he was silent and jerked and waved when he spoke.[7]

Harland's wife, Aline, was treated with a little more sympathy.

The wife was a dark pale tired timid little thing, with a secret and the voice of a nightingale.

This last observation, at least, was true, for Aline Harland was a trained soprano, and often sang for the odd mixture of people assembled in the Cromwell Road flat.

Opinions differ as to how much of what happened was due to Harland's enterprise and how much to John Lane's shrewd eye for a good publishing proposition, but between them they proposed the setting-up of a magazine which would reflect the new spirit of the age. Newness, in the dying decade of the nineteenth century, was coupled with nostalgia and the desire for escape, forming an elusive style, half-dissenting, half-decadent, which had caused Harland's antennae to quiver with excitement. H. G. Traill, in an article on *The New Fiction*, had declared glumly that "not to be *new* is, in these days, to be nothing". Harland agreed, but with enthusiasm. John Lane's imagination was equally fired by the idea of a New publication, and a month later, at a riotous dinner party held at the Devonshire club, the proposal was agreed. The new magazine would be livelier than any of the staid quarterlies and monthlies already existing – even Henley's *National Observer* was dismissed as fuddy-duddy. It would be something closer to a book than a journal, a striking, irreverent, immensely high-class production, a show-case for the work of the best of the New writers and artists. There was already a penny weekly with the title of *The New Age*, published "with a humanitarian and radical objective" (and there would be another *New Age* of a far more prestigious nature, funded by Shaw, in 1907) but Harland's brain-child would not stoop to compete for any such self-descriptive titles. The new production would be distinguished by a daffodil yellow jacket embellished by a Beardsley drawing, and it would be called, with lofty simplicity, *The Yellow Book*.

When the founder-members had recovered from the hangovers resulting from the celebratory evening at the Devonshire club, work started in earnest, Lane having undertaken to publish *The Yellow Book* from The Bodley

Head. Two months later, in April 1894, the first number appeared. It contained contributions from Max Beerbohm, Richard Garnett, George Moore, A. C. Benson, Henry James, Richard Le Gallienne and several others well known in their day. Harland himself contributed two brief stories, one about the death of an old man, somewhat in the style of Guy de Maupassant, and the other a fictionalised memory of white mice owned in childhood. If imitation is flattery, then Grahame should have afforded himself a pat on the back.

The drawings included in the book were not illustrations. They co-existed with the letterpress contents on a level of equal importance, each one shielded by a sheet of fine tracing paper. Walter Sickert contributed a sketch of a woman reading and a lithograph of the Old Oxford Music Hall, and there are solidly competent offerings from such worthies as Sir Frederic Leighton and Will Rothenstein, but Laurence Housman put in a Gothically decorative drawing called "The Reflected Faun" which is simultaneously badly drawn and, for its time, quite astonishingly sexual. While the faun on the bank of the pool (a hornless Pan-figure with pointed ears) attends with rapturous interest to a plucked water-lily, his counterpart in the water is locked in naked embrace with an abundant-haired nymph. This, as much as anything else, was probably responsible for the howl of disgust with which the first *Yellow Book* was received, and yet, both at that time and now, Aubrey Beardsley has been thought of as the figure most centrally identified with its supposed decadence.

Beardsley's drawing on the jacket of this *Yellow Book* represents a fat, periwigged figure, mouth split in a mirthless laugh, eyes reduced to two mocking dots behind the black carnival mask. Peering from behind the sweeping curve of the hat she wears (if indeed this figure is feminine) lurks a lean-faced, saturnine figure, slant-eyed and black-capped, his mask drawn back into points which suggest hidden horns. Inside the book, Beardsley contributes a couple of stylish female portraits, one of them a book plate, and an equally poised and precise satirical drawing called "L'Education Sentimentale", in which a fat woman in an ostrich-feathered hat is listened to demurely by a girl whose mass of black hair drops seductive tendrils over her bare shoulders as her eyes wander inattentively. Her arms are submissively behind her back, but a black-slippered foot with a life of its own has moved sideways under her slinky gown.

Lane had not been entirely happy about the jacket design. It was, to those in the know, a recognisable portrait of Mrs Whistler, and he was worried that Beardsley might have incorporated into the curlicues of his design some "neat little obscenity", as Lambert puts it. The editor was occasionally to be seen poring over the drawings with a magnifying glass – just in case. But Beardsley had been at his most persuasive over the use of the jacket design.

Yes my Dear Lane I shall most assuredly commit suicide if the fat woman does not appear in No. 1 of the Yellow Book. I have shown it to all sorts and conditions of men – and women. All agree that it is one of my very best efforts and extremely witty. Really I am sure you have nothing to fear.

Grahame already knew Beardsley, but there was no basis for any real friendship between the two men. Beardsley was very young – at the time of the first *Yellow Book* he was twenty-two and at the peak of a short life which would end four years later. Unlike Grahame, he was pushy and cocksure, brought up to believe himself a prodigy. He had launched himself in London by walking, with his sister, Mabel, into the house of Edward Burne Jones, who was dining with Oscar Wilde, and demanding the master's opinion of the portfolio of drawings he had brought with him. Wilde was fascinated by the boy, then eighteen, with his white face "like a silver hatchet", as Rothenstein said, under the sharply contrasted mass of chestnut hair. In all that has been written about Beardsley, there is little trace of real sympathy and liking for him, but a letter from Helen Thorp (*née* Syrett) to Grahame's widow does much to redress the balance.

We knew the Beardsleys very well, in fact some time before Aubrey was known at all. My sister Netta taught in a school with Mabel. She was beautiful, really lovely, like an orchid, pale with red hair & a tall and graceful figure. She was as brilliant as Aubrey, deeply read & full of knowledge. Aubrey was remarkable in appearance, he had a straight fringe, beautiful long hands, & was spotlessly *clean* & well-groomed – one was *impressed* [her italics] by his cleanliness as Netta says. Both Mabel & Aubrey were the kindest people I ever met & Aubrey the most cultured, & Aubrey always insisted upon me shewing him my designs and life drawings. I was only a little art student, yet he took an enormous interest in my work, in spite of people crowding round him & his great success. Netta & I knew he was a genius the moment we saw his drawings – it was unmistakable. His line is the most beautiful I have ever seen, apart from the Chinese & Japanese drawing. We often went to tea in their orange room, with black paint, & one white plaster cast of the "smiling girl". . . . They were all very gay, very witty, very brilliant, they were like a flame flashing up & then going out – too brilliant to last – too unreal – artificial – yet the Beardsleys were much kinder than people like the Meynell group. The Meynells I hated – yet they were & are, oh, so correct!
. . . The Yellow Book of course died out after Aubrey. He did all his work before he was twenty-six, became a R.C. & died in the south

of France. He had haemorrhages often all the time we knew him. He always drew his designs at night, I believe.[8]

Despite his kindness to "a little art student", there was a quality of ruthlessness about Beardsley which Grahame would have found alarming, even though his friend Evelyn Sharp said in defence of the young artist that "he seemed to me a shy and simple youth in whom it was uncommonly difficult to suspect dark tendencies towards mysterious vice". At this period of his life, she may well have been right, although Beardsley's later work, with its giant phalluses blooming in the foreground, was perilously near to pornography and he asked on his deathbed for such drawings to be destroyed – a request which was shamefully ignored, and which has sullied his reputation ever since.

There is a touching story by eye-witnesses of an evening when Aubrey Beardsley brought his drawings for *The Rape of the Lock* to a gathering where Whistler was present. The great man had always disliked Beardsley because of the caricature of Mrs Whistler on the first *Yellow Book* jacket, but, as he looked through the drawings, he said slowly, "Aubrey, I have made a very great mistake – you are a very great artist". And the boy burst out crying. All Whistler could say, when he could say anything, was "I meant it – I meant it – I meant it." The hosts on the occasion were Elizabeth and Joseph Pennell, who later wrote *The Life of James McNeill Whistler*.

For all his vulnerability, however, Beardsley was immensely assured of his own abilities and, as barely more than a teenager, the quality of revulsion which is present in his work seems to represent the distaste which the artist felt for his subject. This distaste found its most marked expression when Oscar Wilde, who had taken the new artist under his wing since their first meeting at the evening with Burne Jones, commissioned him to do a set of drawings for *Salome*. Whether Wilde had made homosexual advances towards his young illustrator is not known, but Beardsley could not conceal the fact that he found both the subject-matter and the author repellent. His first set of drawings contained depictions of Wilde himself, his corpulent figure and heavy-lidded eyes instantly recognisable, in such compromising positions that Wilde was compelled to reject the most offensive of them. The *Salome* illustrations made Beardsley's reputation, but his dislike of Wilde was such that, when asked to design *The Yellow Book*'s jacket, he made it a condition of his acceptance that Wilde would never write for the publication. Harland was dismayed, for Oscar Wilde was high on the list of prestigious potential contributors – but John Lane had always disliked Wilde, and he backed Beardsley strongly. Harland had to agree to the ban. The literary world was enjoyably shocked, but Grahame gave no sign that he relished such arm-twisting tactics. With his perpetual caution about the workings of the adult world in which he found himself, he may well have regarded its in-fighting with alarm and distaste rather than amusement.

The Yellow Book itself, however, appealed to him immensely, and Harland's circle was a step up the Bohemian ladder from Henley, who was locked in perpetual battle over the future of the *National Observer* with its hapless and increasingly impoverished owner, Fitzroy Bell. Grahame was more than ready to accept an invitation from Harland to contribute to the second issue of *The Yellow Book*, and offered him "The Roman Road", one of the best of the childhood stories. Kenneth had received the proofs of this story at the time when his sister Helen and Mary Richardson came to visit him in the Chelsea Gardens flat, and Mary remembered him reading the story aloud, commenting that he had a very beautiful reading voice.

Grahame's enthusiasm for the new publication was understandable. As Holbrook Jackson wrote in *The Eighteen Nineties* (1913),

> Nothing like The Yellow Book had been seen before. It was newness *in excelsis*, novelty naked and unashamed. People were puzzled and shocked and delighted, and yellow became the colour of the hour, the symbol of the time-spirit. It was associated with all that was *bizarre* and queer in art and life, with all that was outrageously modern.

They were heady days, full of excitement. From Grahame's point of view, the switch to a new publication happened just in time, for Henley's quarrel with Bell beame so virulent that the owner at last lost patience and withdrew his support. Grahame published one more story, "Sawdust and Sin", in the *National Observer* within a few days of its closure at the end of August 1894. Meanwhile "The Roman Road" had appeared in the July *Yellow Book*, to critical acclaim, and Grahame had moved into a new group of young writers, far more exotic than Henley's bright young men had ever been. There were, perhaps, times when he would willingly have turned the clock back to the fatherly, if autocratic rule of his old editor; Henry and Aline Harland had no intention of providing that kind of stability, and could not have done so if they had tried. The regular Saturday night gatherings at their Cromwell Road flat were unpredictable affairs. While aiming at formality, the Harlands were apt to be absent-minded over the necessary organisation, so that it was not unknown for dinner guests to turn up in full evening dress to find Henry and Aline sitting in the kitchen over a couple of chops, having forgotten all about the invitation. "I must have been drunk," Henry would say. "You know Aline, I never remember a word of anything that happens when I am drunk."[9] They were, by Victorian standards, terrifyingly uninhibited about expressing their feelings, and would quarrel in public with a total disregard for the embarrassment they caused. Netta Syrett recalled an occasion when three guests whom the Harlands had invited to join them at a restaurant waited patiently for the end of a husband-and-wife wrangle about which restaurant to go to, only to have

Henry snarl, "All right, we won't go anywhere at all". They sulked and threw tantrums, and Henry wrote in pyjamas and dressing gown, bearded and unkempt, giving rise to a general impression of squalor which spread to John Lane's respectable publishing house itself and caused the waspish *Punch* epigram, "Uncleanliness is next to Bodliness".

Evelyn Sharp's autobiography dwells with fond recall on how upset Grahame was by this calumny. He tried to persuade Lane to take legal action against *Punch*, but the publisher remained unruffled, wisely refusing to fall into the trap of taking a joke seriously.

The women in the *Yellow Book* group shared a universal affection for Kenneth. Netta Syrett commented on "his complete freedom from the affectations which so puzzled me in the other men of the set". His kindness and Scottish seriousness could not be compromised; although he had a keen sense of humour, he could not find the tormenting of other people funny, and had firm words with Harland over his teasing of Evelyn Sharp.

Evelyn clearly became a close friend, and might perhaps have wanted the relationship to blossom further. She wrote frequent letters to Kenneth with invitations to tea or to the theatre or a lecture, most of which he turned down, but always with wit and affection, though at one point a hint of exasperation crept in.

24 Feb 97
. . . I was very sorry about the theatre, but really you must not *rush* me in this sort of hysterical way.

You remind me of a Spanish bull-fight, somehow – a flash of white horns, hot muzzles, a streak of red, a jump, a shout, – & all under a glittering Southern sun – or a St Moritz toboggin [*sic*] run. – or a Bandersnatch.

Relenting, he added,

As to the queen, – you are quite right. I don't care a – whatever it was you said – about seeing the queen drive in a park.

Evelyn's appearance was far from anything which might conjure up visions of a bull-fight. A photograph of her taken at this time shows a huge-eyed, slightly gaunt-faced girl with a wide, whimsical mouth, her hair bundled up a little untidily, with tendrils escaping across her forehead. Since leaving school at "barely sixteen", her passionate wish to go to college had been denied, and she had spent what she called "the desert years" in her parents' home in "the muddy lanes of Buckinghamshire". She had, however, visited Paris for four months with her two elder sisters in 1900, and returned with increased impatience to the dull life of an unmarried daughter. She had come to London in January 1894, with ten pounds in her pocket, five of it borrowed from her brother and five saved from her slender dress-allowance, to take the unheard-of step of trying to earn her own living. She had sent, she says simply, "a short story to the 'Yellow Book' and a novel I had written before I left home, to the Bodley Head, both of which, as it turned out, were suitable destinations". She therefore found herself a member of London's fast set, where "the personal and often unconventional relationships of acquaintances were discussed sometimes with a frankness that at first embarrassed a country-bred person like myself".

Grahame, however, recognised her innocence with some fellow-feeling, and was always kind to her. She, in turn, liked him immensely. Kenneth Grahame, she said, was

> like nobody but himself, though it is possible that he was somebody quite different in his official capacity at the Bank of England. I cannot be sure even of this; for when I wrote to congratulate him on gaining some new and still more important post at the Bank, and supposed flippantly that he would now dress in red-and-gold and ride in the Lord Mayor's Show, he wrote back to say that he should do nothing of the kind, not because he hadn't a right to, if he liked, but because he couldn't ride. He was at the same time, he added, having gold braid put on the collar of his frock-coat and round his silk hat. I feel sure this was not the Kenneth Grahame known to his colleagues at the Bank of England.
>
> But I knew him best as one of the most delightful contributors to the "Yellow Book", a writer of stories about children after my own heart, the creator of the "Olympians", and one who had a sense of humour that made his few and brief letters worth treasuring, and better still, sometimes caused him to laugh at one's own silly jokes – the most endearing of all qualities in a friend. No, not the most endearing in his case, for I remember with all the keen gratitude of a very raw person that once, in Brussels, when I let fall a remark revealing my unbelievable ignorance of the world, an indiscretion that I recall with far more shame than many things I have said and done of which I ought really to be ashamed, he would not allow Henry Harland to tease me about it. But he did not hesitate to tease me himself when I gave him a loophole to do so without malice; when, for instance, I pleaded spring-cleaning in my minute flat in Knightsbridge (to which I had moved with a fellow member from the Victorian Club) as a reason for not accepting some invitation, and he wrote to say that, "considering the vast range and acreage" of my premises, "the Pope must experience similar feelings when the time comes to clean the Vatican."[10]

Frederick Rolfe, by reason of his own suspicious and uncharitable nature, had never been part of the group, and he remembered Evelyn Sharp only as "a thin wide-mouthed suffragist of thirty, coy and silent, whose huge black eyes yearned for the secretary of a bank". Evelyn married only towards the end of her life, after an extraordinary career in the course of which she was imprisoned twice as a suffragette. In a letter to John Lane, she wrote, "I came out of prison a fortnight ago: it was a very terrible experience, but not so bad as I expected on the mere physical side".[11] She seemed quite undeterred, and badgered Lane on behalf of the cause with a confidence of which her frail appearance gave no hint.

> I believe you pretend to be an Anti, but I am sure you are not, really. You were a pioneer in the glorious eighties, so be a pioneer now and send me some books for my bookstall in the Christmas Suffrage Fair at the Portman Rooms. Then you can come to the Fair and buy them back at exorbitant prices . . .[12]

Kenneth's letters to Evelyn were relaxed and amusing, sometimes rambling, though never exceeding a single sheet of folded paper. At one point he asked her,

> Do you remember a small domestic poem which tells how a little girl mixed up several sorts of poison, all fatal, & administered a large dose to her mother, who expired on the hearthrug, tied up in the most inelegant & unladylike coils? I remember the poem ended
> 'Papa he was *extremely vext*.
> 'Sarah, child,' he said, 'What next?'[13]

More usually they were excuses. On 1 April 1897 he was dining with an ex-Vice Chancellor of Oxford, to his own amazement.

> It sounds like Alice in Wonderland, but it really came off, & we drank old port, the Ex-Vice & I, till all was blue – not to say purple.
> I repeat that I am truly sorry and ashamed; but the port was '47.

His meals were not always so exotic. Three weeks previously, he had written,

> Dear Miss Sharp [he never addressed her as Evelyn]
> I am very much obliged to you for the Water Colour ticket. Until an advanced hour today I hoped to use it: in the end it proved impossible & I only just got home in time for a Private View of my frugal water-coloured dinner.

When Evelyn rented a flat of her own for the first time, she evidently had some difficulty in explaining to Kenneth where it was.

> Sunday.
> My dear Miss Sharp,
>   Why on earth didn't you mention the *Redcliffe Arms* before? I may be ignorant of London, but surely *you* know that cabmen & loafers steer by the pubs? *Now* I know where you are, more or less, & of course I'll come to tea, if I can, though you strange creatures never seem to understand that "afternoon tea" simply doesn't come into a working man's scheme of life, except by accident. As for me, I generally have my meals brought me by one of the kids, in a yellow stone-ware basin tied up in a handkerchief . . .
>   I like your map, which shows so clearly that there are only three civilised people living in these parts. The rest is "still unexplored". The theory that it is inhabited is only a presumption.
> Yours very truly,
Kenneth Grahame

Light-hearted though it is, this is a revealing letter. For all his years in the City and his steady promotion within the Bank of England, Grahame still looked on society at large as the Wild Wood, and flirted with the idea of the humble pudding basin as an antidote to the formality of the Bank dining-room.

In March 1898, he suffered one of his bouts of recurrent illness.

> My dear Miss Sharp
>   Very many thanks for the kind condolences & enquiries & offers of Royal Humane-Society aid. I've had a pretty bad week, but am well now – or as near it as doesn't matter – & hope to be going about my business in a day or two. And I HAVEN'T got a fevered brow!!!!

One wonders whether Evelyn had offered to come and soothe it. In the same letter, he thanked her for offering to lend him books, saying that he was happy with "Mr Jorrocks" and wanted nothing else.

The last letter in the series was written in November 1899, the handwriting perceptibly wobbly.

> . . . I'm a trifle shaky still & can't do much work or shove my nose out of doors at night.

By that time, everything had changed, and Evelyn was moving into the work which took her on many travels, including an extraordinary journey to the frozen, famine-stricken south-east of Russia, where the sledges were pulled by camels.

The friendship covered five incredibly productive years, during which Grahame moved from being a slightly baffled spectator to the inner core of *Yellow Book* contributors, among whom such a fellow-feeling developed that they took to making forays abroad together, to France or Belgium. A favourite spot was Dieppe, "which at that time", Evelyn recalled, "before it had begun to attract the English in the mass, might have been termed the summer holiday resort of the 'Yellow Book' group". Aubrey Beardsley had been there with Arthur Symons, and their writing and drawing inspired by the seaside town appeared in the first issue of *The Savoy* in 1896. Evelyn and Grahame, with the Harlands, also spent the Christmas of 1895 in Brussels, and the following Christmas in Boulogne. Kenneth, she said, was "the perfect traveller, and those two Christmas weekends stand out in my memory as perfect holidays".[14]

She was something of a connoisseur of people's behaviour when travelling, and noted shrewdly how Henry Harland kept up a fantasy of himself as a world citizen, hoping to pass as a native of whatever country took his fancy. He claimed variously to have been born in Paris, Rome, Berlin and St Petersburg, and, although American, tried hard to be taken for an Englishman when in France. Kenneth, on the other hand, could never be anyone but himself. He was, Evelyn said,

> so very Scottish; and I could feel, when my sister Mabel came to see us off at Victoria station, on one of these occasions, how relieved she was to find that someone looking so unlike the editor of the "Yellow Book" was also to be of the party.

It is not easy to see how the honest and kindly Grahame could feel at ease with Harland, but Evelyn Sharp puts her finger on the common ground between them in her analysis of Henry Harland's "endearing and whimsical personality". He was, for all his mannerisms, utterly un-Olympian. Most of the *Yellow Book* contributors were young, but Evelyn wrote of herself and Grahame:

> by comparison with our editor, who, whatever his actual years, did not appear to have yet begun to grow up, we felt almost hoary. Like any other nice child, Henry Harland could become a responsible person when a responsible judgement was expected of him, when literary standards were at stake, when one of us sent him a piece of work that he thought supremely good or supremely bad . . . and that was what lent the more effect to his freakish humour and often such wisdom to his wit, making him one of the most lovable creatures in the story of modern letters.

Jean Cage (later White) wrote that she remembered Kenneth as

> *solid* − & that not only in a physical sense. He answered my idea of a
> *man*. I suppose half-consciously (for I was young for my age & much
> of what I saw and heard at the Harlands' was uncomprehended) I was
> comparing him with the more or less effeminate type of young man
> met there. He was sane and normal.[15]

Once he got used to the informality of the Harland household, Kenneth
enjoyed the Saturday evenings, when Aline would sing and the conversation
ranged from the passionate to the absurd. There was one evening, Evelyn
Sharp recalled,

> when a typical argument about some obscure French poet or artist
> merged into an equally warm dispute as to the right way to make an
> omelet, and the whole company crowded into the tiny kitchen of the
> flat to watch Stanley Makower make one while the rest of offered
> conflicting advice.[16]

It was a cheerful time − perhaps the best time of Grahame's adult life. He
was achieving success in both of the oddly contrasting spheres of his life,
and he was appreciated and cherished by his new circle of friends. For once
in his guarded, wary life, he could be happy and relaxed.

On one particular evening, he took happiness and relaxation to excess,
as he confessed afterwards to a Bank friend, Alan Lidderdale, whose father
had been responsible for Grahame's entry into the Bank sixteen years ago.
Alan wrote:

> Years ago Kenneth told me how late one night, after a very cheerful
> dinner, he, in full evening dress, walked out into Piccadilly, and seeing
> a vegetable cart making its way eastward, ran after it, and climbed up
> behind, made himself comfortable among the vegetables. He was then
> overcome by an "exposition of sleep". He woke in broad daylight. He
> was still in the cart, which, now empty, was moving down Piccadilly
> in the opposite direction. That is all. It was one of the regrets of
> Kenneth's life that he never knew what happened in the interval.[17]

It was a rare lapse. Despite the gaiety of the *Yellow Book* evenings and the
scandalised reception of the publication itself (which continued long after it
ceased publication, and colours its reputation to this day), there was, as
Evelyn Sharp argued, "not enough impropriety to cover a sixpence". Seen
through the wrong end of our twentieth-century binoculars, the little group

of young people who were so excited about their "new" ideas are revealed as an innocent and vulnerable coterie. Evelyn set it accurately in place.

I arrived on the crest of the wave that was sweeping away the Victorian tradition, and I see now that what kept our delirious iconoclasm sane, and preserved a sense of beauty in the most decadent among us, was the high standard of taste bequeathed to my generation by the great Victorians.

But at the time, they would have died rather than admit it.

The lasting influence of the group has been phenomenal. At a 1993 exhibition of 1890s work called *High Art and Low Life*, staged by the Victoria and Albert museum, a self-styled expert was holding forth as he gazed at Beardsley drawings. "They were so *determined* to be decadent!" he proclaimed. But there was more to them than that. The collective desire of the *Yellow Book* group was, perhaps for the last time, an attempt to make a stand against the commercialisation which was about to engulf the country, and it represented an international movement of elegaic horror. Its products are still immensely popular, for out of that mood of despairing nostalgia came the posters of Toulouse-Lautrec and Alphonse Mucha, the designs of Morris and Rennie Mackintosh, the illustrations of Walter Crane, and the sinuous, decorative style which had been so widely imitated and which is finding yet another renaissance in the architecture and design of the late twentieth century.

Grahame was the least likely member of the group to be aware of such portentous concerns. Though a meticulous craftsman, he was never a conscious stylist, as his next, somewhat maladroit offering proved. He finished his long-laboured-over piece called "The Headswoman" in time for the 1894 October number of *The Yellow Book*. It seems to have been received with baffled (or perhaps tactful) silence, and he never wrote anything like it again. It coincided with his promotion to Acting Secretary at the Bank, and this success may have given a brief ascendancy to the would-be adult side of his nature. At about the same time, he moved out of the Chelsea flat with its lighthouse stairs and its view over the Thames, and, with Tom Greg, took a joint lease on 5 Kensington Crescent. He must have had a higher opinion of Tom than he had for the legal profession as a whole, to judge by Jeanne's words to a lawyer in "The Headswoman". She demands,

"What does your profession amount to, when all's said and done? A mass of lies, quibbles, and tricks, that would make any self-respecting executioner blush!"

In our own time, it would be at least suspected that the basis on which two men share in the purchase of a house could be a homosexual one, but there is no likelihood of it in Grahame's case. The social taboo was so strong that homosexuality hardly existed in the public awareness, and probably neither he nor his fellow purchaser entertained the possibility of being thought sexual partners. The two bachelors were looked after by Sarah Bath, who came originally from Somerset, and had long been family housekeeper to the Gregs. She came to Kensington Crescent when Tom moved in there with Grahame, and had rigid ideas about the respectability of her young gentlemen. In addition to having worked together in Whitechapel, both of them had contributed to the *Pall Mall Gazette* and the *National Observer* –they had very probably met at one of Henley's At Homes – but Sarah disapproved of this literary streak. Writers, she said, using a current idiom of the time, were "loose fish". "And I suppose bankers are goldfish?" Kenneth enquired. We do not know whether she laughed.[18] We cannot even be sure that the story is true, for, as the notes to this chapter show, previous biographers have been the victims of Grahame's widow's irresponsibly creative imagination.

According to Annie Grahame, it was largely for the services of Miss Bath that Kenneth left his flat in Chelsea, where he either had to cater for himself or go out for meals. Though a careful and capable cook, he had no taste for self-service, and much preferred to be waited on. When Tom Greg got married and left the house Sarah stayed on, no doubt to Kenneth's relief. Tom was succeeded by Gregory Smith, who commented that Miss Bath made him "very comfortable".

Grahame was enjoying the larger house, filling it with the carefully chosen objects of which he had long dreamed. Tom Greg was a collector of pottery and, in an essay of his own called *In Varying Mood*, he dwelt lovingly on the Grès de Flandres tankards and the salt-glaze teapot which he could show to visitors, and, too, on the two-volume first edition of Grimm's *Fairy Tales*, complete with their Cruikshank illustrations and their Zahnsdorf morocco bindings. These, perhaps, were Grahame's contribution, bearing in mind his earlier yearning for particular editions which had eluded him because of their expense. He was now no longer poor. On the front wall of the house, between the drawing-room windows, he had fixed the Della Robbia plaque he had brought back from Florence, a Madonna and Child which, as Annie remarked, "served as a shrine for the Italian organ-grinders, who, Kenneth said, used to come and perform their devotions in front of it and then go down into the area and demand alms from Miss Bath, who, however (having travelled in Italy herself), was quite equal to them and sternly refused to give them anything, whereupon they departed muttering curses and shaking their fists at her . . .".[19]

Meanwhile, success seemed to fill the air. Just at the time when Kenneth had formed his fruitful association with *The Yellow Book* in 1894, his cousin, Anthony Hope Hawkins, a barrister who had also contributed an occasional article to the *St James's Gazette* in the days of Kenneth's tentative beginnings as a writer, had sprung to fame with a romance called *The Prisoner of Zenda*. Dropping his surname, Anthony Hope was known throughout the reading world as the man who had invented Ruritania. He abandoned the Bar and became a full-time writer, but never produced anything of equal popularity. Although he was knighted towards the end of his life, it was for services at the Ministry of Information in World War I. Nevertheless, his literary triumphs in 1894 must have added to his cousin's feeling that all things were possible.

For a few months, it might have seemed that Grahame was at last about to become a fully paid-up member of adult society, living a sophisticated life in a capital city and hobnobbing with its avant-garde set – but at heart he had not departed from the convictions which had underlain *The Romance of the Rail*, in which he had written that "a man's stride remains the true standard of distance; an eternal and unalterable scale". He made full use of trains and cross-Channel ferries in response to the call of the south which came so suddenly and imperiously at least once a year, and yet he recognised the effect which "the severe horizon" has in limiting and calming the mind's "infinite considerations". He was always ambivalent about travel, simultaneously loving it and regarding it as a fit of madness. Even the comforts of the Kensington house made him a little uneasy, as if they left him floundering in a featherbed of boundless potential which frightened him with its formlessness. Somewhere at the centre of his consciousness, he wanted the bare bones of the countryside. "To all these natural bounds and limitations it is good to get back now and again, from a life assisted and smooth by artificialities."

Meanwhile, *The Yellow Book* went on, combining poems by Anatole France with heavy stuff from Henry James and social agonisings from Arnold Bennett. Arthur Waugh, father of the more famous son Evelyn, attacked Swinburne for the decadence of *Dolores*, with its sado-masochistic overtones, and pleaded for decent reticence – but he might as well have tried to stop a runaway horse, for Swinburne was hell-bent on shocking the upholders of conventional morality – and he succeeded. The public, in fact, wanted to be shocked. Inevitably, it had responded to the crumbling of the old order by seeking a scapegoat to blame for it, and had fixed on the new young writers as a symbol of all that had gone wrong. In a simplistic equation, it seemed satisfactory to hold that disrespect and fresh thinking had caused the collapse, whereas the reverse, in fact, was true. To be horrified seemed to be the virtuous response, as if an attack on the new style was a defence of the old, so the public was eager to express shock and revulsion.

Harland was dismayed to find that he had created a cause of outrage. As an American, he had no grasp of the hidden subtleties of British thinking, in which emotion is disguised as reason, and he was stunned when *The Times* called *The Yellow Book* a "combination of English rowdiness with French lubricity". He had promised in the pre-publicity that the publication would be "beautiful as a piece of bookmaking" and would preserve "a delicate decorous and reticent mien and conduct". John Lane was sure that The Bodley Head had published a book which was true in all respects to these standards, and Arthur Waugh confirmed his innocent intentions, saying that *The Yellow Book* was to be ". . . representative of the most cultured work which was then being done in England, prose and poetry, criticism, fiction and art, the oldest school and the newest side by side, with no hallmark except that of excellence and no prejudice against anything but dullness and incapacity".[20] Nevertheless, the *Westminster Gazette* found Beardsley's drawings so disgusting that it demanded "an Act of Parliament to make this kind of thing illegal", and Max Beerbohm, a then-young *Yellow Book* contributor who was still at Oxford at the time, said with some glee that "so far as anyone in literature can be lynched, I was".

Punch sniped from the sidelines, usually in verse.

How doth the little busy Lane
Improve the Bodley head
He gathers round him, Day by day,
The authors who are read.

There were many such laborious parodies, and, at the time, they were greeted with immense amusement.

Sir Frederic Leighton had been happy to contribute a drawing to the "delicate, decorous and reticent" publication, but quickly dissociated himself when the howl of protest broke loose. Henry James expressed his distaste for "the horrid aspect and company of the whole publication", but continued to offer long and densely written contributions which Harland accepted. James did not, however, favour the despised company with his presence again, for which there may have been some gratitude. Evelyn Sharp recalls the occasion when he came to tea, saying that

we sat in dumb humility while the famous American walked up and down the room seeking the word he wanted for the completion of his sentence. I am sure we all knew the word, but the sacrilege that would be implied in our intrusion upon his mental travail by mentioning it was undreamed of. It was, of course, an immense honour to have been invited to worship at the shrine; but the atmosphere cleared pleasantly when he left and our editor became himself again.[21]

Harland had been paralysed with respect, and always referred to James as "*mon maître*".

Some of the other worthies stayed on despite the storm. The young Maurice Baring, who later worked for the Foreign Office in Moscow and was responsible for introducing Chekhov to the British public, was a regular contributor, and so was Sir Charles G. D. Roberts, the "father of Canadian literature". Arnold Bennett remained constant, and articles were contributed by H. G. Wells, John Buchan and George Gissing, as well as George Saintsbury, an established academic, and Arthur Benson, who, bizarrely enough, wrote the words for Elgar's *Pomp and Circumstance*, "Land of Hope and Glory". An interesting side-light occurs in a letter from Sidney Ward, Grahame's friend at the Bank, who said,

> One of Maurice Baring's brothers once said to me, "Yes, Maurice can write all right when he takes the trouble." No one could say that of Kenneth. He always "took the trouble".[22]

For all its protestations of respectability, however, *The Yellow Book* was stuck with a reputation for Bohemian lunacy. A century later, the madness is difficult to identify, for the writing itself hardly transcends the dull. The magic quality was perhaps a visual one, present in the look of what was going on rather than in any coherent opinion. Ella D'Arcy, whom Lambert calls "an earnest Yellow Book groupie" was, in fact, the publication's assistant editor, and her reminiscences of the time give a clue to the delight which the contributors found in each other.

> Harland was the most brilliant, witty and amusing of talkers, the sweetest-tempered of companions. Never were there such evenings as those long-ago evenings in Cromwell Road! I see him standing on the hearth-rug, or sitting on the floor, waving his eye-glasses on the end of their cord, or refixing them in his short-sighted eyes, while assuring some "dear, beautiful lady!" or other how much he admired her writing, or her painting, her frock, or the colour of her hair. He would re-christen a golden red-headed woman "Helen of Troy"; he would tell another that her eyes reminded him of "the moon rising over the jungle", and thus put each on delightfully cordial terms with herself . . . and with him.
>
> The large drawing-room, lighted by lamps and candles only – in those days electricity had not yet become general – would begin to fill up about nine o'clock.
>
> Two or three would have dined there. Others dropped in to coffee and cigarettes. One might hear Kenneth Grahame, Max Beerbohm, Hubert Crackanthorpe, Evelyn Sharpe [*sic*], Netta Syrett, Ethel Colburn Mayne, the Marriott-Watsons, Victoria Cross, Charlotte Mew, George Moore, Richard Le Gallienne, Arthur Symons, occasionally Edmund Gosse, and Henry James.[23]

There is no mention of Frederick Rolfe, who could not make himself pleasant to anyone. He had described Ella D'Arcy as "an intellectual mouse-mannered piece of sex",[24] and his pen-name of Corvo, the crab, was well chosen, for he was armoured against any approach from the outside world, no matter how kindly intentioned.

Richard Le Gallienne was at the opposite extreme from Rolfe. His conviviality and wildly poetic appearance added a considerable frisson to the group, though it must have given the suspicious public additional cause to suspect the *Yellow Book* coterie of being infiltrated by homosexuality. In fact, there is no proof that Le Gallienne himself was a homosexual, even though Oscar Wilde wrote to him following the publication of a book of verse, "I hope the laurels are not too thick across your brow for me to kiss your eyelids". Le Gallienne had come from Liverpool, where he had heard Wilde lecture on "Personal Impressions of America and its People", and the effect on him had been cataclysmic. He had already produced a book of poems, printed "on cream paper with rough edges" (and paid for by his indulgent father), but Wilde enchanted him, and he took to broad-brimmed hats and flowing cloaks and general theatricality. He had been born plain Gallienne, but added the "Le" as a suitably poetic conceit. He was a beautiful young man, described by Swinburne as "Shelley with a chin", but for all his foppishness, he had a devoted wife, whom he adored. Lane recruited him as literary adviser for The Bodley Head, where his imaginative perception added much to the list. He was a prolific and rather bad poet, and yet he was capable of touching the wistful, almost desperate turning-back to nature which was so central to the group. A typical verse comes from "Tree Worship".

> With loving cheek pressed close against thy horny breast,
>   I hear the road of sap within thy veins;
> Tingling with buds, thy great hands open towards the west,
>   To catch the sweetheart wind that brings the sister rain.[25]

Inevitably, in that insecure, hyper-sensitive group, there were casualties. Ernest Dowson, whose *Apple Blossom in Brittany* reflects his passion for the twelve-year-old Adelaide Foltinowicz, was described by Yeats as "timid, silent, a little melancholy". His parents committed suicide within a few months of each other, after which he travelled endlessly and without clear purpose, continuing to write his world-weary poetry. Others did not achieve even such partial survival. Hubert Crackanthorpe and John Davidson both committed suicide and George Gissing, for all his apparent conventionality, was obsessed by prostitutes. Lionel Johnson, a close friend of Yeats, had published a full-length study of Thomas Hardy in the year of *The Yellow Book*'s appearance, but became a hopeless alcoholic, and Arthur Symons, who wrote that he knew twelve men who had killed themselves, ended his life in the same asylum as Charles Condon. Beardsley himself, as all his contemporaries recognised, would die young of the tuberculosis which was consuming him.

Somewhere at the centre of this grotesquely disparate collection of writers and artists was the small group, many of them women, who found life challenging and delightful. Henry Harland, "the Yellow Dwarf", as he called himself in his open letter of criticism to his own publication, provided an energy and a faith in their own potential which kept the group intensely alive, and Kenneth Grahame, while alarmed by their unpredictability, was warmed and nurtured by them. As 1894 drew to a close, *The Yellow Book* had survived its scandalised reception and seemed set for a successful future. The early issues were, in fact, so popular that Lane reprinted them. It was only in 1974, when Fraser Harrison edited a *Yellow Book* selection published by Spring Books that The Bodley Head admitted with a blush that the reprints had been put out as continued first editions.

Such mild duplicity was perhaps a sign of John Lane's anxiety to ensure the publication's success rather than an effort to make the maximum profit even though the house was, as usual, struggling to keep afloat. He, rather than the contributors or even the editor, was at the forefront of the public's reaction, as he was to find the following spring. Meanwhile, a magically productive coterie had been established, with Grahame as one of its most treasured members. Many years later, Evelyn Sharp was to write to Kenneth's widow in affectionate nostalgia, both for her friend and for the "brilliant and amusing circle", although she prudently withheld the more personal letters.

He was, perhaps, shy among strangers, always looked away hastily if he caught you looking at him, simply hated being lionized but liked to talk about his work if he knew you were sympathetic and not likely to gush about it . . . He was very kind and courteous, but had not an ounce of humbug in him. Very sensitive but would die sooner than let you think so if he could help it, and in many ways reminded one of the nicest kind of schoolboy except that he had a fine taste in literature instead of a passion for sport. He had a charming sense of humour and was a great tease. In the *Yellow Book* set we all admired him tremendously, and the appearance of one of his sketches in the Y.B. would be hailed as an event and discussed at length the next Saturday evening . . .[26]

For all its mixture of absurdity and narcissism, *The Yellow Book* retains an oddly endearing quality. If Beardsley and Le Gallienne gave it decadence, Grahame and his friends gave it warmth and humanity, and this endures, for those who care to investigate it, to this day.

8

An End to Childhood

In February of 1895, John Lane published Grahame's *The Golden Age*. It consisted of the six stories retrieved from *Pagan Papers*, plus a dozen additional ones, all of them centred on the fictionalised family of Kenneth's childhood. The book was an instant success, and made him famous in his own time. The narrative balance is delicate, the tone gently self-mocking, as befits a successful banker who looks back with amused compassion to what he once was, and yet there is no breaking of faith with the child world. Not once is there the slightest hint that the eight-year-old's interpretation of adult behaviour is silly or even immature. It is presented with absolute aplomb, all opinions endorsed as perfectly reasonable by the grown-up child who writes the record.

The Victorians adored it. Swinburne, of all people, wrote two columns of rapturous babble about the book, quoting from it extensively and confessing a special liking for Harold, the youngest boy of the family. The whole achievement was, he said, "well-nigh too praiseworthy for praise". He was not a regular reviewer, and this unprecedented expression of ecstasy in the *Daily Chronicle* was enough on its own to guarantee the book's success. Richard Le Gallienne gave it a generous puff in the *Star*, as did Israel Zangwill in the *Pall Mall Gazette*, and the women's magazines embraced it as necessary reading for all British parents, advising that "they will understand their own children the better for doing so".

In the wake of such popular enthusiasm, the intellectual press began to carp. It was precisely the finely balanced duality of the narrative voice which upset them, and Professor J. Sully for one found the central boy-character thoroughly irritating. Sully himself had written a book called *Children's Ways*, which Green described as "monstrously patronising", and regarded himself as an authority on child behaviour. Writing in the *Fortnightly Review*, he could hardly restrain his desire to administer a caning to both child and man for their joint "air of superiority" and their tendency to go "wandering forth into the fields alone to indulge in precocious poetic raptures . . .". Sully is outraged by the idea that a child could have been "capable of reading into a scene in which figure his little sister and her two dolls, a significance which could only have occurred to an experienced adult".

The story in question is "Sawdust and Sin", in which the older brother watches Charlotte acting out nursery discipline with her two dolls, black-haired Japanese Jerry and Rosa, who was "typical British, from her flaxen poll to the stout calves she displayed so liberally". As the narrator says, "I suspected Jerry from the first . . ." and it is his designs on Rosa which caused such apoplexy in Professor Sully.

> He was nestling against Rosa's plump form with a look of satisfaction that was simply idiotic; and one arm had disappeared from view – was it round her waist? Rosa's blush seemed deeper than usual, her head inclined shyly – it must have been round her waist.
> "If it wasn't so near your bedtime," continued Charlotte reflective-ly, "I'd tell you a nice story with a bogy in it . . ." Here Rosa fell flat on her back in the deadest of faints. Her limbs were rigid, her eyes glassy. What had Jerry been doing? It must have been something very bad, for her to take on like that.

The anthropomorphism of the dolls was deeply disturbing to an academic who took refuge in a safely objective stance. Sully himself, on the same subject, had written,

> The punishment of the doll is an important element in nursery life. It is apt to be carried out with formal solemnity and often with some-thing of brutal emphasis.

The tone is exactly that of Sir James Frazer, who had taken the same lofty attitude in *The Golden Bough* when writing about the religious beliefs of the tribal people he called "savages":

> Small minds cannot grasp great ideas; to their narrow comprehension, their purblind vision, nothing seems really great and important but themselves. Such minds hardly rise into religion at all.

Grahame had broken through the barrier of difference which separated children (or tribal people) from the self-styled "civilised man". The effect, for stiff-minded men like Sully, was as shocking as if a Zulu, complete with spear and body-ornaments, had been found at a drawing-room tea-party.

Central to the horror of "Sawdust and Sin" was the unmentionable el-ement of sex. Jerry's intention towards Rosa was clearly dishonourable, and the idea that a child should recognise it as such was utterly dismaying. In actual fact, of course, Grahame is careful to make it plain that the boy narrator does not know what it is that Jerry may have in mind. His com-ments betray only that grown-ups regard hanky-panky between the sexes as naughty. Just why it is naughty (or whether it is naughty at all) is a conjecture in the mind of the adult reader. Sully falls into the trap of being outraged by his own interpretation. The story itself has Charlotte responding with impeccable Victorian propriety to the Japanese doll's dubious behaviour. She puts the sinning Jerry across her knee and spanks him, while her brother turns his head away in wincing sympathy, for "the outrage offered to the whole superior sex in Jerry's person was too painful to witness". Perhaps that, too, offended the professor.

The episode offers an interesting parallel with the outragè caused by *The Yellow Book*, in that the pent-up Victorian potential for seeing something nasty in the woodshed fastened so eagerly on the slenderest of opportunities for prurient interpretation.

Sully worked himself up into a passionate tirade about Grahame's book, declaring it to be "a dishonour done to the sacred cause of childhood" and, in doing so, revealed exactly the Olympian attitude which Grahame had identified. The conventional Victorian view of children was that they must be sweet, pretty and, above all innocent, kept utterly separate from the dark grown-up knowledge of sex which was thought only suitable for male conversation when no ladies were present. There can have been few periods in history when human access to understanding of its most fundamental motivation was so fenced about with taboos, and anything which threatened, even in the lightest and most innocent of ways, to break down these rigidities triggered an anger which disguised something very close to terror. Just as women who had for years been used to the "support" of corsets feared to cast off their stays and reveal their natural (and perhaps, they thought, unacceptable) shape, so the casting-off of social prohibitions seemed likely to unleash all nature's ugliness.

For Grahame, nature had never been ugly, and his acceptance of a truth which was simpler and more profound than human convention was embraced by all but the most hide-bound. The *Golden Age* children endeared themselves to thousands of readers, and the critic of the *Academy* said, "so typical are their thoughts and actions, misgivings and ambitions, that *The Golden Age* is to some extent every reader's biography".

Suddenly, Grahame was famous. All the society hostesses wanted to include him in their guest-lists, and he dined out on far more evenings than he was at home in the house with the Della Robbia plaque. Somehow, he managed to find the time to go on writing, for the rich seam which had yielded the *Golden Age* stories was still productive. In the spring, he went to Allassio, on the Italian Riviera, perhaps to get away from the remorseless round of socialising, and stayed with an Italian family in what was then an undisturbed fishing-village, watching the catch come in or walking in "the great olive woods".

The April edition of *The Yellow Book* carried one of Grahame's most thoughtful pieces, touched by the angst of the *fin-de-siècle* mood which was making itself so universally felt. "The Inner Ear" reflects very accurately the need to escape from London's bustle and noise which drove him periodically to seek quietness in some remote place, where the inner ear could re-tune to a finer perception of small sounds. With this process, he claimed, came a shrinking of self-importance.

Here it is again, this lesson in modesty that nature is eternally dinning into us; and the completeness of one's isolation in the midst of all this sounding vitality cannot fail to strike home to the most self-centred. Indeed, it is evident that we are entirely superfluous here; nothing has any need of us, nor cares to know what we are interested in, nor what other people have been saying of us, nor whether we go or stay.

With unusual passion he hammers the point home:

The more one considers it, the humbler one gets. This pleasant, many-hued, fresh-smelling world of ours would be every whit as godly and fair, were it to be rid at one stroke of us awkward aliens, staggering pilgrims through a land whose pleasant places we embellish and sweeten not at all. We, on the other hand, would be bereft indeed, were we to wake up one chill morning and find that all these practical cousins of ours had packed up and quitted in disgust, tired of trying to assimilate us, wearying of our aimlessness, our brutalities, our ignorance of real life.

In an age when the Darwinian notion of a universal upwards struggle for supremacy had set the pattern of thinking and convinced all ambitious men that their natural place in the world's scheme of things was at the top, this was revolutionary thinking indeed – and yet it was at the same time very ancient. The basis of all mysticism is founded in the letting-go of self-importance.

Grahame's need for occasional retreat was balanced by a relentlessly active life in London. His old friend, Bill Henley, had reappeared after a year in the literary wilderness following the closure of the *National Observer*. Undeterred, he was now editing the *New Review*. Grahame had been casting about for a magazine outlet which would give him more frequent publication than *The Yellow Book*'s quarterly appearance, and had contributed a story to *Phil May's Illustrated Annual* and another, more ambitiously, to the Chicago *Chapbook*, but he gladly gave Henley three of the stories which were destined for *The Golden Age*, and the editor smartly rushed them into print in his new publication before the book appeared. Grahame, meanwhile, was still thinking about Italy, and it was during this period that he used the incident on the Venice Lido, which had so much influenced his thinking, and shaped it into "Long Odds", for inclusion in the summer *Yellow Book*.

That edition was destined to be very different from its predecessors. On 5 April 1895, Oscar Wilde was arrested at the Cadogan Hotel, and the gleefully scandalised London papers ran headlines which read, "Arrest of Oscar Wilde, Yellow Book Under his Arm".[1] A detailed report declared that Wilde, when apprehended, had "grasped his suede gloves in one hand ... Then he picked up from the table a copy of *The Yellow Book* which he placed in security under his left arm". In fact, the book which Wilde had picked up was a yellowish-jacketed French novel, *Aphrodite*, by Pierre Louys which, ironically enough, was probably far more exotic than *The Yellow Book*. John Lane had always disliked Wilde, even though he knew that the brilliant, flamboyant young man was London's hottest publishing property. The Bodley Head had already published *Salome*, *Lady Windermere's Fan* and a volume of poems, and yet all Lane's instincts warned him that contact with Wilde meant trouble. Beardsley's insistence that Wilde should have no input into *The Yellow Book* had hurt more than the author would admit, and he wrote to a friend, Charles Ricketts, about the publication, "I bought it at the station, but before I had cut all the pages I threw it out of the window". To his lover, Lord Alfred Douglas, he wrote, "It is dull and loathsome: a great failure – I am so glad".[2]

Now, even if inadvertently and tragically, he had his revenge on The Bodley Head. An outraged London took the supposed association with a notorious homosexual to be the final proof of depravity. A mob stoned the windows of the offices in Vigo Street.

John Lane was, at the time, in New York, together with Le Gallienne, setting up his own company in America. He sent a cable to Chapman, who was holding the fort in London, ordering that Wilde's books should be withdrawn from the list at once. William Watson had already demanded this, and so had the Meynells ("oh, so correct"), threatening the withdrawal of all their own books unless it were done. Lane's gesture was not enough. At the trial, it emerged that Wilde had been on scandalously intimate terms with a boy called Edward Shelley who had been employed at Vigo Street, and the tacit implication was that Lane had brought the two of them together. Despite Beardsley's loathing for Wilde, the artist's effeminate appearance convinced the public that the two of them were locked in a homosexual alliance, and more authors on the Bodley Head list demanded that the house should purge itself of the association. From New York, Lane gave reluctant orders that the forthcoming *Yellow Book* should not contain any Beardsley drawings, while doing his best to defend the young artist.

If Beardsley is attacked I hope someone will suggest that he has been the modern Hogarth in pointing out and, as it were, lampooning the period and its customs, *and chiefly in the Yellow Book*.[3] [His italics]

It was a forlorn attempt. Very quickly, it became obvious that Beardsley would have to go. Lane said afterwards of the Wilde episode, that "It killed the *Yellow Book*, and it nearly killed me."[4] It quite literally killed Wilde, who never recovered from the jail sentence imposed on him, and the loss to readers of English literature is incalculable.

The Yellow Book kept going for a further eight editions, but it could not survive the loss of Beardsley. It had, as E. F. Benson put it, "turned grey overnight". The piquancy had gone, together with the decorative, subtly over-ripe flavour. The replacement drawings, though worthy, were dull, and the offerings of the young contributors were not strong enough to stand on their own without the exotic quirkiness which had been supplied by Beardsley's visual setting. The inner group continued to cling together in a mutual support which was more than ever needed in the face of public opprobrium, and Harland strove to increase his publication's respectability. Henry Janes, who had never liked it, was frank (at least, in a letter to a friend) about his motives for continued contribution. "It is for gold and to oblige the worshipful Harland."

The more devoted *Yellow Book* contributors did not write primarily for "gold". They were exploring, as best they could, the changing assumptions which were affecting everyone's lives. Their stories were unsophisticated, for all their efforts to appear worldly-wise, and their poems were wistful and often sloppy. Without Beardsley, the publication had turned from a sharp, sprightly circus poodle into a spaniel. Respectability had won, "Castle Ennui is the Bastille of modern life . . ." Harland wrote in July. "You can only escape from it at the risk of breaking your social neck, or remaining a fugitive from social justice to the end of your days."

From that time, Grahame's rate of story-production began to slow down. After "Long Odds", he contributed "The Iniquity of Oblivion" to the October *Yellow Book*, and the story about Selina and Trafalgar Day, "The Twenty-First of October", appeared in the *New Review* in the same month. After that there was nothing for the rest of the year, though he enjoyed the Christmas spent in Brussels with Evelyn Sharp and the Harlands.

1896 saw a slow continuation of the stories about the *Golden Age* children. John Lane had a natural interest in them, hoping to bring about an equally popular sequel, but Grahame had reservations about the wisdom of this. A. A. Milne had written to him, urging the production of "a second wind", as he called it, and Kenneth sent him a cautious reply. "Sequels," he said, "are often traps which the wise author does well to avoid, if he wants to go, like Christian, on his way singing!" He was nearing the bottom of the barrel, and was not sure what would happen when he had used up his store of childhood memories. The fear of "running dry" haunts every author, and Grahame was no exception. "Dies Irae" appeared in the January issue of *The Yellow Book*, but he made no further contribution to it that year. Henley published "Saturnia Regna" and "Mutabile Semper" in the *New Review*, and *Scribner's Magazine* took "The Magic Ring", but Kenneth wrote nothing else during those twelve months.

1896 was in many ways a negative, depressing year, a low point which affected not only Grahame but many others. To compare its emptiness with the years which preceded it and followed it is to be struck by the contrast. 1895 had seen a flurry of publication from Grahame's circle: Yeats and Belloc had both produced volumes of poetry; Henry James's autobiography, *The Middle Years*, had appeared; George Moore had written *The Celibates* and H. G. Wells *The Time Machine*. The first public film show had taken place in Paris and the London School of Economics had been founded. In music, Richard Strauss had written *Till Eulenspiegel* and Mahler his Second Symphony, and Tchaikovsky's *Swan Lake* had been produced for the first time (although posthumously) in St Petersburg. Marconi invented radio telegraphy. Gillette invented the safety razor blade and Oscar Hammerstein was born. Conrad had entered the London literary scene through the help of Edward Garnett, and published his first book, *Almayer's Folly*.

The year following the dismal 1896 was highlighted by Queen Victoria's Diamond Jubilee, but it was also richly studded with new work from Kipling, Wells, Galsworthy, Edmond Rostand and the Webbs. Conrad produced a second book, Shaw wrote *Candida* and Sir Henry Tate gave a new Art Gallery to the nation.

1896 itself, on the other hand was marked by deaths. Paul Verlaine and Edmond de Goncourt, Harriet Beecher Stowe and, most fatefully, William Morris all died, and so did Thomas Hughes, author of *Tom Brown's Schooldays*. The counter-balancing advances were not ones which Grahame viewed with any enthusiasm. The *Daily Mail* was founded, representing a first move in the direction of a populist press, and the motor car, previously banned from public roads, was granted the right to make its noisy way across Britain, provided it did not exceed the speed of twelve miles an hour. The National Portrait Gallery was moved from its original site in Bethnal Green to the more prestigious one which it still occupies, just north of Trafalgar Square. The interests of money were gaining fast, and Pan's music would soon be obliterated by the roar of car engines.

The Yellow Book of January 1897 was to be its last appearance. In it, instead of a story, Grahame published the lament for a puppy, "To Rollo" (see page 60). There is a poignancy in comparing this with "Sawdust and Sin", where "Rollo, the black retriever, just released from his chain by some friendly hand, burst through the underwood, seeking congenial company".

It was the end of an era. The sad, unnecessary public savaging of Oscar Wilde had cast a long shadow, and as the century ticked away through its closing years, no good seemed to lie ahead. The only story Grahame managed to write was "Its Walls Were As of Jaspar", in which the Golden

Age boy is taken visiting and, managing to escape from the drawing-room, finds in the library a magnificent book "in a stupid foreign language", with pictures of knights and ladies and a detailed, exploration-inviting town under "the deep blue of a cloudless sky". Lugging the book on to the hearth-rug and weighting the stiff page down with a lump of coal, the young hero gets engrossed in a medieval dream – and is soundly chastised when discovered.

The story has none of the conviction of the earlier ones. Although Selina makes a robust appearance at the beginning, the twice-repeated offence with the coal has a false note, with an uncharacteristic wink-and-nudge to the adult audience. More significantly, there is a complete break from the narrator's boyish, romance-despising attitude when the picture story introduces some young women, coyly described as "angels", one of whom is "chatting to a young gentleman, with whom she appeared to be on the best of terms". The young reader decides that

no doubt they were now being married, He and She, just as always happened. And then, of course, they were going to live happily ever after; and *that* was the part I wanted to get to. Story-books were so stupid, always stopping at the point where they became really nice; but this picture-story was only in its first chapters, and at last I was to have a chance of knowing *how* people lived happily ever after. We would all go home together, He and She, and the angels, and I; . . . and then the story would really begin, at the point where those other ones always left off.

The artlessness here is self-conscious, and the pushing towards sexual information much more forceful than the doll-play of "Sawdust and Sin" which so upset Professor Sully. Innocence, once lost, is not easily regained; something had brought the child-narrator not merely to adolescence, but to a positive curiosity about the previously despised female sex.

The change seems to stem from the fact that Kenneth's younger brother, Roland, had recently married Joan Feiling, a young widow with two small sons. For a man approaching forty, with no sexual experience whatever (as far as we can tell), Grahame must have been considerably intrigued and disturbed by his brother's plunge into matrimony. This was too close to write off as an unknown aspect of Olympian behaviour. Joan was a real and likeable woman, with two very real small boys, Anthony and Keith. It was Kenneth's first confrontation with love between two people within his own world, and with a sexuality which could not be kept separate from the secret child-being deep inside him.

Previously, Grahame had always regarded women with a deferential respect not unmixed with fear. At best, he could achieve a trust in a particular woman which could ripen into a warm friendship, as it had done with his cousin Annie, and with Evelyn Sharp. Despite Henry Harland's strenuous match-making efforts, described in Evelyn's book, Grahame had shown no sign of wanting a deeper relationship. In the dreary year before Roland's marriage, he had met Helen Dunham at a society lunch, and with her, too, he had struck up a confiding friendship. She, like so many others, wrote to Kenneth's widow at the time of his death, and recalled how she had confessed to him in 1896 that she was "afraid that he might grow up". At the time, it was a perceptive observation, sparked by the change in Grahame's writing. He himself refuted the idea at once, saying, "No – I don't think I shall – I've just been writing about a circus and I found I didn't feel a bit grown up."[5] But Roland had been part of Kenneth's childhood, intermingled with the Harold of the *Golden Age* stories, and he was now a man, taking Joan Feiling to his bed, and enjoying a happiness which was palpable between them, as real and immediate as the "various outdoor joys of puddles and sun and hedge-breaking" which Roland-Harold had shared with Kenneth. The wall which Grahame had erected against the grown-up world was breached, and the virginity of his outlook was lost.

The change which it brought about in his writing has been attributed by previous biographers to Grahame's meeting with the woman who was to become his wife, but in fact his new sensitivity to feminine charms predates this event by at least a year. Grahame was one of London's most eligible bachelors, and there must have been many young women more than ready to fall in love with him; it was only the sudden abandoning of his defensive innocence which made it possible for one of them to succeed. Without the predisposing effect of Roland's marriage, Kenneth might well have remained in his virginal mental childhood throughout his life.

Allowing for the obligatory long engagements of the Victorian era, Joan Feiling must have a significant place in Kenneth's awareness throughout the months of 1896, and there are clear signs of it in "Saturnia Regna", published in March of that year. The return to the "Stevensonette" style is marked, though Stevenson himself had by now died in Samoa, but there is an additional, very adult concern about the workings of the young mind.

> This mental aloofness of the child, – this habit of withdrawal into a secret chamber, of which he sternly guards the key, – may have been often a cause of disappointment, of some disheartenment even, to the parent who thinks there can be no point, no path, no situation, where he cannot be an aid and an exposition, a guide, philosopher and friend; . . .

This may well have sprung from discussion with Roland about the responsibilities and difficulties of taking on two stepsons.

133

"Mutabile Semper" (Always Fickle) had appeared a month later, and was even more openly concerned with attraction between the sexes, although the story is set within the *Golden Age* idiom. The boy narrator, trying to ingratiate himself with a girl (who is never named) offers her access to all his most treasured imaginings – the boats, the Chocolate-room, the little railway, the soldiers – only to be upstaged by "the parson's son from the next village". The narrator consoles himself with the reflection that "I was beginning to feel my liberty of action somewhat curtailed by this exigent visitor I had so rashly admitted into my sanctum". He regains his kingdom with a sigh of relief.

By December, grasping at the seasonal theme of Christmas as flagging writers will, Grahame was, as he told Helen Dunham, writing about the circus. In "The Magic Ring", he recaptures the ecstasy of childhood excitement with absolute authenticity, and yet, the female element enters once again, in the form of Coralie, the bare-back rider, followed by the even more exotic Zephyrine, the Bride of the Desert, with whom the watching boy falls instantly in love.

In a twinkling we were scouring the desert – she and I and the two coal black horses. Side by side, keeping pace in our swinging gallop, we distanced the ostrich, we outstrode the zebra; and, as we went, it seemed the wilderness blossomed like a rose.

In this story, there is no rejection of the fantasy, and no return to the robust self-sufficiency of boyhood.

When at last my head touched the pillow, in a trice I was with Zephyrine, riding the boundless Sahara, cheek to cheek, the world well lost; while at times, through the sand-clouds that encircle us, glimmered the eyes of Coralie, touched, one fancied, with something of tender reproach.

The publication of these stories caused no outrage from such worthies as Professor Sully, for the sentimental romanticism of the time had been adopted, and the idea of love had moved from the suspicious enquiry about doll behaviour to a lofty symbolism. The waves are very nearly crashing on the shore, but the implications can be safely ignored. The writer is an adult, not a child, and the conventions are being observed. Kenneth Grahame had, at least partially, grown up.

In 1897, much of the Bank's business was still done through personal contact. In the absence of a telephone network, it was quite customary for a leisured visit to be made for the discussing of business. On some such errand, Grahame, it is said, made his way to a grand house in Onslow

Square and asked to see its owner, a wealthy barrister amed John Fletcher Moulton, who had been Liberal MP for Clapham in 1885, but lost his seat the following year, regaining it for only a further single year in 1894. At the time of Grahame's visit, he was again in the political wilderness, working hard at securing a safe seat, and he was seldom at home. Kenneth was received by Moulton's stepdaughter, Elspeth Thomson, who ran the house and her father's social life with equal efficiency. She was thirty-five years old.

Despite her considerable aplomb, Elspeth had about her a suggestion of the wild thing disturbed in some bosky glade. A portrait of her painted by Sir Frank Dicksee when she was a girl shows a long, slightly comical face with a firmly closed mouth, the corners tucked into a half-smile above a determined chin. The eyes have arched lids, but they are set under level, obstinate eyebrows. The post is formal, and yet she looks unsettled, as if detained on her way to do something else. The expression is somewhere between petulance and whimsicality, and seems to shift continually between one and the other. There is no record that Grahame was instantly enchanted by her, but she undoubtedly was by him.

Kenneth at this time was a slightly florid man of thirty-eight, his hair receding a little at the temples, and his flamboyant moustache giving panache to a face which, without it, would have betrayed its dismay. His eyes still had their hare-like stare, and his eyebrows peaked in the middle to give him the startled expression which was his main characteristic. As Evelyn Sharp put it, he looked "as if he thought you might be going to bite if he wasn't very careful!"[6] Kenneth was by now a man of considerable presence, impeccably dressed and groomed, and beautifully courteous, yet still possessed of an endearing trace of diffidence – and he was famous.

Elspeth was not unused to famous people. Like Kenneth, she had been born in Edinburgh, one of a family of four. She was the second child, born on 3 January 1862, and her father, Robert William Thomson, had been a successful inventor, having taken out a patent on the first floating dock. He had also designed a steam-driven road vehicle, not to mention such oddities as a glass-nibbed fountain pen, but his fame rests mainly on having devised the pneumatic tyre, a step which was an immense breakthrough for the infant motor industry. He perhaps did not realise the importance of his invention, for the first pneumatic tyre patent was taken out later by J. B. Dunlop. Robert had married Clara Hertz, who came from a background as passionately artistic and literary as his was devoted to practical creativity, and their house in Moray Place was always full of distinguished visitors. L. A. G. Strong confirms that the young Elspeth was quite capable of coping with such notabilities as Mark Twain, who arrived unexpectedly at the Edinburgh house on one occasion, to find that the Thomsons were away from home. The children, however, were in the nursery, with the staff of servants. Elspeth was still quite small, but, says Strong, as the eldest daughter, she

> received the visitor and offered him tea. He replied that he drank only whisky. Undaunted, and with rare social sense, the little girl ran down with the teapot and persuaded the butler to fill it with whisky, which the guest drank neat.[7]

Like her mother, Elspeth's particular ability lay in bringing talented people together, and she cultivated the famous with an uninhibited energy which usually amused them and secured their presence in her circle of friends. At the age of ten she met Tennyson in Pontresina, where her mother had taken the children in 1872 after her husband's death from locomotor ataxia. Elspeth tickled the distinguished poet's fancy to such an extent that the two of them formed a genuine and long-lasting friendship. She had an openness which was irresistible, specially when a more mature person realised the vulnerability of the whimsical world which she offered so unreservedly. As a little girl, she had obviously been enchanting, and knew it, but the truth was that Elspeth had little to fall back on when her charm, as a grown woman, ran thin. At first glance, she looked very much like the young Evelyn Sharp, but there was one fundamental difference. Elspeth was not clever.

She disguised this fact through her airy toying with great names and through the affection which famous men genuinely felt for her. Sir John Tenniel, for instance, wrote Valentines for her year after year, the last being dated 1907, when he was eighty-seven, although he had complained three years previously of being "in the clutches of the 'Fiend Rheumatism', unable to use pen or pencil". A typical example was this one, written in 1898, at which time Elspeth had already met Grahame.

> In blank despair I tear my hair —
> (Alas! There isn't much of it!)
> And as for wit, forlorn I sit —
> I've not the merest touch of it.
> The muse is dull, my brain is wool,
> I can't arrange a rhyme at all —
> Vainly I try — the pen goes dry
> And nothing comes sublime at all.
>
> I made a verse — and bad means worse —
> Confirming incapacity.
> I cannot thank you half enough —
> In Truthfullest veracity.
> I only know, my heart's aglow

With gratitude, and joy decennial!
You're once again my Valentine!!!!
And I'm – devotedly – J. Tenniel.[8]

He was not as light-hearted as his versifying suggests. Prey to bouts of deep melancholy, he was by 1900 very near to a breakdown and his doctor forbade him all work, including the writing of letters – and yet his communications to Elspeth were always conscientiously cheerful, often illustrated with such zany conceits as the Furious Flycycle, a pedal-powered flying machine. He wrote to her, in fact, as one writes to a child.

One must suspect that this waif-like immaturity was the secret of Elspeth's charm. She clung to the appeal which had been hers as a little girl, failing to grow out of it through fear or ignorance of the adult world. Like Kenneth, she had lost her father while still young, and had thus been robbed of that most natural contact with a mature man who could have provided an easy introduction to grown-up society. Instead, she was flung into the business of entertaining and providing for the needs of men, and learned that what they liked was her girlishness and lack of artifice.

Elspeth was thirteen when her mother married again, three years after Robert Thomson's death. It was a love match, for her new husband, John Fletcher Moulton, was a penniless young barrister, though confident and masterful. For Elspeth, it meant that the years of her early adolescence were spent in watching her clever, vivacious mother succeed in attracting a powerful man through the deployment of charm; the fact that Clara had been left a rich woman by Robert's inventions would have been buried deep in Victorian taboo. One did not discuss money matters in front of children.

Moulton was an ambitious man, and a lucky one, for Clara was not only rich, but highly astute in business matters. As her new husband began to rise in his profession, she bought a house in London, 74 Onslow Gardens, with her own money, and furnished it with the contents of her house in Edinburgh. Strangely, this move has not previously been recorded. According to Elspeth's younger brother, Courtauld, Fletcher Moulton's contribution to the new household "consisted of a cabinet and a few chairs, a silver soup ladle and odds and ends from his Cambridge rooms". At that time, Clara's investments were bringing in "about £2,000 a year", and, having arrived in the capital city of England, she speculated shrewdly in London property. Having, as her son said, "quite a genius for this kind of thing, she increased her income until it was nearly £3,000 a year net".[9]

Clara quickly became a popular hostess. Hugh, Fletcher Moulton's son by his previous marriage, wrote about his father and stepmother with admiration.

They were both keenly interested in literature, science and art, and their circle included practically all the mid-Victorian leaders in these subjects, notably Swinburne, Browning, Oscar Wilde, Lord Kelvin, Spottiswoode, Lord Leighton, Frank Dicksee and Tenniel, as well as many visitors of great interest from continental countries, since Mrs Fletcher Moulton as well as her husband spoke French and German perfectly.[10]

The similarities to Grahame's own background are striking. Clara Hertz and Bessie Grahame had both been Edinburgh girls of immense talent as hostesses, and in both cases there had been a move away from Scotland, coupled with an early loss of the father, one through death and the other through alcoholic incapacity. Both Kenneth and Elspeth had been born into a family of four children – but there the similarity ended. Whereas Kenneth had been left largely to his own devices, and had built up a private world which was more real and vital to him than any social interaction, Elspeth had grown up in a household where to be socially active and successful was everything. Her mother, unlike the unfortunate Bessie, had lived on triumphantly, and Elspeth had been twenty-six when Clara died in July 1888, not long after Kenneth's father had met his sad, obscure end in France.

Shortly before Clara's death, the family had moved to a more prestigious house in nearby Onslow Square. This transaction was made by Fletcher Moulton, who had derived substantial benefit from his wife's shrewd financial management. He told Courtauld at the time that he had saved between £40,000 and £50,000. The house, run in lavish style, incurred annual costs of about £3,500, of which Clara paid £3,000. The balance was made up by her husband, but he had been able for some years to retain almost all his earnings of between £10,00 and £20,000 for his own use.[11]

Standing by Clara's deathbed, Fletcher Moulton promised his stepson, Courtauld, that he would be "more than a father to you and your sisters". The elder brother, Harold, seems not to have been present on that occasion.

Events were to prove that promise an empty one but, at the time, there was no change in the opulence with which the house was run. Courtauld remembered that "entertaining was resumed on a larger scale than ever". Elspeth and her younger sister, Winifred, filled their mother's place efficiently, though the new house was a large one, and though, in the absence of Clara's effective financial provision, money became curiously elusive.

Green, writing in 1959, is censorious of Elspeth, claiming that she "set about playing her fish with dogged ruthlessness". She was, he said, "a woman of dominant, almost obsessional personality, which could absorb even so canny a politician as Justin McCarthy: there is no reason to suppose that Kenneth Grahame was any more immune from her hypnotic self-projection". The truth is, perhaps, more subtle. Elspeth had been overshadowed by her immensely popular, capable mother, with whom she could not compete. Her letters build up a picture of a confused, badly educated girl (despite the efforts of a French convent) who had little grasp of how the world worked and only the most sketchy knowledge of history and literature. Her spelling was erratic, and it was quite typical of her to make a verse translation of Ronsard's poem to his mistress (for she spoke French well, and also Flemish) but to call the poet Rousard.[12] Things came disconnectedly to Elspeth, for she lacked analytical intelligence, and coped as best she could with the multitude of impressions which life seemed to offer her. The situation was not improved by the fact that her younger sister, Winifred, was a talented artist and musician, and that her brother, Courtauld, showed from an early age the capability which would make him an eminent man. When Courtauld was only four years old, Robert Thomson had said to Elspeth, his eldest daughter, "Some day baby will be a great man in business".[13] He was right. Poor Elspeth, however, could do little but reveal her muddled, affection-starved personality and hope to be loved.

Looked at from the logical, conventional point of view, it must seem that a woman of thirty-five, already "on the shelf" by Victorian standards, would spare no efforts to catch one of London's most eligible bachelors – but Grahame was not simply an innocent fly caught in the web of a scheming spider. He contributed his own readiness to be ensnared. Following his younger brother's happy marriage, he was, for the first time in his life, ready and almost eager to find his personal princess-playmate as Roland had done.

His sudden vulnerability in his late thirties seems bizarre, specially in these days of worldly-wise children who move into sexual activity almost as soon as they have shed their milk teeth, but it must be remembered that Grahame had not experienced adolescence as we now define it. Sent to school at nine, he had defended himself from a frightening outside world by retreating into his "little territory", coupling it with the behaviour and self-control of a grown man. He had moved into employment at his uncle's firm where he was again expected to conduct himself in an adult way, and his subsequent post at the Bank had reinforced the necessity to conform with the expected standards of respectability. He was not one of the uninhibited young tearaways who could throw pass-books around the room; the child in him was alarmed by such rowdiness in adults, while his adult persona despised them for being so immature. He was never that specifically identified being called "a teenager", and had never found the half-grown self which these days is so obviously engaged in experimenting with adult life (often to the dismay of parents and the anguish of the young person him or herself). There are complex potential arguments as to whether this clearly identified stage is now too respectfully recognised, but the present point is simply that Grahame did not have it. His defensiveness against the adult world butted right up against his involvement in it as an adult himself, and there was no gap between the two; indeed, they had for years co-existed, resulting in two sharply differentiated aspects to his personality. Now, a new possibility had touched his secret child-self, a late, half-formed awakening which aroused in him all the confusion and vulnerability which more normally occurs at puberty.

There is nothing more seductive to the female psyche than a suddenly perceived seam of weakness in a strong man, and Elspeth was no exception. This assured, broad-shouldered young banker in his well-fitting formal clothes was, despite the military moustache and the gold watch-chain, as uncertain in the field of sexual encounter as she was herself. In this most fundamental matter, there was perhaps a sense of recognition and fellow-feeling which linked the pair of them. Despite her cosmopolitan education and her blue-stocking pseudo-intellectualism, Elspeth had not established a position of her own in the world, and she remained sheltered by her step-father's affluence and restricted by his expectation that she would take her dead mother's place as housekeeper and hostess, helped by her younger sister, Winifred. Elspeth was very different from Grahame's female *Yellow Book* colleagues who had struck out on their own into the hitherto debarred world of professional work – though she had certainly entertained some literary ambitions. In 1888, the year of her mother's death, she published a penny novelette called *Amelia Jane's Ambition*, under the pen-name of Clarence Onslow. It was, perhaps, an attempt to establish herself as a professional writer; she was assiduous in seeking publication for the bad verse which she produced in large quantities, even though her offerings tended to come back with withering comments pencilled on them. "This is not quite English", somebody wrote on one, and on another, "I do not like it".[14]

Elspeth, with none of the professional resilience which enables a writer to learn, even from the most unpleasant of experience, simply felt hurt. The rejections were, perhaps, further proof of her suspicion that the world was a cruel place, needing all one's powers of coaxing and placating if painful encounters were to be avoided. Her stepfather, it turned out later, had kept her very short of money, since her mother's death, and she may have become well used to wheedling her way into his favour when presenting him with tradesmen's bills to be paid.

Kenneth probably saw, with sympathy, that Elspeth worked unremittingly in Fletcher Moulton's service, supporting him in his political campaigns and entertaining his friends in a constant round of luncheons and soirees, tea-parties, and dinners. Grahame's kindness utterly disarmed her, and she fell in love with him, as helplessly as a child. To her, it seemed quite simple. She accepted the conventional Victorian image of her sex as the weaker one, needing a man's financial support, for which she would give admiration, love, domestic organisation, children, and unguarded access to the deepest inner recesses of her soul.

Elspeth, in fact, far from conducting a calculated campaign, won by utter capitulation. Like the dog which rolls belly-up in order to make its defence-lessness plain, she gave Kenneth the open, childish truth of the way she saw things. She was so vulnerable and so artless that to repel her would have been brutal, and Kenneth, who was always kind, even to those who irritated him, was half-honoured and half-horrified to be given stewardship over the feelings of one who had voluntarily torn down all her own barriers. He was locked with her in a mutual admission of vulnerability, very much like the "bears and squirrels" world of Jimmy Porter and Alison in John Osborne's *Look Back in Anger*. Once weakness has been offered and accepted as the basis of a relationship, it is impossible to break the trust which has been established, for everything depends upon it.

In a dusty cardboard box, among dinner invitations from people long dead, I found a poem in Elspeth's sprawling early handwriting. Whether she showed it to Kenneth or not must remain conjectural; she probably did, for she was proud of her poetry, and besides, the rambling eager verses had a purpose. With a touch of classical presumption, she called her creation *O Tempora! O Mores!*

In knowing you, I've one regret
(That is not much, one might have more)
I wish that you and I had met
Some time ago, when I was four!

Think of the joys we could devise
To fill my being with delight
And I should think you great and wise
And always good, and always right

You could have told me tales you know
Of ladies shut in stairless towers!
And whispered legend long and low
Of talking-trees and flying-flowers!

Of course you'ld be too old for toys
Like tops, or marbles blue and red,
They're only fit for silly boys –
I'd let you play with me instead

For you should pinch my cheeks, and take
Me in your arms, or on your knee
Like some big doll, that would not break
Think what a plaything *that* would be

I'd give you presents, too, of course,
Daisies without a trace of stalk
And make you take, almost by force,
Some broken bits of billiard chalk

I'd work you samplers with blue birds
Perched proudly on a crimson tree
And underneath, in crooked words
"With my best love to you, from me."

I'd serve you tea in my doll's cup
(With a lead spoon to stir it by)
And if you didn't drink it up
Be sure I'd know the reason why!

And out of nutshells we would make
The dearest little boat with sails,
The nursery-bath would be our lake
And oh the wreckage and the gales!

And I should *never* be afraid
That any grown-up lady's charms
Would make you slight the little maid
That you could gather in your arms

Because, you see, you would not care
For heads fenced round with diamond bands
When you could seize my flowing hair
And pull it freely through your hands

But what would be their studied grace,
Their painted smiles, what could they mean
To you who'd helped me wash my face
In May-day dew upon the green

Their sweeping skirts, their lofty locks
Their forms encased in flounce and frill
Could never rival curls and frocks
That you could tumble at your will

So I'd be sure when you went down
To dinner with some lady fair
With rustling robe and jewelled crown
You'ld still look backward up the stair

At me in my poor pinafore
But with bright hair ablaze like gold
And I should know you loved me more
Than any lady young or old

I'd make you tie my sash and shoe
At least a hundred times a day
And when you'd other things to do
I should be vastly in the way

Till nightfall came, and then I'd keep
So still, and lean my tired head
Against you, but afraid to sleep
Lest they should whisk me off to bed.

Ah, yes! If I were only four
I could of course do that, and this,
But then you seek for something more
So you might take it all amiss.[15]

Kenneth did not keep any of Elspeth's letters, and until now there has been no clue as to her side of what was to be an extraordinary courtship. The poem, while overtly artless, is charged with sexuality; it also touches astutely on Grahame's own weakness for the defenceless, unsophisticated world of childhood. It even refers specifically to the imagined voyages in a nursery-bath which had formed the subject-matter of a *Dream Days* story, "A Saga of the Seas". She could not have laid her finger more precisely on the secret nerve of his being.

Everything indicates that Kenneth found his involvement with Elspeth Thomson simultaneously precious and embarrassing. He was touched, perhaps, by Elspeth's early efforts at writing, and by the ineptness of her one published piece. This tale of a virtuous working-class girl matched his own uneasy experience at Toynbee Hall, and, like him, Elspeth could achieve no confidence that she might understand East End life. She found it more natural to write about the French convent where she was educated, and here she managed to be evocative, even though the vocabulary verges on the purple and the punctuation is sketchy.

There was a strange glamour about the garden and indeed about the whole place. The silences, the clamour – the brilliant youth and high spirits, the calm and self-abnegation. The cold stone stairs with the faint warmth of incense, the chapel with the white veiled scholars, and the black shrouded teachers the tall misty candles the formal altar flowers the lovely chanting voices, then the garden, especially in an autumn haze was magical. Frosted wheels of spider web, dew glittering on the Christmas roses, a strange hint of incense blended with flower breaths.[16]

The writing, like its author, is impulsive and emotional, showing no sign of self-scrutiny or revision. This is not the phraseology of a calculated, self-aware woman, but of a turbulent girl, at the mercy of her own emotions. Such people are more dangerous to those involved with them than the deliberately malign, for they go about their way in the passionate conviction that they know the truth of the world, and that all those who take a different view must be deluded.

There is no detailed record of meetings between Elspeth and Kenneth during the remaining months of 1897, and Grahame's only publication during that time was a review of Evelyn Sharp's book for children, *All the Way to Fairyland*. This appeared in the *Academy* on 18 December, two weeks after that periodical had included him in its list of literary profiles headed *Some Younger Reputations*, among them Yeats, Gissing, Wells, Beerbohm, Quiller-Couch, W. W. Jacobs and Grahame's cousin, Anthony Hope. The article on Grahame had been quite unreserved in its praise.

> It matters very little whether or not Mr Grahame writes any more. In *The Golden Age* he has given us a book, a four-square piece of literature complete in itself. Many a literary man writes hard all his life, and never a book – in the best sense of the word – is forthcoming. Mr Grahame made one the first time.

The writer was obviously unaware of, or indifferent to, the existence of *Pagan Papers*. Grahame's own first effort at reviewing is curiously evasive. He cannot seem to bring himself to the point of any objective evaluation, but instead takes refuge in a general essay on "The Invention of Fairyland". The tone is jocular but slightly frantic, and it is difficult not to see a certain identification of the all-powerful fairy with Elspeth. Fairyland, Grahame asserts, with the faith of the true pantheist, cannot possibly have been invented by people, so the opposite must be true. Fairyland invented us. Therefore,

> they have us at their mercy, and, as soon as they are tired of thinking about us, or want a new manuscript – puff! – we shall go out and *that* will be over. Fortunately, fairies, as all records agree, are loving, irrational, and not easily wearied; and, after all, humanity must possess many humorous points for the outsider that escapes the encaged observer within . . .

The last phrase is telling, with its overtones of Wordsworth's "shades of the prison-house", and so, too, is the attempted placation of these ethereal creatures which wield such terrible power. Grahame's images for women always have a touch of the other-worldly about them; they are princesses or angels or fairies, and in his early work they were inevitably dismissed with scorn – but those days were over. Elspeth could not be ignored. Although he continued to keep in touch with Evelyn Sharp and his other friends, he must have been aware of the child-woman who ran the big house in Onslow Square and who gazed at him with all her hungry soul, for subsequent events showed that there had been a continuing contact between them. Elspeth, as her later letters revealed, found her own gawky, inept way to express her passionate yearnings, but knowledge of her infatuation was, perhaps, an embarrassment rather than a pleasure. Kenneth's health had always tended to break down when he was under pressure, and the stress of feeling responsible for Miss Thomson's painfully love-lorn state had its inevitable effect. Although the year was in other respects a successful one, his letters to Evelyn told their own tale of recurrent colds and influenza.

The output of stories had slowed to a painful trickle. In 1898, only a single one appeared, and that was the one so eagerly seized on by Elspeth, "A Saga of the Seas", in the August issue of *Scribner's Magazine*. It is a curious piece. Although ostensibly about the *Golden Age* children, it begins with an account of female visitors in the drawing-room who are indulging in a ferocious grumble about men.

> In tact, considerateness, and right appreciation as well as in taste and aesthetic sensibilities – we failed at every point, we breeched and bearded prentice-jobs of Nature; and I began to feel like collapsing on the carpet from sheer spiritual anaemia.

Banished for complaining when a long skirt knocks his toy soldiers over, the boy takes refuge in the attic, there to play at ships in an old bath-tub. There ensues a long and detailed fantasy about piracy on the high sea during which the boy rescues a princess, and when all celebrations are over, retires with her into the cabin and locks the door.

The privacy mocks the prurient reader, for the young couple's enjoyment is firmly set in the child-world. They play the musical box, make toffee, run the toy train "round and round . . . and lastly we swam the tin iron-clad in the bath, with the soap-dish for a pirate". Eyebrows might well have been raised, had any reader known of the existence of Elspeth in Grahame's background – but nobody did. "A Saga of the Seas" ends with the departure of the female visitors, leaving the boy triumphant.

> Man was still catching it, apparently – Man was getting it hot. And much Man cared! The seas were his, and the islands; he had his

frigates for the taking, his pirates and their hoards for an unregarded cutlass-stroke or two; and there were Princesses in plenty waiting for him somewhere – Princesses of the right sort.

The note of defiance is new, and the final phrase sounds like a coded message of warning to Elspeth. Was she nagging him to commit himself? It is impossible to be sure; but the story is full of panicky desire to escape. The princess has been allowed into the secret child-world, but there is a delicate hint that the boy-hero has begun to recover from his first calf-love. There are more princesses where this one came from, and if she is to retain her place in his dreams, she must be as he dreamed her. Any sign that she may turn into a drawing-room grumbler will destroy the magic, and that is not to be tolerated.

The new access of confidence may have been in part due to Grahame's promotion to the post of Secretary of the Bank of England. At the age of thirty-nine, he had succeeded G. F. Glennie, taking over early in 1898, almost exactly eighteen years to the day since the foggy morning when he had first groped his way to Threadneedle Street. He had now moved into the ruling élite, even though his function within the Bank had little to do with its commerce. A. W. Dascombe, himself Secretary in the late 1950s, defined the job for Green's benefit, but there is a certain vagueness even in his description.

> At this period the Secretary, whose office dated back to 1694, was at one and the same time the Secretary to the Company and Secretary to the Governor. In the former capacity he was largely concerned with the constitutional side of the Bank's administration: he was present at meetings of the Court of directors to take minutes, and it was his duty to see that the decisions made were subsequently carried out. He dealt also with all those duties which did not fall within the scope of the two other senior officials, the Chief Cashier and the Chief Accountant: he dealt with visitors and he organised staff. As Secretary to the Governor his position was rather more vaguely defined: he was not primarily concerned with implementing banking policy but was, ideally, not so much a banker as a lay adviser: the Governor's conscience, so to speak.[17]

It is a fascinating concept, and one which fitted well into Grahame's ambivalent attitude to the Bank's activities. In a time of vast investment in trade and transport, he could find no enthusiasm for the development of railways and the increasing sprawl of factories, together with the slum dwellings which housed their workers. "There, 'mid clangour, dirt, and pestilence of crowding humanity," he had written, "the very spirit of worry and unrest sits embodied."[18] He had been frank about his hatred for what was happen-

ing to his beloved countryside, claiming in a *Pagan Papers* story, "Deus Terminus", that his generation had become "Romans of this latter day", with
a passion for demarcation and for "possession and domination'. We are, he
said,

> fain to set up the statue which shall proclaim that so much country is
> explored, marked out, allotted, and done with; that such and such
> ramblings and excursions are practicable and permissible, and all else
> is exploded, illegal, or absurd.

Holding such views, one wonders what contribution Grahame made to those
directors' meetings, if any. In dealing with Olympians, he was always circum-
spect, feeling, as he said in "The White Poppy", that a man must never be led

> in his anger to express himself with unseemliness, and thereby to do
> violence to his mental tranquillity, in which alone, as Marcus Aurelius
> teacheth, lieth the perfection of moral character.

Sidney Ward was loyally supportive of his Bank of England friend.

> In all the push & bustle of a great institution, the conflicting interests
> of different departments and the personal jealousies, sometimes, of
> their chiefs, Kenneth was just the man to hold the balance. Always
> there, always wise, never too busy to see anyone, a sound advisor of
> the Governor, never "rattled" and universally respected – he was a far
> greater force than most men imagined at the time, and as those of us
> who have lived the best part of our lives know, it is the silent forces,
> not the noisy ones, which guide the world.[19]

Even if he said nothing, Grahame's very presence, with its aura of honesty
and "mental tranquillity", must have had an effect. There is a hint that his
poetic, non-exploitative view of the world irritated some of his colleagues.
The Bank's Consultant Physician, Dr Kingdon, was a recipient of confidences, and he had known Kenneth and his family for a long time. Nearly
twenty years before, he had commented that the boy's Uncle John did not
seem to understand him,[20] but now he expressed some concern. As he put it,

> Kenneth's a dear boy, a *very* dear boy, but he doesn't think half enough
> of his position in the Bank and in the City. They tell me that he *writes
> tales*. So did Charles Lamb – but what of it? Maybe Charles Lamb
> didn't think much of his position at East India House, but what after
> all was his position in the City to Kenneth's? Kenneth should think *less*
> of books and *more* of being what he has come to be in the City.

The doctor must have been disappointed to see his advice blatantly ignored. Within a year of Kenneth's promotion, in December 1898, *Dream Days* was published.

The book sailed into public favour, being a sequel to *The Golden Age* and featuring the same children, now such a favourite with Victorian readers. Most of its stories had already been published in magazines during the four years which it had taken to accumulate enough material for the slender book, but "The Reluctant Dragon" was new, and has something of the feel of a make-weight, being a longish folk-tale spun to the children by their old friend, "the circus-man", he who had taken them so unexpectedly and wonderfully to "the magic ring".

As a whole, the book is elegaic and deeply sad despite its humour. Grahame knew that his fund of childhood memories was exhausted. He had written his way through that whole magic store, and had come out into emptiness. It seemed unlikely that he would ever write again. The last story in *Dream Days* is called "A Departure", and it is also a farewell. In it, the children are told that they are now too old to be the owners of such things as "a hoop and a Noah's Ark". Their toys are to be handed on to a children's hospital in London.

> Why does a coming bereavement project no thin faint voice, no shadow of its woe, to warn its happy, heedless victims? Why cannot Olympians ever think it worth while to give some hint of the thunder-bolts they are silently forging? And why, oh why did it never enter into any of our thick heads that the day would come when even Charlotte would be considered too matronly for toys? Each fresh grammar or musical instrument, each new historical period or quaint arithmetical rule is impressed on one by some painful physical prelude. Why does Time, the biggest Schoolmaster, alone neglect premonitory raps, at each stage of his curriculum, on our knuckles or our heads?

The protest is passionately felt by the thirty-nine-year-old author. Grahame had never recovered from that final robbery of his childhood happiness, and the revealing of it makes agonising reading. His house in Kensington contained a vast collection of toys, for he had begun to buy them compulsively once his salary allowed it, but the grown man could not make up for what he had lost.

> There was old Leotard, for instance. Somehow he had come to be sadly neglected of late years – and yet how exactly he always respon-ded to certain moods! He was an acrobat, this Leotard, who lived in a glass-fronted box. His loose-jointed limbs were cardboard, card-board his slender trunk; and his hands eternally gripped the bar of a

trapeze. You turned the box round swiftly five or six times; the wonderful unsolved machinery worked, and Leotard swung and leapt, backwards, forwards, now astride the bar, now flying free; iron-jointed, supple-sinewed, unceasingly novel in his invention of new unguessable attitudes . . .

And there was the spotty horse. The children had

dug our heels into his unyielding sides, and had scratched our hands on the tin-tacks that secured his mane to his stiffly curving neck.

It was just before *Dream Days* was published that Grahame wrote to Evelyn Sharp about being shaky and unable to work, but the whole year had been a bad one in terms of health. In the spring, with his mind running on the elegaic tale of "A Departure", he had written to Grace Dunham, sister of Helen Dunham who had been so supportive about his dream room:

I am shaking with influenza myself, and feel like Shem or Japhet out of the Ark – left by a careless child on the carpet – trodden on by a heavy-footed housemaid – and badly mended with very inferior glue.[21]

But the Noah's Ark had gone, together with "its haunting smell, as well as that pleasant sense of disorder that the best conducted Ark is always able to impart", and so had the dolls. "Where was old Jerry? Where were Eugenie, Rosa, Sophie, Esmeralda?"

The story tells how, that night, the children raid by moonlight the "grim big box" where the toys wait for dispatch for London. They take out "a small grey elephant and a large beetle with a red stomach", a bull called Potiphar ("my own special joy and pride"), and Rosa, the doll. They know they cannot keep these old treasures, and dare not take any more " 'cos we'll be found out if we do". They carry them into the moonlit garden, where a pre-dug grave is ready.

The earth was shovelled in and stamped down, and I was glad that no orisons were said and no speechifying took place. The whole thing was natural and right and self-explanatory, and needed no justifying or interpreting to our audience of stars and flowers . . . The Noah's ark might be hull down on the horizon, but two of its passengers had missed the boat and would henceforth always be near us; and, as we played above them, an elephant would understand, and a beetle would hear . . . Potiphar . . . was spared maltreatment by town-bred strangers, quite capable of mistaking him for a cow.

As to Rosa, her book

was finally closed, and no worse fate awaited her than natural dissolution almost within touch and hail of familiar faces and objects that had been friendly to her since she first opened her eyes on a world where she had never been treated as a stranger.

The end of the story, and of the book, is heartbreakingly bleak, despite Grahame's efforts to be jocular and optimistic.

As we turned to go, the man in the moon, tangled in elm-boughs, caught my eye for a moment, and I thought that never had he looked so friendly. He was going to see after them, it was evident; for he was always there, more or less, and it was no trouble to him at all, and he would tell them how things were still going on, up here, and throw in a story or two of his own whenever they seemed a trifle dull. It made the going away rather easier, to know one had left somebody behind on the spot; a good fellow, too, cheery, comforting, with a fund of anecdote; a man in whom one had every confidence.

In the darkness of December, Kenneth went to stay with Roland and Joan for Christmas, to watch the little boys Keith and Anthony play, and to get used to the idea that he was no longer of their world. In a garden which belonged to someone else, the moon still shone on the small grave of his childhood. Ahead lay 1899, and the Bank and Elspeth Thomson.

9

Dino and Minkie

1899 looked uncompromisingly realistic. The Golden Age had now been set firmly in the past, written into finality. That fund of memory had been used up, and there was no more escape into the dream days of yesteryear. In the self-using way of all writers, Grahame had lost a private territory through making it public. He stared bleakly into a future which seemed to consist exclusively of his Bank duties and occasional pages of reviewing, coupled with the inexorable presence of a princess who increasingly threatened to become a real and impatient woman. She continued to intrigue him, and yet the awful, undefended availability of her heart and soul was a terrifying imposition. If he married her, what was to happen to his treasured solitude?

Five years after he published *The Wind in the Willows*, Grahame wrote an article for the Jubilee Commemoration Number, July 1913, of his old school magazine. It was, of course, deeply retrospective, and its plea for solitude and private communing with the natural world had been realised too late. In 1899, trapped by a confusion of sexual attraction and a fatal mixture of love and pity, he could not formulate a coherent statement of his needs and communicate them to Elspeth, and neither could he explain that in an increasingly commercialised and untrustworthy world, it was only his love of the countryside which remaind confident and untainted by fear. At that time, he was perhaps not even aware of what he would later on express so clearly. He called the piece "The Felowe that Goes Alone".[1]

> For Nature's particular gift to the walker, through the semi-mechanical act of walking – a gift no other form of exercise seems to transmit in the same high degree – is to set the mind jogging, to make it garrulous, exalted, a little mad maybe – certainly creative and supra-sensitive, until at last it really seems to be outside of you and as it were talking to you, while you are talking back to it. Then everything gradually seems to join in, sun and the wind, the white road and the dusty hedges, the spirit of the season, whichever that may be, the friendly old earth that is pushing forth life of every sort under your feet or spell-bound in a death-like winter trance, till you walk in the midst of a blessed company, immersed in a dream-talk for transcending any possible human conversation. Time enough, later, for that – across the dinner table, in smoking-room armchairs; here and now, the mind has

shaken off its harness, is snorting and kicking up its heels like a colt in a meadow. Not a fiftieth part of all your happy imaginings will you ever, later, recapture, note down, reduce to dull inadequate words; but meantime the mind has stretched itself and had its holiday. But this emancipation is only attained in solitude, the solitude which the unseen companions demand before they will come out and talk to you; for, be he who may, if there is another fellow present, your mind has to trot between shafts.

In the London winter of 1899, the refuge of solitude seemed to be cut off, for Elspeth was very much present. The eager woman, simultaneously elf-like and clumsy, was so easy to hurt that Grahame shrank from her like one who has a new-hatched, featherless bird placed in his hand – but he could not hurt her. Green compares her with "Thurber's monolithic *ingénue*, who bursts into a drawing-room announcing that she comes from haunts of coots and hern", and certainly Elspeth had a streak of theatrical self-presentation which caused a friend to remark that she "had a happy indifference to the lesser conventions of the social world".[2] Unconventionality in itself was no bar to Grahame's liking for Elspeth; he had always been attracted by the bizarre and exotic and un-Puritan, but if the woman he cared for had a tendency to overdo it, he would have cringed for her in an agony of embarrassment, and been doubly protective as a result.

The bars seemed to be closing round him. He wrote nothing. Meanwhile letters arrived from Elspeth, most of which do not survive. One, however, on paper headed with the Onslow Square address, was preserved – perhaps because it was the first. It is an extraordinary document, written in a wild pencil scrawl, very characteristic of Elspeth in those days, and signed, not with her own name, but with a tentative rendering of what looks like Mai – the capital M is plain, but the rest wanders off the edge of the paper.

Zur,

Plaze to vorgive that I make so bold as to write-ee. Sithee wen I parted from ee – all i the garden green – ee spook kine to mee – so thought I – sure and certain-sure, will he send me some writin – kine (like the words he spoke i the gardin) to say may-be he wanted me back there where the flowers grow and the birds sing cheery – or that he's think o' me like he thinks o' the flow'rs and the green things i th' gardin.

But now 'ee don't think o' me do 'ee? Happen ee forgets the gardin and all that stood in't now ee are back i th' town and the streets, and among gay folks. Happen ee has one mind for t'country, and t'other for th'town. Happen some dame with dimonds – dimunds that shine more than the dew drops has caught thy notice. And then the Play-houses and the Singing-places, and gran sights and the fine meat and drink – what chanst has the gardin – what chanst have I? But ee spook kine, and the trees heard ee, and I remember – an sithee! – ee may look at the Theatre-ladies – ee may listen to the singing-ones – ee may spake to the Dimund-dames in the fine houses, ee may sport, and ee may do what ee will so thee save thy heart for me – will ee? Ee hast no need of it in London-town from what folks say, and I need it sore, for mine goes but halting.

Zur, I am too simple to know how ee should be wrote to. I would never have been so bold to write to ee now, but that ee onct spook kine to me in t'gardin – for kine 'ee spook.

Zur, if so be as ee will pardon my venture and write me kine – do and remember to save thy heart for me –

thy little   Mai –[3]

Grahame must have been immensely touched by this letter. It both revealed and covered up Elspeth's secret dread of her own imperfect grasp of English. How could she approach a famous man of letters except by disclaiming any competition in his field? She had never competed with her mother's worldly sophistication or her sister's artistry or the competence of her two brothers, particularly Courtauld, who had already built up his first business, the design and manufacture of light coupé carriages with pneumatic-tyred wheels. Defining her own ground was a matter of retreat to the small, half-imagined territory which nobody else could want or reach. For Kenneth, it must have seemed that this big-eyed girl understood, as he did, the words of Marcus Aurelius. That she was willing to share her kingdom with him, was, he knew, an act of the utmost faith – and to accept her offer would be a terrible responsibility. Knowing Yeats as he did, the dark-haired poet's words might have come urgently into his mind:

I have spread my dreams under your feet;
Tread softly, because you tread on my dreams.

To tread softly enough seemed to demand almost superhuman powers of wisdom and care – but he had to try, for the sensitive carpet of dreams was already in place, and to reject her would be a stamping on it with hob-nailed boots. In February she sent him a Valentine.

Dear Sir i umbli begs to say
Thit Vallingtine's is as Today
So should *you* see no reason not
Why i've no wish to be forgot!

But if you've got anuther flame
Why never mind 'tis all the same
For I'm not one to sulk nor pout
Becos a feller won't walk-out –

So reely i won't rite no more
Except to menshun as beefore
That 'tis Snt Vallingtine's today
And that is all *i* has to *say*.[4]

She inscribed a row of fourteen childish kiss-crosses along the bottom of the paper.

The peasant-girl fantasy was becoming firmly established. Had Elspeth and Kenneth been able to spend a reasonable amount of time together, it might have led gently into a growing acceptance of reality, but the rigid Victorian sexual mores forbade this. Each of them thought with romantic yearning (and on Grahame's part at least, some fear) of the "gardin". Perhaps more through circumstances than choice, they were both firmly bound by the conventions, though Elspeth, for whom the dream was everything, had more courage in this respect than the young Secretary of the Bank of England. Grahame was not a Dickens, and Elspeth no Nelly Ternan, prepared to be kept as a famous man's mistress. Both of them lived lives of the utmost probity, Grahame in Kensington Crescent under the eagle eye of Miss Bath and the decent, neutral presence of Tom Greg, and Elspeth in her eminent stepfather's house, carrying out her duties as organiser and hostess. They were a guileless pair, quite incapable of the subterfuge – and panache – with which such men as Wilkie Collins, together with countless other upright Victorians, ran an illicit ménage.

Of the many illnesses which afflicted Grahame in these two years, by far the worst was the chest infection which began shortly after St Valentine's Day, 1899. It began in a common enough way, with a cold and a persistent, exhausting cough, bad enough to keep him from work, but it worsened rapidly. It is impossible to avoid the suspicion that his ill-health at this time was largely brought about by intolerable stress. In later years, Elspeth, naturally enough, was adamant in blaming the near-fatal scarlet fever of his childhood, which probably had in truth left a weakness of the chest, but during the busy, enjoyable *Yellow Book* years, he had been well, full of energy and enthusiasm. Now, despite his success both at the Bank and with *Dream Days*, the future was frightening. He lay in a warm room and wished himself a child again, free of the dreadful decision-making which pressed upon him.

As if in sympathy, Elspeth, too, was ill, though still able to bombard her loved one with letters and gifts. She sent him a copy of Melville's *Moby Dick*, provoking a letter of thanks from a man who had retreated as far as he could from the active grown-up world. He had no doubt written to her on previous occasions, but this is the first note which survives and it comes as a shock. He had joined her in the artless child-world of her fancy, and wrote in a baby-talk which makes embarrassing reading.

> Darling Minkie Ope youre makin steddy progress & beginnin ter think of oppin outer your nest & facin a short fly round. I ad nuther good nite & avnt ardly corfd torl terday – but it aint so nice a dày, & doesnt tempt one out . . . Feel orfle slack still but am wearin down the cold grajily. Wish the sun wood cum out fer a bit, Im very dull & bored ere. Spose youre a bit dull'n bored were *you* are, aint you? But you've got a maid, & a poodle, (tho they're bicyclin most of the time) & your friends do drop in sumtimes. Easter is always detestable. Your whale-books a rippin good book, wif lots of readin in it, & it sor me froo Good Friday triumphantly. Spose youve got a sort o mudie box spread out on *your* quilt.
>
> This aint much uv a letter my deer but aint got no spirits and dont take no interest nor no *notice* just yet. But Im wishing you elth & appiness my deer & a speedy recuvry & peece and quiet. Goodbye darlin from you own luvin
> Dino.[5]

If in fact the letter was meant as a single effort to be amusing, written in a nadir of weakness, he had calculated wrongly. The Dino and Minkie Show was set to run and run.

Despite his declared lack of spirits, Kenneth got up after he had finished writing to Elspeth and, on the following morning he presented himself at the Bank, staying on in the evening for a directors' dinner. The next day, he was in bed with a serious relapse. The chest infection developed into pneumonia and empyema, and he was taken to hospital, where he underwent an operation involving section of the ribs. If his subconscious wish had been to escape, it very nearly succeeded to the ultimate degree, for he hovered between life and death for some days.

Eventually he was sent home to Kensington Crescent and, his sister, Helen, came to look after him, helped by the devoted and deeply alarmed Sarah Bath. His progress was slow and erratic. It was the end of May before he was able to write a short note to Fletcher Moulton, thanking him for "your *second* most kind consignment of ancient Port". He was, he said, just able to "crawl about with a stick".[6]

There can be little doubt that the gift of the port was provoked by Elspeth, who was a frequent caller, bringing grapes and carnations.[7] Helen took an instant dislike to her, evidently sensing the visitor's more than conventional concern, and made her feelings known to Kenneth in no uncertain terms. Helen was very unlike her brother, having inherited Bessie's practicality rather than Cunningham's poetic inwardness. She had not had the experience of being sent away to school, or the disappointment of thwarted ambitions, and could feel no sympathy for Kenneth's seeking of refuges from reality. For her, the day-to-day business of life was interesting and acceptable, and her medical training predisposed her to see Kenneth's retreats into a private haven as pathological symptoms rather than expressions of a hyper-sensitive awareness. The repeated arrival of a tremulous, flower-clutching Elspeth triggered all Helen's protective sisterliness, both as nurse and sibling, and she was outraged that her brother, after years of respectable virginity, should now fall for someone so obviously silly, who would encourage him in what Helen regarded as his worst characteristics. She did not tell him of Elspeth's visits.

Within four days of his note to Fletcher Moulton, Kenneth was tackling longer letters.[8]

Darling Minkie This is just a *smuggled* line – for I'm not supposed to sit up writing letters yet – to say I've begun coming down in the afternoon and *seeing* my *friends*. I did not even know you had not gone away for the holiday, till this morning – and indeed while I was in *quod* I was told nothing about anybody. The surgeon has done with me – says I've made a famous recovery as far as *his* share of the thing goes – but says I must go away the moment I can – in a very few days if possible – & for a *long* time, so as to get through the winter without a breakdown. My dearest I mustn't write any more – but I wonder if I shall see you? It's been a bad two months.

Your loving   Dino

The return to a normal adult style is interesting. Evidently the need to retreat into babyhood had gone, perhaps because Fate had called his bluff. Kenneth had escaped with his life, but only just, and the experience had been a sobering one. On the same day as his letter to Elspeth, he wrote to another woman, a Miss R. M. Bradley, whom he had known for several years, and who was safely cast in the role of friend rather than lover. Miss Bradley's father was the Dean of Westminster and her uncle the Dean of St Paul's, a man who had been moved to tears over his first reading of *The Golden Age*. "You see," he had said, "I, too, was brought up by an aunt."[9] Throughout Grahame's courtship of Elspeth Thomson (or hers of him) he confided in Miss Bradley, who remained dispassionate and sensible, refusing to get drawn into any partisanship. On 25 May, Kenneth complained of Helen's unco-operative attitude, making it clear that his correspondent knew about the affair with Elspeth. "No object in talking things over with my sister *now*," he said. "*Irresponsive* is not the word." To Miss Bradley, his style is relaxed and easy. "I've been having a desperately bad time of it, but am going to be stronger than ever some day."[10] The contrast between this and his letter to Elspeth could not be stronger. In writing to the woman he supposedly loves, even in plain language, he strains to achieve a kind of extra simplicity, underlining words as if to explain them to a child.

Elspeth responded with alacrity to the letter from her loving Dino. Yet another consignment of wine arrived at Kensington Crescent, together with a note from Fletcher Moulton suggesting that Grahame should avail himself of the Moulton carriage when he felt able to take an outing. This suggests that he had no idea that his stepdaughter had anything more than a charitable hostess's concern for the young Secretary, for the suggestion, which almost certainly came from Elspeth, offered a chance of physical proximity which would be unthinkable except between people whose relations were of the most formal and impersonal. Grahame on this occasion declined the offer, but was glad to accept the port, and wrote a letter of thanks which showed a return to his more usual "man's man" image.

> Like Lord Rosebery I am regretting the possession of only one stomach – and one head; and I think of the historic Scotchman who never could sleep a wink as long as there was a drop of whisky in the house. It will be hard indeed for me to go back to the humble "four ale" – which more properly belongs to my lot in life.[11]

Later, he changed his mind about the carriage.

> Dear Mr Moulton,
>   Thank you very much – it *is* a tempting day, & a drive *would* be a sort of lark. I should be ready at 3.30, since you are so kind as to "stand by" your offer.
>
> > Yours very truly,
> > Kenneth Grahame[12]

It is hard to imagine that a man who could write such an urbane, modestly assured letter could have become a prattling toddler for the benefit of the woman who wanted to make him her husband. On the following day, he scribbled a note to Elspeth;

> Darling – come when you can, tomorrow afternoon – I rather think my sister's going out about 3.30 or so, for the rest of the afternoon – anyhow come.
> Your lovin own   Dino.[13]

The word "lovin", spelt with its missing letter, told Elspeth all she wanted to know. The secret world was still intact. She and Dino were back in business, and what's more, they were now condoned by Dino's alter ego, Kenneth, who was prepared to risk the scandal of an unchaperoned visit in order to be with her.

There is no record of what transpired at this furtive meeting, or what Sarah Bath must have said, although she made her disapproval plain later. Helen had gone out in order to finalise arrangements to take Kenneth down to the West Country to begin his convalescence, and obviously knew nothing of what had happened when her back was turned. The following day, Helen put her plan into operation. She sensibly broke the journey at Torquay so as not to overtire her patient, and they stayed there for ten days. Elspeth knew where her beloved was, and bombarded him with letters. Kenneth's responses were written in pencil, which suggests that he scribbled letters secretly instead of sitting in the usual way of Victorian letter-writers, at a desk properly equipped with blotter and ink-stand. His first letter to her, dated "Wensdy artnoon" (7 June), is a full return to baby-talk, even though he points out to her that " 'digestible' aint got no hay in it". Perhaps such a rebuke would have been impossible to make except under the cover of their private language. Again, the fear of hurting turns the whole letter into a prolonged cringe, even on such practical matters as trying to fend off well-meaning visitors sent round by the anxious Elspeth.

Dont bovver to let loose enny muvverly large people on me I dont want to be muvvered just now if I do theres a chambermade wot'll take it on . . .

He stresses the chamber-maid, mentioning her again in the course of a general complaint about Torquay:

. . . shall move on nex week unless sumfin ideal in chambermades turns up. I wanter get down to the shore & paddle & this place is too Tory orltogevver for that.

The teasing attempt to make Elspeth jealous is atoned for in the last paragraph.

Goodbye darlin pet & I wish you were here we wood go crors the bay in the little steem ferry bote & *not cum back* – there is poppies t'other side. Your lovin Dino.

The sudden poetic evocation of a special place which is encapsulated in the last bit of information gives a clue to Grahame's bereft mental state. With the completion of the *Golden Age* canon, he had lost any form of imaginative outlet. Although the stories about Selina and Harold and the others had been based on memories, they were also works of fiction, given actuality by a strongly functioning creative process, and this now could find no form through which to express itself. The Dino and Minkie scenario was a poor substitute, a fantasy-world of flimsy promise, a spider-silk life-line which produced a sense of frantic inadequacy and yet was better than the bleak alternative of implacable reality.

Elspeth's letters of this period do not survive. Whether Grahame prudently destroyed them as they were received, or whether Elspeth herself retrieved them and suppressed them is not known. Their loss is tantalising, for it would have been fascinating to know whether she responded to Kenneth in the same baby-language, or whether she wrote in plain English. The single Dino letter which she permitted Chalmers to quote in his 1933 biography was scrupulously transliterated into standard spelling, and it was an impersonal one about Helen's humourless observation of a rat. There are hints that Elspeth was beginning to find Grahame's wilful childishness irritating. It was time, she seems to have felt, that he pulled himself together and attended sensibly to the business of getting better and furthering their relationship. Kenneth, feeling himself railroaded, was in turn irritable, telling her not to

> jor me no more bout diet cos you are mixin me up so fritefly. I eets wot I chooses & wot I dont want I dont & I dont care a dam wot they does in Berlin thank gord I'm British.[14]

This bad-tempered outburst must have produced contrition, for on 1 June Kenneth is back to fantasy, expressing adolescent toyings with the erotic, dreamed up as he shelters from the "eesterly" wind on the leeside of the cliff.

> I could play at frowin you over − over the cliff I mean, but I woodn't do it reely − and you cood play at bandonin me artlessly for nuther − but you wouldn't do that neither . . .

He goes on to exercise a more conventional sexual fantasy.

> Chambermaid [spelled correctly this time] don't share your views − ses she aint paid to old ands orl nite − & she'd lose er karacter besides − she ad on a nice wite gown wif pink spots this mornin, wot "stood out" wif starch and virtue. Praps if you starcht your gowns you woodnt tork so lightly bout spendin orl nite wif dinos − but praps you'd better not starch 'em!

Evidently Elspeth had written a letter of considerable passion, throwing Kenneth into an agonised effort to respond in kind. It is interesting that a "dino", minus capital letter, seems to be accepted here as a lover in a general sense rather than as Grahame himself. The letter continues:

> Was interrupted ere by bein dragged orf owlin to "go for a nice drive". So it *was* nice, but I ate bein chained to a orse chariot. Flowers was pink & blue & beautiful, but the lanes wos ment to walk down arm in arm, not drive.

His remark about Elspeth's mis-spelling of "digestible" had evidently touched a raw nerve, for whatever she said caused him to apologise, saying,

> it wos rarver bad o me to fly out at you bout "digestable" . . . but sumow the word aroused my worst pashins.

It was hardly surprising that the pair of them stuck to the safe idiom of baby-talk, within which the "pashins" aroused were mostly of sentimentally veiled sexual desire.

The correspondence wandered on throughout the weeks of Kenneth's convalescence. Helen took her brother on to Fowey, where he cheered up considerably.

> Dear Sweetie (sounds as if you wos a goldfinch, dont it?) it was enterprisin of you to get orf a extry stamp letter (*and* a paper) yestdy. I seem ter see you flying round the corner in a dressing gownd just afore lunch, wif your bare feet in slippers. Your idea of a Love-Post is a xlent wun but clients will ave to be purvided wif cards wif L.P. on em to stick in their dinin-room winders so's to be able ter lay in bed & write till 5 minits to 2.[15]

(Some readers may remember the cards with a bold C.P. on them, the display of which resulted in the fairly instant services of a passing Carter Patterson van.)

Elspeth wanted to know what he meant by the pink and blue blossoms he had mentioned, and he responded obligingly.

> bout lane-flowers – they is pink, yaller & blue like the botes. There's valerian, in masses of pink, wot shows up the blue of the sky like wot the Judas-tree does in Itly.

He did not bother with further detail. In the same letter, though, he dismissed a couple more queries in the same relaxed manner.

> You arst me long time ago if I liked the Rhine & I meant to tell you

160

never bin near the thing ony I olds with Ock. And you arst me wevver
I'd read Wuvrin Ites & I menter say I never took no stock in Brontës.

He added, "Dunno wot you wd do if you wos ere, my love-child, seein as
you don't smoke." Despite his addiction to tobacco, he was recovering well
from the operation, confiding that

> yestday I rowed the bote fra bit by way o spandin the lung and wasnt
> nun the worse – & the sides so nearly eeled that we speck to take orf
> the dressin tomorrer for good & all.

He did not date his letters to Elspeth, marking them merely "Mundy" or
"Wensdy", but noted meticulously that it was 21 June 1899, when he wrote
to her stepfather to thank him for a copy of *Contes Drolatiques*.

Shortly after this, he started to call Elspeth by the name of whatever little
boat took his fancy in Fowey harbour – "Ki-wi", "Silverseas", "Dashing
Wave". "Nanny" particularly caught his imagination, and he used it for
several letters, retaining it even while apologising.

> So glad you're corled "Elspeth", nannie, coz I didn't no it & I like it
> so much. Shame corl you nuffin else . . .

Throughout the series of letters there is an almost comic mingling of boat-
talk with Grahame's sparse references to the wedding arrangements which
he is clearly being urged to make.

All this increased Elspeth's impatience. She meant business, offering nothing less than her whole self, and by contrast, Dino gave her nothing but
mildly salacious titillation and chat about boats. The immaturity of it provoked her into protest, and she wrote to him in evident exasperation. Even
then, Grahame could not respond to her with the maturity she was trying
to elicit.

> It sums it up, wot you say "bout 'abit o not bein interested" speshly
> wen its cuppled wif much natral "gaucherie" wot as never been strove
> gainst.

It is difficult to imagine what Elspeth had said to provoke his next response,
but evidently she had been moved to some forceful expression.

> Your remark bout wastes in lanes is simply indecint & never will I trust
> myself alone in the same lane wif you – at least not in my presint week
> state.

The positions had become reversed. It was now Grahame who paraded his defencelessness, pleading his puppyish innocence, "cuppled" with the lassitude of his illness as an excuse for his lack of assertiveness. In fact, he was enjoying every minute of his stay in Fowey. He was away from the City and the demands of his new job (which, despite the admiration of his friends, may have frightened him more than he would admit), and he was able to pursue a dilatory flirtation at a safe distance. A black-and-green-painted boat called *Nanny* was much less alarming than Nanny-Elspeth. He wrote with provocatively Calvinistic approval of the bed in his room at the Fowey Hotel. It was, he said, "a nice narrer soft one instead of a brord ard one that leadeth to destrickshin".

The June days passed idyllically. Grahame loved the little Cornish town. "I felt summow 'sif I was coming 'ome from boardin-school at Torquay", he had written. Helen saw to it that he did his exercises to reinflate his damaged lung, and tried hard to get him to join in social activities, obviously in an effort to wean him away from the influence of the constantly arriving letters. She took her brother out for walks and gave him her care and her company unstintingly, but her disapproval of Elspeth and all that she stood for were so strong that she was more than usually practical and humourless.

My sister went along the cliffs & climed down to a little cove & as she sat there a big rat cum out & sat beside er & ett winkles! I sed did ee buy them orf of a barrer & drop em in is at but she looked puzzled & seriouse & sed no ee only scraped in the seaweed wif is little pors & fetcht em out. Then I began agin was it a *black* pin – but by this time she evidently thort I was *ravin* so I dropt the subjick.

It was this episode which Elspeth later allowed Chalmers to reproduce in a corrected form, perhaps with a touch of malice against her sister-in-law.

One of Helen's well-meaning social introductions had a long-lasting result. In a house called The Haven, looking out across the harbour, lived Arthur Quiller-Couch, better known by his pen-name of Q. A Cornishman by birth, he was a graduate of Trinity College, Oxford, and had been working in London as a journalist for some years, but had abandoned the city in 1892, settling in Fowey to try and live from the proceeds of his novels, then three in number. In the seven years of living in Fowey, he had produced only two books, both volumes of poetry, but, younger than Grahame by four years, he was infectiously happy, writing in a leisurely way and paddling about in the creeks and backwaters in his little skiff, the *Richard and Emily*. Kenneth and Q became instant friends, and Helen was obviously much relieved to have handed over some of the responsibility for her troublesome brother to such a sane and healthy-seeming man. Like her uncle John, Helen tended to regard imagination as the product of under-exercise and lack of fresh air, and thoroughly approved of Q's river picnics and fishing expeditions. Her relaxation caused Kenneth to write to Elspeth that "sister as bin distinckly more amiable". Charitably, he added, "reely I fink it is ony er sort o' 'awkwardness' ".

Things began to look up. Immensely cheered by his new friend, Kenneth found himself part of the Fowey boating fraternity, through which a second fellow-spirit was discovered. This was Edward Atkinson, "Atky", as every-one called him, the Commodore of the Fowey Yacht Club. He owned thirty boats and a huge collection of *objets d'art*, the surplus of which formed the basis of a Fowey Art Gallery. To Kenneth's special delight, Atky also had a passion for mechanical toys of all kinds. His riverside house, Rosebank, was crammed with them, and joy of joys, instead of stairs to the bedrooms, he had a rope ladder. Elspeth did not like the sound of Atky, as described in Kenneth's letters. He was obviously encouraging her beloved to behave like a little boy instead of a grown man. Kenneth's account of a trip up-river with Q to Atky's house was particularly depressing, with its incoherent babble of how "we found a drore full of toys wot wound up, and we ad a great race tween a fish, a snaik, a beetle wot flapped its wings & a rabbit".

The Atkinson family were famous for the manufacture of fine soaps and perfumes — "Atkinson's Lavender" must be an evocative image for thou-sands of present-day people — and so the Commodore could afford to be carelessly luxurious and eccentric. He was sixty-two when Grahame met him, and had never married. He lived a bachelor existence with a devoted housekeeper, Miss Marsden. Distinguished and grey-bearded, he generally wore, Green says, "an exquisite and idiosyncratic hat ordered from Paris". He sounds to modern ears rather like a nautical version of Quentin Crisp, but Kenneth found him enchanting — and, at last, with Atky and Q, he could unburden himself of the problem about Elspeth. To these men, he was able to confide (as he could not to Helen) that he and this young woman had spent time alone together — albeit only a single afternoon in London — and that an unspoken agreement existed between them that marriage would take place sooner or later. Perhaps, among fellow males, he could bring himself to confess that sexual desire was causing him uneasiness and discomfort, but that he was not sure if he was the marrying kind. Q, realising that his new friend was already deeply compromised, had no doubts. Grahame could not wriggle out of it.

Q himself was happily married, with two children, and Kenneth's mis-givings faded a little. Maybe all men felt like this as they approached the unknown, almost supernatural mystery of sexual fulfilment, he may have thought. Perhaps, in his free-wheeling imagination, he pictured himself liv-ing a Quiller-Couch life, sailing and writing and introducing a son of his own to the joys of the sea.

There is a small "Q" or rather "q" boy of $8^1/_2$ oo lives a bote-life & don't care bout nuffin else much as yet. It's a jolly place for a boy to first know the world in, as it'll be "cumpny" fer im orl is life.

It was a tactless thing to say to "Nanny", who had begun to feel jealous of Kenneth's carelessly flaunted love-affair with the outdoor world, and she began to complain about it, with little success. In an abruptly ended letter which Grahame excuses because Q has just called, he says,

You are a marter to tides my deer but mustn't complane its the moon wot done it. Goodbye for now, I am your lovin
Dinetto

Elspeth adopted a new tactic. Resentment had failed to shift Kenneth out of his retreat into "gaucherie", but his one truly reliable characteristic was his kindness. She knew he could not bear to hurt her, and, probably without conscious strategy, launched a different appeal. From Grahame's response, it is obvious that she had complained about the unending drudgery of her life, with its constant routine of work on her stepfather's behalf, organising his house, entertaining his friends, making the obligatory social calls and undertaking the good works which were an expected part of any upper-class Victorian woman's duty. This time, the effect was immediate. After some murmurings of concern, Dino summoned all his courage. On 22 June, he wrote to say that he had made up his mind.

I'm ritin to your farver today cos I think it is time you was "brort to your bearins" & got a chance of actin for your own future & not rampagin bout for uvver people.

For all its decisive start, however, the letter tailed off into a fantasy of Elspeth as part of his sea-side dream. By the time he got to the end, she was again identified with a sailing boat.

And if it all goes well, my dear, do take yourself in bofe hands – rest, – arrange wot is best for bofe of us. And if you can come down ere for your rest, wy that wd be the best fing on erf – but do just as you think best my own deer nanny. My sister is frettening to go on to the Lizard, to see friends, & probbly wont return to me, and you & me wd be free, my deer. Now I must say goodbye, Oran Picotee (crimson bote, wite inside) cos Mr Q as just corled, to arst me to cum a sailin.
Your best
Lovin Dino

The promised letter to Elspeth's father was duly sent, and there was a long, stunned silence. Kenneth did not seem over-concerned. Q had given him the little skiff called the *Richard and Emily*, and the resulting happiness could not easily be dispelled. Elspeth, however, was less than euphoric, and must have written back without enthusiasm for Dino's scheme to get her down to Fowey. Kenneth wrote soothingly.

> I kwite understand bout your bein "wifin corl" & my deer its puffickly easy to be discreet and sensible. Go easy, like wot I dus wif the Richard & Emily, wich I intend ter be a reel benefit ter me tho' I could easily make it kwite the oppsit by fergettin for 5 minutes that I woon't stroke in a eight. Ain't erd from farver yet but I kwite understand.

The delicate reminder that he was a sick man did not have the desired effect. Elspeth was irritated by the torrent of boat-news which formed the bulk of his letters, and there are signs that she had no intention of being cast as the active and responsible one of the pair. Kenneth's attempts to let her "arrange wot is best for bofe of us" were based on his perception of her as a capable housekeeper and organiser, which she undoubtedly was, but Elspeth wanted her Dino to look after her as her stepfather and her dead parents had never done. She entered into a competitive invalidism which was to become habitual, perhaps hoping to provoke him into taking the lead, lamenting that she could not possibly undertake such taxing activities.

Tension was building, and it was not helped by Fletcher Moulton's response to Kenneth's letter. He was outraged. Possibly his stepdaughter's cajoling of gifts of port and the offer of the carriage suddenly crystalised into the realisation that an affair had been going on behind his back. A barrister who finds himself duped is likely to be an angry man, and Moulton was very angry indeed. At thirty-five, Elspeth could reasonably have been expected to have settled into the duties and benefits of an unmarried daughter. It would make him a laughing-stock, a woman of that age flitting off to get married at short notice like any common housemaid. And how was he to replace her? The younger sister, Winnie, had already abandoned him in favour of Courtauld.[16] The ridicule and sheer inconvenience of the situation were intolerable.

Letters hurtled to and fro. Two days later, Grahame thanked Elspeth for her latest communication, but even in this crisis, he was unable to write to her in plain words, and sounded horrified by the "shouts & the crash of battle soterspeak". There were urgent matters to discuss, but Elspeth, having achieved her objective, was now panicking at all the rumpus she had caused, and she in turn was trying to retreat into the illusory safe ground of non-commitment. Her loving Dino became peevish.

My dear it is so easy, I know, to misunderstand letters . . . but the drift of your larst simply seemed to be "o do for goodness sake leave me be, wif my notes & invitashuns & sum day wen the coste's clear I'll send you a wire & run down and settle up your little affair" wich is orl very well but – if I may insult you by common detales – unless you're bound for a registrars, & even then, some notice & lapse of time is legally required, & in our case a speshle license wd ave ter be obtained, wich probbly carnt be done by wire.

Righteous indignation produces a couple of sentences of correct spelling, but he soon returns guiltily to the shared fantasy and to the "speshle" license.

The Quiller-Couches were offering practical support, and Grahame was beginning to nerve himself to the necessity for elopement – and then, on 26 June, Fletcher Moulton wrote a stiff letter to say that he had reconsidered the situation and would agree to his stepdaughter's marriage. One can imagine that the presence of a distraught and weeping Elspeth in the house had been enough to change his mind, but Fletcher Moulton was a single-minded man who did not like to be upstaged. Within a few weeks, he announced his own engagement, as if to demonstrate that he would have no difficulty in replacing his daughter with a new mistress of the house in Onslow Square.

The change of heart did not seem to fill Kenneth with joy, for he still seems to have been more interested in the prospect of getting Elspeth down to Cornwall without formalities.

My sister went orf erly this mornin to the Lizard for a week or so but nounced that she was a coming back! I sed nuffin one way or tuther . . .

It was only after this that he announced the big news.

Me deer Ive ad an streemly kind & nice letter from your farver – & now I mus leave the matter ntirely in your fare ands & I will say nuffin till you tells me to, cos we gets no further with discushins – on paper.

Straight after this came a complaint about Elspeth's preoccupation with clothes, which he confusingly spells "close".

I see you were thinkin orl the time but close wile pore me wos ony angshus to fulfil the requirements of the lor!

His next letter was all about boats, ending casually, "sorry you don't 'see fit' to cum down".

A battle for the privilege of being the artless one of the pair was now in full cry, though Grahame probably did not realise it. Elspeth, in her new role as bride, was not going to have things left in her "fare ands". She retreated to the unassailable position of an Elizabeth Barrett-Browning, lying on a couch in helpless incapacity, and was sharp with her Dino when he wrote irreverently,

My deer, I'm *not* sorry you've got to "lay up on the mud" & wen youre launched again you must nurse yourself a bit . . .

The nautical imagery was not what she wanted, and her rebuke produced a slightly unrepentant apology. "I'm so sorry my dear I was 'not so kind as I mite be.' " He goes straight on to an account of seeking Q's advice and getting in touch with "a tame curick" who would conduct the service. "Then I wired to Courtauld." With this handing of things over to Elspeth's brother, Kenneth reverted to boat-talk for the rest of the letter.

Helen had been away in the Lizard, most probably to see her friend Mary Richardson and make arrangements to continue Kenneth's convalescence there, and the first she knew of the change of heart was the engagement announcement in the *Morning Post* of 1 July 1899. The date of the wedding had been set for exactly three weeks later, on the 22nd of the same month. She came back to Fowey speechless.

She's just sed she'd seen it, & that was abslootly orl. There must be sumfin at the bottom of er sullen sort o silence wot I ain't got at yet.

A few hours later, Helen, ever practical, had decided what to do. She tackled Kenneth, asking if he *really* intended to marry Elspeth Thomson, and he said despondently, "I suppose so; I suppose so".[17] As far as Helen was concerned, that was the end. She announced that "she was goin ome on Toosday wereat I bowed my edd in silence, saying nuffin". Q and his wife went on being helpful, finding a curate who was prepared to marry the couple at short notice, and taking Grahame into their own home after Helen's departure. The question of the honeymoon arose, and the Qs suggested that the couple should just go away to Newquay "from the Satty till the Mundy". Here, acquired ideas about sex as a bedroom farce suddenly blocked all practical suggestions. Kenneth objected, ludicrously, to the suggestion, claiming that "Wensdy to Friday wd a bin orlrite not bein a 'weekend' ". In the same letter, the last flickers of the sexual fantasy which was fast being overwhelmed by practicality found a brief flare of expression. "Darlin ow'd you like ter go on livin at Ons: Sq: & cum away wif me fer week-ends?"[18]

For a man on the brink of marriage, this is lack of commitment of a high order. Shaken perhaps by Helen's departure (the breach between them was to be almost permanent), Grahame may have cast about desperately for a last-ditch compromise: some way in which he could retain both the love of his darling Minkie and of Helen-Selina, the sister who had kicked his shins in their childhood and had stood on the quarter-deck of the *Victory* while the cannon-balls flew. The split was deeply painful, and the only compromise lay in a wild dream of Minkie as mistress instead of wife. Without any real hope, he suggested to her that a relationship based on illicit weekends would be "so nice and immoril & yet nobody coodnt find no forlt not even arnts".

The barely serious bid for irregularity came, of course, to nothing, and yet Grahame continued to brood over it. He wrote to Martin Conway, who had congratulated him on his coming marriage: "My beastly virtue has been my enemy through life, but once married I will try & be frankly depraved, and then all will be well".

As the fateful day approached, his nervousness increased. He tried in vain to get some sense out of Elspeth about what she would wear, expressing his own preference for "a blue serge soot and soft 'at", but Minkie had gone fey about the whole thing and refused to commit herself. There had arisen between them a fancy for an informal, spur-of-the-moment wedding of the kind described by Dickens in *Great Expectations*, where the lawyer's clerk, Wemmick, suddenly marries Miss Skiffins, but Grahame was having some difficulty in coming to terms with the reality of such a proposal.

Fowey'd be orl rite, for a wemmick-marriage – but I wish you'd tell me *ow much* [his italics] of a wemmick-marriage its got ter be.

Elspeth, vacillating wildly between her child-of-nature dreams and the conventional celebration planned by her relatives, could not enlighten him. She had a curious hatred of jewellery, and flatly refused to wear an engagement ring, and this provoked Kenneth to one or his most extraordinary actions. He had kept in touch with Miss Bradley throughout the fraught days of hesitation and of Fletcher Moulton's anger, and she had done her best to be consoling, while preserving a balanced neutrality. ("Papa is quite distressed that there should have been so much anxiety and trouble . . . and wishes he could have helped you . . .") Now, in the face of his intended bride's refusal to wear a ring, Grahame sent one to Miss Bradley instead. His letter is in marked contrast to those he was writing to Elspeth, sounding as if it was written by a man years older and already a little sad.

Dear Miss Bradley, – Elsie refuses to have anything to do with an engagement ring of any sort. And I respect unconventionality of any kind too much to even protest. But I do feel strongly that there ought to be a ring in the business *somewhere* – to appease the gods – and circumstances seem to mark *you* out for it clearly. So I hope that you will not refuse to accept the one I am sending along with this. It is of no value, unless it will sometimes remind you of a friendly action – and if you do friendly things you must put up with being reminded of them.

Yours most sincerely,
Kenneth Grahame.

Quite what Miss Bradley had done to merit such a sensitive expression of gratitude remains a mystery. She represented, perhaps, an interlude of tranquility which was now lost for ever, for Chalmers quotes a letter in which she mentions that her father was devoted to Kenneth

and recognised in him a master of English prose. Not least did he appreciate his boyish mind. The regard was mutual. Together they would sit, the old churchman and young banker, and quote their favourite passages from the classics or else the younger man would listen to reminiscences which went far back into the first half of the nineteenth century.

Kenneth, while "not manifestly a Christian", had deeply religious instincts, and his gift of the ring was, as he said, placatory. The idea of penance and absolution was not far from his mind, for Catholicism had been a strong influence among his *Yellow Book* friends, several of whom had embraced the faith. Pantheism contained a self-evident element of cause and effect, and Grahame obviously felt, as so many people do today, that the power-seeking activities of mankind would ultimately reap a grim harvest. Huxley had described the Neo-pagan attitude as "Catholicism with the Christianity taken out", and this neatly encapsulates Grahame's sense of humility and superstition. Symbolism, which lies at the heart of both poetry and religion, was intimately mingled with his thinking, and his need to give a symbol of commitment, and perhaps of atonement for the proposed exercise of lust, was a very deep one.

Ironically, Elspeth abandoned her anti-ring stance in the face of opposition from her relatives. Grahame wrote with gloomy triumph:

Fort youd get inter trubble bout engagement ring – you ortera *ired* one fer aunt-pupposes cos aunts spec such fings . . .

There was no doubt that a wedding-ring must be obtained. He wrote a long letter to Minkie in the train to "Plymuff" where Q had told him there was a very good shop. It is an odd mixture of business and nostalgic yearning.

Bout ouse – I ony pays £70 p. ann. & of course woodnt want more'n my money back till next Lady Day, wen my greements up.

He would not take his bride back to Kensington Crescent. The future was getting uncomfortably close. As always, Grahame took refuge in a child-hood fantasy.

Darlin, its gettin on ter nex week aint it – & then we'll fink o nuffin for a bit, but you & me – & you'll let me paddle in pools wich ave bin left by tide, cos they gets as ot in the sun as a warm barf, an I'll let you tadpole – wifin reesnable limits.

It is pathetically obvious that he can envisage no relationship except that which links child to child or child to authority-figure.

The same letter is continued in Plymouth, following the visit to the jewel-ler's shop. Grahame's need for a symbolic gesture has overcome caution.

Deer own Minke – I *noe* yr nonconformist views bout joolery, but ope you wont *mind* a pendant wot I'm sendin you frum ere – cos I seen you wearin' things on chanes & I'd like you to wear sumfin from *me* sumtimes, dearie – & as you've got your dino on a string you mays well wear is pendant remind you ee's a angin very near your art . . . It's being sent sepritt, by jooler. I've got a ring . . . Twos bout as narrer a ring as they ad, & jooler didnt kwite approve – which makes me think it'll be orl rite . . .

The letter's pencilled words are almost illegible, much scuffed from having been carried about for a long time.

The last letters of the series are increasingly desperate as the pair struggle to establish workable terms. Elspeth was already fearful that she would never be as central in her Dino's life as he was in hers, and Grahame's response was not reassuring.

Wensdy nite – my darlin Nannie Elspeth of Fowey . . . I'm not afrade of your finkin that I frow you over for *botes*, my deer, tho it reeds like it, cos I noe you feel wif me that I must make bein in the open air & takin reglar excise my first thort . . .

Within the childish language, the riposte is a stern Victorian reminder of wifely duty. Where fantasy ended, convention began.

The penultimate letter of the series is a nervous one, hoping that Elspeth will not mind too much about the pendant, then going on to an unrepentant description of the surrounding boats – for he is writing in the *Richard and Emily*. It ends, with sudden courage:

. . . I'm agoin' ter be pashnt my pet & go on a dreemin a you till youre
a solid reeality to the arms of im oo the world corls your luvin
Dino

Grahame had taken a long lease on a house in Campden Hill, 16 Durham
Villas. He had hoped that Sarah Bath would come to be the housekeeper
there, but that lady had not forgiven Elspeth for the impropriety of forcing
her way, unchaperoned, into Kenneth's presence, thus, in Sarah's view,
deliberately compromising his honour and forcing him to marry her.
Grahame's request to his housekeeper resulted in a strongly worded letter
of refusal, and he found some difficulty in explaining this tactfully to Elspeth. His fear of upsetting Minkie led to a hypocritical betrayal of his real
standards. From a man who had consistently upheld the unpretentious virtue of agricultural labourers and domestic servants ("Martha is a real lady"),
there is a hollow sound to his assertion that Sarah "aint kwite the person
for us, and she *as* got 'erself' on the brane – those peeple of the *pesant* clars
orfin ave". Here is a true social chameleon at work, hiding his fear of people
under a desperate effort to be ingratiating. The interesting thing about the
self-deception is the way it reveals Grahame's estimate of Elspeth's social
outlook. Despite her professed Liberal leanings, she would not blink at this
disparaging description of the "peasant class", but it is impossible to imagine Grahame using the same phrase to his friend Q, with whom there was
no pretending.

The last letter before the wedding alludes again to Sarah Bath, and
struggles to make sense of the somewhat chaotic arrangements for the
coming Saturday.

Fursday, a brite blowy mornin
Darlin Nannie – *Fort* I shd get into trubble bout that there ornymint.
But Im very sorry & now I'm goin' ter be good.

Look ere my sweetie – furrin affairs cums curst. Bishop's very sorry
but can't manidge it – too much engaged. But vicar's a nice chap. Ad a
tork wif im yestdy & he'll fall in wif ennyfing we wants. Mr Q ses Im
t'arst you wevver Im t'order (1) orgynist (2) flowers (3) bell-ringers. I sed
adnt even fort of em fer a "Wemmicker". *She* sed she'd give way bout
flowers but stuck to organist & bells. [This probably refers to Mrs
Quiller-Couch, whom Grahame disliked.] So you mus tell me jus wot
you'n farver wood like. Sarah rites sivilly nuff, but wants to quit, & run er
own show . . . [illegible] I'm glad I was fairly "nice" to er cos she's reely
ony a summersetshire pessant & carnt be xpected tave a brord mind.

There follows a long paragraph about rowing, and the letter ends with a
slightly clumsy outburst of ardour.

Goodbye sweetie and dont sorst yourself cos its a long journey down
& I want ter do the sorstin of you wen you gets ere.

The day of the wedding arrived. Elspeth, with her sister and her two
brothers, her stepfather, her maid and her pet poodle, had come down to
Fowey on the previous evening, and Grahame, even if he had abandoned
the blue serge suit, was horrified to see the formality of the guests' clothes,
and the dressmaker's boxes carried carefully to protect the finery within.
His cousin, Anthony Hope, was to be his best man, giving Fowey's residents
an extra thrill as the presence of two famous authors among them was
realised, and Hope took charge of the traumatised Kenneth and of the Q
household, even hiring an organ-grinder to play his hurdy-gurdy outside
The Haven as an early alarm-call the following morning.

The bridal half of the party was installed at the Fowey Hotel, and rose
in more sober style for its breakfast, though slightly perturbed by the absence of Elspeth. The guests were at the toast-and-marmalade stage when
the door burst open. There stood the bride, her old muslin dress dew-wet
from a morning walk and a daisy-chain round her neck, eyes shining with
limpid fervour, demonstrating a communion with nature which out-
Grahamed her husband-to-be. She would, she announced, get married
exactly as she was.

And so, on Saturday, 22 July 1899, Kenneth Grahame married Elspeth
Thomson at St Fimbarrus's Church, Fowey, in front of embarrassed relatives in formal clothes, the bride dressed artlessly – some would have said
tastelessly – in less-than-fresh white muslin and slightly withered daisies.

Afterwards, the couple went to St Ives for three days while their respective families returned to London, then came back to Fowey and the more
congenial company of the Quiller-Couches. Q, however, despite his support
for Kenneth's intended marriage, had been dismayed when he met the
bride herself, and Elspeth knew it. A mutual dislike was palpable between
them from the start, and added to the stress of the situation. Q hated
pretension of any kind, and sensed in Elspeth an artificial straining to be
sweet and natural, which denied her real skills of management and organisation and made her seem dishonest. Kenneth, utterly unable to be
what Elspeth demanded while Q watched the pair of them and refrained
from smiling, solved the problem ruthlessly. He kept faith with Nature, his
genuine first love, returning to the "messing about in boats" and the long
walks along Cornish paths sweet with harebell and valerian, and closed his
mind to the fact that his newly wed wife fretted alone in the house of
unsympathetic strangers.

Despite the increasing ardour of the Dino letters in the days before the
marriage, we may suspect that the sexual encounter itself was almost certainly less than magic. Neither partner had any experience, and both were

filled with ethereally romantic notions of love, compared with which the physical act of lovemaking must have seemed difficult, crude and embarrassing. For Kenneth, it destroyed the dream. A private imagining had been made real, and there was a sense of loss rather than gain. Nothing could now mitigate the embarrassment of his mismatch, and he fled from it to the safe world of male companionship and boats.

10

Durham Villas

As July came to an end, practicalities could no longer be avoided. After four months, first of sickness and convalescence, then of honeymoon, Kenneth was due back at the Bank. Installed in the Campden Hill house, Elspeth was deeply unhappy. She, no less than Grahame, had suffered the loss of a dream, but for her nothing could replace it. There was no professional life to occupy her days, and she did not even have the busy routine of organising Fletcher Moulton's social calendar. Kenneth regarded social occasions as work, and his reluctant presence in the house in order to preserve the conventions in front of invited friends was no comfort to her. The Dino and Minkie love affair was over, and she suspected that the ashes, as far as Kenneth was concerned, were cold. He had nothing to say.

In despair, Elspeth turned to a female friend, Mrs Thomas Hardy, who seemed to cope equably with her husband's self-absorbed life. Elspeth's letter is lost, but Emma Hardy wrote back with some down-to-earth advice which verges on the cynical. Her letter is dated 20 August 1899, at which time the Grahames had been married for barely a month.

It is really too early days with you to be benefited by advice from one who had just come to the twenty-fifth year of matrimony ... I can scarcely think that love proper, and enduring, is in the nature of men – as a rule – perhaps there is no woman "whom custom will not stale". There is ever a desire to give but little in return for our devotion, and affection – theirs being akin to children's, a sort of easy affectionateness and at first man's feelings often take a new course altogether. Eastern ideas of matrimony secretly pervade his thoughts & he wearies of the most perfect and suitable wife chosen in his earlier life. Of course he gets over it usually somehow, or hides it, or is lucky!

Keeping separate a good deal is a wise plan in crises – and being both free and expecting little, neither gratitude, nor attentions, love nor *justice*, nor anything you may set your heart on – Love interest, – adoration, and all that kind of thing is usually a failure – complete – someone comes by and upsets your pail of milk in the end – If he belongs to the public in any way, years of devotion count for nothing – Influence can seldom be retained as years go by, and *hundreds* of wives go through a phase of disillusion – it is really a pity to have any ideals in the first place.

This is gruesome, horrid, you will say – & mayhap Mr Grahame is looking over the bride's shoulder as bridegrooms often do. But you have asked me.[1]

Emma went on to advocate a submission to Christian philosophy, accepting a life of selfless service, and ended with a note of caution about the folly of imagining that a husband genuinely shares his wife's outlook on life. "Similarity of taste", she said firmly, "is not to be depended on."

Her words must have been cold comfort to poor Elspeth, as they would to any woman who was still painfully and helplessly in love. Elspeth was not capable of Emma Hardy's stoic self-sufficiency. She poured out her feelings in bad verse:

When I go out, you stay at home,
No sooner am I in
Than you desire at once to roam,
I vow it is a sin!

Oh! It really is unbearable
And would provoke a saint!
By all oaths that are swearable,
There's reason for complaint![2]

The couple now had nothing to share except the unhappiness they caused each other, and they could not even explore that stony ground, for they had no means of knowing what lay at the heart of their terrible mistake.

The most significant factor was undoubtedly Grahame's profound ignorance of the female sex, together with a set of irrational prejudices and fears which had grown up to fill the void. He was, though he perhaps did not realise it, very frightened of women. Men, in his experience, could be ruthless and unreasonable, but at least their intentions could be talked about and protested against, however uselessly. Women, although ostensibly helpless, held an irrational power which could not be defined, much less contested. There is no doubt that Kenneth, brought up in Granny Ingles's largely female household, had overheard a lot of the contemptuous talk of the kind he reported in "A Saga of the Seas", where

the burden of their plaint was Man – Men in general and Man in particular. (Though the words were but spoken, I could clearly discern the captial M in their acid utterance.)

Uncle John's parsimony may well have given Granny Ingles a legitimate

175

cause for complaint, but the children could not see anything more than the pursed lips and the sense of mysteriously justifiable anger.

As far as Grahame was concerned, femaleness was a fate which overtook girl children even if they had seemed to be quite reasonable people. In "A Departure",

> Charlotte, on entering one day dishevelled and panting, having been pursued by yelling Redskins up to the very threshold of our peaceful home, was curtly informed that her French lessons would begin on Monday, that she was henceforth to cease all pretence of being a trapper or a Redskin . . .

From not understanding femininity, Grahame quickly adopted the more active defensive position of not wanting to understand. Netta Syrett, a *Yellow Book* contributor, had written that Kenneth "was immensely pleased once when I had the cheek to say that I did not like his little girls, that they were not *real*, like his boys".[3] A *Golden Age* piece called "What They Talked About" expresses the prejudice, and the underlying uncertainty.

> "P'raps they talk about birds'-eggs," I suggested . . . "and about ships, and buffaloes, and desert islands; and why rabbits have white tails; and whether they'd sooner have a schooner or a cutter; and what they'll be when they're men – at least, I mean there's lots of things to talk about, if you *want* to talk."
>
> "Yes; but they don't talk about those sort of things at all," persisted Edward. "How *can* they? They don't *know* anything; they can't *do* anything – except play the piano, and nobody would want to talk about *that*; and they don't care about anything – anything sensible, I mean. So what *do* they talk about?"
>
> "I asked Martha once," put in Harold; "and she said, 'Never *you* mind; young ladies has lots of things to talk about that young gentlemen can't understand.' "

This has the authentic ring of what was all too commonly said to Victorian children. Grahame himself confesses in "The Magic Ring", a *Dream Days* piece that

> we had known the outward woman as but a drab thing, hour-glass shaped, nearly legless, bunched here, constricted there; slow of movement, and given to deprecating lusty action of limb.

The Grahame children had, of course, lived in a particularly sexless household, where no hint of carnal love ever penetrated the dispassionate, faintly bitter atmosphere. No matter how "bunched and constricted" a woman might be, in the presence of a man who finds her sexually attractive, she – and he – will always give off a certain warmth and spiciness which children pick up as part of their pre-pubertal awareness, but Kenneth and his sister and brother had none of this. Roland, being five years younger, spent more of his formative years in other households. He had been no more than a baby during the free-running years at The Mount, but after the move to Fern Hill Cottage and Kenneth's departure to school, he came in for more attention from the newly married David Ingles, the kindly curate of the stories, and went with his older siblings to stay with Jack or with Uncle John, both of them family men. Willie had died at sixteen, leaving a gulf which can only be guessed at, for Kenneth never made overt reference to it. The absence of the elder brother, however, perhaps contributes to the elegaic quality which pervades the later *Golden Age* stories, many of which centre round the loss of Edward. Although it is school rather than death which has claimed the fictional boy, there is still a strong sense that the narrator and his remaining siblings feel bereft. Edward – or Willie – has gone away into the mystery of an unknown state. In real life, because of Willie's death and Roland's extreme youth, it was the two middle children, Kenneth and Helen, who had suffered most from their grandmother's monastic regime. Helen accepted it as the norm. She never married, and her intense disapproval of her brother's entanglement may have been as much provoked by a mistrustful fear of sexuality itself as by any specific dislike of Elspeth.

As to Kenneth, his fantasies of the ideal woman were based on the sugar-plum creations of circus and pantomime. It was Coralie, the bare-back rider, with her "more than mortal beauty" who first opened his eyes to the fact that a woman could be glamorous and alluring. Even though she was almost immediately ousted by Zephyrine, her influence remained, as he wrote in "The Magic Ring":

> In one of those swift rushes the mind makes in high-strung moments,
> I saw myself and Coralie, close enfolded, pacing the world together,
> o'er hill and plain, through storied cities, past rows of applauding
> relations, – I in my Sunday knickerbockers, she in her pink spangles.[4]

Was it Coralie who had reasserted herself in the form of the Fowey "chambermade" with her "nice wite gown wif pink spots"? In those desperate last days before a marriage which he could not escape, Grahame's subconscious mind may well have turned back to an ideal of love in which, he, the mundane boy, would be lifted and transported into a Coralie-world "past rows of applauding relations". The mental construct is all there, complete in a dream-match which would at one stroke stun the Olympians into admiration and release Kenneth himself from the sexual uncertainties imposed on him by an increasingly insistent woman who, for all her feyness, was firmly rooted in actuality.

That it should have happened the other way round, in the real world instead of the dream one (as adult reason must have told him it would), still came as a shock. Coralie was grounded, the lights were out, the music did not play. His princess had been reduced to the ludicrous state in which the children had observed Miss Smedley, their governess, at a time when she had managed to ensnare Uncle George, even though "she had neither accomplishments nor charms – no characteristic, in fact, but an inbred viciousness of temper and disposition".[5] The magic spell had not worked, as he had known in his heart that it could not do. One should not subject magic to the test of literality. Now, recovered from what seemed in retrospect to have been a long madness, he was saddled with the result. Landlocked in London, there was not even the escape route of the sea-going company of Atky and Quiller-Couch.

There was, however, one friend, the painter, illustrator and playwright Graham Robertson. He, like Kenneth Grahame himself, was a Scot of aristocratic lineage, descended from the Chief of Clan Donnachie. Sargent's portrait of him in the Tate Gallery shows an almost waif-like sensitivity, though Robertson had a robust good humour. He writes of Kenneth in revealing reminiscence:

He was then in Durham Villas, Campden Hill and I was in Argyll Road, just round the corner; a two-minutes walk lay between us and the path soon became well worn.

His special room in No. 16 was most characteristic; it looked like a nursery. Books there were certainly, but they were outnumbered by toys. Toys were everywhere – intriguing, fascinating toys which could hardly have been conducive to study and may have accounted to some extent for their owner's very occasional literary output.

As his house was full of toys so was mine full of dogs, and we each found the other's surroundings quite normal and satisfactory.

Anyone who wants to know Kenneth Grahame may still find him in *The Golden Age* and *Dream Days*, the eternal boy, keenly alive to the beauty and wonder of the world around him yet shy of giving expression to the strange happiness that bubbles up within him. In those long ago days when we saw much of each other, I always felt that, with all the frankness and jollity of his boyishness, there was also the boy's reticence and half-unconscious withdrawal into himself; and then again, beyond the boy, was a man known by few, remote, but very much to be reckoned with.

I was but touching the fringe of a great personality. As we were such near neighbours, he would happen in casually to dinner or later in the

evening, and though we often spoke hardly more than did the som-
nolent dogs crouched at our feet, yet memory seems to give me back
hours spent in long and intimate conversation. We never wrote to
each other, but I always felt that I had his friendship, and it was very
precious to me.[6]

This tribute comes from a contribution which Robertson wrote for inclusion
in Chalmers's book, as an excerpt from a letter (probably to Grahame's
agent, Curtis Brown)[7] makes clear:

I've been worrying and licking my Kenneth Grahame bit until I dare
say I have spoilt it and made it mannered and "precious", but I rather
like it myself at present. The man who is writing and compiling the
book is coming here on Friday for the day. What he expects to get
from me I can't imagine. He tells Mrs Grahame "Atmosphere". But
I haven't got any of Kenneth's atmosphere about me, and I personally
think that – as he never met or even saw Kenneth – he would do well
to stick to letters & accounts of K. by people who did know him, and
not try for "atmospherics" and psychologising on his own account.
Oddly enough (for he was a most attractive man), Kenneth had few
friends. He simply didn't want them. He would say rather wonderingly
to his wife, "You *like* people. They interest you. But I am interested
in *places*!"

Robertson's "worrying and licking" comes very naturally from a man so
passionately doggy. Many of his letters dwell in affectionate detail on his
canine friends, and he could write, without affectation, of his eldest sheep-
dog,

Bob married twice. His first choice fell on a pretty, rustic maiden in a
neighbouring village, and of their union was born Portly . . .

And of Portly was born the baby otter of *The Piper at the Gates of Dawn*.

Poor Robertson was to be disappointed by the form in which his long
tribute to Grahame appeared in the book. Stoically, he said, "I think Chalmers, from his point of view, was right to cut my stuff up – it would have
bulked too large otherwise. But from *my* point of view it is perhaps a bit
spoiled, as one does try to get a certain beat and cadence running through
a thing and to make each phrase and paragraph lead on to the next."[8] He
did not, at the time, realise that it was Elspeth, rather than Chalmers, who
had made the excisions.

Meanwhile, in 1899, Elspeth, doing her wifely duty as she saw it, tried
hard to get her husband more interested in people. In the early months at

Durham Villas, she entertained in her accustomed Onslow Square style, and by all accounts did it well. The faithful Miss Bradley was a frequent guest, and many years later wrote that "the easy informal hospitality at the Grahame's house on Campden Hill will be remembered with peculiar pleasure by many of their intimate circle" – but the letter was to Elspeth, and it was to her that she continued,

> Kenneth's mind was not ruled by the ordinary conventions. He made little attempt at small-talk but his silences were curiously companiable: & presently the thought would flow . . . He was a good – sympathetic – conversationalist because he was as genuinely interested in the person he was talking to & in the latter's views as in his own – he was entirely without pretensions or affectations of any description. Never a great talker in a mixed company, he would sometimes give utterance to his least conventional sentiments wih genial but unhesitating conviction.[9]

Robertson was less constrained by courtesy. Genuine as Grahame's regard evidently was for Miss Bradley, he could only feel truly relaxed in the company of another man.

> Dogs were a great link between us and we shared other enthusiasms, chief among them, perhaps, a love for the works, pictorial and poetical, of William Blake; and my rather comprehensive collection of Blake's drawings may have lured my neighbour into a neighbourliness that otherwise might have taken longer to develop.

From the privilege of this neighbourliness, Robertson could gain more insight into Grahame's true nature than either Miss Bradley or Kenneth's unfortunate wife.

> He had a marvellous gift of silence. We all know the old rustic who said, "Sometimes I sets and thinks and sometimes I just sets." Kenneth Grahame had reduced "just setting" to a fine art. He would slowly become a part of the landscape and a word from him would come as unexpectedly as a sudden remark from an oak or a beech. He could not have been thinking, because a silent thinker is, socially speaking, quite as disturbing to serenity as a motor cyclist. No, he was "just setting"; in other words he was on the threshold of Nirvana; his brain was receptive but at rest, a great peace was with him and about him and his companion was drawn into it.[10]

Robertson's observation was perceptive. From this point on, Grahame began increasingly to detach himself from what surrounded him. Quite apart from the shock of his marriage, he had nearly died of the illness which had struck him down in the previous spring, and such a close brush with oblivion has a tendency to change the perspective of the survivor. Worldly ambition had never been high in Kenneth's priorities, but now it was virtually abandoned. He had been in no hurry to return to his new post as Secretary of the Bank of England, which he had hardly tackled before illness removed him from it, and he resumed his duties with a distinct lack of enthusiasm.

Mr H. A. Siepmann, a distinguished banker of his time, confided to Green that the general view of Grahame among his colleagues was a poor one.

> The tradition is that he was a very dilatory and lackadaisical Secretary. Perhaps that is the reason why so little has been said about his activities in the City. I rather think that, in quite a few ways, he fell short of the Bank's standards – such as they were.[10]

Although he was writing nothing of his own, Grahame was not entirely out of touch with the literary world, for John Lane seems to have been using him as a reader and adviser, as a later letter from Baron Corvo (Frederick Rolfe) makes clear.[11] This minor gesture towards a vanished creativity did little to rouse him from his state of habitual remoteness, and he showed no signs of finding any genuine excitement in Elspeth's announcement, after only a few weeks of marriage, that she was pregnant.

The winter and spring in which a new century began saw no improvement in Elspeth's relationship with Kenneth. He remained locked in a private childhood and, as she prepared a nursery for the coming baby, she must have looked at her husband's room full of toys and wondered how a forty-year-old boy would cope with a child of his own.

Kenneth continued to seek the company of Grahame Robertson, who, as an old Etonian, understood absolutely how a boy of particular awareness could be driven by a ruthlessly convivial society into what small refuge he could find within himself. Both men thought themselves to be sane in a mad world; perhaps they were. They shared an absolutism of judgement which had nothing to do with conventional acceptability, and Robertson was prepared to be guided by the opinion of his three bobtail sheepdogs as to the suitability of his friends. They accepted Grahame unhesitatingly "and welcomed him with effusion whenever he appeared". Animals, in general, Robertson averred, "loved him. They felt safe with him, and indeed his presence ever brought a sense of security, like the shelter of a hill or the shadow of a great tree. His quiet strength soothed and sustained."[13]

Though Grahame was child-like, he was never childish – except in the single case of Elspeth, where he had leaned over backwards to accommodate someone he sensed to be even more vulnerable than himself. It was a pitifully wrong approach, for Elspeth, despite her well-earned reputation for organisational ability, had lost her father at an early age, and was in desperate need of a kindly, capable man who would look after her. Within a couple of years, it would be revealed that John Fletcher Moulton had been a stepfather notably lacking in these qualities, and that there were good reasons why Elspeth was deeply insecure.

Meanwhile, Kenneth appeared to be almost literally "away with the fairies". His visits to Grahame Robertson's house were, Elspeth realised, an escape, and she could only assume that they represented a desire to get away from her – but there was more to it than that. Grahame was still not writing, and the evenings spent in companionable talk – or silence – with his new friend were a small substitute for the loss of expression of a private world, for Robertson could out-match him when it came to the devising of credible fantasies. As he said,

> Another tie was our mutual interest in fairyland, upon the manners and customs of which country we could both speak with authority; and we would discuss the points of view, proclivities and antecedents of its inhabitants with all the passionate earnestness displayed by really sensible people when speaking of Latest Quotations, Lunch Scores or Cup Finals.[14]

The gentle irony about the enthusiasms of the "really sensible" would not have been lost on Grahame. He and Robertson clung to a belief, now seriously under attack in the increasingly commercialised world, that decency and the beauty of the mind's imaginings had been designed as the ruling principles of mankind. In their fairy-trusting way, they wrestled earnestly with the problems of establishing a tenable ethical standard which would take account of ancient myth and legend.

> For us the Folk of Fairy Tale were genuine historical characters and we always tried to enter sympathetically into their feelings, but I remember that we sometimes found the morals of the virtuous heroes and heroines, though much insisted upon, not a little complicated and perplexing.[15]

Elspeth, thirty-eight on 3 January 1900, may well have found the same difficulty in deciphering the ethical standards of her husband. Imprisoned in her passionately romantic view of him, she had no hope of understanding the reasons why he sought the company of another man, with whom he prattled of toys and fairies, when she herself was trying to cope virtually alone with the tiredness and fear which a late first pregnancy must engender.

Over the years, Elspeth's handwriting changed from a fly-away scrawl to

Bessie Grahame, née Ingles

Mary Ingles, known to Bessie's
children as 'Granny Ingles'

The Mount, Cookham Dene

Bonham's, Blewbury

Church Cottage, Pangbourne

Alistair Grahame as a baby (COPYRIGHT COURTAULD THOMSON
TRUST, DORNEYWOOD)

Miniatures of Elspeth and Alastair Grahame, painted by Elspeth's
sister, Winifred Hope Thomson

Kenneth Grahame, from a drawing by John Sargent, RA
(COPYRIGHT BODLEIAN LIBRARY, OXFORD, SH REPRO/93/165)

Alastair Grahame at Blewbury *circa* 1912

Alastair Grahame as an undergraduate

Elspeth Grahame
circa 1930

Kenneth Grahame aged about sixty

a close, cautious hand with a curiously deliberate graphic quality. It mirrors the gradual effect of the shock in which she lived after her marriage, when her reliance on girlish charm turned out to be groundless, and she seemed to be without any resource except the tormenting love she felt for the man whom everyone admired. Her poems written during this first year, many of them typed out and decorated with patterned lines of ampersands and dollar signs, dots and stars, tell their own story. One of the earliest is called "Accepted".

> I love thee so – that all beside
> Is lost, forgotten, and unknown
> Of all things in this world so wide
> I think of thee, and thee alone.
>
> My life, before I saw thy face
> Must in some other sphere have passed
> Some planet poised in distant space
> Where all was bleak, and dim, and vast.
>
> But now of light there is no dearth
> Or radiant warmth, and bliss divine
> I hardly feel I tread the earth
> I only know that thou art mine![16]

An untitled composition may have been written before the rapturous paeon of "Accepted", for it is more cautious. If it was written afterwards, then it is a foreshadowing of strain.

> Look not on love with curious eyes
> Or else he flies, or else he flies
> With all the speed that in him lies
>
> But hearken to his rustling wings
> The song he sings, the song he sings
> And seize the perfumed flower he flings
>
> Then he will fold his wings and stay
> Full many a day, full many a day
> Perchance for ever, and for aye.[17]

For all its lack of polish, Elspeth's poetry at its best has a genuine lyrical quality, and embodies a sadness which disarms mockery. This one is called "Alas!":

You let a flow'r fall from your hand last night,
That hand which I may never hold,
I gathered it up and hid it from sight
As a treasure rarer than gold;
    For I thought it was meant for me − for me −
    I thought it was meant for me.

You let a word fall from your lips last night,
Those lips which I may never kiss,
And I listened to it full of delight,
In the hope it might bring me bliss;
    For I thought it was meant for me − for me −
    I thought it was meant for me.

You let a tear fall from your eyes last night,
Those eyes which may never regard me,
And there was an end of my vision bright
For I knew you would discard me;
    For I knew it was meant for me, alas!
    I knew it was meant for me.[17]

Elspeth's wild bird of a husband could not be tamed. There is never the slightest suggestion that he was unfaithful to her, and the later letters of their marriage continue to be phrased in the loving child-language of their courtship; but Kenneth was complete within himself, and could not understand that his wife belonged to that other group of human beings, who need to see themselves reflected through others in order to be certain that their existence has any significance. There was, however, one consolation for Elspeth. The child which would be born in the spring was the tangible outcome of the love between Minkie and her Dino. The long, burdened months of sickness and sadness would end in triumph.

11

Mouse

The baby was born, a little prematurely, on 12 May 1900. He was a small, delicate thing whose barely fleshed fingers and pinkly convoluted, almost translucent ears at once earned him the nickname of Mouse. Kenneth, with his deep regard for animals, could not have given his son a more affectionate title, and it suited the little creature far better than his gravely Scottish official name of Alastair. There is no record of how long his delivery took, or of Elspeth's state of health afterwards, but there must be a suspicion that she found the birth traumatic, and did not recover from it for a long time. Previous biographies have suggested that sexual relations between her and Kenneth hardly existed after the honeymoon, and have ascribed this to Grahame's unsuitable choice of wife and his growing coldness towards her, but it may well have been that she was terrified that she might become pregnant again. Contraceptive advice was only just becoming available through the work of such pioneers as Annie Besant and the Malthusian League, but it was not a matter that could be talked about between a husband and wife as inhibited and charged with sexual embarrassment as the Grahames.

Elspeth perhaps found herself in a terrible impasse. She had staked everything on the love of her Dino, and yet its results had been traumatic and agonising, and she now felt compelled to avoid the very thing she had so much wanted. The only safeguard against further pregnancy was the sad, self-damaging one of separation from her husband, but, since the fear of his attentions could not be admitted or even mentioned, her action had to be explained in terms of physical incapacity. Throughout her years of invalidism, Elspeth's symptoms were never easily defined. There was much talk of nervous debility and obscure muscular pain, and since she had shown no sign of any such complaints before the birth of the child, it seems obvious that it was this event which had triggered a dramatic change in her capabilities.

She wrote of her dilemma in a limping, broken-winged metre which is no less touching for its ineptness.

Dear, leave me for a while,
Endeavour to forget
Dance with the rest and smile
You may be happy yet

But I have fought with fate
And fallen in the strife,
Your love dear comes desolate
Leave me to live my life

I cannot keep your love
I may not give you mine
Take up your flowers and glove
Let others see no sign

Forget your grief and me
But I'll remember you
Your tender sympathy
So innocent and true.[1]

The poem exists only in draft form, in a pencil-written notebook where the completed lines emerge from a thicket of crossing-out and amendment. It is very different from the dismayed, angry verse she had poured out in the previous year, complaining of her husband's indifference as he sought Graham Robertson's company rather than hers. This is written out of tragic paradox, in the grip of a fear which she had never previously imagined possible.

Elspeth's practicality, however, had not completely deserted her. During one of the long periods which she spent away from home, taking a "cure" at Woodhall Spa, she began to make down-to-earth enquiries. Among her papers is a letter from a Muriel Bure, to whom she had evidently written in search of information about birth control, for the reply is firm on the question of prescriptions, saying that no doctor would prescribe except for his own patients. It is bizarre to reflect that Elspeth was at the time being attended by no less than three doctors, on friendly enough terms with two of them to be exchanging chatty informal letters – and yet she could not bring herself to ask the fundamental question which probably lay at the heart of her malaise.

Her correspondent went on to advise Elspeth, that she could buy "some things called quinine pessaries", and also recommended that she should use a small sponge soaked in antiseptic. "As it is difficult for a woman to know when a man wants it, she can without doing herself any harm put one in every evening . . . If you should feel nervous about getting the sponge out you can fasten a little silk cord to it, to take it out with." The ultimate reassurance, however, came in her last words. "If it is put up high enough, he never needs to know that it is done."[2]

At the time of Alastair's birth, even this inadequate knowledge had been denied to Elspeth. The shock of what she had been through had been compounded by another circumstance, which undoubtedly added a further burden. As the baby's eyes begen to try and focus on the things around him, it became evident that something was wrong. He had been born with a congenital cataract in his right eye, which was completely sightless. The other one, afflicted with a pronounced squint, was also suspect. When Mouse was eighteen months old, Dr William Collins, later knighted for his expertise in ophthalmology, wrote to Grahame to confirm that the "good" eye was what he called "over-sighted". The little boy was, in fact, more than half-blind.

He was to be the Grahames' only child, for, whether by accident or design, Elspeth did not conceive again. She was almost constantly ill or exhausted or upset, demonstrably unable to pick up the domestic reins. Her capable housekeeping dwindled into a narrow reluctance to spend money, and she made no attempt to keep her own appearance attractive or even presentable. From being unconventional, she began to slip towards a slatternly eccentricity. Every outward sign indicated that the birth of Alastair had been a traumatic shock to her, not least because the baby, on whom such hopes had been pinned, was the victim of a physical handicap.

Typically, the disaster was one which the Grahames would not face. Elspeth in particular denied the distress which her physical state made so plain, declaring that Mouse was the perfect child, not only normal, but talented to a breathtaking degree. Her later writing about him reads like worship. He was, for her, the equivalent of Elizabeth Barrett Browning's Pen, a brilliant, beautiful boy who could only have been created by genius parents. Kenneth, too, had no way of coming to terms with his son's disability. He did not carry self-deception to Elspeth's rhapsodic extent, but he ignored the problem. His function in the child's life was to be a good father, as Kenneth understood fathers. He would tell him stories and recite poems, and once the delicate little creature was old enough and strong enough, he would take him for walks and introduce him to the books which spelled magic.

By the time Alastair was a year old, Elspeth's family background had changed considerably. Fletcher Moulton had remarried in 1901, and, faced with the prospect of a new mistress for the house in Onslow Square, Courtauld and Winifred had decided to remove themselves elsewhere. Courtauld bought a house in Pont Street, number 59, and recalled later that he and his sister had gone into rooms at 12 Old Burlington Street until the house was ready. Their stepfather's wedding had taken place in Italy. "We decorated the house with flowers for his return," Courtauld said.[3] From that time onward, Winifred lived with her brother and kept house for him, while pursuing her own artistic career. The older brother, Harold, had already left home, so Fletcher Moulton was effectively separated from his stepchildren in any domestic sense.

Alastair, meanwhile, grew slowly into the theatrical role in which he had been cast, and found that he was expected to be nothing less than an infant prodigy. He was cared for by a nanny whom he might bully as he wished, and every word he uttered in the presence of his strangely tense and excited mother was seized upon with rapture, to be quoted again and again. Visitors found themselves obliged to join in the chorus of praise. Chalmers, writing in 1933 under the strict eye of Elspeth, ventures no dissenting note, depicting Mouse as unreservedly saintly. He was, he said "of that rare infancy who come, we cannot know why though we humbly presume that it is for some high purpose . . .". Arthur Quiller-Couch, seeing the baby for the first time, reputedly said, "Never be afraid for a boy with a head shaped like his".[4] In all the worship, only one small girl, a few years later, put in a word of criticism. "You are only a baby who has swallowed a dictionary," she said, though Elspeth interpreted this as a compliment to her son's "beautiful" speaking voice.[5]

The enforced perfection makes it difficult to see what the child himself was really like, and it is odd that the considerable bulk of his early letters have not previously been drawn upon as evidence. In his infancy, Mouse had a Dutch nanny who left no written record of those first years, but his later governess, Miss Naomi Stott, was a fluent, perceptive writer who contributed some valuable insights. "He lived a great deal in an imaginary land of his own making," she said. "He called it 'Puppyland where it is never silly to be silly'."[6] The irony is tragic. Kenneth Grahame, famous throughout the country for his insight into the perceptions of children, had a small son so pressurised by the necessity to live up to his parents' expectations of him that his "little territory" had to be a land where one could romp as freely as a young animal, with no need to be sensible or clever.

Despite her professed delight in her son, Elspeth, through her continued weakness, maintained a centre-stage position in Kenneth's concern during these years. It has previously been thought that the couple never left home during Alastair's infancy, but the little boy's first letters, written in wobbly capitals with a black dot between each word, are to his absent parents. "Dear Mum I was sad when you went off", "Dear Dad I hope you like Devon", "Please come home soon". The letters are not dated, but the writing is that of a very young child, obviously helped by an adult. One of them is surprisingly long.

Dear Mum & Dad Will you tell me what you keep in the Xmas box
I gave you at Xmas Since you went away the house hasn't been so
chirpy. I wish you'd come back from Mouse.[7]

Grahame's own undated letters imply that Elspeth was away on a cure at quite an early date, for Mouse is still young enough to be put in a pram.

The writing is a continuation of the Dino style, though in letters of this period Kenneth signs himself as "Monty" or "Mont".

> . . . I devoted ole aternoon to im & walked wif im to gardens, played, ad tee togever under tree . . .
>
> We played a good deal on Albert Memorial steps, watched & criticised motors, & practised yumpy-yumps & trick-climin. Then ee wos wheeled orf & ad tea in pram, wile I ad a well-earned sigrette in a green arm-tare [chair] by is side; & once e ad got is mouf well stuffed wif brednbutter ee sed softly "now tell me about the mole!" So the ole of the time I ad ter [s]pin out mole [s]tories. Eee is cummin on tremenjus both in ideas & language, & misses nuffin – there was a tory in which a mole, a beever a badjer & a water-rat was characters & I got them terribly mixed up as I went along but ee always stratened em out & remembered wich was wich.

This letter is filed immediately after a very different one on Bank of England paper, dated 24 November 1903, written for an urgent purpose.

> Darling M. – just a line to tell you not to be alarmed at any rumours or statements on posters & c. There was a lunatic in here this morning, "shooting free" with a revolver, but *nobody* got hurt at all, except the lunatic, who was secured after some trouble.
>
> Yrs
>
> M

The actual events were bizarre. At about eleven in the morning, a respectably dressed man came into one of the offices in the Secretary's department, giving his name as George F. Robinson. He asked to see the Governor of the Bank, whom he named as Sir Augustus Prevost. Prevost was, in fact, no longer the Governor but this seemed no cause for alarm. Mr Robinson was asked whether he would agree to see the Bank Secretary instead, to which he consented, and he was then shown into a waiting-room while someone went to fetch Kenneth Grahame.

When the Secretary arrived, Mr Robinson fixed him with a stern eye and repeated his original request to see the Governor. Grahame explained that he was not in the building, and Robinson nodded. "I suppose you're in charge, then," he said. He then thrust a large roll of manuscript towards him, ordering him to read it. Grahame took the roll in one hand, but was irritated by the man's behaviour and refused to look at the documents, asking Mr Robinson somewhat curtly to state his business. From that moment onwards, the events were surreal.

'Well, if you won't, then –" and Robinson produced a service revolver.

189

Grahame fled, slamming the door behind him, colliding as he did so with one of the Directors who was just about to enter. From inside the room, Robinson fired three shots. The door was not locked, and he burst out of the room and fired a further shot at a messenger in the corridor, then bolted into the Directors' Library, where the head doorkeeper had the presence of mind to turn the key on him. Grahame had by this time sent for the police, but Robinson threatened to shoot anyone who came in, and eventually the fire brigade was deployed to knock him off his feet with a powerful hose-jet. It turned out later that his only three "live" bullets had been fired at the Secretary and the others were blanks, but this, of course, was not realised at the time. A frantic struggle ensued, but Robinson was finally strapped into a strait-jacket and thrust into an ambulance. He was decanted at Cloak Lane police station and charged with "Wandering in Threadneedle Street: deemed to be a lunatic". *The Times* of the next day reported the affair in loftily dispassionate terms, remarking that "from statements made by the prisoner, he appears to hold Socialist views". Other press reports were more explanatory.

The prisoner pleaded that his rolled documents had been tied at one end with a black ribbon, at the other with a white. These documents had been presented to Mr Grahame length-wise. It had therefore been open to Mr Grahame to grasp either one of the two ends. Instead of the innocuous white end Mr Grahame had preferred to take the end bound by the black ribbon, thus proving that Fate demanded his immediate demise. Mr Robinson looked upon himself as a mere instrument in the matter and quite without prejudice or guile.[8]

He was committed to Broadmoor.
Elspeth received a concerned letter from her stepfather:

We both send you our deepest sympathy in the shock and anxiety which you have had today. Nothing but the promptness and presence of mind of your husband could have avoided a terrible calamity and you must be very proud of his having shewn himself so cool and courageous. But don't let yourself brood over it – such an outrage cannot occur again. It was an accident that he was the one in danger & it is not possible that such carelessness will be allowed in future on the part of the Bank servants.[9]

His was not the only letter. That the author of *The Golden Age* should have been put in such mortal danger horrified hundreds of devoted readers, and the Bank was inundated with expressions of sympathy and outrage.

For Grahame, the incident was frightening in symbolic terms rather than

190

in actual ones. Evidently, there was no longer any stability. *Punch*, putting an ironic finger on a popular metaphor of the time, remarked that "Mr Kenneth Grahame is wondering what is the meaning of the expression, 'As safe as the Bank of England' ". It seemed now that none of the grand old institutions could feel themselves to be unassailable. Their solidity and old-ness and accumulated layers of flavour and tradition were no longer enough to ensure respect.

The episode started Grahame on a new train of thought, much of which would eventually find expression in the book for which he is known in our own time. Defensiveness and definition of values was not a new theme to his contemporaries, although he found them alarmingly unfamiliar. Twelve years previously, in April 1891, the *Quarterly Review* had carried an article on "The Prospects of Conservatism in England", which, dwelling on the coming election, looked with sober foresight at the future political conflict. The outcome, it said, would depend

> upon the extent to which the wealthier classes by their public spirit, and practical sympathy with their poorer neighbours, justify to the people the existing bases of society.[10]

Justification was a new idea to Grahame, as it was to thousands of instinc-tive Conservatives who were in fact closer to being conservationists than members of the political right wing. Previously, he had always assumed that the experiencing of a richly flavoured life, complete with all its traditions and mysteries and nonsensicalities, was a good thing – but now there seemed to be a new idea abroad, that an imposed system of equality would be better than all the muddle and unfairness of a system which was not in essence systematic at all. For Grahame, life could not be detached from nature, which was self-evidently perfect. He had begun to understand this as a child, at a time when he was completely without money or the power of self-determination, but his lack of social authority made no difference to his instinctive pantheism. To him, the natural was the only significant good. So why, he reasoned, did people think that having money would put them in touch with the delight of natural life? One either appreciated it or one did not, and the difference lay in the quality of the appreciation, not in the thing appreciated. But now, there was a demand for definition, as if life's glory had to justify itself in the eyes of those who were not sure if it was worth wanting. As he had pointed out in *Pagan Papers*,

> The sylvan glories of yonder stretch of woodland renew themselves each autumn, regal as ever. It is only the old enchantment that is gone, banished by the matter-of-fact deity, who has stolidly settled exactly where Lord A's shooting ends and Squire B's begins.[11]

Madmen were in the streets. Nothing was sacred.

The sense of needing to defend all that he held precious began to grow slowly in Grahame's mind, but still he wrote nothing. He was never a polemicist, and could not start now to put down abstract ideas. These, to him, were no more than scaffolding rods, gradually accumulating in his mind, ready for whatever material should eventually clad the structure they would make. The cladding would have to come from something as personal as his own childhood, just as it had done to give form to *The Golden Age*; but nothing presented itself. It was five years since he had published anything, and that had been the review of Evelyn Sharp's book. It seemed a long time ago.

The public, however, had not forgotten him. Letters of appreciation continued to trickle in, most of them unanswered, but one particular communication tickled him immensely. In an essay called "Marginalia", published in *Pagan Papers* eleven years previously, he had expressed a liking for broader margins in book design, expanding the idea into the suggestion that the ideal page would be one which was all margin and no text. Josephine Hoveed, a young woman from San Francisco, took him at his word, sending him a one-sheet essay called *Margin* which consisted of entirely blank paper. This merited a reply.

> Dear Madam: Please accept my sincere thanks for the beautiful copy wh. had reached me of your new work 'Margin' — a copy which I understand exhausts the Edition & baffles the clamorous public. Nothing cd be more charming, or more acceptable, than the binding, lettering and general bodily format of
>
> But the format must give place to the pleasure the contents have given me. For your verse has a limpid spaciousness, a clarity, & a breadth wh. soothes while it satisfies, and throughout there is a haunting suggestion of broad heaths, moonlight, wind-swept spaces & the Open Road. To these positive virtues one must add the negative qualities — an absence of all that frets or jars — the superior English of the Printer's Reader — the Celtic Twilight or the Split Infinitive. Such verse as yours must it seems to me go far — it must arrive. Indeed it has done both. Hence this line.[12]

When the gunman incident happened, Mouse was away in Broadstairs, staying with Mrs Merrick, a cousin of Elspeth's, who wrote from Goodwin Cottage, Shuttle Road, to thank the Grahames for their telegram to assure her that all was well. It was not his first visit, for there is a photograph of him at perhaps eighteen months old, taken by a Broadstairs photographer, showing the child befrocked and petulant, frowning near-sightedly at the camera. When Elspeth's sister Winifred painted a portrait miniature of

Alastair, she slimmed his fat cheeks and amended the gaze of puzzled suspicion which is so like his father's, showing instead an elfin, curly-haired
child whose unblemished eyes stare with almost Beethoven-like intensity at
something beyond the frame. The rosebud mouth and firm little chin combine to give him a look of authoritative charm.

At three-and-a-half, however, the child was not easy to look after. He had
devised a game which involved lying down in the road in front of approaching motor-cars, thus forcing them to a halt, and it may be that it had
seemed prudent to send him away from London. The steeply sloping traffic-
free streets of the little seaside town were better suited to a small boy obsessed by a potentially lethal game.

The dating of the incident also makes it clear that the stories which would
later be incorporated into *The Wind in the Willows* were already well known
to Mouse. Elspeth's own recollection of their beginning is, according to her
own evidence, a good six months later. The Grahames were to go out to
dinner, and Elspeth was waiting for her husband in the hall. Growing impatient, she sent the maid, a Wiltshire girl called Louise, upstairs to find out
why the master was taking so long, and was told, "He's with Master Mouse,
Madam, he's telling him some ditty about a Toad".[13]

In Elspeth's book of reminiscences, *The First Whisper of 'The Wind in the
Willows'*, this is stated to be the earliest sign of her husband's classic work,
but the letters make it evident that Kenneth and his son had enjoyed a close
literary association for many months previously. Elspeth herself was
wretched. In a miniature painted by Winifred, she appears with her hair
cut short in the modern manner so that it curls like her son's but her face
is sadly changed. The eyes which were full of curiosity are now dark-circled
as if from much weeping, and the eyebrows have a lift which was not there
before, denoting a weary surprise. The mouth is formless, its half-smile
obliterated by the effect of a shock which has left it tremulous. By the time
Alastair was two years old, his mother was spending an increasing amount
of time in bed, or reclining on a couch, drinking hot water.

Later in life, Elspeth proved herself to be extraordinarily resilient, taking
the lead in all practical affairs, but at this stage, she had withdrawn completely. Though she and Kenneth believed absolutely in the reality of her
illness, there is every sign that her troubles were psychosomatic in origin.
External stress resulted in instant nervous collapse, and it seems all too plain
that she was subconsciously seeking an escape from her place in a trio which
had polarised into a close partnership between father and son, with wife/
mother as the odd one out. If she were terrified of the results of further
sexual intercourse, the natural righting of the balance through the husband-
and-wife relationship was denied her.

Kenneth was always simplistic about her sufferings, and saw only that his
wife could not take an active part in the family. It was therefore doubly his

job to provide Mouse with parental care. The child's physical needs were well met by the nanny, whom he called in his letters "Dutchy" or "D", plus a staff of servants, but Kenneth took an almost obsessive fatherly interest in his son. Every scrap of childish conversation is recorded, with no apparent sense of irony, in the mawkish nursery-language that continued to be the means of communication between him and Elspeth. Continuing his account of the Albert Memorial outing, he said,

> I erd im telling D arterwards "And do you no Nanny, the Mole saved up al is money & went & bought a motor car! gave hundreds of pounds for it! fancy, an *animal*, Nanny!'
> You will perceive by this that Mr Mole has been goin the pace since he first went his simple boatin spedishin wif the Water Rat. Arter that we ran races on the grass. Poor little fellow! he said, wif one of his *shivers*, "O I am enjoying myself!" I'm sure the pleasures offered im were simple & tame enough. Then we walked ome quietly . . . Ope you down by now, & soon fit again.[14]

At about this time, probably early 1904, Grahame's letters began to dwell on the idea of renting a cottage in the country. He spoke of house-hunting in South Ascot ("there don't seem to be any *shops*"), and was attracted by a house called Woodside, though he was dismayed to find a new vicarage being built to the rear of it, "close to invisible devil-building". He enclosed a sketch-map which made it clear that he meant the church. As a daily commuter to the City, he was evidently beginning to yearn for a more rural setting in which to spend his hours of freedom.

> I'm sure you understand, that it not *house* I in love wif, but situashun
> – ouse is small, & we may ave to put up wif minor inconveniences.
>   Ever lovin
>   Monty

For the most part, though, his letters were concerned with the precious minutes spent with Mouse.

> Mouselin got the start of me this mornin & a ee went downstares I erd im shoutin "I will wait for you at the corner Daddy!" Then I erd some female gigglins & then, in accents of orfle contemp, "Now, mind, I'm not goin out wif *you*! I'm goin out with my deer daddy" ("*You*" was poor white female trash.) We jogged along to corner togevver, then ad to leeve him, as so late; ee wave angkercher contentedly.

On another occasion:

I ad ter run, it bein late, & Mousekin ee make a break fer the open country, & last thing I see was two full grown women oldin im in air, neck n'eels, like a sack of taters, & ee rorin larfter.

Grahame's own barely concealed contempt for women communicated itself to his son, and the little boy obviously felt that he had an ally in his father. One morning, Kenneth reported with some pleasure, he "made desprit tempt to brake down door of barf-room (I wanter see you in your barf, daddy". The child's behaviour, however, was becoming intolerable to everyone else.

Arter tea of corse ee was furiously norty – that's is bad time. Eee as a way of usin is *boots* on the form & edd of a defenceless female wich ee must ave picked up in the East End, & one or twice British public neerly interfere.

In another letter:

greeve say came upon im in very act of violence, slappin very small girl (stranger). He splane that ee "wanted to" & I ad no argment set up gainst that. I arst if ee often did it, & D. ses ee as a leanin that way & – this is perfetic – Wee-wee, oo very fond of im, is little frade of im, & ses evasivly, "You *wouldn't* hit me, would you, Mouse?"
"Yes I wood," ee says – & often does. On other and, there are two girls [nameless] oo ee meets mornins & them "ee never slaps, cos they stand up to im."

It is, by today's standards, breathtaking that a man can say he has no argument to set up against his son's slapping of a small girl because he wanted to. Grahame's detachment from the moral judgement which he might have considered "Olympian" was total. A few days later, he mentioned a heated discussion "as to wevver ee was to walk to gardins (wich ee maintane) or go in pram & I ad no time to argue so left him kickin is D. about body". He added, in one of the throwaway lines so characteristic of him: "Sined Woodside greement today".

The letters contain no reference to any opinion expressed by Elspeth about the Woodside house – or, indeed, about anything else. She is as neutral as a vase of flowers. At one point he says sternly, "You ad better make up mind to come back Monday 3rd, & so get all the good out of the place you can". The place in question was probably Woodhall Spa, where Elspeth certainly went for a long cure in May 1904, but it seems certain that this was not her first visit.

Meanwhile, Mouse's attacks on small girls continued.

Dutchy tell me ow fritefle ee beave little girls – ow ee not only smack them but dig is ten fingers deep into their tender flesh – ow ee let little boys severely alone, from motives of prudence – ow the Keepers ave made fishle report that ee worst boy wot enters Gardings daly. Report gone in to (1) Ranger (2) Office of HM. Works (3) London County Council – & akshin expected shortly.

Kenneth's admiration remained undimmed, although Mouse was making himself unpopular. The child's growing contempt for those who could not control him extended even to his father.

Wen ee cum down ee say wot you doin wile you waitin fer me – I say umbly I readin mornin paper – ee say contempshus wy don't you read a *book*! Spose I shall be ordered t'ave mornin' prayers nex.

Grahame perhaps made the mistake of assuming that his son was himself all over again, endowed with the same sensitivity, and the same careful, self-regulatory awareness. He forgot, or did not recognise, that his own childhood was devoid of the indulgent adults who provided Mouse with a rapturous (or, at least, silently enduring) audience for every precocious utterance. In his eyes, Mouse could do no wrong. In a letter postmarked 1 July 1904, he strikes the familiar note of besotted tolerance.

. . . Larst I sor of im ee runnin up Broad Walk tords me, a little white dot, larfin, & Gnädige frau flat-foot a very bad second.

In the same letter, he goes on to give Elspeth worldly advice on how much to tip the staff at the Spa, suggesting 5/- each for the second chambermaid, two young waiters, page, kitchen boy and stillroom maid, with 10/- for the band. "Barfwoman will probably be £1 to 30/- or £2," he added, and concluded in a mixed style of expression, "I expect I'd better send you £15, to cover all possibilities – which I do tomorrer."

Kenneth's tendency towards baby-talk increased in direct proportion to the embarrassment caused by the subject matter. Anything to do with sexuality produced instant regression, but so did all references to his eminence as a writer. He obviously felt that this touched on the sore point of Elspeth's slightly erratic spelling and the derisive rejection of her poems. When a correspondent of *Tit-bits* interviewed him, he was thrown into a state of near-incoherence when telling Elspeth about it and he followed his account with a Dino-gabble which is barely comprehensible.

Ope Mink will go on walkin in parves were hevver & banks & things cos woodland orter be bewtifle in ortum – As mink got room to likin? And ow they *feed* er? & wot table mink titt at? & is ed water tober?

Being translated, he wants to know what table Elspeth sits at and whether the head waiter is sober, but he reduces it to gibberish, and it is hard to remember that the writer is the Secretary of the Bank of England.

Elspeth's release from Woodhall Spa had not lasted long. In the spring of 1904, there had been a new and additional reason for her nervous prostration. An extraordinary upheaval had begun to make itself felt in Elspeth's family. Her youngest brother, Courtauld (who was destined to become Lord Courtauld-Thomson), had always been particularly astute, and now, a successful businessman in his own right, he began an investigation into the will his mother, Clara, had left at her death in 1888. Robert Thomson, the father of all her children, had left her a wealthy woman in her own right, and she still had the income resulting from the patents on his various inventions. This income was left in trust to John Fletcher Moulton, to be divided among the four children.

Uncharacteristically, Clara had not been very specific in her will as to how the funds should be administered. Death does not always come tidily, and it may have been that, at the last, she found herself overtaken unexpectedly and without ceremony. In the emotion engendered by the deathbed scene in which Fletcher Moulton promised to be "more than a father" to his stepchildren, the last thing anyone thought of was a legal formalising of the financial arrangements, and it would have seemed graceless to cavil at the fact that Clara's will was made out in John Fletcher Moulton's handwriting.[15]

Gradually it became evident that the head of the household, far from being the perfect father-substitute, was in fact pathologically mean. At Elspeth's marriage, he gave her just £250, although Courtauld had expected a settlement of £5,000 or an allowance of £300 a year, which would be more appropriate for a man of his wealth. He reflected bitterly that Fletcher Moulton "never offered me a single memento of my parents of which his house was full. I remember asking if I could have three pictures of my father's for my new house and his objecting on the grounds that he would have to repaper the walls of the room in which they were if I had them. Eventually he gave them to me. I then gave him in return a silver tea service for which I had paid about £100."[16]

Courtauld discovered that no written arrangement existed as to the administration of the trust. Fletcher Moulton was, in fact, the sole trustee. Asked by his stepson to produce an account of payments to Elspeth and Winnie, Fletcher Moulton flatly refused.

Elspeth realised for the first time that during the years of living in her stepfather's house and managing his social programme on a scant allowance which left her nothing for her own clothes and expenses, she should have been receiving £300 a year from her mother's bequest. Her marriage did not invalidate the allowance; accumulated over the years since Clara's death, she was owed a lot of money. Fletcher Moulton tried to steamroller the thing through, but Courtauld was adamant that justice should be done, and, in his sisters' names, he brought a civil action against their stepfather.

At this point, Courtauld became an important influence in Grahame's life, and remained close, both as an adviser and friendly brother-in-law, for the rest of his life. The two men were not unalike in their creative, self-motivated attitude to life, though Courtauld had a breezy confidence which Kenneth could never aspire to. Despite their similarities of outlook, their upbringing could not have been more different; whereas Kenneth had been deprived of parental support at an early age, Courtauld had been the dar-ling baby of the family. His very name augured success, for it was given by Samuel Courtauld, co-founder of the silk-manufacturing firm which was to grow into a worldwide corporation, as the condition on which he consented to be the boy's godfather.

Courtauld was no academic. He escaped into Eton, where his prowess on the games field did something to offset his poor scholastic record, but he was threatened with expulsion unless his handwriting improved. With wry humour, he recalled a school holiday spent in practising pot-hooks under the eye of a writing master, the result of which was that the school could then realise "how inadequate my answers were to their questions".[17] He had a shrewd eye to the benefits of association with fellow pupils, however, particularly those with titled or influential parents, and this pragmatic suc-cess-seeking enabled him to benefit from an education to which he was academically quite unfitted. He was accepted for Magdalen College, Ox-ford, but failed his exams and was sent down, though the influential Clara managed to win a reprieve for him, and he went on to get his degree. Fletcher Moulton tried to get him into the legal profession, but that was pushing things a little too far. Courtauld abandoned the Inner Temple, preferring to accompany his beloved mother on her expeditions to buy antiques and attend to her various business ventures. It was thanks to being bumped about in a carriage with iron-clad wheels that he decided to design his own vehicles, and he quickly made a success of the Coupé Company, which sold light, quiet, well-sprung coaches, running on the well-sprung tyres which his father had invented.

The delay in tackling Fletcher Moulton about his shabby financial treat-ment of Elspeth and Winifred was caused largely by the fact that Courtauld had gone to Alaska. Having set up the coach company, he had been asked by a firm of financiers to go out to investigate a gold-mine interest in which, they suspected, they were being defrauded. Fletcher Moulton lay behind this suggestion, for, with his usual bad business judgement, he had invested heavily in the enterprise.

During this time abroad, Courtauld began to realise how narrow and grasping his apparently affectionate stepfather really was. "I managed sev-eral pieces of business for him (chiefly trying to rescue money for him which he had put in rotten concerns)," he said, "but he never paid me anything for doing so."[18] Conversely, when Fletcher Moulton had put money into Courtauld's carriage business, he had demanded five per cent compound interest, and had asked his stepson £200 a year for living in the Onslow Square house, which Courtauld paid.

It was against the background of growing resentment and disillusion that the lawsuit against Fletcher Moulton was brought, for when Courtauld returned to find his sisters struggling to run their stepfather's house on an utterly inadequate allowance of money, he ran out of patience. The case took a long time to prepare. Meanwhile, a charade of good relations was maintained. Courtauld managed the household's carriages and horses, and was assiduous in promoting his stepfather's career. He claimed in a legal statement that Fletcher Moulton's success in winning the parliamentary seat at Launceston was entirely due to him, for, having heard of the vacancy, he had ridden through the night to attend the selection committee and persuade them of his stepfather's suitability as a candidate.

As preparations for the case neared completion, Elspeth, married by now, and in the state of debility which had followed the birth of Alastair, was thrown into panic. The thought of appearing in court terrified her, for it ran completely counter to her usual technique of relying on helpless charm. In the summer months of 1904, there is an interesting exchange of letters between Grahame and Courtauld Thomson. Writing from the rented cottage, Woodside, Kenneth reveals that, on receiving a letter from her brother on 3 March 1904, Elspeth took to her bed with "an acute inflammation of the tissues of the neck". Her condition remained incapacitating. On 7 August, Kenneth wrote to his brother-in-law.

. . . you & Waterhouse ought to know as early as possible how soon & to what extent you can count upon E in regard to evidence possibly in the witness-box. Briefly, she has been very ill, since the spring, from nervous shock – has undergone one cure at Woodhall Spa, which has done her great good & is recuperating steadily. But her Doctor, who was down here last week, is sending her back to W. Spa for another course of baths when she leaves this, & does not think that for this year at the very least she can face any nervous strain or excitement. . . . I know you don't think that he [Moulton] will come into court – but we have always gone on the assumption that he will, hence E's desire that you should know as soon as possible how she is situated.

Five days later, he wrote again, in a flurry of self-deluding denial.

I fear I have expressed myself badly, or imperfectly, in a letter written solely to foreshadow a contingency which may never occur. E is *not* worrying or bothering about the case at all, simply because she has not been either asked or allowed to do so.

Again, the psychological ignorance is astounding, together with the assumption that a woman would only feel that which her husband allowed her to. However, working on that premise, Grahame did not hesitate to send his wife a communication from their solicitor, Harper. Significantly, the meat of the letter is conveyed in standard English.

> Darlin M. Here is a letter from Harper, with "proof" of his evidence. You will see what he says about altering freely & so on.
> I have thought it better not to make any notes or communicate myself, but on p. 10 he [Harper] seems to have gone a bit astray as to the dinner in August 1902, so I have altered that bit in pencil, but if I'm not right please alter it further.
> > Ever lovin
> > > Mont

The following day, he wrote to say that Harper thought it *extremely unlikely* (Grahame's italics) that the case would come on before February 1905. This, he said, came from Linklater, the opposition solicitor, "which may imply that they are not particularly anxious to face the music".

Elspeth was not reassured, despite her husband's instructions to "dimiss the matter from your mind at present". A few days later, he wrote with barely concealed irritation to point out that

> you have been assured that you will not be asked to attend in Court unless *quite* physically fit, so I am sorry that you still worry, as is evident from your letter. Please do not do so any more.

He goes on:

> Of course we should all have liked to have had it, say next week, & have got it over; but the fact that the postponement (wh. we can't help) seems to emanate from the other side, looks rather as if, now they know you intend to go into Court, (of wh. they were previously more than doubtful) they are "sparring for wind" & we may hear from them shortly. Nothing more from Harper today.

It seems that Elspeth never lived in the South Ascot house with which Kenneth had so impetuously fallen in love. On 6 August 1904, when she was at Woodhall Spa, he wrote to Courtauld:

This little house is in the pine woods & very cool & restful – though Mouse says frankly that he finds it dull. Perhaps he's right. We have got it till the 15th Sept., after which date we are rather indefinite.

In fact, he and Mouse went for the second year running to Broadstairs. In an earlier letter to Elspeth, he had mentioned how the little boy, mistaking the Serpentine for the "river wot mole & water rat got upset in", still referred to oars as "row-sticks" – "as ee did at Brorstairs".

From the Royal Albion Hotel in the little Kentish seaside town, Kenneth wrote to his wife about Mouse's rather odd reaction to the holiday presents he had been given. He inspected them in silence then repacked them in their bag and "started down street, cryin out 'But I've got to catch a trane!' " This phrase he had obviously picked up from his commuting father. "Ee then went down sands & played wif orl of em quite delighted. Ee was watchin a baby cryin & ee say ter me *so* sentenshus, 'There's nothin' but crying in *this world*, is there daddy?"

This letter is dated 21 September 1904, when Grahame had evidently begun his annual holiday. Mouse was as precocious as ever, for, taken to see the catch of fish being gutted,

> waded in, took possession of bucket & fish, & kept andin of em out to fishermen wot clean, saying patronizinly, "Now you've got *somebody* to help you, haven't you?" D. was orror-tricken, but ee kep on till bucket empty – & then want to play wif – well wif wot was formerly intide the fitt [inside the fish] – but I drew the line at that.
>
> I was so glad to see im playin wif nice natchral fings instead o eternal toys . . .

Within the week, Grahame had gone back to London, for he had other plans. For the first time since his marriage, he intended to go abroad, and he wanted a congenial companion to go with him. Ingenuously, he wrote to Elspeth –

> Atky as turned up 10.30 unexpected & is setting now in my chare jorin for all ee worf. Eee very keen apparently. Tommorrow we go into maps & fings.[19]

Elspeth evidently knew of the plan, but she may not have been too happy to hear that the Fowey yacht commodore, whom she detested, had "got 'kit' orl lade out on mink-bed . . .". With mounting incoherence, Kenneth went on,

> We start Friday mornin, & probably go by Newhaven & Dieppe to Pallit [Paris], were Atky got some low haunt of its own were ee bin fer 26 yeers.

Elspeth may well have turned in relief to a more sensible letter from Eliza Blunt, housekeeper at Durham Villas, who assured her that "Mr Grahame and Mr Atkinson went off to Paris this morning, left the house soon after 9 o'clock in a fourwheeler cab both gentlemen well, bright and seemed very happy". The capable woman had even managed to retrieve the hot-water bottle which Kenneth had left in the Albion Hotel in Broadstairs, by means of the magically fast post of the time.

> I hope Dear Madam you are feeling better for the Beautiful Weather but its rather foggy mornings here.
> With my duty to you, Dear Madam, I remain
> Your Humble Servant,
> Eliza Blunt

Elspeth, however, needed more than the solid support of faithful servants. She collapsed into self-pity.

> I wonder when you said good-bye
> So lightly – almost with a smile –
> If you remembered, Love, how I
> Should miss you all the weary while.
>
> For days to you like hours seem
> The hours as moments only
> And so you neither think nor dream
> Of me so sad and lonely.
>
> I wonder when we meet again
> If you'll come gaily with a smile
> As if forgetful of the pain
> I've suffered all the weary while?[20]

Kenneth wrote every day to tell Elspeth of their itinerary and to fret gently over Mouse, lamenting that "no one take im to play wif fish-guts now I'm gorn". He also, in a splutter of embarrassment, ventured to defend his friend against Elspeth's criticisms.

> Atky behavin pretty well – You ave a orfle "down" on im, but make no allowance for treemenjis convenience of avin man os dlited [who's delighted] look up time-tables, pay otel bills, do orl tippin &c &c.

It was almost as though Kenneth and his wife were locked in a competition to be the more childlike. She won most of the time by forcing him to tell her how to manage such mundane matters, but he won by relying on Atky. As if in triumph, he added that outside the hotel in Bourges was a "fountain in treet wish make nice plattin noided". If Elspeth was able to decipher that he was talking about the splashing noises of the fountain in the street, she was still left feeling that she had been out-toddlered, and she may with good reason have felt some satisfaction that her husband found Bourges the "dullest ole in Crittendom". Even the guide-books, he asserted, "admit it 'manque d'animation' wich trong langwidge for a guide-book".

On the first Sunday he attended High Mass at the Cathedral, and on the Tuesday they moved on to Mauriac. "I hope somebody rites to you from Broadstairs occasionally & say ow little sand-eel gettin on", he wrote.

The weather worsened, and the two explorers had a nasty bus journey with a peasant woman who had in a basket half a dead sheep, which she cut up and distributed to the "cutomers ong roote", but the Hotel de Bordeaux in Brives cheered them up "wif electric lite in bedrooms wich is marvellous".

From Rodez, Grahame wrote with a trace of impatience that "Atky continues to be gentle & amiable, & does *all* disagreeable work so that I feel like bride on onnymoon, but carnt get im down souf quite farst nuff. We shall not reech Tooloose till Tersday . . ."

A postcard showing Notre Dame des Voyageurs sitting on a cloud above a railway station, with sunbeams and cherubs, is written in impeccable English, being open to the public gaze, and talks of visiting an old chateau near Cahors owned by one of Atky's many friends. In Toulouse he wrote that he was longing for a letter and news of Mouse, but interrupted himself to say that a letter had just arrived – "very 'belated' – a week old – but that not mink fault". They went out to visit the chateau of "an old legitimist Cafolic family whose quaintance Atky made 28 years ago" – but the glass was falling and dark clouds were piling up. The next day, it snowed, and there was a "cuttin wind wot seem to get inside all *organs* & play on their pipes". If it were an ill omen, he was soon to know the reason why. Elspeth sent him a telegram to say that Mouse was critically ill with peritonitis.

Elspeth abandoned her cure at once and rushed down to Broadstairs, where Alastair had been taken to hospital for an emergency operation. Kenneth joined her there, conscience-stricken, in desperate anxiety about his little son. Once the crisis was past, Elspeth relapsed into invalidism, and was incapable of answering letters from the many concerned friends who had written to wish the child a speedy recovery. To Mrs Lane, Kenneth wrote of Elspeth,

It is a bad set-back for her. She had to cut short her cure just when she was getting most benefit from it, and the anxiety and strain have been very great . . . I stayed at Broadstairs till the worst danger was over, and then came back to work. The poor little fellow has suffered a great deal of acute pain, but his pluck and cheerfulness have been wonderful. It is a pathetic thing that little children are not *resentful* about undeserved pain thrust upon them, but rather apologetic than otherwise.

The last phrase may strike most parents as a little unnatural. The average child is not apologetic for being ill. If this were Alastair's response to his affliction, it suggests that he was acutely aware of the high expectations which centred round him. Coupled with his self-destructive behaviour in the path of motor-cars and his cruelty to younger and weaker children, there must be some suspicion that his life was far from stress-free.

The operation had taken place during September but, four months later, Alastair was still being cossetted in Broadstairs, it being considered impossible to risk moving him back to London. Kenneth went down to join him and Elspeth for Christmas, and wrote a conversational letter to Q on 3 January 1905.

Very many thanks for the beautiful Christmas book you have sent to poor Mouse. He is devoted to picture-books, and they are most useful now that he is mentally active again & has such long hours to get through each day. I am glad to say that since the wound healed entirely, he has forgotten his pains and terrors, and "rots" everybody all round as before. The other day when the doctor arrived he cocked his eye at his nurses whom he knew to be modest and shamefaced women beyond the ordinary, & began cheerily; "Hello doctor! Are your bowels open today?" One of the women stupidly begged him not to refer to such things – "it wasn't nice". This gave him the opening he wished for. "Not nice?" he said furiously, "then what does he say it to me for? I didn't begin it, he said it first!" And thenceforth he chanted the enquiry in plainsong, till the doctor was hustled out of the room.

There seems to have been not much wrong with Alastair at this stage, but his parents had had a terrible fright, and were taking no chances. The faithful but somewhat maladroit Miss Bradley sent the four-year-old a book of her father's Addresses, and Kenneth wrote back with a gentle irony which she did not perhaps appreciate, "It shall be put by for him beside his Horace;" he promised, "& later on it shall be read to him, but before the Horace I hope." He added, "We are rather Pagans here, by temperament; but so long as the shadow of Scotch-Calvinist-devil-worship does not cross his path I am content." This was written on 22 December 1904, and it is one of Grahame's most revealing statements, firmly deleted by Elspeth from the 1933 biography.

During that autumn and winter, Kenneth continued his Bank duties, living at Durham Villas and cared for by Eliza Blunt and the other servants Edith and Gertrude. Elspeth, despite her inability to answer letters, did not return to Woodhall Spa, but stayed in Broadstairs at the Albion Hotel, where she was able to see Mouse each day. Meanwhile, the law-suit against Fletcher Moulton continued to rumble on. Kenneth had in August written to Courtauld in uncharacteristically waspish terms about Elspeth's step-father.

I can quite imagine that M is busy providing his friends with theories to account for so preposterous a proceeding as an attempt by anyone to recover their own half-crown out of his trousers-pocket . . .

In a further letter to his brother-in-law, written after one of Kenneth's weekend visits to Broadstairs, he obviously felt that his wife was much better, and declared, "I am going to suggest to her to come back to town for a bit, as things are going so well."

Elspeth, however, proved difficult to dislodge from her new bolthole by the sea.

Darlin Mink
    I fink we ad better agree to spend one more weekend at Albion & talk it over . . . there's a good deal in what you say, though not quite so much as wot you peer to fink.

There is no clue as to the subject at issue, but a further letter pointed out, a little peevishly perhaps, that when the final bill was settled, Kenneth would have paid the Albion "bout £150 in all". Another detailed list of people to tip followed, ending with "£1 to useless pageboy".

In a letter dated 30 January 1905, Grahame sent Courtauld a cheque for £60 as Elspeth's share of Counsel's fees, and said he had returned that day from Broadstairs, where Mouse was "doing very well". Elspeth's address, he reported, was now King's Mead, Eastern Esplanade. Kenneth himself, however, had been getting increasingly depressed as the winter wore on. He admitted to a "a certain amount of 'run-downedness'", and added, "I always get that way arter turn o year. One unfailing simtum is I shirk my work − set & look at it & swear orfle but not do it." Perhaps in an effort to make good the shirking, he did not always get down to Broadstairs at the weekend, pleading that " 'affairs of state' got to be called on". He was glad to hear that Mouse was "running about room" and sent him a tode-pote-card (toad post card) which he thought the boy would like better than Cupids. Defensively, he protested that he had "not forgot sisters burfday, but not seen or fort of nuffin yet". He wrote of staying in bed until one on a Sunday, of getting more bookshelves made and then of "working like a ort" (horse) putting the books on them, but the despondency is never far below the surface.

Would like go feater or somefink for divertissement, but too bloomin cold. Detestable time o year, this – not take "no joy" in ennyfink.

The absence of joy was all too evident in Grahame's letters at this time, grumbling at Elspeth for having sent an express letter which arrived at seven in the morning when he was still asleep and conceding that a "non-press" letter which came at 9.30 did *not* wake him up. He promised, as requested, to send chocolate, said without enthusiasm that Elspeth's "Aunt Annie & Uncle Arry" had called, and complained that "the base Towny promised to take me to Peter Pan, but ave erd nuffin of im on it". This probably refers to Graham Robertson, who was the most likely person to organise such an outing.

Grahame always worried about the weather and about the possibility of catching a cold, not surprisingly after his near-fatal chest infection in the spring before his marriage, and fretted about having adequate supplies of "one-day cures and quinine". He was also curiously helpless about domestic details. In an exceptionally childish plaint to Elspeth, he said, "Mittit Blunt tay I'm out of toof-powder & you may like order a tin to be tent. You see I mention fings in order as they occur to me."

In a similar infantile confession, he expressed the fact that he missed the company of Mouse.

It teem to trange [seems so strange] not to ave him arst wot the mole & the water rat did anuvver day – keeps finkin sumone arts me suddingly evly minit – Bluntie, or pleetman [policeman] or burglar, or sumone.

In the midst of this comes a throwaway line which seems quite at variance with everything else: "Ope transmigration o souls cum orf orlrite".

This is the first clue that Elspeth was beginning to dabble in spiritualism. Kenneth makes only this single dry reference to it and, with the slowly lengthening days of February, his spirits rose a little. He sent Mouse a Valentine, but apologised for not being able to find a suitable one for Elspeth, both because "so wet this evnin" and, more oddly, because he could not find one of a red-nosed policeman kissing a smutty-faced cook. Thanking his wife for her "very buteful & chaste" offering, he declared that

Mont ee perfer the late-middle-Victorian [s]tyle now ektinkt –
    A dirty slut wif a face like thine
    Shall never be my Valentine!

This hint of a Hogarthian approach to sexuality may explain something of Elspeth's nervousness and her obvious disinclination to return to the marital home at Durham Villas. On 22 February Kenneth wrote that (the language being translated) he had been *very* busy that week with tiresome things which he detested. A week later, however, it became evident that he was determined to bring his wife and son back to London. On 2 March, he wrote to Courtauld,

> Mouse has been getting on hand over fist, & indeed I was arranging for his return this week or next. Unfortunately he has just lately developed a sore throat – there seems to have been a slight outbreak of this among children at Broadstairs. It has alarmed us somewhat, but this morning's accounts are very good, & I hope that he will be able to come up by the end of next week or not much later.
>
> And I hope his mother will then come also. She has been much agitated, of course; & has been upset in consequence. I think they will both be better up here, but the weather there has been so beautiful that they have hung on.

Five days later, the faithful Eliza Blunt wrote to Elspeth for instructions on "what food Master Alastair will want", and confirmed that she would meet the boy at Victoria Station. Elspeth, however, was remaining at Broadstairs. Perhaps she still had some hopes of avoiding the impending court case, which continued to fill her with terror. Meanwhile, Kenneth was happily reunited with his son, and resumed his gaily gabbling letters about the minutiae of life at Durham Villas.

> I told im I was orf to Titty [the City] but ee sed, "No, not yet; first you have to take my hand & say one, two, three & away, away away! & we run together down a grass hill." He is determined that the play shall be played just as it was all written down last year.

Elspeth's prolonged invalidism had put her on familiar terms with her doctors. There were long, gossipy letters from Dr Hector Mackenzie during her time at Woodhall Spa, referring to Mouse as "baby" and advising Elspeth to keep on with the head-raising exercises and to try cold soup with cream. There was no doubt that her medical advisers equated her illness with what would now be called stress. After Mouse's operation, Mackenzie wrote,

> I comfort myself with the thought that you must be in a much better condition to stand such a strain as this now than you would have been if it had come six months earlier.

207

She was attended also by Drs Moon and Gough, and the latter wrote to her frequently, with painstakingly detailed advice as to her diet, bath treatment and exercise. It is tempting to reflect that she must have been a wonderfully profitable patient.

In April 1905, the Fletcher Moulton affair finally came to court. Elspeth went into the witness box, and painted a picture of life in Onslow Square which must have fascinated and scandalised the society people who had frequented the house. Elspeth and Winifred had no money of their own, and frequently borrowed from the servants in order to supply themselves with some necessary petty cash. They also ran accounts with the butcher and other tradesmen which they paid when their carefully rationed housekeeping allowance arrived, and against which they borrowed when in desperate need of money. Elspeth admitted that she often supplied herself with up to £3 10s a week through these unofficial sources – the equivalent of sixty pounds or more at present values.

It seems extraordinary that Fletcher Moulton should have allowed these details to be brought to public knowledge. He was obviously an arrogant man, and perhaps assumed that his own connection with the legal profession would carry enough weight to get the case dismissed. He was very nearly right. Courtauld presented calculations drawn up by a professional accountant to show that Fletcher Moulton owed his stepdaughters something in the region of £10,000, but the defence claimed that the allowance for Winnie and Elspeth was set against their personal expenses "including clothes, journeys, cures, pocket money etc, etc" and that the girls had agreed to this. They denied it, but the judge ruled in favour of Fletcher Moulton, laying down that he was "to have credit for all the monies provided by him that were received or expended by the children for their own benefit".[21] With a little creative accountancy, that could have been taken to mean virtually all of it.

Courtauld threatened to appeal, but gave his stepfather a chance to settle out of court. There is a letter from the plaintiffs' solicitors dated 11 August 1906 which offers to terminate all litigation provided "the defendant shall pay to the plaintiffs the sum of £8,250 in full satisfaction of all claims . . .". Fletcher Moulton turned it down, and so the proceedings went grinding on.

It was while the appeal was pending that John Fletcher Moulton was appointed a Judge of the Court of Appeal, which added a certain piquancy to the case. From Fletcher Moulton's point of view, it was perhaps too much piquancy, for he at last gave in, after some bluster about taking the affair to the House of Lords, and settled out of court. It was not until January 1909 that the Figures of Final Adjustment appeared, written in the beautiful calligraphy of the day.[22] Moulton drew £6069-9-8 from the Temperance Building Society, and it was split between the sisters in the proportions of five-ninths to Elspeth and four-ninths to Winifred. Elspeth ended up with

£3118-1-10 and her younger sister with £2494-9-5. Their bill from the solicitors, however, was £1596-9-3, and Charles Harper wrote from the firm of Waterhouse in some apology, pointing out that Moulton had employed "a small but very highly paid army of K.C.s . . . thereby making our expenses much heavier than they need otherwise have been".

However, the business was over. Kenneth had escaped without any embarrassing personal publicity, having made only one brief appearance in court, to deny emphatically that he had any part in the case against Fletcher Moulton. If one accepts the somewhat dubious premise that his activities were all on his wife's part, the statement may just about pass as true. He had, however, been intimately involved in the negotiations, writing numerous letters to Courtauld and at one point drawing up a suggested apportionment of his own devising, which his brother-in-law did not approve. He hated to be badly thought of, and managed to emerge from the affair without any smirch on his reputation for fair dealing.

It had been a depressing winter for him during the bachelor months at Durham Villas. His good friend Graham Robertson had provided company, and he had been to Anthony Hope's wedding at St Bride's, but Bill Henley had died, and it seemed that things were giving way to a bleak new era. The turn of the century had seen the death of the old Queen, and of Ruskin, and of Arthur Sullivan. The speed limit for motor cars had been raised again, this time to twenty miles an hour, and frightening new art was being produced by Picasso and Gauguin and Cézanne. The age was no longer Victorian, and things were changing too fast for comfort. Edward's reign had brought a style curiously stripped of decoration and of leisure, a slicked-down, smoothed-out culture, half-American and half-European, in which Englishness seemed to have been forgotten. Lewis Carroll was dead and so was Oscar Wilde, leaving "De Profundis" and "The Ballad of Reading Gaol" as a combined epitaph for a man crucified by respectability. Strange foreign names had come to join Shaw and Wells and Conrad − Rostand, Strindberg, Brecht, Gorki, Ibsen, André Gide.

Although the court case had not come to a final conclusion in the spring of 1905, the worst of it was over, and the Grahame family was together again in London. Now that she had confronted the thing which had so terrified her, Elspeth was evidently in much better health and spirits.

In May, Mouse's fifth birthday was celebrated effusively, and Grahame wrote to Mrs Lane of "a visit to the Zoo − a Maypole − and a gipsy caravan with brushes and baskets which he has been selling ever since, at somewhat inflated prices". No details are offered as to whether this caravan was a toy one or life-sized but it took its place in the accumulating mental heap of material which Kenneth would use when he began to write again.

In the same year, the family went on holiday together, for what seems to have been the first time. They stayed at what Elspeth described vaguely (or evasively) as "a famous old castle", but it was in fact a return to Inveraray. Kenneth evidently took up the old family connection with Argyll, and it was during this visit that he went back to the house his father had built some forty years before. In a small notebook of reminiscences, Elspeth had jotted down that her husband "asked by Lady Constance if he wd like to be *shown* his old nursery unerringly found it for himself".[23] For some reason only known to himself, Kenneth did not enjoy the holiday, grumbling in a letter to Q that Scotland had "gone down-hill considerably since I was there last – anyhow, I didn't much care about it". The whole visit had been, he said, "a stupid idea".

Mouse, however, was having a great time. "Dutchy" had been discarded at some point during the ups and downs of the past year, and he was now looked after by Miss Naomi Stott, whose later letters are detailed and often very revealing.

> I remember how interested he was once at Inverary in an old woman who lived at a Lodge. The boy had been bathing & rain came on – it turned very cold & to try to get him warmed up, I went to the Lodge for a drink of hot water. I said, "I am sure you will befriend a Grahame." That old soul said "I remember Sheriff Grahame." So I told Mr Grahame & she was delighted & made up the fire to get the hot drink for the Sheriff's grandson. On that occasion I said "Perhaps a tot of whisky would be a help." "What?" said Mouse – "Make me lose £100?" That had been promised him if he avoided such indulgences until he was of age. I remember the pair of vases he bought as a keepsake for that old dame.[24]

Bearing in mind that money was worth perhaps twenty times as much in 1905 as it is today, the bribe was enormous, and says much about Kenneth's horror of the fate which overtook his father. It was a skeleton in the family cupboard which had been kept well hidden. Even as close a cousin as Reginald Ingles was to write later of Cunningham that he "came to grief in some way, (I never heard what it was) & went abroad".[25]

Mouse was enjoying the holiday enormously, and referred to it often in later years, urging his father to take them again to Scotland. The stories at bedtime had been reinstated, and Elspeth mentions how a fellow guest in the "famous old castle" had overheard an episode of the saga, punctuated by the child's interruptions.

Miss Stott had on arrival been subjected to the full recital of Alastair's brilliant sayings, most of which were somewhat unattractive. His resistance to being "babied" was enshrined in a train-journey vignette when, encouraged by his nurse to "look at the pretty boats", he said pettishly, "Oh, Nannie, do leave the boats in the water, they look very well there."[26] Miss

Stott herself recounted how he was asked at the end of a particular day whether he had been good enough to deserve a treat. "Yes," he said, and then admitted, "but there was a good deal of vulgar eating and arms on the table."

Poor Alastair is difficult to like, and yet he was almost certainly a deeply sensitive child, trying his best to respond to the highly charged circumstances in which he found himself. While still very young, he asked in despair, "Why is there trouble in the world?" Chalmers' account of him, written when Elspeth was still alive, is sentimental to the point of nausea, referring to him as "this brilliant little child", but there is every sign that he was pert rather than brilliant, and that he had inherited his mother's romantic tendency to self-enhancement, complete with her fears of being exposed as less than exceptional. The myth-making was a constant process, building him up as a prodigy. Of his early letters, for example, Elspeth picked the one which declared simply,

Dear Mum   I have been thinking

                                  A. Grahame

This was, she claimed, the first letter he ever wrote, but this is not true. It was the first one which features joined-up writing, but is clearly predated by the series inscribed in childish capitals, and there must be a suspicion that Miss Stott's influence had been at work, as it so often was in the boy's earlier compositions. She was an astute woman, well able to know what would please her employers.

A photograph of Mouse taken at about this time shows him seated, legs dangling but feet nonchalantly crossed, in a dark oak chair with barley-sugar-twisted armrests and legs. His head is turned aside so that it is seen in profile, perhaps to avoid revealing his eye defects, and his hair is cut in a long pageboy bob with a heavy fringe. He is dressed all in black, with a belted Russian tunic fastened at the side with huge white buttons. The overall appearance is foppish and poetic and curiously isolated. One could not imagine such a boy, in his black stockings and shiny black patent-leather shoes, entering into the rough-and-tumble of school life.

The Christmas of 1905 was a big improvement on the traumatic one spent at Broadstairs the previous year. Mouse was now in good health, despite the continuing handicap of his partial-sightedness, and the house was much visited. Old Sir John Tenniel came to see Elspeth, whom he still regarded as the little girl he had known years ago, and another old friend from the Onslow Square also arrived – Anstey Guthrie, the F. Anstey whose *Vice Versa* had put in a strong word for children when Grahame was still an anonymous young clerk. Sympathetic or not, on this occasion he chased young Alastair up to bed, growling like a wolf.

At about this time, Graham Robertson, who was a playwright as well as an artist, invited Mouse and his father to the dress rehearsal of his play for children, *Pinkie and the Fairies*, at His Majesty's Theatre, where Ellen Terry played the part of an elderly aunt. Mouse remarked, "I should have liked her very much if she had been Cinderella or the Fairy Queen, but she was only an Aunt." Robertson himself, recalling the episode, went on:

> As the author of *The Golden Age* was the greatest living authority upon Aunts ... I was naturally much wrought up by his presence at the performance and enormously relieved when he expressed approbation.
>
> And I think he really enjoyed himself – anyhow, he said less than ever afterwards, which I knew to be a good sign.

What follows is, perhaps, the best evocation of Grahame ever written.

I had hardly ever, before then, met Kenneth Grahame amongst a crowd, we had nearly always been alone together, and I remember, as he came towards me through the press, realising how distinct he was from the people round him. There was something not abnormal, but supernormal in his presence – he was the slightest bit over life-size (any painter will know what that means) – there was a splendour about him that was both of the body and the spirit. He was a being of a different race, or perhaps a throwback to what our race may have been before it became stunted and devitalised. It was the impression of a moment but I never forgot it. His good looks I had thitherto taken as a matter of course – it seemed natural that the writer of such books should look like that – but, as I then saw him, towering above his fellows, his beauty took on a new significance, showing him as the lost Arcadian, the wanderer from the Country of the Young, one who had looked into the eyes of Pan and listened to the Piper at the Gates of Dawn.[27]

The words were written in the grief of the days following Grahame's death, and were a heartfelt tribute, but Elspeth vetoed their publication. No reference to Kenneth's pre-Christian attributes were permitted.

In the following May, Mouse was six. Kenneth had perhaps been comparing his son's experience of life with his own, realising that he himself at that age had been in the middle of the two blissful years at The Mount, in Cookham. Alastair, conversely, was being brought up as a London child, in an atmosphere murky with the smoke of coal fires and now increasingly polluted by exhaust gases from the noisy and ever more popular motor-car. For him, Grahame had realised, there would be no Golden Age. Other, larger considerations loomed as well. The General Election of 1906 had produced a Liberal landslide, and, even more ominously, there were now fifty-three Labour MPs in the House. Horatio Bottomley, described by Green as a "hearty, flamboyant, gabby vulgarian", was becoming established as a public figure. London suddenly seemed impossible. It was no place in which any child, let alone Mouse, should grow up.

As always with Grahame, there was no agonising over the right decision. The solution presented itself, intact and perfect. They would move to Cookham Dene, the village of his childhood.

Within a few weeks, Kenneth had found a furnished house, The Hillyers. With a reckless disregard for the impracticalities of living in Berkshire and working in Threadneedle Street, he moved Elspeth and Mouse down there, keeping Durham Villas as a *pied à terre*. The family was installed by 27 August 1906, when Kenneth wrote to Courtauld and said they would be "staying on here for some time longer".

Mouse was delighted. His liking for the countryside was perfectly genuine, and appears consistently throughout his life, but there must be some doubt about the authenticity of a remark credited to him by his adoring mother. Anstey Guthrie, according to her, ventured to say something about the pleasures of Kensington Gardens, and the boy replied disdainfully, "Kensington *Gardens*! Simply starchy with perambulators!" The remark duly appeared in Chalmers's book, ascribed to Guthrie's memory of the boy, but in fact it appears in one of Elspeth's own notebooks. These small launderings of the truth are so common that it is tempting to discard her evidence altogether – and yet, of course, mythology is seldom totally fictitious. A lively imagination was at work somewhere, and whether in the mother or the son, after all these years, hardly seems to matter, for the pair of them were locked in the quasi-reality they had created.

Grahame himself was almost equally myth-seeking, for it never seemed to occur to him that his superiors at the Bank might not be happy about his move to Berkshire. Since his near-fatal illness, he had not really settled back into a thoroughly dutiful regard for the Old Lady and her doings. The appeal of absence through illness was enormous, and he tended to work short hours and take time off whenever he felt prompted to do so. A younger member of staff wrote later,

> I was too much of a junior to have any personal contact with him in the Bank. My only recollection is of a tall figure striding through the Secretary's outer offices shortly before four o'clock, bound for Paddington and Cookham Dene. Even in those more leisurely days it seemed an unconscionably early hour for such an important figure to be leaving for home . . .[28]

Chalmers, ever influenced by Elspeth's manufacturing of the best possible image, holds that continuing ill-health was the cause of Grahame's uncommitted attitude to his work, claiming that a Harley Street opinion had advised that Grahame should give up his sedentary City life. The story could be apocryphal, for there is no supporting evidence for it, but if it is true, the advice was soundly based. In a self-feeding syndrome, Grahame's loss of interest in the Bank was itself causing his lassitude – but Cookham Dene unleashed all his enthusiasm. Within a few months, he had found a larger and more beautiful house, Mayfield, low and rambling, thatched and meadow-bordered, an idyll of elms and buttercups and old red brick. This, surely, would be the place where he could come back to the beginning and regain touch with all that really mattered.

The rest of the year passed in busy practicality as the Grahames settled into their new surroundings. But Cookham, inevitably, had changed. The sleepy rural life of forty years ago had been infiltrated by a newly rich, faster-living set who had "discovered" the village and moved in to enjoy its charms. The old feudalism had given way to a more edgy and hyper-sensitive social system, based on an assessment of wealth and class which was in itself a new cleverness, requiring the shrewd instinct of a bridge-player. Kenneth wanted none of this. His fame no doubt brought a lot of sycophantic attention from Cookham society, but he had not come for attention – quite the reverse. He had sought to rediscover childhood secur-ity, but even here, the march of what was called progress could not be avoided. The village was no longer remote and secluded, for the process of suburbanisation had begun, bringing with it a rash of new houses, owned by people who, like Grahame himself, were daily commuters to London. Increasingly, the bedtime story for Mouse represented an interlude of sanity in a mad world.

12

The Wind in the Reeds

1907 was a year of endings and beginnings. Grahame's lack of interest in his work at the Bank was beginning to be widely obvious and, when a new Governor was appointed in the spring, the lackadaisical performance of the Secretary immediately came under his scrutiny. William Campbell Middleton was well known in the City as a man of ruthless efficiency, a tough, no-nonsense administrator who took an attitude very different from the gentlemanly tolerance of the past. While professing a conventional sympathy for a man afflicted by ill-health, he must have looked with consternation at Grahame's record of absence and short-time working. On paper, it was clear that the Bank was not getting value for its money as far as the current Secretary was concerned.

Kenneth himself seems to have been unaware of any storms ahead. He had arrived at the ultimate promotion, and now had nothing further to aim at. He was one of the Bank's established figureheads, a fixed and immutable part of its ongoing tradition, well paid and well respected. On 23 April, he was visited by the children of the Prince of Wales (later King George V). He entertained them with a magnificent tea, and allowed them to sign banknotes, each one valued at £1,000. They wrote him a simple letter of thanks from Marlborough House on the same day, signing it Edward, Mary and Henry. There had been something regal about the visit, on both sides.

Chalmers declared, with typical fulsomeness, that a later Bank Secretary had told him how, in all the Bank's history, "no visitor, whom she desired to honour, had been received so worthily as in the magnificent reign of Kenneth Grahame".[1] A certain complacency had perhaps set in; but a rude awakening was in store.

As a senior Bank officer, Grahame could count on a generous holiday allowance, and this year he was impatient to escape from even the sketchy compromise of his City attendance. He proposed to be away from May to mid-June, down in his beloved West Country which, perhaps, he hoped to find untouched by the smartness which had tainted Cookham Dene. William Campbell Middleton meanwhile had something to say. Grahame emerged from an interview with the new Governor a shaken man – so much so that he was jolted out of a nine-year silence into a barely disguised declaration of his feelings.

It was Mouse who unwittingly provided a vehicle for this expression. Part of the family mythology is that the "brilliant little child" editeda magazine called *The Merry Thought* during the years at Cookham Dene, mostly written by himself, but also contributed to by his parents and their friends. There is a play, *Beauty Born*, written in rhyming couplets, which Chalmers declares to have been Alastair's work. "It seems," he observed, "that a little boy who, barely out of the nursery, could perpetrate such a plot and action might have gone far. "Beauty Born" remains for me as remarkable a piece of 'child literature' as ever I read." Chalmers's book was closely supervised by Elspeth but, in the absent-mindedness of her later years, she refers to "our own small boy, not yet able to write, who dictated his material to his nursery-governess". The literary talent may have been that of Miss Stott, for its rather conventional rhyming and phraseology are quite un-child-like. At least one piece bears the stamp of Kenneth's own invention. "Hunting Song" could not for one moment be considered a product of the nursery.

Ye Huntsman winds ye clarion horn,
   Ye dappled hound doth yap,
Ye poacher plods his weary way,
   To set ye rabbit trap.

Ye rabbit leaps o'er thorn and bryre,
   Ye poacher to avoid,
Ye wrathful keeper seezes him,
   Ye poacher is annoyed.

Ye angler waiteth patiently,
   To catch ye bonny trout,
His patience is rewarded,
   And he hooks him by the snout.

Ye Scottish Laid to pot ye grouse,
   His neighbours all doth ask,
Ye canny Scottish gillie
   Doth drain ye whiskey flask.

Ye fat red-faced policemen,
   Ye suffragette pursue,
Ye magistrate says, "fourteen days",
   Ye suffragette says "Booh!"

Ye huntsman Cupid shooteth
   At lovers with his dart.

It never pierceth through the head,
  But always through the heart.

I pause, for now ye angry mob
  Disturbe ye poet's peace.
"Ye stocks, ye horse pond," is the cry,
  And I perforce must cease.

Kenneth Grahame had long held a conviction that poets were the natural butt of the common herd. "The fact is," he had said fourteen years ago in *Aboard the Galley*,

> the poets are the only people who score by the present arrangement; which it is therefore their interest to maintain. While we are doing all the work, these incorrigible skulkers lounge about and make ribald remarks; they write Greek tragedies on Fate, on the sublimity of Suffering, on the Petty Span, and so on; and act in a generally offensive way. And we are even weak enough to buy their books; offer them drinks, peerages, and things; and say what superlative fellows they are! But when the long-looked-for combination comes, and we poor devils have risen and abolished fate, destiny, the Olympian Council, early baldness and the like, these poets will really have to go.

Similarly, Kenneth had taken a keen (if somewhat alarmed) interest in the progress of universal suffrage, his conscience jolted by such partisan friends as Evelyn Sharp and Beatrice Harraden. In this year of 1907, Austria had granted all its citizens, male and female, the right to vote. Mouse was encouraged to read the newspapers and take an interest in current events, but the neatly compressed satirical version of them is not the work of a child of primary school age.

A better authenticated record of Alastair's actual standard is supplied by his answers to "coaching" questions set four years later by his father, just before the boy went to school at eleven years old. Asked what he knew of the Phoenix, Mouse wrote the following:

> The Phenix is an inshurance co. There is only one at a time. Before it dies it lights a bonfire and roosts on it and when it is dead a new Phenix pops out of the ashes – but is it a new one? peradventure it is the same old bird all the time?? tut-tut! a strange bird it lives 100 years.[2]

It is clever stuff for a child of his age, light-hearted and confident, but of a very different order from "Beauty Born" or "The Huntsman".

217

Whatever its authenticity as a Mouse production, *The Merry Thought*, circulated in holograph only, and offering no pay to its contributors, published a story called "Bertie's Escapade" which Kenneth signed. The piece is written with no idea at all of appeal to a larger public, for the animal characters were, Elspeth asserted, all real and well known to Mouse. This seems to be true, for it was written just after the real-life family pig had escaped from its sty, and there are references to places where Alastair had been, such as "the cliffs at Broadstairs". The story concerns Bertie the pig, who decides to go carol-singing, and sets out with the pet rabbits, Peter and Benjie, for company (Beatrix Potter's *Peter Rabbit* and *Benjamin Bunny* had appeared in 1901 and 1904 respectively, and had made their mark). The animals, seeking a quick way up the cliff, are guided by Peter down a tunnel which

> ended suddenly in a neat little lift, lit up with electric light, with a seat running round three sides of it. A mole was standing by the door.
> "Come along there, please, if you're going up!" called the mole sharply.[3]

It is not the diffident, artless Mole we later came to know and love, but it is a mole of sorts: gestation for a major character of more richness has been established. The story continues with a swift return to Mouse's real-life territory, for the carol-singers make such an unmusical noise that the dogs are set on them, and they (together with the mole lift-keeper) go looking for a compensatory supper. The resourceful pig knows where it can be found, confiding that

> there's a window in Mayfield that I can get into the house by, at any time. And I know where Mr. Grahame keeps his keys – very careless man, Mr. Grahame. Put your trust in me, and you shall have cold chicken, tongue, pressed beef, jellies, trifle, *and* champagne . . .

Kenneth, like many children sternly rationed in childhood, had an immense weakness for food, and the lists of goodies have a familiar ring to any *The Wind in the Willows* reader.

> When they got back to Mayfield, the rabbits took the mole off to wash his hands and brush his hair; while Bertie disappeared cautiously round a corner of the house. In about ten minutes he appeared at the pig-sty, staggering under the weight of two large baskets. One of them contained all the eatables he had already mentioned, as well as apples, oranges, chocolates, ginger, and crackers. The other contained ginger-beer, soda-water and champagne.

The involuntarily hospitable Mr Grahame was, meanwhile, having a bad night, half-woken by Bertie's raid on the larder. Kenneth's description of his dream is astonishingly revealing. It begins with a confused impression of burglars "ransacking his pantry", but he is unable to move a muscle to do anything about it.

> Then he dreamt that he was at one of the great City Banquets that he used to go to, and he heard the Chairman propose the health of "The King!" and there was great cheering. And he thought of a most excellent speech to make in reply – a really clever speech. And he tried to make it, but they held him down in his chair and wouldn't let him. And then he dreamt that the Chairman actually proposed his own health – "the health of Mr Grahame!" and he got up to reply, and he couldn't think of anything to say! And so he stood there, for hours and hours it seemed, in a dead silence, the glittering eyes of the guests – there were hundreds and hundreds of guests – all fixed on him, and still he couldn't think of anything to say! Till at last the Chairman rose, and said "He can't think of anything to say! *Turn him out!*" Then the waiters fell upon him, and dragged him from the room, and threw him into the street, and flung his hat and coat after him; and as he was shot out he heard the whole company singing wildly, "For he's a jolly good fellow – !"

Apart from a brief concluding passage about the pigsty being a dreadful mess the following morning, that is the end of the story, and the dream episode stands as its main theme. The implications are devastating. The Chairman is a very obvious metaphor for the Governor, who had perhaps, in cataloguing the Secretary's sins of omission, asked if he had "anything to say". Without a significant improvement in performance, he had implied, the Bank might, with regret, have to seek a new Secretary. And Kenneth had not been able to find a reply.

The massed company of guests with their "glittering eyes" and their barely suppressed taste for rowdy carousal, evoke the stoats and weasels who form such a nightmare presence in Toad Hall, and it is suddenly clear that Grahame, throughout his City life, had regarded the bulk of the people by whom he was surrounded as a threatening, untrustworthy rabble, their bloodthirsty instincts only lightly veiled by a veneer of good manners. They, with their greed for money, and their contempt for fine feeling, were the denizens of a Wild Wood where everyone seemed to be "running hard, hunting, chasing, closing in round something – or somebody?"[4]

The nightmare lies in the baffling, contradictory quality of the banqueters, who at one moment "held him down in his chair" to prevent him from making his "excellent speech" and at the next, were ruthlessly standing him on his feet in order to demonstrate that he had nothing to say. There is, too, a terrible sense of isolation and of being in some way on a different plane, as if in waking life there had been a feeling that the Bank was part of a continuing dreadful dream. At the banquet, like Alice, Grahame was larger and more real than the dream-figures which had wielded such authority, but he had not the confidence to stand up as she did and declare "Why, you are nothing but a pack of cards!" Lewis Carroll had somehow had the insight to see that Alice belonged absolutely to herself, whereas Grahame, for all his sensitivity and intuition, lived at least partly in the structures of the orthodox world, and could not deny their power.

At the beginning of May, a few days before his seventh birthday, Alastair, with his governess, Miss Stott, went off to Littlehampton for seven weeks. Just why he should have been dispatched at this point, without his parents, is unclear – but there is a clue in the first letter Kenneth sent him, dated 10 May 1907. Chalmers quotes the sender's address as 11 Durham Villas, which is strange on two counts. The Grahames lived at number 16, not number 11 – but, more fundamentally, the letter had in fact come from the Green Bank Hotel, Falmouth, as did a second one written on 23 May. Kenneth had gone on holiday with his wife, but without his son. He wrote to Alastair with anxious, apologetic affection.

> MY DARLING MOUSE, – this is a birthday letter to wish you very many happy returns of the day. I wish we could have been all together, but we shall meet again soon and then we will have *treats*. I have sent you two picture-books, one about Brer Rabbit, from Daddy, and one about some other animals, from Mummy. And we have sent you a boat, painted red, with mast and sails to sail in the round pond by the windmill – and Mummy has sent you a boat-hook to catch it when it comes ashore. Also Mummy has sent you some sand-toys to play in the sand with, and a card game.[5]

There is an underlying implication that Kenneth was not free to do as he would have liked, but the reasons for this are open to speculation. It seems obvious that the Grahames had made a deliberate decision to go away without Alastair, and the tinge of regret in Kenneth's letter implies that the insistence was not his. Elspeth had evidently recovered from her years of lassitude and was now prepared to take a positive hand in the relationship which was still the central focus of her life. It is interesting that she was able to respond to Mouse's illness so promptly, abandoning Woodhall Spa rapidly and permanently, and that the resolving of the Moulton case left her fit and well and eager to travel. The contraceptive advice she had so furtively sought may also have given her fresh confidence during the still-vulnerable years as she approached fifty.

She and Kenneth were in Falmouth for a couple of weeks and then moved on to Kenneth's beloved Fowey. Mouse's early letters prove that the couple had been away in the West Country before, but there is no indication that they had revisited Fowey. The boy mentions Devon, but not Cornwall. It may have been that Elspeth was hoping for a rekindling of the Dino and Minkie affair, but Kenneth was probably in search of a reassurance which was, to him, more fundamental. Having been disappointed by the outcome of the move to Mayfield, which had revealed changes in Berkshire life that made his childhood seem more remote rather than closer, he may have been thrown into a retrospective search for something – anything – which would prove itself to be enduring. Cornwall, being further from ʰhe influence of London, could have preserved its character intact. There is little sign, though, that Kenneth returned to Fowey in the spirit of recaptured honeymoon. His preoccupations were too inward and private for that; tragically for Elspeth, they always had been.

Mouse, when told of the arrangement, was not pleased. He would be deprived for seven whole weeks of the nightly story-telling sessions in which he could wrangle pleasurably with his father over the likelihood of what the characters would and would not do, and Miss Stott, for all her kindness, had no hope of being able to fill this gap. Kenneth had promised frequent letters to his son, in which the stories would be continued. He was as good as his word. The first letter, sent with his birthday gifts, continued with an episode from the ongoing saga.

Have you heard about the Toad? He was never taken prisoner at all. It was all a horrid low trick of his. He wrote that letter himself – the letter saying that a hundred pounds must be put in the hollow tree. And he got out of the window early one morning, & went off to a town called Buggleton & went to the Red Lion Hotel & there he found a party that had just motored down from London, & while they were having breakfast he went into the stable-yard & found their motor-car & went off in it without even saying Poop-poop! And now he has vanished & everyone is looking for him, including the police. I fear he is a bad low animal.[6]
Goodbye, from
Your loving Daddy.

There had obviously been a change of heart about what Toad is up to. The early stories must have seen many wanderings through various possibilities – but writing a narrative down, however informally, is very different from the transient process of telling it orally. In fifteen letters written during the course of that summer and autumn – for the promised reunion for "treats" did not happen until September, except for occasional weekends – the adventures of Toad began to be established in their final form.

Kenneth, meanwhile, had resumed his acquaintance with Q and Atky, and was spending happy days at sea or on the river. What Elspeth was doing is not recorded. Her husband's idea of enjoying himself did not need her presence to complete it. The whole question of holidays seems to have been a particularly difficult one. Before his marriage, Kenneth had been an addicted traveller, heading south every time an opportunity arose, but now, apart from the single abortive trip to France with Atky, he had not set foot outside Britain for eight years. It is easy to jump to the simple explanation that Elspeth would not let him travel without her and yet did not want to come, but far more difficult to imagine what tensions can have made such a situation possible. If the trip to Fowey was an attempt to make a new start, then it achieved no great success for, within a few years, visitors to the Grahames' house would report that the couple lived in bizarre and total separation.

While in Fowey, Grahame made a new friend. This was Austin Purves, an American from Philadelphia who was visiting Britain with his wife and five sons, Dale, Austin Junior, Edmund, John and little Pierre Marot. The mutual liking between the two men was so strong that when this youngest child was christened, Kenneth was a godfather, with Q as the other. Grahame was delighted by the ceremony, which "was unusual in that old Cornish customs were carried out, a procession to the Church and the presentation of the Kimbly cake to the first person encountered".[7] The Purves boys were later adamant in their claim that a boat trip up the river, undertaken by themselves with Atky and Grahame, was the inspiration for Mole's river picnic with Rat, and this seems to be correct, for at the very end of his life, writing to a schoolgirl called Ann Channer from Instow in North Devon, Kenneth said, "I hope you recognise the 'Fowey' bits of 'The Wind in the Willows'."[8] Certainly the Mole and Rat episodes were written as a later adjunct to the Toad saga.

Whether based on the dabbling at Fowey or not, Toad's adventures continued to be relayed to Alastair in letters, at first always addressed to "My darling Mouse". By the fifth one, however, Alastair was being addressed as "Robinson", the boy having taken it into his head to give himself a new name. There is something macabre about the fact that the man who had tried to shoot Kenneth at the Bank had been called Robinson. The name must have been mentioned in the house at the time and, even if Mouse had picked it up in all innocence, his insistence on adopting it for his own use is slightly horrifying. Despite his enjoyment of the bedtime stories, there is no evidence that Alastair found his father in any way remarkable or admirable for composing them; on the contrary, a certain contempt begins to creep into his attitude, and his announcement of a new persona as Michael Robinson was, at its very least, expressive of a firm refusal to consider himself a Grahame. Kenneth said mildly that he could not find himself capable of affection to a complete stranger, so he refrained from signing his letters, ending them merely "to be continued".

At this stage, there is no hint that the correspondence was anything more than a placation of Mouse's demands. The Toad adventures had been worked into a fairly complete shape, but Mole, Rat and Badger were peripheral, shadowy characters, not yet needed in the ongoing entertainment. Alastair was not only mollified, but thoroughly enjoyed himself in Littlehampton, described by Grahame later as "a rather horrid little place, which he adores".[9] When the seven weeks of the boy's holiday came to an end, Mouse and Miss Stott returned to Cookham Dene, and Elspeth left Fowey and went home as well.

Chalmers claims in his Elspeth-dominated biography that the Toad letters were all written within the seven weeks of Alastair's absence, and that Kenneth then went back to Mayfield with his family, but this is not true. From Fowey, Kenneth in fact returned to the London house in mid-June, where he lived alone except for occasional weekends spent in Berkshire, until at least mid-September, and the later letters were sent from Durham Villas to Cookham Dene.

The implications, both of Kenneth's whereabouts and of Elspeth's later efforts to misrepresent them, are significant. Bearing in mind that Grahame's traumatic interview with the new Governor had taken place shortly before he went on holiday, it seems obvious that he had been given firm instructions to buckle down to his job on return. Living in London, he could present himself at a reasonable hour in the morning and stay at his work rather longer than his accustomed mid-afternoon departure time. The only other possible explanation for his return to a London-based bachelor existence could be that his relationship with Elspeth, far from being revitalised by the return to their honeymoon haunt, had entered a new stage of impossibility.

Either way, the history of that time was firmly rewritten by Elspeth in *The First Whisper of "The Wind in the Willows"*. She claims that the letters written to Alastair were preserved by his nursery governess, who "posted them to me for safe-keeping, knowing full well that, if restored to the author, they would merely be consigned to the waste-paper basket". In fact, at least half the letters were directly received by Elspeth herself after her return to Cookham.

By the time *First Whisper* appeared, Elspeth was a very old lady, and some vagueness of memory may be assumed to have set in – and yet there is a consistency of outlook which cannot be ignored. Events are telescoped or discarded in order to present a smooth picture of herself as the perceiver and facilitator of her husband's classic book, and the records of other people's comments are all given in a rhapsodic, over-blown style which is so characteristically hers that it almost invalidates the evidence. Her account of the overheard Inveraray story-telling session, for instance, is typically rose-tinted. According to her, the visitor said,

"I heard two of the most beautiful voices, one relating a wonderful story, and the other, soft as the south wind blowing, sometimes asking for an explanation, sometimes arguing a point, at others laughing like a whole chime of bells – the loveliest duet possible and one that I would not have interrupted for the world. But the subject under discussion was so entrancing that I only wished I could have taken down every word of it, so that others – indeed a world-ful of others – might have the chance of enjoying the story as much as I did."[10]

The same narrative voice is audible in Elspeth's account of "the coming together of Kenneth and Mole". The facts are simple. While dressing for dinner one night, Kenneth saw a flurry of small activity going on in the garden and ran down, bare-footed, to discover a robin and a mole arguing over possession of a large earthworm. He grabbed the mole and, intending to show it to Alastair the next day, put it for safe keeping in a box with a heavy iron weight on the lid, and left "the temporary prison" on top of the grand piano. In the morning, the mole was gone, having shouldered its way out, and Mrs Blunt, "our dear old housekeeper" admitted to having killed "a young rat with my broom this morning very early, just as he was making for the back door". So far so good – but Elspeth's rendering of Mrs Blunt's apology to Kenneth is unlikely in the extreme.

"Oh, but, sir, couldn't you just make the mole into a story for Master Alastair, and I know then he would see it plain as plain, and how I know is, that when Nanny goes out after his bath and lets me fold up his little clothes, and put the room straight, I listen to your stories and know how real they are to Master Alastair. I am there in my cap and apron, and you know I am big and solid, and I am not real to him, I am not there at all, even though the floor creaks beneath my weight. But the least little thing in the story, even if it were light as a bird or butterfly, is there in the room with him, and for me too, as you tell it. And I only wish that Nanny would go out every night, instead of once in a blue moon, so that I could listen to more of those wonderful stories. So if you could just tell him a story about a mole, I feel it would come alive again and go on being alive, and that I had not killed it, which I am so dreadfully sorry about."[11]

It is a fine flight of poetic perception, but it does not sound like Mrs Blunt, who wrote practical and unimaginative letters, and who, besides, was the daughter of a gamekeeper, and inclined to deal firmly with vermin.

A larger inaccuracy is Elspeth's version of how the "Toad Letters" came to be thought of as a book. According to her, this, too, was a result of her own initiative. As she puts it,

> possibly no more would ever have been heard of Otter, Badger, Mole, Toady, Ratty and all the other "Characters", but that a lady-agent for an American Firm of Publishers arrived in a taxi from London at the house in Berkshire where we were living, to proffer a request that Kenneth would write something for them on *any* subject and at *any* price he desired.[12]

The "lady-agent" was Constance Smedley, who lived at Bray, not far from Cookham Dene, and who arrived during one of the weekends which Kenneth was spending at Mayfield. Elspeth condenses the events:

> the lady seeming very disappointed at failing in her mission, I bethought me of the bedtime stories now more or less in manuscript form, and after some discussion, it was decided that the adventures of Toad, Mole, and Company should go farther and be published in America.

This cuts out the main protagonist from the picture almost completely. Constance Smedley was, in fact, as charismatic an influence as Furnivall or Henley or Harland. Among other activities, she was the European representative of the American magazine, *Everybody's*, and her editor, John O'Hara Cosgrave, had written to her, suggesting that she should make a determined approach to Grahame. John Lane had spent years in such blandishments, and had given up in despair. There had been any number of approaches from publishers both in Britain and the USA who had begged to be favoured with something from the author of *The Golden Age*, but without result. It was nine years since Kenneth Grahame had written anything, and Miss Smedley knew that her mission was unlikely to achieve any positive result.

She went about her task with subtle care. Although she was an ardent feminist and the author of a book called *Woman: A Few Shrieks*, she deployed gentle and reassuring tactics. She was, she pointed out engagingly, a relation of the governess called Miss Smedley in *The Golden Age*, and felt particularly closely involved in the book. Whether it was literally true or not, Kenneth was delighted by the idea, and began to accept that this young woman was one of the same ilk as Graham Robertson, a believer in the lovely world in which fairies could exist, and in which one did not have to grapple with the imponderable ideas of the Olympians. Constance did, in truth, have an immensely fey side to her character, and this helped her towards an intuitive understanding of Grahame which was quite genuine, but she was at the same time careful not to show him the efficient entrepreneur which also formed part of her character. Knowledge that she had co-founded the Women's International Lyceum Club might well have frightened off her quarry.

Kenneth, nudged gently towards the idea of a new book, resisted. Writing, he said, was sheer physical torture, and he hated it. Miss Smedley was sympathetic and did not push the point. But she was still in the house at Mouse's bedtime, and learned how he and his father shared, as she herself related,

> an unending story, dealing with the adventures of the little animals whom they met on their river journeys. The story was known to him and Mouse alone and was related in a bed-time visit of extreme secrecy . . .

Evidently, she was able to penetrate this secrecy, for she observed (after only a few hours of Alastair's company) how

> Mouse's own tendency to exult in his exploits was gently satirised in Mr. Toad, a favourite character who gave the juvenile audience occasion for some slightly self-conscious laughter.[13]

Miss Smedley moved in for the kill. The work was already done, she pointed out to Kenneth that evening. The years of trying out various permutations on the theme during the story-sessions with Alastair had represented a painless way of tackling the drafting process which is so onerous and tiresome. The thing was as good as written. All he had to do was expand it into a book.

Slightly startled, Grahame found himself agreeing. Miss Smedley, as if to minimise the impact of the work she had suggested, turned the conversation to more general things and talked of her admiration for the reclusive Thomas Hardy, so resistant to uninvited visitors that the local cab-drivers would not set a fare down within a mile of his house. Elspeth, whose social instincts were always keen, revealed that they knew Thomas and Emma Hardy well, and offered an introduction. If Miss Smedley was going to see them, she continued, would she take a few poems with her? Constance Smedley said she would be delighted. She climbed into her car, carrying Elspeth's verses carefully, and drove off.

She arrived a day late for her appointment, and Thomas Hardy was clearly somewhat stunned by her. In a letter to Elspeth dated 31 August 1907, he remarked,

> I do not care much for rushing across England in a motor-car, but a great many people enjoy doing so just now.

About the young female driver, however, he was more enthusiastic, commenting that "she is most bright and interesting, and we had a long talk". His letter closed with a polite reference to Elspeth's verses. They were charming, he said cautiously,

> and certainly remarkable for being made in the top of an omnibus, where my attention is always too distracted by the young women around me in fluffy blouses to be able to concentrate on inner things.

Emma Hardy may have been right in her shrewd suspicions of "Eastern ideas of matrimony".

Grahame, however, had returned to a bachelor existence, at least during the week, and in the solitude of his life at Durham Villas, he began to transcribe and expand the toad letters into what would eventually become *The Wind in the Willows*. Most of the letter-narrative went straight into the book, unchanged, and the two versions are virtually identical. The character of Toad himself was now very clear, and Grahame had perhaps become consciously aware that his concern for the bombastic, simple, over-indulged and deeply insecure creature was the concern he felt for his own son, venturing forth with arrogance and vulnerability into the world that lay ahead. Unwittingly, Kenneth had found a vehicle through which all the sides of that concern could be expressed, through the opinion of wiser or nicer animals. Just as the finding of access to his own childhood had unlocked the opinions which glowed through *The Golden Age*, so Alastair's childhood had provided a metaphor through which Grahame's view of the future could be set in the context of all that he held precious about the present and the past. The work absorbed him. Although he had told Constance Smedley that he found writing a painful process, he had in fact been at his happiest and healthiest during the productive years of the *National Observer* and *The Yellow Book*; it had been the idea of writing, and the terrible confrontation with an inability to set anything down, which had caused him such agony since the last stories of *Dream Days*. Now, the blockage had been swept away. His anxiety about Middleton and the Bank receded to the level of a minor concern; he was again a writer. It became apparent later that his change of self-definition did not go unnoticed in Threadneedle Street, for Courtauld wrote afterwards to the then Governor, "Though possibly these books were not all written during banking hours, his duties as a Secretary may have suggested the titles *The Golden Age* and *Dream Days*".[14] Disapproval was building up, but Kenneth ignored it, or was oblivious. The book was all that mattered.

Grahame's newly recovered confidence had been boosted immensely by a bizarre result of his meeting with Austin Purves at Fowey in the summer. Purves, "a fine, hearty, jolly-looking man of big build and jovial countenance", was a successful businessman, well known in America as a collector of books and pictures and as a lover of music and literature. Among his wide circle of acquaintances was Theodore Roosevelt, who had been elected President of the United States two years previously, in 1905. In June, Purves wrote to Grahame:

The President and Mrs. Roosevelt again alluded to your book and Mrs. Roosevelt informed us that she was now engaged in reading *The Golden Age* and *Dream Days*, for about the tenth time, to her children. The President requested me to write to you and say that he would esteem it a great privilege and compliment if you would send him an autographed copy of your books and that in return he would be very proud to send you an autograph copy of works of his own. He also requested me to say that if you ever visit the United States during his term as President, he would be delighted to have you spend a weekend with him at the White House in Washington.

Kenneth sent the books as requested, and in each, he wrote:

To President Theodore Roosevelt
with highest respect and in grateful
recognition of his courtesy
from
Kenneth Grahame

A letter of thanks came back promptly from America, in cobalt blue typewriting:

The White House,   Oyster Bay, N.Y.
Washington   June 20, 1907
Personal

MR DEAR MR. GRAHAME, – I am sure that no one to whom you could have sent those two volumes would appreciate them more than Mrs. Roosevelt and I. I think we could both pass competitive examinations in them – especially in the psychology of Harold!

Now there are two people from Scotland whom we especially wish to see as guests in the White House while we are still there to be hosts. One is Oliver, who wrote the best life of Alexander Hamilton that has ever been written; and the other is yourself. Isn't there some chance of your coming over here?

With renewed thanks, believe me,
Sincerely yours,
THEODORE ROOSEVELT[15]

Mr Kenneth Grahame
England.

Grahame was well used to fan mail, and ignored most of it, replying only to children and an occasional West-countryman, but an accolade of such authority came as a valuable boost at a time when he was groping his way into a new phase of his creative life. Toad's adventures became more complete, working their way towards the rescue operation staged by his friends when his recklessness had brought him to the brink of disaster, and their author, faced for the first time with a book-length narrative, was also faced with the problem of fleshing out the setting in which the plot unfolded.

The Toad saga had been brought to a stage of near-completion in the series of letters to Alastair, but the hero of the story existed at first in a vacuum. To depict the complex truth of his outrageous personality, he needed to be set within his own society. Just as the *Golden Age* narrator had found expression through interaction between himself and the fictionalised characters of Edward, Selina, Harold and Charlotte, so Toad could only achieve a convincing reality through his relationship with the scandalised and yet protective River Bankers. The necessity was doubly pressing because Toad was not the narrator. He, of all the book's characters, is the only one through whose eyes the author cannot see. The others reveal themselves very clearly as embodiments of Grahame's own awareness. Mole is the most central of them, born from the Freudian darkness and narrowness of his underground home into the dizzying delights of sunshine and meadow and river, and he remains ever naïve, stunned by the beauty of it all. He has a centrality of vision and feeling which the author uses to depict the other characters, so that the Water Rat can at first appear impressive in the way he manages boats and packs picnic baskets, a dapper, confident, well-funded figure, a compound of Atky and Q. And yet, Mole perceives the fallibility and romanticism which underlies all the smartness, just as Grahame was aware that a worldly-wise element in himself was prone to collapse into a wild and irresponsible wanderlust. The social aspect of his being embodied an unstable element which, seeking enjoyment, was apt to be caught up with it and swept away.

The counter-balance is in Badger, earth-based and suspicious, utterly unconvivial. Mole emerges from his subterranean and truly much-loved home to be enchanted by Rat, the dweller in a clearly lit reality shared by others, but he is also grounded and given stability by the larger, older creature who lives at a deeper level and understands ancient truths which are only fleetingly glimpsed by the vulnerable and ever-young Mole. In Grahame's own experience, Badger surely springs from Marcus Aurelius, whom he discovered within his own darkness when the shared public world of school provided no comfort or private refuge. The symbolism of the Wild Wood is striking. What terrifies Mole is not the wilderness itself, but the knowledge that it is full of people, active and unseen. "They were up and alert and ready, evidently, whoever they were!" Nothing actually happens

to Mole, but the conviction that Wild Wood society is dangerous is reinforced by the unknown rabbit, a member of the victim class, defenceless
and preyed upon, who comes bolting through the trees. " 'Get out of this,
you fool, get out!' the Mole heard him mutter as he swung round a stump
and disappeared down a friendly burrow."

When Rat comes to the rescue of the "exhausted and still trembling"
Mole, he reads him a brisk lecture on the management of the Wild Wood,
explaining that

> there are a hundred things one has to know, which we understand all
> about and you don't, as yet. I mean pass-words, and signs, and sayings
> which have power and effect, and plants you carry in your pocket, and
> verses you repeat, and dodges and tricks you practise; all simple
> enough if you know them, but they've got to be known if you're small,
> or you'll find yourself in trouble.

As a City man, Grahame knew all this to be true. He was well aware that
what is said may mean something quite different to those "in the know".
At his level in the Bank, he would undoubtedly have encountered Free-
masonry, with its rituals and secrecy, but even on a normal day-to-day basis,
the offering and accepting of cigarettes and drinks were the equivalent of
the "plants you carry in your pocket", and the "dodges and tricks" of the
City constituted the basis of normal commercial life, as they still do. Rat is
the urbane (though fallible) side of his nature, Mole the central, rawly aware
poet, and Badger the deep-lying Taoist philosopher. But Toad, however
affectionately cherished and protected from his self-destructive instincts, is
somebody else. There is a touch of the Horatio Bottomley about him and
a suggestion, perhaps, of the flamboyance and tragic vulnerability of Oscar
Wilde, but Constance Smedley put an unerring finger on the truth when
she perceived that Toad was, above all, Alastair. Grahame, like all deeply
introverted people, had assumed that his own way of seeing was an absolute
truth, shared at least by all people close to him. He had come to realise
painfully, and with a gradual process of shock, that his son was not an
extension of himself, sharing the same awareness. He was somebody else.

Alastair was, in fact, like his mother, measuring himself by the effect he
had on others, a social, extrovert person, expecting the external world to
accept and admire him, and thrown into helpless confusion when it did not.
Kenneth loved his son, but he could not understand him, any more than
he could understand Elspeth – or Toad. That character could only be
depicted through the perplexity of those who believed in a different world,
unconcerned with the struggle to possess and impress. The problem of
justifying such a belief presented itself again, but this time in a clear literary
form rather than an abstract polemical one. The characters were their own

defence. They lived in a world of careful decency, trying at all times to avoid arrogance and the causing of unnecessary suffering. They spoke to each other with unfailing courtesy and, above all, they recognised themselves to be a small, integral part of the natural world, a totality so mystic and real as to constitute the immanent God.

Grahame was no conscious self-analyser, and yet the order in which his book developed reveals the process of his thinking. The Toad narrative was laid down first, then the chapters which precede it and establish Mole and his meeting with Rat and Badger. Last of all came "The Piper at the Gates of Dawn" and "Wayfarers All", which give the book its mystic quality of connection to larger forces. These two chapters address Grahame's profound belief in pantheism on one hand and his love-affair with travel and the lure of the South on the other, and act as the poles between which the scope of the book is set. Superficial readers have said that these are irrelevant additions which can well be skipped, but to omit them is to miss the essential import of what Grahame is writing about, and what he lived for. They were added, not as an afterthought, but as the logical conclusion to the philosophical statement which forms the whole structure of the book.

By Christmas, *The Wind in the Reeds*, as Grahame called it, was finished, and he packed it up and sent it to the eager Constance Smedley, who despatched it to her editors, waiting with no less excited anticipation in New York. After a stunned silence, they turned it down flat. They had been expecting a further volume of *Golden Age* essays, and could not look with fresh eyes at what they had been given.

Grahame's agent, Curtis Brown, also found the book's departure from the previous formula a huge disadvantage. The Bodley Head, despite Grahame's long association with John Lane, and the continuing brisk sales of his three previous books, firmly rejected *The Wind in the Reeds*. Curtis Brown seemed to think it might be easier to try and sell the book in single episodes, much as the *Golden Age* essays had originally appeared, but even here he had no success. As he confessed, "I tried it with magazine editors all over England and America. They thought it too fantastic, and wouldn't have it."[16]

The failure of the new book was ironic, specially when contrasted with the success of its predecessors. In America above all, Grahame was enjoying immense popularity, and a later letter from the indefatigable Austin Purves reported an unexpected fan.

You will be interested to hear that in the Kaiser's cabin, on the royal yacht *Hohenzollern*, there are only two books in the English language. One of them is the Bible and the other is Kenneth Grahame's *Golden Age*.

Grahame does not seem to have been unduly impressed. He was more sympathetic to letters from the most "ordinary" readers, and replied to a selected few. Among them was a letter from a little girl who had read *Dream Days* but wanted to know the meaning of *res augusta*, and what was meant by "weekly books". Grahame wrote her a sensible and straightforward explanation, plus a word of bankerly advice.

> *Res augusta* is Latin for a very small income. The "weekly books" are the tradesman's account books which are supposed to be paid weekly, and when they aren't there's trouble, sooner or later. They are tiresome things and, when *you* reach that stage, I advise you to have nothing to do with them, but to pay cash. It may be troublesome, but it brings mental ease and peace![17]

He answered, too, a letter from a man who wrote disarmingly that

> It is Sunday morning and the deadly hideousness of the Californian scenery has been, as it often is, much on my nerves – you see I come from the Wye Valley and from South Devon and from some years spent upon the high seas beneath the old red rag . . .[18]

Such an appeal was irresistible and the letter is marked "replied to", although Grahame's response itself is lost.

Quite apart from the presidential invitation to stay at the White House, there had been offers of immensely lucrative lecture tours in the United States, but Grahame never went. Perhaps the "deadly hideousness" was enough to keep him near his spiritual lifeline of the English countryside. Meanwhile, *The Wind in the Reeds* languished. Graham Robertson pointed out that W. B. Yeats had just published a collection of poetry by that title, and enclosed some alternative suggestions;

Down Stream, With the Stream, The Lapping of the Stream, The Babble of the Stream, "By Pleasant Streams" (Blake), "By Waters Fair" (Blake), The Whispering Reeds, In the Sedges, Under the Alders, Reeds and Rushes, Reeds of the River, River Folk, The Children of Pan . . .[19]

We may be grateful, perhaps, that none of these appealed to Kenneth.

Robertson had been the first to read the book, and he had drawn a frontispiece for it, depicting three naked babies and an otter dabbling in a waterfall in a sub-Kelmscott kind of way, above the woodcut-styled words, *And a River Went out from Eden*.

Grahame settled for *The Wind in the Willows*, but not until after Methuen had reluctantly agreed to take the book. The firm would pay no advance, being utterly unconvinced that there would be any public enthusiasm for such an uncharacteristic Grahame production, but Curtis Brown turned their misgivings to advantage, pointing out that if it didn't sell, there would be no harm in offering Grahame a generous rising royalty. This they agreed to do, with enormous subsequent benefits to the University of Oxford and particularly the Bodleian Library, to which the copyright eventually reverted.

Graham Robertson was still troubled by the lack of enthusiasm for his friend's book. He himself had been enchanted by it, and wrote later of his excitement and of his own self-doubts as an illustrator.

> I well remember my joyful enthusiasm when I first read the MSS. It was wonderful to be allowed to witness and even, in a tiny way, to assist at so happy a birth. There was then some talk of my providing illustrations, but time was lacking and, moreover, I mistrusted my powers, for I could not number an otter or a water-rat among my acquaintances though I had once known a mole almost intimately and had several toad friends . . .[20]

In fact, Robertson had drawn a beautifully naturalistic otter in the frontispiece; what deterred him was probably the strange cross-identity of animal and human which makes it difficult for any artist to sort out the problems of scale. Toad is hardly a toad when he sells a horse for six and sixpence and as much as he can eat of the gipsy's stew, made from "partridges, and pheasants, and chickens, and hares, and rabbits, and pea-hens, and guinea fowls . . .". But Robertson had a shrewd head when it came to perceiving the difficulties people had with *The Wind in the Willows* (Methuen had advertised the forthcoming book as *The Wind in the Reeds* but changed the title at the last moment, after the book had gone into production because of Yeats' forthcoming volume of the same name). "Don't you think," he wrote to Grahame,

> that Methuen himself, in his preliminary announcement of the book should mention that it is not a political skit, or an Allegory of the Soul, or a Socialist Programme or a Social Satire? It would save critics a good deal of unnecessary trouble.[21]

Robertson was, of course, trying to suppress his own perception, in sympathy with his friend's unawareness of what he had revealed. Grahame had written from the deepest recesses of his own psyche, and either could not or would not recognise that he had made a powerful plea for what he saw as good and that it was therefore a political statement. If he had tried to establish a King Canute-like stance against the unstoppable tide of all that was vulgar and ruthless, he did not want to be cast in the role of that ultimately misunderstood figure. He was, he insisted, just a story-teller.

Relations with Elspeth seem at this time to have improved. She was immensely proud of the new book, regarding it as "hers" in a sense which the earlier ones, written before she met Kenneth, could not be. It must have troubled her that, having married a famous writer, he immediately ceased to write, and had not produced a word throughout the nine years since their wedding in 1899. Now, she could recognise the genesis of *The Wind in the Willows* through the stories told by her husband to her son, and felt triumphant. Kenneth was back at Mayfield, and she was in better spirits altogether. It may well have been in 1908 that she wrote a surprisingly witty Valentine for her husband after failing to buy the traditional blank card on which to inscribe one's own verses.

Exit Amor
A Valentine I went to buy
I trudged the drear Macadam
Yet ever met the same reply
"We do not stock them, Madam."

I said, "You know the kind of thing
They've been the same since Adam
Hearts, roses, Cupids on the wing"
"We do not stock them, Madam"[22]

As ever, her punctuation was vague, but the whole thing has a panache which is quite different from her usual morbid verses.

Constance Smedley, though mortified by her editor's failure to see the merits of the book she had prodded Kenneth into writing, remained a family friend, and visited the house often. It seemed from her recollection of it that Kenneth had recovered his confidence and that Elspeth was again deploying her talents as a hostess.

I remember the sloe gin poured into tiny cordial glasses . . . the ceremony of the salad, served in a great basket with herbs and flasks of condiments and solemnly prepared by Mr. Grahame; the rows of tear-bottles of Bristol glass, the peasant toys from all countries, the wonderful collections of old glass and china used, not only looked at. One night I remember being greatly intrigued. Some very tall glasses with a curious convoluted edge were before us through which one saw everything as through the wrong end of an opera glass. They were most fascinating to drink out of; Mr. and Mrs. Grahame appeared like animated toys miles away across a miniature dining table. When I left, the housekeeper was waiting with one of these glasses most beautifully packed up and tied. "It is the custom," said Mr. Grahame, "to give your guest the cup he has drunk from."[23]

The hospitality was not all on Kenneth's side. Miss Smedley, as founder of the Women's Lyceum Club in Piccadilly, devised an extraordinary event which she called a Fairy-Tale Dinner, to which Kenneth was invited. Everyone was to dress up – Constance herself appeared as a Fairy Princess decked in a "bower of autumn foliage" – and the general idea was to create, at least for one evening, a world of magical innocence. As she put it, using a vocabulary surprisingly artless for the European representative of *Everybody's*,

> The princes and princesses, the goose-girls and swineherds love and mate in simple kindliness.

It would be, she insisted,

> the world of William Morris without its cruelty, savage passions and fighting and its somewhat heavy sexuality.[24]

This was supposed to appeal to Grahame, who had said in advocacy of his new book that it was "clean of the clash of sex", but it is not recorded whether he enjoyed the evening, at which toasts were drunk in rowan wine and each guest was presented with the Order of the Golden Rabbit. Certainly he found the idea engaging, for he allowed Miss Smedley to take him shopping for the dinner. This must have been no easy task, since the menu included goldfish, cream tarts and gingerbread, but, with his weakness for the eccentric, he probably enjoyed it.

His employers, meanwhile, were not happy. What further interviews took place between Middleton and his erring Secretary is not known, but the facts speak for themselves. In June 1908, four months before the publication of *The Wind in the Willows*, Kenneth Grahame resigned from the Bank. The timing is significant. As far as he knew, the book was doomed to failure; there was no question of abandoning his bank career in the certainty of good royalties. Chalmers, no doubt relying on Elspeth's information, claims that Kenneth was offered a year's sick leave on full pay, but no hint of any such offer can be found among the otherwise complete Bank correspondence, and there is no reflection of munificence in the eventual offer of retirement terms, couched in the coldest of official language in a letter dated 2 July 1908. Grahame's pension was to be £400 p.a., a low sum for a Bank officer of his eminence, and even that was qualified by the stern statement: "All persons pensioned before they are 60 years of age shall, until they attain that age, be required to satisfy the Court, from time to time, that no material change has taken place in the circumstances under which the pensions were granted."

Meanwhile, Elspeth, following the successful outcome of the case against her stepfather, was far the better off of the two. The balance of power had begun to swing the other way. With the end of her husband's banking career and the sale of the London house, Elspeth, for almost the first time in her married life, found herself permanently at home with her husband. He was only forty-nine years old and by all conventional standards, his professional life had been cut short by at least ten years.

Later, a memoir of Grahame published in the Bank's quarterly, The Old Lady, includes a couple of genuine paragraphs amid much fulsome verbiage:

> It was my privilege, when a junior in the service of the Bank, to come into personal contact with Mr Grahame both before and after his appointment as Secretary, and I have pleasant recollections of many small kindnesses he showed to me and of the considerate manner in which he criticised my early efforts to adapt the Queen's English to the purposes of official letters. My impression of Mr Grahame was of a shy, reserved man, with a fine presence and charm of manner, who did not fit in with my preconceived notions of a Bank Official; . . .[25]

However, it was at last over. Uncle John's sentence of bank servitude had been discharged, with remission for good – or bad – conduct. Kenneth retired to Mayfield, to take Alastair for long walks in the country round Cookham, and lay some plans for the future. With limitless freedom ahead, there was a tempting prospect of travel – if the problem of Elspeth could be solved. She had still never set foot outside Great Britain with her husband.

There is something very strange about this, for Elspeth herself had travelled quite extensively in Europe before her marriage. Apart from her French convent schooldays, she had been to the Rhine, as her early letters to Kenneth made clear, and seemed enthusiastic about revisiting it. Grahame himself was (at least in his Sea-Rat persona) devoted to the south. He hated cold winters and feared the physical effects of northern dampness and chill, and yet, with the single exception of his doomed expedition with Atky, he had remained Britain-bound for the whole nine years of his marriage. It may have been, quite simply, that Elspeth was never well enough to travel, but, considering that she had spent long periods of time away from her husband, Kenneth's own restraint from travel is more difficult to explain. His nature-fearing, Catholic-inclined religious sense, however, may have laid at the bottom of it. Elspeth had obviously objected strongly to his trip with Atky, and the guilt he felt about going was compounded by the fateful coincidence of Mouse's illness. He had sinned, and was punished through the child. The fear of divine nemesis may well have inhibited further venturings abroad; the long years cooped up in London had been a kind of penance. It would take courage – and, perhaps, the support and companionship of Elspeth – before he would risk it again.

In October 1908, *The Wind in the Willows* was published. Several other notable books appeared in the same year. There was Arnold Bennett's *The Old Wives' Tale*, G. K. Chesterton's *The Man Who Was Thursday*, E. M. Forster's *A Room with a View*, and another children's book destined for fame, L. M. Montgomery's *Anne of Green Gables*. The quality of Kenneth Grahame's book, however, was not easily recognised. The reviews were guarded, if not downright baffled. *The Times* said,

> Grown-up readers will find it monstrous and elusive, children will hope, in vain, for more fun. Beneath the allegory ordinary life is depicted more or less closely, but certainly not very amusingly or searchingly. As a contribution to natural history the work is negligible.

The fact that the heroes were animals was one which most reviewers found indigestible. *The Saturday Review of Literature*, striving for a touchstone, said, "His rat, toad and mole are very human in their behaviour, and remind us of undergaduates of sporting proclivities". The *Nation*'s reviewer, H. W. Nevinson who, many years later, was to marry Evelyn Sharp, made the same point. "All the animals had a very stirring time, and but for their peculiar shapes they would well pass for first-rate human boys." *T.P.'s Weekly* clung to a view of the book as an exercise in natural history and said sniffily that most of its episodes "will win no credence from the very best authorities on biology."

Arthur Ransome, writing for *The Bookman*, grappled hopelessly with his incomprehension.

> *The Wind in the Willows* is an attempt to write for children instead of about them. But Mr Grahame's past has been too strong for him. Instead of writing about children for grown-up people, he has written about animals for children. The difference is only in the names. He writes of the animals with the same wistfulness with which he wrote of children, and, in his attitude towards his audience, he is quite unable to resist that appeal from dreamland to a knowledge of the world that makes the charm of all his books, and separates them from children's literature. The poems in the book are the only things really written for the nursery, and the poems are very bad.
>
> If we judge the book by its aim, it is a failure, like a speech to Hottentots made in Chinese . . .

Graham Robertson had been right in predicting that a lot of reviewers would regard the book as allegorical. *Punch* was shrewd enough to forestall any indignant denials from Grahame. "Some grown-up readers may find in the story a satirical purpose which its author would probably disclaim," it said. And Arnold Bennett, an old colleague of Grahame's on *The Yellow Book*, tackled the question head-on.

> The book is fairly certain to be misunderstood of the people. The publishers' own announcement describes it as "perhaps chiefly for youth", a description with which I disagree. The obtuse are capable of seeing in it nothing save a bread-and-butter imitation of *The Jungle Book* . . .

Bennett, however, was entirely persuaded that the characters were "meant to be nothing but human beings". He went on: "The book is an urbane exercise in irony at the expense of the English character and of mankind. It is entirely successful."

The "publishers' announcement" which Bennett refers to was in fact written by Grahame himself. In July 1908, he wrote in response to a request from Methuen:

> I will jot down on the fly-leaf of this some material for a descriptive paragraph for the announcement list, though probably any one else would do it better.
>
> "A book of Youth – and so perhaps chiefly *for* Youth, and those who still keep the spirits of youth alive in them: of life, sunshine, running water, woodlands, dusty roads, winter firesides; free of problems, clean of the clash of sex; of life as it might fairly be supposed to be regarded by some of the wise small things
> " 'That glide in grasses and rubble of woody wreck'."

In a generally unappreciative reception, the only bright point was a long and thoughtful review by Richard Middleton in *Vanity Fair*, in which he, alone among his colleagues, identified the pantheistic faith which forms the underlying subject-matter.

> The book for me is notable for its intimate sympathy with Nature and for its delicate expression of emotions which I, probably in common with most people, had previously believed to be my exclusive property. When all is said the boastful, unstable Toad, the hospitable Water Rat, the shy, wise, child-like Badger, and the Mole with his pleasant habit of brave boyish impulse, are neither animals nor men, but are types of that deeper humanity which sways us all. To be wise, an allegory must admit of a wide application, and the man has read his *Pilgrim's Progress* in vain who does not realise that not merely Christian but Ignorance, Talkative, and Justice Hategood himself, are crying for

mastery in the heart of us all. And if I may venture to describe as an allegory a work which critics, who ought to have known better, have dismissed as a fairy-story, it is certain that *The Wind in the Willows* is a wise book.

Elspeth was dismayed by the generally unperceptive and indifferent reception of "her" book, and did her best to pull a few strings. She wrote to Anstey Guthrie, begging him to review it, but he replied in guarded terms, pleading that "I am, as you see, away from town, but even if I were not, I could do very little, as I do not review for any paper, and though I belong to a literary and artistic club, never go to it, and am not on intimate terms with any reviewer." He never did mention the book in any of his writing.

Grahame, meanwhile, had sensibly sent a copy of *The Wind in the Willows* to Theodore Roosevelt. The effect was not immediate, but the President, unlike most of the British critics, was an open-minded man, willing to accept new ideas, even though he modestly denied that very quality in his first paragraph.

> *The White House,*
> *Washington,*
> *January 17th 1909*

Personal

My Dear Mr Grahame, – My mind moves in ruts, as I suppose most minds do, and at first I could not reconcile myself to the change from the ever-delightful Harold and his associates, and so for some time I could not accept the mole, the water-rat and the badger as substitutes. But after a while Mrs Roosevelt and two of the boys, Kermit and Ted, all quite independently, got hold of *The Wind in the Willows* and took such a delight in it that I began to feel that I might have to revise my judgement. Then Mrs Roosevelt read it aloud to the younger children, and I listened now and then. Now I have read it and re-read it, and have come to accept the characters as old friends; and I am almost more fond of it than of your previous books. Indeed, I feel about going to Africa very much as the sea-faring rat did when he almost made the water-rat wish to forsake everything and start wandering!

I felt I must give myself the pleasure of telling you how much we had all enjoyed your book.

> With all good wishes,
> Sincerely yours,
> Theodore Roosevelt.

Roosevelt seems to have accepted the book in the same simplistic spirit with which it was offered. Grahame, in his accompanying letter to the President, had written with typical (and in this case, self-deceiving) protestations of innocent intent.

> Its qualities, if any, are mostly negative – i.e. – no problems, no sex, no second meaning – it is only an expression of the very simplest joys of life as lived by the simplest beings of a class that you are specially familiar with and will not misunderstand.

At first sight, it is difficult to see why he should have been so categorical in refusing to admit his book's deeper meaning. The only possible explanation can be that he was embarrassed by the idea of detailed self-revelation, and wanted to forestall any questions based on a personal interpretation. He was, after all, a very shy and private man. The denial was perhaps a necessary defence.

Curtis Brown, still pursuing the seemingly hopeless search for an American publisher, had just sent the manuscript to Scribner and had been told that "it wouldn't go". But then, as Brown recalls in his memoirs, Scribner got a letter from President Roosevelt, saying that *The Wind in the Willows* was "such a beautiful thing that Scribner *must* publish it".

With an apologetic cough, Scribner did. The way was paved, at last, for the book's success.

13

A Difficult Freedom

The first months of Grahame's retirement produced an overwhelming lethargy. The compulsion to attend the Bank was ended, and *The Wind in the Willows* was written and published. As the autumn of 1908 wore on, there was nothing to do except answer letters and take Mouse for walks, and Kenneth's enthusiasm for both activities was flagging. A photograph of Alastair taken at about that time shows a somewhat overweight boy in a suit and waistcoat, head held back at a slight angle because of his partial-sightedness, but with a broad, faintly contemptuous grin on his face.

Kenneth was becoming increasingly disenchanted with Cookham, and wrote grumblingly about its villagers, who "were ever child-like admirers of Progressive Stunts – and not given to nostalgia". Possibly his efforts to engage in reminiscence over a couple of pints in the local pub had proved fruitless. Innovation is always more interesting than things long-accepted and, in the first decade of the twentieth century, the talk would have been of motor-cars and telephones rather than Harvest Home and the visit of the mummers at Christmas. These, indeed, still came, but they, too, were afflicted with modernism. "Hardly any of the good old 'St George and the Dragon' play left," Grahame lamented. "Instead, cheap comic songs from the London music halls. But Mouse liked it."

This complaint was made in a letter to Austin Purves, who was still beavering away on Grahame's behalf in America, and who wrote a constant stream of letters to Mayfield, undeterred by Kenneth's tardiness in replying. Only occasionally could the lethargy be overcome, as Grahame confessed in a letter dated 3 November 1908.

MY DEAR PURVES, – your most welcome and amiable letters continue to reproach me daily, as they bulge in my pocket like a visible bad conscience. I must be allowed to dwell on their amiability, because you have every right to be "shirty" to any extent – yet no "shirtability" has appeared up to the present date.

The fact is, when one has written letters for many years for one's daily bread, and suddenly finds oneself free of them, a revulsion sets in which must be allowed to work itself off. You will understand and make allowances.

He thanked Purves for a review of *The Wind in the Willows* which "was perfectly charming and is bound to be helpful," and then turned to the question of travel, saying that he was

> hoping to manage it after the New Year – in Switzerland to begin with, and then perhaps a drop into the northern part of Italy, for colour and anemones and Chianti and so on.
>
> We had a beautiful summer here, and now we are having an equally beautiful autumn – still and misty and mild and full of colour. I had a jolly day at Oxford a short time ago. Everything in full swing and the river covered with men doing "tubbing" practice. The old place was just as beautiful as ever, and I bought some youthful ties and some "Oxford sausages" in the delightful market – they are a small species without any skins on their poor little persons – and took a walk down Mesopotamia, and explored many old haunts.
>
> We can't extract any Fowey news from Q, who is probably mighty busy, and neither Atky nor Miss Marsden have given any sign of life for a long time. I wish we could get down there for a bit before the year closes. Perhaps it may yet be possible.
>
> This is not much of a letter, but look on it as a makeshift and I will try and do better next time. Our kindest regards to Mrs. Purves and all the family, and hearty thanks for all you are doing to help a struggling author to get an honest living . . .

Chalmers deleted from this letter a revealing reference to Elspeth. Grahame had outlined a plan for a Mediterranean trip, but conceded that it would only be possible if he could "get E. sufficiently patched up for the journey". His next sentence made it clear that his wife was still debilitated and almost pathologically withdrawn." By the way, about her photo. She has not been done for many years, and now absolutely refuses to undergo the process until she is less of a Living Skellington . . . The reversion to Dino-speak is interesting, and so is the indication that Elspeth was painfully thin, and so unhappy about her own appearance that she would not face a camera. The nine years of cold soup and hot water and sulphurous baths had evidently taken their toll.

Instead of the hoped-for trip to Fowey, Kenneth found himself taking Elspeth to Devonshire. There is no explanation for this change of plan, but it was not what Kenneth had wanted. Despondent in the denial of his heart's craving, he again fell ill. His next letter to Purves, written on 17 December, has a slightly desperate striving for good cheer, admitted in the last paragraph to be a transparent effort.

> DEAR PURVES, – It occurred to us that you might possibly care to

have a copy of the English edition of "The W. in the W.", so I have sent you one, instead of a Christmas card with two robins sitting on a steaming plum-pudding with an intoxicated church in the background. I should like to have sent Mrs Purves a tiara and each of the boys a steam-yacht or a motor-car, but that will have to come some other Christmas. We are just back from Devonshire and miss the sea and the sunshine. My influenza was apparently a slight one at the time, but the after weakness and general grogginess still continues, and I can only walk a mile or two, and then an armchair and slumber till dinner-time, which is a nuisance. We find deep mud everywhere and leaden skies overhead. But my faithful tame robin was waiting on the doorstep next morning and came for his currant as if we had not been away a day.

E. is Christmassing for all she is worth [Here Chalmers omitted the words "and is not precisely sane at the present season"]. We have had no Fowey news this long while. Well, this is a dull letter, written like Hon'ble Poet Shelley's stanzas "in a moment of depression". But it wishes you all good things, including a Happy New Year, "jointly and severally", for you and Mrs Purves, and all the boys, and Jerry.

The "Jerry" he refers to is the Black valet, much esteemed by Austin for his skill in preparing a lobster. Grahame had ended his previous letter to Purves with "remembrances to Jerry (I eat a *cold* lobster every Sunday for lunch and mournfully think what might have been if you were all over on this side and lobsters were cheap)."

Two days later, Grahame wrote again to Purves, distressed and upset by a letter he had received from Trant Chambers, an old school-fellow from St Edward's, now down-and-out and begging for money. Kenneth had sent him a cheque by return of post, but appeals were to continue to arrive intermittently over the next two years, sometimes asking for help in finding journalistic work, sometimes starving and suicidal (at which times Kenneth recommended him, unsuccessfully, to a charitable organisation). Grahame saw him as an appalling product of the squalor and degradation which lay in wait for those who found themselves overwhelmed by life's roughness, and the alcoholism was an uncomfortable reminder of Cunningham, the lost father whose ghost warned against weakness and loss of self-control. The importuning, embarrassing letters served to increase Kenneth's conviction that decent restraint was a fast-vanishing quality, for Chambers did not hesitate to pile on the agony. He was, he said, "light-headed for want of food", living in a "fireless garret, the rent for which is sadly in arrears . . . After putting a stamp on the envelope, I have only twopence left in the world."[1] After a silence of seven years, a final missive was to arrive together with a copy of the *St Edward's Chronicle*, to say that Trant was being sheltered by the Revd A. B. Simeon, Kenneth's and his former master at the school, and to hope that "you are flourishing in every way you could desire in what is for most of us a rather hard and perplexing world".

Kenneth, in his own way, might have shared the view of the world as hard and perplexing, but there was no possibility of explaining such a thought to a man who could truthfully describe himself as "friendless, hungry, penniless, shelterless and without immediate prospect of any kind".

1909 began, and Constance Smedley wrote to Kenneth to tell him of her engagement, asking him to keep it a secret for the time being. With the weakness for a fey, confidential correspondence which had been so evident in his courtship of Elspeth, Kenneth wrote back to congratulate her on choosing Gloucestershire for her intended home, and plunged into a string of jokes about such mythical counties as Double-Gloucestershire.

Cheshirecatshire is another delightful one, and Yorkshirepuddingshire and Devonshirecreamshire are first-rate to live in. Lie-in-Bedfordshire is warm and sheltered, an excellent county for a prolonged stay. Ten-to-forfarshire is chiefly inhabited by retired government officials: you would not care for that. But Hunt-the-slipperingdonshire has lively society, and several packs meet in the neighbourhood.[2]

He was, perhaps, subconsciously rehearsing the forced joviality with which he would tackle the prospect of travelling with Elspeth, for the pair were, at last, about to undertake a Continental tour. They left in February for three months, visiting Switzerland and Italy as Kenneth had planned. This time, there would be no letters to Mouse about the adventures of Toad. Those stories were now public property, and, at nine years old, Alastair had moved out of the nursery stage. There is no mention of any further bedtime storytelling sessions. On the contrary, Mouse's parents seem to have departed on their long trip without a backward glance.

Kenneth came back to find a pile of fan mail waiting for him, much of it forwarded from the Bank of England. One of the most impressive – and perceptive – came from the Hon. Alfred Deakin, Prime Minister of Australia.

January 28, 1909

DEAR MR GRAHAME, – I have never been able to forgive myself for having neglected the opportunity afforded me by my only visit to the Bank of England (in 1907) of at all events acknowledging my debt and that of my family to you for *The Golden Age* and *Dream Days*, which I read to them years ago. But after *The Wind in the Willows* I can no longer deny myself the pleasure of congratulating you upon an even higher and still more original achievement – a prose poem perfect within its scope and style and sentiment, rising to its climax in the vision of Pan – a piece of imaginative insight to which it would be hard to find a parallel anywhere. Certainly one would only look for it among the rarest flowers of literature in that vein.

If this language appears to you strained, let me assure you that it is not by intention. I have read the book as a whole twice; once out loud, and passages such as that mentioned "Mole's Xmas Eve", and the "Sailor Rat's Reminiscences", &c., several times.

It is now three or four weeks since I was under the glamour, so that my verdict represents what lawyers call a considered opinion, and, so far as I am concerned, is binding. Nor am I the only beneficiary; my wife and daughters were equally fascinated, as were several friends upon whose judgements I am accustomed to rely.

Please therefore accept this spontaneous and informal note of hand, just for what it is – an expression of gratitude and admiration from some of the many Australians who find in your book a delicate and delicious insight into nature and human nature, enriched and inspired by that "natural magic" which touches the deepest chords of poetry and of the soul with the simplest and most artless sincerity.

As, after all, I am writing this off-hand – merely a line of thanks – I will only ask you to accept it, not as an attempt to discharge, but a recognition of a continuing debt. When with your Governors at the Bank, my mind, alas, was full of other debts in other spheres more material and yet perhaps more evanescent than this.

Yours sincerely,
ALFRED DEAKIN

In contrast to Deakin's studied literary phrasing, Kenneth wrote back with simplicity.

April 23rd, 1909
DEAR MR DEAKIN, – It was most kind of you to write me such a welcome and more than generously worded letter about *The Wind in the Willows*. If I have ever received a pleasanter or more encouraging appreciation I do not remember it.

It is not exactly logical, but somehow to have given pleasure to readers very far away seems to bring a special satisfaction which one cannot feel about the opinion of the man round the corner. And as for the animals, though they might well look for recognition down here, with their native Thames a few hundred yards away, yet they are aliens in Australia, and would have no right to grumble at prompt deportation; but your friendly greeting will make them feel adopted and at home among relations; and I hope they will stay.

I am just back from a Continental wandering of nearly three

months, which has delayed my reply. With many thanks again, and all good wishes,

                    Yours very sincerely,
                        Kenneth Grahame

As if in reprisal for the months of winter holiday, the summer was cold and wet. Alastair went happily enough to "his favourite seaside resort", Littlehampton, leaving his parents at Mayfield. He had hardly seen them at all that year. Elspeth was suffering from inflammation of the optic nerve in one eye (which Green suggests may give some credence to the suspicion that Alastair's semi-blindness was hereditary) and claimed that she could not stand the glare of coastal light. There seemed to be some pricking of the Grahame parental conscience about the increasing amount of time spent apart from their son, for Kenneth wrote, "I wish our taste in places were similar, so that we could be together . . .". It is not clear what Grahame had in mind. It could imply that Elspeth, after her "Continental wandering", had had quite enough of holiday locations and wanted to stay at home. On the other hand, the slightly lame excuses could have disguised the fact that both parents found themselves in need of a prolonged break from Alastair. Perhaps they were, at last, enjoying each other's company. Kenneth was happy in his release from City bondage, and Elspeth was evidently in better health and free of her various fears. She told Chalmers that she and Kenneth travelled abroad every year after her husband's retirement, and although Green declared this to be utterly untrue, Mouse's letters are certainly addressed to absent parents, journeying in France or Italy or Switzerland, dated from 1910 to 1914, though there are many more which have no year-date. The boy's developing handwriting, however, indicates that a good many years passed during which he saw his parents only intermittently, though this was in part because he himself was away at school. Whether at home or not, he was always cared for by paid professionals, and his parents, like most upper-middle-class people of their generation, felt themselves free to enjoy their own lives.

On 27 July 1909, Grahame broke a long silence to write to Purves and thank him for a batch of press cuttings. His excuses for non-communication are engaging, and all too recognisable to those of good intentions and flagging energy.

DEAR PURVES, – Your letters, welcome as they are, always hit me on a very sore spot on my conscience – and a spot that had not had time to skin over properly since the last one knocked it raw. And yet, do you know, I *do* write you any quantity of truly magnificent letters. In my armchair of evenings, with closed eyes, or strolling in the woods of afternoon – or with head on pillow *very* late on a thoroughly wet and disagreeable morning. I see my pen covering page after page of cream-laid parchment-wove extra antique. Such good stuff, too – witty, anecdotal, pensive, pathetic – I feel myself lick the envelope – I see myself running to the post – I hear the flop of the letter in the box. It's all so *real* – to me – that I was quite surprised to find that you weren't asking me to limit them to, say, three a week. Please believe that, if they never reach you, it is not my fault.

We have had two surprise visits from "Atky" this summer. He just dropped from the clouds, without notice, ate a hearty lunch, talked a great deal, and flitted away again into the outer darkness. He seems to have been very poorly all the winter as a result of influenza, which sapped his strength, but he was distinctly on the mend when he came here, and is probably all right by now. We were deeply disappointed to hear from you that there was no chance of your coming over this summer, but of course we quite understand. After all one's "affairs" must rank first, and you want, when you come, to bring an easy mind with you. And Fowey and the Thames will wait . . .

Quiller-Couch, Grahame's other Fowey friend, was deeply involved in politics, and was far too busy for social visiting. A passionate supporter of the Liberal cause, he was solidly behind Lloyd George, whose People's Budget had caused reactions ranging from ecstasy to apoplexy, though its demands were remarkably mild. The main point at issue was the proposal to levy a super-tax of sixpence in the pound (2.5 per cent) on incomes of over £3,000. Bearing in mind that Grahame had retired on less than a sixth of this amount, it was not excessive, but Lord Rosebery held it to be out-and-out Socialism. It was, he thundered, "the end of all – the negation of Faith, of Family, of Monarchy, of Empire".

Grahame, too, regarded the rise of democracy with a tremor of alarm, though he was able to write to Q with a certain wry humour: "I must not wish you luck in your nefarious designs of our savings, our cellars, and our garden-plots; but I do hope you'll get some fun out of it".[3] The other Liberal proposals centred on new land taxes and a slight increase in the duty on spirits and tobacco (hence Kenneth's comments about cellars and gardens), and Q did get some fun out of it, for he was knighted the following year for his services as a Liberal campaigner during the run-up to the General Election of 1910.

The Grahame household, like many others, was riven by political dissent. Kenneth regarded Socialism as a kind of Puritan wet blanket which would extinguish forever the colour and flavour of life under a soggy weight of officialdom, but Elspeth had been brought up in the Liberal tradition, for Fletcher Moulton had been a Liberal MP and she was well used to active political campaigning. Alastair supported his mother's view, though Elspeth naturally had it that the boy formed his opinions from an intelligent reading of the newspapers, but the People's Budget caused the pair of them to revise their collective opinion. Kenneth wrote to Q in gloomy triumph about his son's change of heart, even though he himself did his best to take a balanced view. Alastair, he said,

after being a staunch Liberal all his life, has lately crossed the floor of the House. "I had been having doubts for some time," he said: "and this Budget is the last straw." I tell him that there are many good points about the Budget; but he only replies that he has failed to detect any.[4]

Mouse was also failing to detect many good points in his parents at this time. They were away somewhere in the autumn of 1909, and he sent them press photographs of a local *Midsummer Night's Dream* production, declaring, "I have made up my mind to run away to the stage". At about the same period, he wrote twice to his parents.

Dear Dad & Co,
    I do want you to come down hear [*sic*] for the week end as I have a bone to pick with you.
                                            A. Grahame

Dear Dad & Co,
    as I cant pick a bone by post & you cant weekend it I must save it up.
                                            A. Grahame

In even more exasperation, he wrote on 29 September: "Dear Mum how dare you not come home on Tuesday".

The Grahames had other concerns, more pressing perhaps than their son's irritation. The lease on Mayfield was running out, and a move elsewhere would have to be made. In a letter to Purves dated 12 January 1910, Kenneth surveyed the situation without enthusiasm, saying that

I want to explain the difficulty I found in answering your last letter, of some months ago, sketching your hoped-for programme for the present year. It found us very busy house hunting and hopeful of being settled in a place of our own by Christmas at least; and now Christmas has come and gone, and we are as far as ever from a house. And our time is up here, and the owner wants to come back. And until this point is settled, all plans are in abeyance. As soon as I have found something and "moved in", I hope to go on my travels with a light heart. We are both somewhat stale and rusty, and I want to smell foreign smells again and drink wine in the country where it grows; but we feel it would be wiser to get our troubles over first. However, I do hope they *will* be over, long before you begin to get a move on you; and then it would be nice indeed if we could stretch our weary limbs under the same marble table outside some sun-bathed restaurant.

I will get E. to write to you about Tyrol, which she knows – I've never been there myself, but I should like to go. Though I can't talk German I *can* drink beer – and it's handy for Venice.

Q. is frightfully busy over the election, propagating his pernicious doctrines throughout the west country. We had a nice letter from his boy, who goes into residence at Oxford next week. Atky recently made a sudden flight into Sardinia, an island I've long wanted to visit. He hints darkly at adventures, but as yet I've had no opportunity of pumping him. Your boys must have had a ripping time. I wish some one would take me on a trip like that.

Well, until we meet, which I hope will now be soon,

Yours most sincerely,

Kenneth Grahame

The two eldest Purves sons had recently completed a grand tour of Europe. Kenneth's mind was still running obstinately on its theme of escape, and for all his courteous mention of Elspeth and her fancy for a visit to Austria, the underlying yearnings break through in his use of the first person – "I want to go on my travels . . . I want to smell foreign smells . . .". In the ten years since his marriage and (one feels more significantly) the blissful summer spent in Fowey, Atky and Q had remained his most cherished friends. The addition of Austin Purves to this close circle was also due to a meeting at Fowey. Nobody from London or Berkshire had penetrated Grahame's privacy to anything like the same extent. Constance Smedley, for all her slightly gushy sympathy, was not in the same league. All else apart, she was a woman, and Kenneth could not be quite relaxed in female company. In the days before his marriage, it was the quiet companionship of a male fellow walker which gave him most pleasure. Sidney Ward, who had worked at the Bank with Kenneth and had also put in some time at Toynbee Hall, reminisced about their shared experiences. Typical was

a weekend which I once spent with him at Streatley, during a cold, sunny spring. A friend had lent him a fourteenth-century cottage in the main street, and we had a grand twenty-mile walk along the Ridgeway, the subject of his "Romance of the Road". If we either of us said clever things that day they are forgotten, but we came home happy and tired, bought some chops and fetched a huge jug of beer from the pub. We cooked our dinner over the open wood fire, and how good the chops were! Then great chunks of cheese, new bread, great swills of beer, pipes, bed and heavenly sleep!

Grahame himself, in the piece Ward alluded to, remarked how

after unnumbered chops with country ale, the hard facts of life begin to swim in a golden mist . . . Tomorrow you shall begin life again; shall write your book, make your fortune, do anything; meanwhile you sit, and the jolly world swings round, and you seem to hear it circle in the music of the spheres. What pipe was ever thus beatifying in effect? You are aching all over and enjoying it, and the scent of the limes drifts in through the window . . .

Elspeth could not supply this kind of companionship, and it is doubtful whether any woman could. Male comradeship had a value very different from female love. Perhaps the lost father lingered in Grahame's yearning for a figure which paced at his side and shared in the exertion and tiredness of a day in the open air, and in the contentment which followed it. Elspeth, with her ailing, querulous unhappiness, had tried to bind her husband close, not seeing that in doing so, she robbed him of all that he loved. Now, in the early months of 1910, they were brought together again in a fretful way over the "troubles" of finding a new home.

Kenneth was fussy. He had once remarked, with perfect truth, that whereas Elspeth liked people, he liked places, and he could not enter into a relationship with a house unless it seemed capable of providing deep and long-lasting satisfaction. Had he gone into his marriage with the care which he lavished on the selection of a home, his life-story might have been very different – but, without the tragic and frustrating elements which Elspeth unwittingly supplied, it seems unlikely that *The Wind in the Willows* would ever have been written.

In his search for a suitable house, Grahame was looking for a retreat from all modernity. At last he found it, hidden away, like Mayfield, among trees, an ancient thatched farmhouse which, together with its outbuildings, had grown with the needs of those who had built it, over the centuries. Mouse and Miss Stott were sent off to Littlehampton on 5 May, to be out of the way, and Elspeth and Kenneth moved into Boham's a week later.

> *Boham's,*
> *Blewbury, Didcot,*
> *England, 20th May 1910*

MY DEAR PURVES, – After exceeding great tribulation we have at last found this little farmhouse, and moved into it a few days ago. Chaos, of course, and we live in a small clearing in a forest of books and furniture, striving vainly to reduce things to some appearance of order. Blewbury is perhaps the most beautiful of a string of pretty and very primitive villages stretched along the northern edge of the Berkshire Downs. It is only about 54 miles from London, but 5,400 years remote from it in every way. This is the heart of King Alfred's Country, "Alfred the Great" who beat the Danes, close by here, about 860, and nothing has really happened since. True, a tiresome innovator, called William the Conqueror, came along some years later, and established a thing called the Curfew bell, which still rings here during the winter months, to the annoyance of the more conservative inhabitants, who say they used to get on very well before these newfangled notions; but this is all that divides us from Saxon times. We are some twelve miles from Oxford, but its culture does not permeate to us; if we penetrate as far as Abingdon or Wallingford we are mighty travellers and have seen great and distant cities.

The village is really a charming one – a mixture of orchards and ancient timbered cottages and clear little streams, and the people are simple and friendly and dignified. The downs lie a mile or two to the south – splendid bare grassy spaces with (so-called) Roman or British "Camps" and "Barrows". The villages along the edge are all beautiful with fine old churches – ours is a beauty, and not much spoilt. We went to a memorial service for King Edward there to-day and the simplicity and genuineness of it all was very touching. As for this little house, it is a plain Berkshire farmer's house, "unfaked" and unaltered, with no special architectural features, with its orchard on one side and its farm buildings on the other. We are genuinely hoping that you may be able to come and see it – and us, and if you have to suffer any minor discomforts (if, for instance, we have to "sleep" you "out", in some dream of a thatched cottage, owing to exigencies of space), I am sure you will bear in mind that Alfred the Great was no better off. I have honestly no fear that Blewbury itself will disappoint you. The Bohams, I may explain, sleep in a row in the churchyard. Only their name remains, attached to this farm and to a road leading from it up onto the downs. I wonder whether your plans still hold good, as already related to us? If so, you will be here about the time that I have hammered in the last tack into the last carpet, and I shall wearily straighten my back and prepare to take a well-earned holiday with you. I suppose you would hardly have time to walk from here, by way of the downs, to Fowey? Atky says six weeks would do it quite comfortably. That peripatetic personage wrote to me the other day from Corsica. Each year his "St. Anthony's fever" seems to agitate his lean limbs more violently. Don't bring any fine clothes or evening frocks to *us*. We are the only people here who dine late at all and we keep it dark.

George V, whose children had come to see Grahame at the Bank of England, was now on the throne, and times were changing. But Kenneth was in full retreat from all that; Blewbury occupied his full interest. Despite the practical work which surrounded him, he wrote copious letters in these first days at Boham's and it is interesting to see how the style of these changes according to the addressee. To Constance Smedley, he uses brief sentences and a simple, almost childish vocabulary:

A little way off, there is a farmer whose family has been here for a thousand years. They are real Saxons. They live in a lovely old farm-house with a ghost in it. Indeed all the houses here are very old. They do not build the horrid little red houses that spring up around Cookham.[5]

Nowhere is his uneasiness with women more evident than in his efforts to write to them. To Alan Lidderdale, conversely, he is urbane and brisk, an ex-Bank man writing of trivia with an amused smile.

We moved into this little old farmhouse a fortnight ago, and have been slaving ever since to get it straight, with very little result – the trouble being that we have got too much stuff for so small a space. I was very sorry to leave Cookham Dean [sic], but there was really nothing there that suited us at all. This is a very beautiful village, in quite a different way, and the Downs are at one's door. I hope for some fine walking when I have finished picture-hanging and falling over rolls of carpet.

Mouse is down at the sea-side, to be out of all this stramash. E. hunts chickens – dead ones – through the village all day, & tries to persuade the farmers' wives to part with provisions of any sort, which they refuse to do.[6]

Elspeth, in fact, was becoming a little odd. She had adopted an autocratic manner, stumping round the village with a stick and addressing people with an abruptness which was not likely to produce offers of chickens or anything else, yet she habitually dressed in "an ancient navy-blue serge coat and skirt, with a frayed cardigan and hand-knitted stockings". Green, who supplies this description, claimed that, according to village gossip, "mouse-nests pro-liferated in the larder" at Boham's, and Elspeth "put Kenneth into special underwear which was only changed once a year". She herself often slept in her clothes, and was seldom out of bed before eleven in the morning. Grahame admitted to R. E. Moody, an artist friend, that "We live here in a state of primitive simplicity which is almost shocking".[7]

Within a few weeks of the move, however, Grahame was obliged to put on respectable clothes and travel the twelve miles to Oxford for, on 7 June,

A DIFFICULT FREEDOM

he was invited by Herbert Warren, President of Magdalen College, to hear
Theodore Roosevelt give the Romanus Lecture in the Sheldonian Theatre.
Warren's other guests were Rudyard Kipling, Andrew Lang, Gilbert Murray and Sir Charles Oman. Kenneth wrote a report of the event to Mouse,
still away at the seaside.

> Last Tuesday I went to Oxford to meet Mr Roosevelt. He was giving
> a lecture there and after the lecture he received his friends at Mag-
> dalen (you pronounce it Maudlin) college where he was staying. I had
> a long talk with him. Rudyard Kipling was there and Lord Curzon
> and a lot of old gentlemen in scarlet gowns.[8]

Grahame's eminent American fan, writing later in the *Saturday Evening Post*,
declared the author of *The Wind in the Willows* to be "simply charming".

There was evidently no hurry to get Mouse back from the seaside. On
10 June, the boy wrote, "Thank you for letting us stay on at Littlehampton
. . . By the way have you and mumy [*sic*] spring cleaned bohams yet? Yours
Bad Boy." This was a self-description which he often used. By 15 June, he
was becoming impatient, and wrote to Elspeth saying, "We are coming
home to you and Dad and Bohams on the 30th without fail".[9]

He did indeed return and, shortly afterwards, yet another American made
himself known to Grahame. He was Clayton Hamilton, a scholar in search
of material on Robert Louis Stevenson, and Kenneth invited him down to
Boham's for the weekend. The visitor recorded a clear impression of his host.

> At Didcot, on the platform, Kenneth Grahame stood waiting for me.
> He was very tall and broad, a massive figure, but with no spare flesh.
> At that time he was fifty years of age. His hair was white, but his face
> was almost beatifically young, and he had the clear and roseate com-
> plexion of a healthy child. He was dressed in knickerbockers, a soft
> shirt, and a baggy coat of tweeds. One could see at a glance that he
> was one of those rare people in the world who look like themselves.[10]

The contact had not been an easy one to make. Hamilton had approached
several writers in the hope of an introduction to Grahame, among them
Edmund Gosse and Andrew Lang, but they all told the same story – that
since his retirement from the Bank of England, Kenneth "rarely came to
town, he never went anywhere or saw anybody – he had adopted, in effect,
the life of a recluse".[11] Hamilton sent Grahame a copy of a *Wind in the Willows*
review he had published in America, and the invitation was a prompt result.

Engagingly, Hamilton recounted how his mind ran to the rhythm of the
train wheels as he mused on Grahame's address, giving rise to "a series of
preposterous couplets, such as:

Boham's, Blewbury, Didcot, Berks,
Fell in the sea and was bitten by sharks.

"One is not at one's keenest on a railway journey," he added. In the nervousness of meeting the elusive author, he "felt a desperate need to say
something unimportant", and he trotted out another of his couplets, linking
Boham's with the name of an American poetess, Josephine Preston Peabody
Marks. Kenneth at once fell into the literary game, remarking that

At Boham's, Blewbury, Didcot, Berks,
She would wake in the morning and listen to larks.

The two men evidently achieved a rare and instant understanding. Hamilton noted that

> before the second day was finished, I became aware of a delicate and
> somewhat strange phenomenon. It was simply, but emphatically, this
> – that Kenneth Grahame was not at home beneath a roof. Indoors,
> he would lapse into a silence that might endure an hour, for – as I
> observed with gratitude – he felt no social compulsion whatsoever to
> keep talking in the presence of a visitor; but, as soon as we started out
> upon a ramble across country, he would break into an easy current of
> cheery conversation.

In an effort to retain as much as possible of what the famous British author had
said, Hamilton noted down what he remembered of the day's talk. Although his
account cannot be regarded as verbatim, it is the most complete statement of
Grahame's philosophy which has been recorded, and it is worth quoting in full.

> The most priceless possession of the human race is the wonder of the
> world. Yet, latterly, the utmost endeavours of mankind have been
> directed towards the dissipation of that wonder. Everybody seems to
> cry out for a world in which there shan't be any Santa Claus. Science
> analyses everything to its component parts, and neglects to put them
> together again. A bare-foot boy cannot go wading in a mountain
> stream without being told that he must no longer spell the fluid that
> sings round his feet by the age-old lettering of W-A-T-E-R, but must
> substitute the symbol H_2O. Nobody, any longer, may hope to enter-
> tain an angel unawares, or to meet Sir Lancelot in shining armour on
> a moonlit road. You have quoted Wordsworth – "It is not now as it
> hath been of yore". But the poet *began* by reminding us that, "There
> *was* a time" ... It is that time which I have attempted to recapture
> and commemorate in *Dream Days* and *The Golden Age*.

Granted that the average man may live for seventy years, it is a fallacy to assume that his life from sixty to seventy is more important than his life from five to fifteen. Children are not merely people: they are the only really living people that have been left to us. Any child will agree with your American poet, Walt Whitman, when he says: "To me every hour of the day and night is an unspeakably perfect miracle."

In my tales about children, I have tried to show that their simple acceptance of the mood of wonderment, their readiness to welcome a perfect miracle at any hour of the day or night, is a thing more precious than any of the laboured acquisitions of adult mankind.

Hamilton questioned him about his use of animals as characters, and about his evident liking for them, and Grahame had this to say;

As for animals, I wrote about the most familiar in *The Wind in the Willows* because I felt a duty to them as a friend. Every animal, by instinct, lives according to his nature. Thereby he lives wisely, and betters the tradition of mankind. No animal is ever tempted to deny his nature. No animal knows how to tell a lie. Every animal is honest. Every animal is true – and is, therefore, according to his nature, both beautiful and good. I like most of my friends among the animals . . . come, and let me show you . . .

Grahame had chirruped to his tame robin, and then led Hamilton on a round of the Blewbury farms and, as the American said, "introduced me individually to each of the domestic animals of that rural district".

Grahame's almost empathetic fellow-feeling for animals is evident in his writing, and his liking for particular ones often spilled over into his books. Portly, for instance, the baby Otter who was found safe between the hoofs of the great god Pan, was named after one of Graham Robertson's dogs. "I hope you don't mind," he had said to Robertson, "but I must call him Portly because – well, because it is his name. What else am I to call him?"[12]

There was, however, an odd inconsistency in his animal-sympathy. Wherever male toughness was to be proved, Grahame withdrew his sensitivity and took a strictly conventional stance. It began with Farmer Larkin's occasional killing of a pig in the *Golden Age* stories. Although the children are shown to be "on the friendliest of terms" with pigs, there is an obligation to regard a killing as a great event. When Edward departs for school, his siblings promise him earnestly that they will ask Farmer Larkin not to kill any more pigs until he is home for the holidays.[13] Grahame offers a pragmatic excuse: "Did you come to love a pig, and he was taken from you, grief was quickly assuaged in the delight of a selection from the new litter."[14]

255

But the bloodthirsty proclaiming of delight in the execution itself was perhaps a test of toughness which no boy could be seen to fail.

The same test applied to the hunting of foxes. During the first autumn at Boham's when out with Alastair one day, Grahame encountered the hounds and huntsmen – and their quarry. There is a touch of braggart defensiveness in his account of it to Purves.

> Mouse and I had a wonderful bit of luck one morning in November, when the hounds ran into their fox at our very feet and we saw every detail of the kill and the "breaking up" and then Mouse shyly asked the huntsman to "blood" him – do you know the nasty process? And this good-natured man did and presented him with the brush as well, and he was proud indeed.[15]

Somehow, a sense of horror hangs over the event. "Nasty" is a word which slips in almost inconsequentially, and yet it more than counter-balances the welcoming of the "bit of luck". Alastair seems to have been the more outgoing of the two, taking the initiative in approaching the huntsmen. In this, as so often, his over-riding motivation seems to have been the desire to make the most of what the situation offered.

Hamilton took Kenneth to task about the ten-year gap between *Dream Days* and *The Wind in the Willows*, and said there should not be such a long hiatus before another book appeared. Grahame was silent for a moment. Then he said, "I doubt very much if I shall ever write another book. A certain amount of what a countryman of yours called *life* must go into the making of any page of prose. The effort is enormous."

Hamilton pointed out that "everybody praises you for your graceful ease" and this observation unlocked a rare flood of opinion on the literary process.

> A sentence that is easy to read may have been difficult to put together. Perhaps the greater the easiness in writing, the harder that task in composition. Writing is not easy; I need not tell you that. There is always a pleasure in the exercise; but, also, there is always an agony in the endeavour. If we make a formula of those two motives, I think we may define the process. It is, at its best, a pleasurable agony.
>
> "I am not a professional writer. I never have been, and I never will be, by reason of the accident that I don't need any money. I do not care for notoriety: in fact, it is distasteful for me. If I should ever become a popular author, my privacy would be disrupted and I should no longer be allowed to live alone.
>
> What, then, is the use of writing for a person like myself? The answer might seem cryptic to most. It is merely that a fellow entertains a sort of hope that somehow, sometime he may build a noble sentence

that might make Sir Thomas Browne sit upward once again in that
inhospitable grave of his in Norwich.

But language – before this ancient world grew up and went astray
– was intended to be spoken to the ear. We are living now in an
eye-minded age, when he who runs may read and the average person
glimpses his daily reading on the run. What is the use, any longer, of
toying with the pleasurable agony of attempting stately sentences of
English prose? Apart from you and myself, who sit alone upon this
ancient barrow, there are not more than six men in the United Kingdom who have inherited an ear for prose.

When Hamilton objected that *The Wind in the Willows* was admired by
thousands of readers, Grahame was prompt in his disclaimer. " 'They liked
the subject matter,' he replied. 'They did not even notice the source of all
the agony, and all the joy. A large amount of what Thoreau called life went
into the making of many of those playful pages.' "

It was a rare admission, pointed in its contrast with Grahame's public
denial of any deeper significance to the story. But the whole statement is
spoken with a sense of finality. It is retrospective, reviewing a past activity.
For all the pleasure of his idle existence in rural Berkshire, Grahame knew
that it was not the stuff from which books are made. He had retreated from
the battle. He had settled for domesticity, even though Elspeth's version of
it was a comfortless travesty. He was, in the fullest sense of the word, a
retired man.

In July 1910, the long-hoped-for visit from the Purves family took place,
though this time the children did not accompany their parents. Kenneth's
plan of setting out on foot with his old friend to walk to Fowey came to
nothing; Purves and his wife professed themselves quite content to potter
about the village, indulging in their new-fangled passion for taking photographs (the results of which were to astonish the villagers later). It could have
been, too, that Mrs Purves had no desire to be left alone with Elspeth, for the
daisy-decked bride of eleven years ago had changed into a tense, wild-eyed
eccentric, convinced that her own idea of normality was in no way odd. It was
some time before the Purveses returned home, for they went on from Britain
to undertake a long Continental tour, but the strangeness of the Grahame
household remained sharp in their minds, and they had a highly entertaining
tale to tell. Their son, Austin Purves Jr, never forgot it. As he wrote later:

I remember clearly my mother's amusement, or consternation, or
both, at the fact that Mr and Mrs Grahame lived in separate parts of
the house. My parents were very connubial and the Grahames simply
expected their guests to enjoy the same household and sleeping arrangements as they did themselves . . .

One remembers Kenneth's uneasy proviso that guests might be asked to "sleep out" in a cottage in the village. Was he embarrassed by the revealing of the gulf between himself and Elspeth? If so, in the interval between his letter to the Purveses and their arrival, he had evidently decided that there was no hope of any pretence, for his wife's eccentricity took so many forms. She hardly ate anything herself, as if in silent disapproval of Kenneth's continued delight in good food and drink, and Mrs Purves was startled afresh to find that "at breakfast after this nocturnal separation of the sexes there was tea and toast and one egg. Mrs Grahame said: 'The egg is for Kenneth'."[16]

Elspeth never managed to understand that she was in any way unusual. Her careful housekeeping, enforced by the years of Fletcher Moulton meanness, ripened into a parsimony of irrational harshness, perhaps aggravated by knowledge that Kenneth's retirement pension had been a small one. Her personal shabbiness acted as a proof that she spent none of her husband's money on herself, even though she had rolls of silk and satin dresses upstairs which she had never unpacked after the move, and certainly never wore. Since the settlement with her stepfather, Elspeth was quite well off in her own right, but she seemed unable to come to terms with this fact.

Austin Purves and his wife had hardly left when a letter arrived from Gordon Home of A & C Black, suggesting to Kenneth that he might like to write a book of some 40,000 words, to be called *Highways and Hedges*. It would be about country life, the editor said, and it could contain "anecdotes, folk-lore, philosophy, political economy, botany, ornithology, and references to anything and everything that rambles in beautiful English country are likely to bring to mind".[17]

It was a tailor-made vehicle for Grahame's views, and he found the idea very attractive, despite his previous pessimism about the prospect of another book. He wrote back to Home with tentative enthusiasm, and proposed that he should have the rights to publish the contents in instalment form prior to the issue of the volume itself, much as he did with the essays which formed his first three books. Home had no objection to this, but he wanted to buy the whole copyright for $50 in lieu of royalties. It was, of course, an outrageous suggestion, and Grahame turned it down. John Lane's young assistant in New York, Mitchell Kennerley, had paid $1,000 to Stone and Kimball for the plates and publishing rights of *The Golden Age*. Reckless though that purchase undoubtedly was, it made the offer from A & C Black seem all the more parsimonious. A writer of more energy and ambition would have mulled over the idea and presented it to a different publisher, but Kenneth was disinclined to settle down to work. Alastair had again been at the seaside during the visit of Mr and Mrs Purves, but he returned later in the summer, to enjoy the long, blossomy Berkshire days.

There was a sense, too, that the company of Mouse was to be treasured, for the boy was now eleven, and the following year, he was to go to school, following which he would, Kenneth anticipated, start to grow up in the way that Edward of *The Golden Age* had done. These were the last months of his childhood, and Kenneth was determined to enjoy them, as if to make up for the long periods of separation. He flung himself into village affairs and into the entertainment of Mouse, with equal enthusiasm. As he wrote to Purves,

> Our great annual social event, the "Fete", came off last Wednesday and Society with a big S was convulsed from top to toe; but is gradually simmering down to quietude again for another twelve months. We made £27 for the Church expenses – Mouse as a "costermonger" with a miniature "coster-barrow", sold sweets vigorously, and cleared 17s 6d. Saunders had a weighing-machine and Mrs S a bran-tub, and made over £2 between them. Dancing and pyrotechnics closed an event of unexampled brilliance, which the *Morning Post*, however, has so far failed to chronicle.[18]

Saunders was the local farmer, whose natural eminence as a landowner put him and Grahame on a similar level. Through him, Kenneth discovered a further delight, recorded in the same letter.

> Yesterday morning we drove over early to East Ilsley (that village we did *not* go to, the day we were up on the downs together) to see the big annual sheep fair. I can't describe it, but it was one of the most *intoxicating* things I have ever been at. The noise of dogs and sheep and dealers, the procession of sheep and men, the droves of flockmasters and dealers in the most fascinating clothes you can conceive, the pubs all gay and busy, and the beautiful little village glittering with movement and humming with the real Berkshire language, beat any Pageant I have ever seen. And all genuine business too – not an "outsider" present except ourselves. *You ought to have been there*. Mouse was soon in the thick of it, but when I sought him and discovered him bidding at the auction for pedigree rams, I had to haul him out of action.
>
> Mouse and Saunders have become very good friends and now call each other "old chap" and he goes to tea there when he likes.

The rest of the letter reverts to the theme of travel, and, despite the charms of Berkshire, a note of wistfulness creeps in.

> The card you sent me of Innsbruck was beautiful, and rather tugged at me. But foreign places all do. We are fixed here for August anyway, and a bit of September. After that – I don't know: there are possibilities.

You don't say if the boys have had all the climbing they wanted. Sooner them nor me. Something with a restaurant on its airy summit is quite good enough for me.

He added a postscript: "E. is most tremendously obliged for the dental silk, wh. duly arrived". Purves had sent prints of the photographs taken during their stay at Boham's, and these, too, are acknowledged with thanks: "They are being gradually shown round the village, and are received with cries of 'Law' and 'Well I never' and 'Fancy now' and careful identification of every paling and bit of thatch".

Such accounts carry a hint of the isolation which an incomer into such a community must feel. Despite the taking up of his natural place in the local squirearchy, Grahame was becoming aware that he could not *belong* to the village except as a respected curiosity. Depression began to set in. The initial work on the house had been done, and the thrill of finding three-hundred-year-old linen-folded oak under the eight layers of paint was no longer new. The thatch and the apple-loft, the granary and the two great kitchens and the trout-streams were there, but a retired banker and his semi-invalid wife could not bring them to life; neither could the dry sexlessness of the house be blamed solely on Elspeth. It was an aspect of Kenneth's functioning which had never developed, and he had arrived at a monastic existence within marriage through his own choice. As he had told Hamilton, he wanted "to live alone". And yet, by the Christmas of 1910, he was expressing some regret, in a letter to Q, that he was no longer part of the major pageant of life. Thirty-odd years spent in intimate involvement and in a capital city leaves a certain familiarity with that rhythm of bustle and interaction, and it is not easily discarded.

The passing of the days was marked by small details. Purves sent a rain-cape for Alastair. "He highly approves of its cut and style," Grahame wrote back, "and so does his governess, who finds it light and convenient to carry." Mouse, it seems, was not expected to carry his own rainwear. His company, however, continued to be a source of happiness to his father.

This morning Mouse and I went to see Farmer Saunders and buy some apples – and first we went up a ladder into the apple-loft, and sampled every sort of apple and filled our pockets – and then we sat in the parlour and discussed circuses, and all three of us agreed that they were the only thing worth living for.

While you have sailed across half the world nothing has happened here except that the Michaelmas daisies have come out . . .

Grahame had, however, taken Mouse to Oxford's St Giles's Fair, "and had a dizzy day riding around on pink bears, swinging to the clouds in Dread-noughts . . .".

On 18 October 1910, he wrote to Purves to return a proffered gift of a bundle of letters from Maxfield Parrish, who had illustrated *The Golden Age*, and whose work Kenneth admired immensely. The youngest Purves boy, Pierre Marot, Kenneth's godson, had sent him a Parrish-illustrated book of fairy stories the previous Christmas, and Austin was obviously trying to raise his old friend's flagging spirits. He had sent him two pictures, to-gether with a pressing invitation to come to America, but the offer of the letters was misplaced, failing to allow for Grahame's scrupulous sense of rightness.

> I received and read the Maxfield Parrish letters with great delight and the consciousness of a vivid personality behind each written word; and I much appreciate your kind offer of them for my own keeping. I am, however, sending them back, for I feel *very* strongly that a letter has a peculiar and direct and special appeal for the recipient, which no one else can entirely share; and you will like to glance over these again, on some happy *idle* day that is surely to come.

Austin, unlike Kenneth, was still frantically active, and his accounts of evi-dently over-packed days were a sharp contrast to the aimlessness of life in Berkshire. On 15 November, Mouse wrote to Elspeth, "Dear mumy How do you like Weymouth?"[19] His parents had clearly not told him that they had gone in search of a prospective school. Kenneth, however, had more idle days than he knew what to do with, and his depression deepened. It was massively increased at about this time by the sudden death of Roland's wife, Joan. She was younger than Kenneth himself and yet a heart attack had ended her life without warning. The cosy security of Boham's seemed a mockery. Grahame went down with bronchitis, and was ill for several weeks. It was 21 January 1911 before he could write to Purves again.

> I have been laid up in bed with a sharp attack of bronchitis, which has interfered sadly with my Christmas duties, and pleasures too for that matter, and other people's also; but that is over for the present, though I have to sit indoors over a fire and not run about over the downs, as I would fain be doing . . .
> We have not had much fun this winter − too much wet for gadding about. But Mouse goes to children's parties and is very happy. He goes to school after Easter and is much pleased and excited at the prospect. It is a nice place in Dorsetshire, near the coast, with beautiful bathing and surroundings. We took a short trip to that part of the country in November and liked it much.

Typically, Kenneth sought to interview the place rather than the people but, on this occasion, his approach worked well. The Old Malthouse School, at Langton Maltravers, near Wareham, on the Dorset coast, was a relaxed, permissive community, ideally suited to Alastair's somewhat over-blown personality.

Only a few months remained before the departure of Mouse would rob Kenneth of his walking companion and fellow enthusiast for fairs and circuses, and he was determined to make the most of it. If Elspeth objected, she was firmly over-ruled. On 7 February, he wrote to Purves:

> We are all four for Cornwall three days hence, if nothing intervenes. First to the Lizard, for two or three weeks, then, I hope, to Fowey. I want Mouse to make the acquaintance of my Cornish haunts, and friends, before he goes to school – then he may like to go back there. So my next letter may be from familiar scenes and contain tidings of gulls and lobsters.

It was three months before he wrote again, with a long and revealing account of the holiday. Sadly, even the Cornish dreamland had not been untouched by change. Fowey had been "discovered" and was suffering from the effect of its own success as a tourist resort. On 15 May, in the emptiness left by Mouse's departure to school, Grahame recalled his sense of let-down.

> I found the arrangements of the house (which was also very full most of the time) very uncomfortable for correspondence, and I may say that we were greatly disappointed in the way that the place was run. I went there because I thought it would be more simple and home-like for the boy and his governess than the hotel, which I should have preferred; but there was a skimping and a pinching everywhere, which was not agreeable. Skimping in food, in lights, in chamber linen, in hot water even. Complaints were general, and for my part I shall not go there again. It is indeed becoming a little difficult to find accommodation at Fowey. The doctors have begun to send convalescents there, the G. W. Ry [Great Western Railway] advertises it assiduously, and although it was still a fortnight to Easter when we left, the place was as full as in summer.
>
> Well, enough of that side of it, the town itself, the harbour, the river, greeted us with all their old charm. Bigger steamers than ever come up to the "tips", the clay is loaded by electricity, and the work goes on night and day. Fowey is prospering, and new houses have been built, out Point Neptune way; but the quays and the old town and the harbour-front are the same as ever – the same mud, the same fish heads and guts (apparently). And the same Q, looking not a day older

and even more beautifully dressed than formerly. Mouse was particularly struck with Q's clothes. I think he then realized, for the first time, that man, when he chooses to give his mind to it, is incomparably the finer animal of the two, and does the greater justice to clothes. (Soldiers and peacocks know this already of course.) He observed solemnly to me, after contemplation of a certain suit of checks – Irish homespun – that "Q. was his idea of a hero of a novel". The "Haven" was "done up" too, last autumn, in a new suit of excellent style and taste, and sparkled with cleanliness and colour.

The Haven was Quiller-Couch's riverside house. He had two children, the boy called Bevil whom Grahame had mentioned when he had gone up to Oxford the previous autumn, and a younger girl called Foy. For those unfamiliar with Cornwall, it is worth pointing out that Fowey is pronounced Foy. Q, unlike Grahame, had given himself wholly to the little salty town of his dreams, and had turned out a steady stream of novels and poetry which had earned him recognition and a good income. Mouse and Foy, Grahame was happy to see, "became good friends at once, and had many teas and walks together, and expeditions to the farm . . .".

Atky too, was very much in evidence, for the same long letter records that

we had several expeditions to Rosebank and had two of Atky's "special" luncheons – i.e. mostly fancy *hors d'oeuvres* and every sort of sausage – and Mouse had several teas, with gramophone, and liberty to potter about among all the books, and objects. He had not begun sailing, but was busy "fitting out" in the boat house. He has been doing a lot of carpentering this winter, and that seems to have done him good.

Even if Atky was busy in the boat-house, it did not prevent Kenneth from getting out on the river.

One specially warm and sunny day I took M. and his governess up to tea at Lerryn "on a tide", sailing up and rowing back. There is to me a tremendous sense of age about Lerryn – if I were painting some thirteenth or fourteenth century incident, I would be content to take Lerryn water-side, with the old bridge, for background: just as it is – indeed, it has probably altered little since those days.

Bevil was back from Oxford part of the time, but we didn't see much of him. He was on the water all the time – sailing, sailing, sailing.

Mouse has asked to be taken back to Fowey some day soon, which is a good sign – but I fancy, on the whole, he liked the Lizard best.

To be sure he went there first, and we had better weather there, but the wildness, freshness and strangeness of the Lizard, its grandeur and sparkling air, probably impressed him more than the slightly sophisticated Fowey; and he liked the simple, friendly people, who were all so nice to him and let him run in and out of their places, and had him to tea, and called me "Mr Kenneth", as I was known to them four-and-twenty years back.

The feudalism evoked by these words evidently suited Alastair who, according to Elspeth, "was always known by the appellation of 'The Young Squire' ". Since she admits that "even new-come owners of great Estates in those regions were never given the title of Squire", it seems that there may have been an element of irony in the villagers' mode of address. Kenneth, indifferent to such social nuances, was, as always, more concerned with the place than the people. The cliffs, he said, were "not really safe for children, so I shall not hurry to take him back till he's a good deal older". Meanwhile, the golden age, such as it was, of Alastair's childhood was almost over.

Since we got back from Cornwall we have been very busy fitting M. out for school and getting him off. The joy and pride of a complete new outfit of clothes – including even "Eton" jacket and trousers for Sundays – no doubt mitigated the pangs. At any rate he made the great plunge last Monday, going off very manfully and composedly and, from what we hear, he is falling into the ways of the new life very well. It is very quiet here now without him.[20]

14

Alastair at School

Chalmers, writing in 1933, depicted Alastair Grahame as an outstandingly talented boy, sensitive, brilliant, witty and unusual. Green, twenty-six years later, rejected this picture as a fabrication of wish-fulfilment on Elspeth's part, and claimed that Mouse was under intolerable pressure from his ambitious parents, and that, far from being brilliant, he was an academic dullard, unable to spare any energy from the struggle of trying to overcome the handicap of his near-blindness.

Neither picture rings quite true. Mouse was undoubtedly cosseted, indulged and admired from his earliest babyhood, and he certainly developed all the unlovable characteristics of the spoiled child; but if he sensed a conditionality underlying the parental rapture, it was not connected at that time with a demand for academic excellence. What the Grahames wanted from their late-born, purblind son was proof of normality. The more "normal" he could be, the better they liked it. They enjoyed his naughtiness and pertness and presumption, and did not jib at his growing arrogance. Like the bemused and scandalised, yet still protective animals of the River Bank who tried to save Toad from his own worst excesses, they did their uncomprehending best for Alastair. Kenneth, in particular, had leaned over backwards not to be Olympian in his attitude towards the boy, always taking the stance of a friend and playmate rather than any kind of authority-figure. Consequently, Mouse, as his later letters made clear, was beginning to despise his father. Kenneth had to earn his son's affection by ever-increasing indulgence.

Elspeth, always the romantic self-deceiver, was able to believe utterly in Alastair's brilliance, and for a long time she managed to keep Mouse's own self-belief intact. She, as the archetypal "weak woman" lying on sofas in a state of frailty, could not be expected, or so her behaviour tacitly implied, to enforce the family's standards. If Alastair had lapses of courtesy or modesty, then the failing must be that of the father who did not do his fatherly duty. If he had successes, then she could take a simple delight in them as a manifestation of the boy's real nature. She did not, perhaps, realise that she had cast her husband in a no-win situation. If Elspeth and Alastair were in sympathy, that was all that mattered. Mouse was thus assured of the love and approval of at least one parent all the time. If they did unite occasionally in a feeling that coping with Alastair was becoming intolerable, they sent him off to Littlehampton with his governess, ostensibly as a special treat. He never knew what it was to be disapproved of and, if his parents' enthusiasm for him seemed to be flagging, it only took some act of flamboyance to blow the spark into active life again. What others regarded as showing off was, to Alastair, life's most important technique.

His prep school was chosen for its indulgent attitude as well as satisfying Kenneth's insistence that the natural setting must be pleasant. This was to be Alastair's first venture into the outside world, and the Grahames took great care that the introduction should be a gentle one. Even the time of year was deliberately chosen, to give him only a single term's taste of being away before the return for the long summer holiday.

As early as 28 May 1911, when he had only been at school for a few weeks, Mouse's letters are cocky and full of confidence. Talking about the form of address he should use, he said, "in future I shall begin – your majesty's humble servant craves your majesty's pardon for not at once answering your majesty's epistle . . .".

There is an unrepentant note here which is not at first easy to understand, but it may well stem from a protest about what he had written earlier, when he had only just left home: "My dear Madam, your humble servant is glad to hear that improvements are coming up like bulbs and that Inferiority is doing some work *at last*!"

It is not the only occasion on which Alastair uses this term for his father, and Elspeth herself formalises it by noting in pencil on the letter, as if for the benefit of the archive, that "Inferiority was his whimsical name for his father at that time".[1] It was a whimsy – if that is the word for it – which she condoned, even though she did not sanction any reference to it in the 1933 biography.

The improvements which Alastair mentions probably refer to Kenneth's work on what he called "my barn". In January 1911, just before the pre-school expedition to Fowey, he had written to Purves that he had "put a good stove in, and most of my books, and it makes a very decent study indeed". He may well have felt in need of a bolt-hole.

Another letter to Purves, dated 16 August 1911, at the end of Mouse's first term at school, takes up the story of his American friend's continued solicitous attention and Grahame's own growing inertia and boredom.

Dear Purves, – Thank you very much indeed for the beautiful Maxfield Parrish colour print you sent me – the pie picture. It is a noble piece of colour, and I am glad indeed to possess it. Of course it ought to have been acknowledged long ago – and your two letters – and there is also Mrs Purves's letter to E. and the two *Print Collector's Quarterlies*, the five magazines, the gift of photos.

We never expected you to write at all during your terrible heatwave. How thankful you must have felt that the boys were away. Here we have been having a bit of a wave too, in our own small English way. People have been crying out, of course – but, to me, it has been the most glorious summer that I remember. I never saw such colour in the crops – burnt to a fierce tawny red. What is getting serious is the drought – practically no rain in these parts for two months, and no sign of it. The farmers are hard put to it to find food for their beasts, and sheep are fetching wretched prices in the market.

We are staying on here quietly, for the present, for Mouse's summer holidays. He seems quite happy and contented here which is as it should be. When he is older, perhaps, he may find it a bit dull. He brought home good reports, and says he liked it from the first day.

We had several pleasant trips to Oxford before the hot weather set in. Since then it has not been possible to make any expeditions – at least it was possible, but it would not have been very wise. I take a siesta, foreign fashion, from 2 to 4, and later, get up on the downs, where there is generally a breeze. I hope soon to get some boating on the Thames; but since I wrote to you, our life has been most uneventful. Not even any fairs as yet. Owing to the coronation, when we poor country folk spent all our hoarded pennies in decorations, &c., the dates of all the village fêtes and fairs have been fixed for as late in the summer as possible, to give us a chance of saving a few more pennies for shows and roundabouts. But when we get our harvest money, we shall be rich again, and the fun will begin. Then we will ride on noble steeds of wood, with their names painted in gold on their necks (they are all named after famous racehorses of old time), and shy for co-coanuts and swing till we are sick – at least, I shall be sick.

Well, goodbye for the present. This is not a real letter. Perhaps later I shall have something more solid to tell you about. Some wild village orgie – or "harvest home".

Despite his efforts to find an identity with people who had to wait for "our harvest money" before indulging in the delights of a local fair, Grahame was isolated, and knew it. He must have been aware that one of his infrequent letters to Purves had already dealt with the subject of the roundabout horses with their names painted on their necks, and that he had, in truth, nothing else to write about.

A few weeks after the August letter, Kenneth suffered the loss of a treasured friend. Atky, out sailing in a heavy sea off the Fowey coast with Q's son, Bevil, was caught in the gale, and the eighteen-footer foundered on the rocks. Atky was knocked unconscious, but Bevil, still at this time an Oxford undergraduate, managed to bring the inert, water-sodden man ashore through the breakers as far as the foot of the cliff. It was night-time, and he could not struggle any further without help. He hauled Atky on to a rock-shelf, then climbed the cliff in the windswept darkness, found a farmhouse and mustered a rescue party – but by the time they reached the ledge where Bevil had left the unconscious man, the mounting waves had washed him out to sea. It was several days before his body was found. On 20 September 1911, Grahame wrote to Purves:

> The sad news of the deplorable tragedy at Fowey has no doubt reached you; but you will naturally be anxious for all particulars so I am sending all that appeared in the *Western Morning News*, in case no one else has done so. We have not yet had any letters from Fowey about it. Please keep the cuttings if you want to.
>
> I loved Atky – in perhaps a selfish way first of all because his special "passions" appealed to me – boats, Bohemianism, Burgundy, tramps, travel, books, and pictures – but also, and I hope and believe chiefly, for his serene and gentle nature, his unfailing good humour and clear, cheerful spirits, and his big kind heart. But you know all these qualities of his as well as I do. And you are mourning him too.
>
> Again and again, in imagination, I get my boat at Whitehouse Steps and scull up the river by the grey old sea wall, under the screaming gulls, past the tall Russian and Norwegian ships at their moorings, and so into Mixtow Pill, and ship my oars at the little stone pier, and find Atky waiting on the steps, thin, in blue serge, with his Elizabethan head; and stroll up the pathway you know, to the little house above it, and he talking all the time and always some fresh whimsicality. I had a letter from him a very few weeks ago, telling of a Yachting Dinner they had just had – he, apparently, in the Chair, and his spirits seemed as buoyant as ever.
>
> Well, I will not write more just now. I feel as if we had all suddenly grown much older. All, that is, except Atky. He couldn't do it, he didn't know how.

The shock was numbing. Once Mouse had gone back to school, Kenneth took a holiday with Elspeth in Pont Aven, in southern Brittany, but it did not lift his spirits. They saw, he said, "a lot of new things, but, to me, that is not the *South* and therefore – nothing. You've got to have the Alps to the North of you before the air begins to have the right feel to it."

There is no clear reason why, feeling as he did, Kenneth chose western France rather than answer the call of his restless blood and go somewhere Mediterranean. Before departing, he had written to Curtis Brown, in an oddly self-excusing tone, saying that he and Elspeth wanted "something fairly cheap – and not too far – and yet properly foreign".[2] Apart from the last stipulation, such concerns sound more like Elspeth than Kenneth. She had been abroad with him for three months in the previous spring, and now evidently was not keen to repeat the experience. Pont Aven was perhaps a compromise. "I want a change of diet and a change of smells," Kenneth wrote in the same letter to his agent, "– and I believe the smells of some of the Brittany ports are very rich and satisfying." But he had lamented on more than one occasion previously that differences in taste made it difficult to holiday together as a family. The differences may well have been between him and Elspeth, for Mouse seems to have enjoyed himself wherever he was taken.

The truth may have been that Kenneth, grieving for Atky, was in no mood for relaxation and enjoyment. A much-loved landscape, once visited in sadness and depression, takes on a shadow which lingers there to be re-experienced; if Brittany was so shadowed, Kenneth did not mind.

Elspeth's allusions to the trip, as set down in her cloying little book, *The First Whisper of The Wind in the Willows*, touch on an episode which sounds more than usually unreal, for it seems to indicate that Elspeth herself was not there at all.

Quite recently a friend, as she has now become, related to me how her first impression of Kenneth came to her on the verandah of the celebrated "Hotel Julia" at Pont Aven in the south of Brittany. He had just arrived there, and while his luggage was being taken up to his room, waited outside to get a glimpse of his new surroundings. But he himself was soon surrounded by a group of small Breton boys who had already induced him to tell them a story which they were drinking in with avidity, while he stood looking far away over their heads and charming them as the song of a hitherto unknown bird might. And there could have been but little more comprehension in this case for the reason that the children – barely of school age – would, although Kenneth spoke French, not yet have mastered that language and only knew their native Breton which even French people living in Brittany for half a lifetime do not understand.[3]

The story is grotesquely unlikely, particularly as Grahame was well known by his friends for his absolute ignoring of strange children. He was willing to answer letters from young people, but he shrank from that avuncular approach which he himself had so disliked as a child. Hinds remembered him on another occasion "ignoring two children who were of the party, but studiously polite to their parents", and the Purves boys spoke with appreciation of his friendly silence. "Nor was there any need for words," Dale said.

Alastair, meanwhile, "undaunted and in high spirits", had taken to the liberal regime of The Old Malthouse with the greatest of aplomb. In a retrospective letter to Purves about the events of the autumn, Grahame wrote that they had "excellent accounts of him and his progress". There was much else which he might have said, but he was unfailingly generous to his son, happy to send decorations for the Coronation celebrations on 22 June, and to forgive the continuing note of contempt in his letters. When Kenneth and Elspeth went off to Brittany, however, it provoked an almost savage outburst of heavy-handed irony.

– To the Artful and Extravagant One –

I hear that you have taken advantage of my absents to make a bolt for France, and I have no dout that before long you will be in *Gay Paris* or Mòntécârló. [The erratic accents are his.]

I am at present staying in a little island known as England [this word is encased in a furiously pencilled box] of which you may have heard, you will find it on the map of Europe, to the west of *France*.

Nothing doing here, at present, England *is* a dull little place!

Yours

Off the Côntinông

A. Grahame

On the reverse of this epistle, he scrawled an imagined account of his father's self-indulgent expenses.

[Bill]

	£	s	d
cigars	0	10	6
chocolate	0	5	3
New hats	5	5	0
cigarettes	0	7	6
motor car (on hire)	10	10	0
orchids (for buttonholes)	2	5	0
Eau-de-cologne		12	6

total

He did not bother to add the figures up.

The resentment and jealousy comes off the paper in waves, and one begins to sense how unstable was the trio in which the family found itself locked. It constantly polarised itself as a two and a one, and Alastair was not used to being the single element. Prior to his departure to school, he had been assured of a close pairing with one or other of his half-estranged parents and, on the rare occasions when they were together, he had been sent on holiday with the faithful Miss Stott, so that it appeared that he was having a treat. Now, he was confronted with the duality of his parents and he was furiously angry, particularly with his treacherous father. He was hardly mollified when his parents came back to Britain:

270

Sunday Nov 5th 1911
My dear Madam,
    I perceive that your present address is at Jersey, which, I suppose,
is on your way home. I am just trying to make somebody sell me
something, so could you please prevail upon inferiority to send some
more £ s d . . .

By the following Sunday, he was slightly contrite, thanking his father for the
ten shillings which "far exceeded anything expected". He followed this with
a conscientious description of a theatre visit. He was in fact greatly attracted
by the theatre, and the next Sunday letter is wildly excited because he is
about to be the hero in the school play: "Yow-yow-yow. I want to yell
badley, so I have to let it off on paper . . ."
    Of the play, he says ". . . an offal lark being in it, but rather a responsi-
bility". Irrepressibly, he ends the letter, "Plonk-tiddly-onk-tonk, Yours, A.
Grahame".
    The advent of Christmas, however, brought out his most beady-eyed
self-interest.

    I also enclose a warning to Inferiority. If he does not take me to the
    Pantomine, and to Monte Carlo, and give me three helpings of Christ-
    mas pudding, and mince-pies, and otherwise show his paternal afec-
    tion [sic] well – I'll let him know it.

Such arrogance perhaps reassured Elspeth that her son would make his own
triumphant way through life, much as Bevil Quiller-Couch was doing. That
golden-haired, clean-limbed young man, known to the family simply as The
Boy, had retained all his enthusiasm for boating despite his traumatic involvement in Atky's drowning. As Kenneth wrote:

    I had a line from Q. just the other day. The Boy had been elected to
    the "Leander" Boat-Club – the premier rowing club of England –
    which I suppose is a great compliment for so young an oarsman. He
    stroked one of the two trial eights this year, but he is not in the
    "Varsity" crew – at least up to the present. I fancy he may be a trifle
    light as yet – those boys run to such a size nowadays. On Latin and
    Greek and such trifles the father was silent.[4]

Bevil, the social and sporting Apollo, was not born for such mundane things
as work. Elspeth wrote of him in characteristically effusive terms.

    The eight-year-old page boy at our wedding was Bevil Quiller-Couch
    . . . – a splendid little fellow who, even at that age, was so clever and

so sensible that his opinion was weighed and gravely taken, as later it came to be sought and valued, alike by towns-people and sailor-men. He grew up to be what he then promised – a tower of strength, ever to be relied on – cheerful, charming – with a genius for friendship in every walk of life, and for those of all ages.[5]

Alastair's opinion, too, had been "weighed and gravely taken", and it is clear that Bevil was the ideal at which Mouse's upbringing aimed. Parents could afford to be silent on "such trifles" as Latin and Greek when their son was popular and adored. Bevil, however, had an eight-year-old sister, Foy, for whom he had a great and protective love, and his parents were blessed with a quite unusual degree of common sense, a quality which underpinned the whole of Q's academic attitude and formed the touchstone of his philosophy. In Alastair Grahame's background common sense was conspicuously absent.

Oddly, Mouse knew nothing of his father's close friend. On Sunday, 11 February 1912, he wrote to his mother: ". . . you said in your letter that Inferiority had revieved [sic] a letter from 'Q'. Who is 'Q'?" Elspeth kept up a constant stream of letters and gifts, and on Good Friday her son wrote to thank her for a case of bananas. She often sent large consignments of foodstuffs, enough for all Mouse's friends, perhaps calculating that this would be a boost to his popularity. The Easter letter ended on a confidential note. "I have a lot of things to tell you and Daddy which I cannot put on paper . . ." Whatever they were, the letter is a first sign that Mouse had worriès of his own.

By this time, Kenneth and Elspeth were beginning to fret over the question of Mouse's continued education. In two years' time, he would have to leave his prep school and go elsewhere. But where? Naturally, his parents wanted "the best", but this was not easy to identify. Both of them were inclined towards the public school, though perhaps for different reasons. Elspeth's upbringing had taught her that the social cachet of a "big-name" school was important. Knowing and influencing people was, to her, the most fundamental skill; even though she now dressed with dowdy eccentricity, she did it as a kind of reprisal for the loss of socialising which her marriage to Kenneth had forced on her. Elspeth had become a walking protest, and she wanted to make sure that her son had full access to the world of amusing and important people which had been denied to her. He must therefore go to a public school, and preferably the best-regarded and most prestigious one. Kenneth, for his part, was entering unknown territory, for his own education had stopped short of such heights, but he wanted for his son all that he would have liked for himself. St Edward's had been a copy of a public school rather than the real thing, and Kenneth's only experience of the great traditional system had been the vicarious one of reading *Tom Brown's Schooldays*, and being swept along by the emotion which Hughes had felt for Dr Arnold, a father-figure who, like Pan himself, inspired fear and love in awesome balance. Grahame had, in fact, been re-reading Hughes at about this time, for he wrote to ask Purves:

> I wonder if you ever read *The Scouring of the White Horse* by T. Hughes, the *Tom Brown* man? It was written, I suppose, about fifty years ago, and gives, in a small way, a rather faithful picture of life in these parts – as it is now, because of course here fifty years amounts to just nothing at all.[6]

Such factors could work on the deepest levels of Grahame's mind, forming an emotional predisposition which outweighed more rational considerations. Nevertheless, the problem remained a pressing one. The Grahames needed advice.

The obvious person to consult was Q. Although he was much taken up with political work, for which he had been knighted, his connection with university and academic life remained strong, both through Bevil and through his own increasingly recognised writing. In the early summer, not waiting for Alastair's term to end, Kenneth and Elspeth headed for the West Country, stopping off first at Lyme Regis for two weeks. Mouse was again resentful.

> Saturday, June 3rd
> My Dear Madam
> I am very interested to hear that you are going to Lyme Regis, but I think it is very mean of you to make a lot of excuses about trains "not running between here and there" indeed!

The following week, he made a scathing reference to The Inferior One, but by 16 June he was in the sickroom, suffering from a cold and deeply cast down because an admired boy, Phil Robinson, who had just gone to Bradfield at the age of fourteen, had died. He was, Mouse said, "the best captain we have ever had or ever shall have"; he and two other boys were making wreaths for the funeral as a personal tribute, additional to the school's organised mourning.

His parents, meanwhile, had moved on to Fowey. The town was, Kenneth wrote to Purves,

> Prosperous, cheerful and full of smiling faces. More steamers up the river than I have ever seen and the jetties working all night as well as all day. Many inquiries after you all, from all classes, and a general feeling of having come home. Q. and miladi are going very strong, the

Boy [Bevil Quiller-Couch] has been at home for a week, but is off again to camp as an Artillery man.

Inevitably, the reminders of Atky were painful: "We have been up to Rosebank – a sad sight rather, with its empty rooms and bare walls ... The place is for sale, not to be let, and I don't think it will sell in a hurry – it's not everybody's home."[7]

In fact, Grahame wanted to buy the house himself, but the scheme came to nothing, and he watched unhappily as Atky's collection of books and mechanical toys and faded, damp-spotted water colours were put up for auction. The dealers, he said, "stood aloof. But the books did well. The enormous stock of clocks, barometers and binoculars (I believe he had 45 telescopes alone) fetched very little." Depressed by this and by the "consistently beastly weather", he and Elspeth went home.

Mouse had discovered a new delight. On 14 July, he wrote "Why did I not learn to swim last summer? I had my first lesson last Tuesday: since then I have been having lessons every day. It is simply *glorious*!"

During that summer, he moved into a new confidence. Swimming was one of the few sports in which he was not handicapped by his poor sight, and it gave him immense pleasure.

The problem of his continuing education, however, remained unsolved. If Q had given the Grahames advice, it had perhaps not been what they wanted to hear. In a letter to Purves dated 8 August 1912, there is for the first time a note of reserve in what Grahame has to say about his Fowey friend – and, more particularly, about his wife.

Q is more full of work than ever at present. A book of original verses coming out, another anthology, and a novel. You really mustn't take it to heart, by the way, if they don't write to you. They never write letters to anybody. For myself, I don't think I have ever seen so much as a pothook or a hanger of her Ladyship's; and as for Q I sometimes have to bother him, for introductions, or information of some sort, and when he replies, which he always does promptly, he gives me a half-sheet summary of the latest gossip – in shorthand. I fancy that professional writers nearly all hate letter writing. The *style* is different and that makes it difficult for them. Lamb was good at it, to be sure, and Edward Fitzgerald – but in a sense they were amateurs.

It was as near as Grahame got to tetchiness. He himself was a reluctant correspondent. Purves was the only man who managed to drag a series of responses out of him, by dint of constant sending of present and books and cuttings as well as copious letters but, in this latest missive, Grahame seems to be clutching at the excuse of being a professional writer, even though he had produced nothing since *The Wind in the Willows* four years ago. There had, however, been a slightly maladroit attempt to dramatise one of his stories, "The Roman Road". A couple of months before the Fowey trip, in March 1912, an American children's writer called Kitty Cheatham, who had visited the Grahames at Blewbury, decided on this project, and master-minded a production in a small London theatre. Kenneth made a rare trip to the city for the occasion, and was greeted rapturously by Kitty, as Curtis Brown recorded in a letter to Purves.

> After it was over, we went around to the artist's reception-room. Kitty was surrounded by a congratulatory throng, but when she saw that beautiful head, she literally leapt through the crowd and landed with both arms round K.G.'s neck, exclaiming: "You Angel Lamb!" Not even pistol shots could have been more startling to his grave dignity; but there was nothing in his attitude to indicate it.[8]

Kitty Cheatham had obviously taken a great fancy to Kenneth, for she wrote him numerous letters, often beginning "Beloved Kenneth Grahame" or "My beloved friend". Nothing, however, could dispel the winter and early spring bleakness of Boham's. Grahame had written to Q about the less attractive side of country living, unperceived by him as a summer walker, but all too real now that he was a permanent resident.

> I hardly get out at all now, as we are surrounded by a sea of mud. I never knew mud was so potent. And gale after gale comes battering down on us. I was explaining to E the other day that wind does not always move in strictly horizontal plane, backwards and forwards, which did not seem to have occurred to her; & later I found myself browsing, before the fire, on Milton, & reading, or trying to read, the *Epitaphium Damonis*; & I came to
>
> <div align="center">at malus Auster
Miscet cuncta foris, et <i>desuper intonat ulmo</i></div>
>
> & that struck me as rather jolly.[9]

The jollity lay in the fact that the wicked Southerly wind which whirled about everywhere *came thundering down on the elms* (Grahame's italics). One wonders whether Kenneth carried the great poet's evidence in triumph to his wife or whether, as seems more likely, he savoured it in private, sharing it only with his trusted friend, Q.

Kenneth's autumnal depression seemed to be particularly bad in 1912, and it was not helped by the fact that Mouse wrote far more often to Elspeth than he did to his "inferior" father. He perhaps complained about this, for an October letter from Alastair shows some signs of contrition: "I am writing to you this week because I have not done so before this term, and because you wrote to me a short time ago, and because of something Mummy told me in her last". Later the boy decided to write to his parents on alternate weeks, "so that there may be no cause for jealousy".

1913 began with a promise of better things, for Quiller-Couch was appointed to a professorship in English Literature at Cambridge. His lectures, reprinted in book form, remain the most readable of his vast output, with much to say which is sharply relevant in our own time. Q was tirelessly prolific, and was troubled by his friend's lethargy and inability to write. He had always disliked Elspeth, and, once installed in Cambridge, he did his best to stimulate Kenneth's interest in the world which lay beyond the claustrophobic smallness of Boham's. In May, he invited him to be his guest, together with A. E. Housman, at the Rustat Audit Feast in Jesus. It was a well-calculated move, for Housman was an exact contemporary of Grahame's, born, like him, in 1859, and there were other striking similarities of background and experience. *A Shropshire Lad* had been published in 1896, and its lyrical, elegaic cadences had entered into the English collective consciousness, giving a resonance of half-familiarity to Wenlock Edge and the bells of Bredon, even to those who had not read the poems. Grahame, Q must have felt, would surely respond to the man who had written

> The troubles of our proud and angry dust
> > Are from eternity, and shall not fail.
> Bear them we can, and if we can we must.
> > Shoulder the sky, my lad, and drink your ale.

Housman had worked for ten years in the Patent Office, though he had during that time published the scholarly work on Ovid, Juvenal and Propertius which, despite an undistinguished pass degree from Oxford, had earned him the Professorship of Latin at London University. If he could do it, Q may have felt, then why not Grahame?

The two writers plunged into a conversation which went on long after the feast was over and, although there is no evidence that any lasting friendship was formed, Grahame did at last break his long literary silence. In the weeks following the Cambridge event, he wrote "The Felowe that Goes Alone", and sent it, rather strangely, to his old school, for inclusion in the Jubilee Commemoration Number of the *St Edward's School Chronicle*. He took the title from Caxton's *Golden Legend*, which he probably came across through Furnivall and the Early English Text Society, for it appeared, Chalmers said, in the ledger diary he kept then, and which was later lost. Kenneth wrote down Caxton's words about an Oxford schoolboy, Edmund of Abingdon, later a bishop and saint. The boy, he said, lefte their felawshyp and went allone into a meadowe and under an hedge he says his devocions. And sodeynlye there apperyed tofore him a fayr chylde in white clothynge which sayd, "Hayle, felawe that goest allone!"

Grahame took the description as appropriate to himself, and used it often. The piece he wrote now was one for which any national magazine would have paid dearly, but "Teddy's" had probably sent him a personal appeal and, with his mind running on the importance of schools (for the question of Mouse's future was not yet solved), he sent the astonished and gratified editor the totality of his recent thinking. It was a profoundly disillusioned essay. Prompted by memories of the defence strategies he had evolved during his school days, Grahame wrote about solitude and, in the passage already quoted on page 151, about the joys of walking alone. "As for adventures," he said,

if they are the game you hunt, everyone's experience will remind him that the best adventures of his life were pursued and achieved, or came suddenly to him unsought, when he was alone. For company too often means compromise, discretion, the choice of the sweetly reasonable. It is difficult to be mad in company; yet but a touch of lunacy in action will open magic doors to rare and unforgettable experiences.

Grahame never did things by halves. When asked to write for the boys of his old school, he gave them all he knew.

It was also doubtless due to Q's influence that the Cambridge University Press asked Grahame to edit an anthology of poetry for children. Throughout 1913, the task of selection and seeking permission continued. It was a long job. By December of that year, Kenneth wrote to Graham Robertson, saying that

I have got my two little volumes about three-quarters done, but am rather stuck for a little more matter, which I can't find to my liking, so I have been rather letting the thing slide; but I shall have to make a push and send the stuff in to Cambridge somehow.

In the summer of 1913 the Purves family again came to Britain, bringing the children with them, even though Austin had not been well. It had seemed, in fact, unlikely that their planned visit would take place, for Grahame had written, on only 11 July:

Of course we are immensely disappointed to hear of the very small probability that exists of your being able to get to England; and we

277

are deeply sorry to hear that you are so pulled down and all the rest. But I want to say at once and right away, that what you are doing is absolutely the right thing, and the only thing, and the thing to make you fit and well again in the shortest possible time. You have got to "slack" as if you were in for a prize for it. Not only must you not think today of what you will do to-morrow, but you must not think in the morning of what you will do in the afternoon. In fact, you mustn't think at all, but sit in the sunshine and let things just happen before your eyes and don't ask yourself why they happen, or any other co-nundrum. Nature will do her work all right, if she's given the chance and a free hand.

We shall probably start for Fowey on the 16th or 17th as we have got to be back here about the 26th, to get ready for our journey to the Highlands in the following week. We continue to have excellent reports of Mouse in every way. I wish we could bring him to Fowey with us, but that may not be.

Alastair's school term was, presumably, not yet at an end. The Purveses made up their minds to travel and arrived in Fowey, where they spent about ten days. Austin Jr remembered their reception with some amusement.

We arrived on the evening train and Mr Grahame was on the station platform. My brother Pierre, whose godfather was K.G., did not of course remember G., but nevertheless kissed him on arrival. G. said, in effect, Pierre it is all right this once, but men don't kiss. Pierre, then aged six, received, for a child, something of a shock.[10]

As with his reaction to fox-hunting, Kenneth had suddenly applied the standards of grown-up male conventionality, even though they seemed quite at variance with his kindly and spontaneous nature. It was not as inconsistent as it seems, for he had throughout his life shuttled between his instinctive childhood self and the formality of learned adult behaviour; but the incident makes Elspeth's tale of his close involvement with the Breton children even less likely. Where Mouse was concerned, however, he could not do enough to make him happy. The boy had never forgotten his Inveraray holiday, and had often begged to go back to Scotland; this year, he was to get his wish.

Purves offered to take Alastair with them on their continued European travels. He may have thought of this only when the Grahames had gone back to Boham's, for Kenneth makes reference to it in a letter written after Purves had returned to the United States.

I wanted particularly, first of all, to thank you for your very kind, thoughtful invitation to Mouse to come and see something of Holland under your auspices. Had he been kicking his heels here, at a loose end, I would have jumped at the opportunity; but the fact is, it would have abruptly cut his Highland holiday off suddenly, and the boy was so enjoying every hour of it, and so eager to be allowed to stay there till the last possible day – which indeed is what we did – that I hadn't the heart. I wish you could have been with us; we were in places which were almost fantastically beautiful, even for the Highlands, and some of it only recently opened up to travellers.

Writing to Graham Robertson, his old friend from the Durham Villas days, Kenneth confided some personal reservations about the trip, even while reiterating Mouse's delight. "Of course," he said,

travelling in August is always infernal, and we had to couch like the beasts of the fields in temperance inns and such. But the weather was magnificent, and we were in the most beautiful country, even for the Highlands. The boy was simply drunk with it all, and grieved sorely to leave it.[11]

Mouse was now thirteen years old, and his grieving was perhaps not merely for the end of a holiday, but for the ending of childhood. He was now afflicted with terrible acne as well as the permanent squinting eye and half-blindness. His voice was breaking, and he was gawky and poorly co-ordinated, given to waving his arms about to emphasise any point. He was also opinionated and precocious, desperately trying to rely on a rapidly vanishing childhood charm, without which his selfishness and arrogance were pitilessly revealed. He had no idea of how else to behave, and his parents still indulged his every whim. His only task appeared to be the production of a satisfactory number of whims.

Shades of the prison-house, however, were closing round Alastair. In a serious conversation about his future, he was told that Rugby appeared to be the best school for him, and that, in order to get a place there, he would have to work hard and pass the entrance examination. The idea of hard work was new to Mouse, and he went back to Dorset to begin the autumn term of his final year without much enthusiasm. From that time on, a dislike of school began to settle in, despite the easygoing attitude of The Old Malthouse. The boy had lost the lightheartedness with which he had written such quips as "When I am a full-blown multi-billionair [sic] I will stand you a sixpenny ice". He now addresses Elspeth as "Dearest Mother", although contact with girls of his own age seems to have filled him with horror:

I consider dancing an extremely idiotic form of amusement, and would rather not make a fool of myself by "Turkey Trotting" round a crowded, stuffy old ballroom, treading on people's toes, and "Buny-hugging" [*sic*] some wretched girl round the waist.[12]

Kenneth, ever indulgent, allowed him to stop attending the dancing lessons.

Drama, however, still had Mouse in its spell. He was again in the school play, and when his parents declined to come to it, wrote to them with a disappointment barely covered by his sarcasm.

> ... of course, it is only an amateur performance, with *very* amateur actors, so I expect you would not think much of it, after seeing Sir Henry Irving & Sarah Berneharte [*sic*] etc. But of course it is very exciting for me because I am actually in it, so please excuse me if my enthusiasm for THE drama has bored you ...

He was impatient, too, with Elspeth's constant preoccupation with the house, and wrote on 23 November:

> ... those improvements are getting on my nerves. I really cannot think what there is to improve. It can't be inside the house, and it can't be in the garden, nor in the barn; in fact, when I left Boham's at the end of the holidays, there was not room, to my mind, for a single improvement.

Money, as always, pacified him, and he wrote on 11 December with great respect to his father:

> Thank you very much for responding so promptly and generously to my rather brief and impolite demand for money. Of course, your idea of giving me half a crown is quite preposterous, so please deduct it from my guinea, according to instructions.

It was probably at the beginning of 1914 that Mouse wrote an extremely odd letter. The handwriting matches with the other letters of the period, sprawly and large, unnervingly like that of the young Elspeth, but the correspondent is unknown.

> My dear Alan,
> I wish you a happy New Year.
> Edith has had strange ideas that people were hurraying in the village.
> Please will you join the Revolution, Alan?
> This is the Revolution because the servants want to get their own way, so Mummy and Daddy will have a fine scare tonight.
>   The servants will come dressed up as ghosts & will seize Mummy

& Daddy & make them pay the money the[y] want although they will ot work for them.

I have a bad cold. It began the day before yesterday.

I know that tomorrow you will be 21 & that you are going to lunch with Eric.

I have got some transfers lately. Numbers, little men and other transfers of all shapes & sizes.

White bear has a cold too. He had a cold first & I caught it from him. He is a very good bear & has to take very nasty medecine [*sic*] & he takes it as he likes it & the Dr & the trainer nurse say that it is a pleasure to look after him.

With good wishes and much love,

Your affectionate   Mouse[13]

This letter has obvious overtones of mental inconsistency, to put it mildly. The boy is obviously writing to a young man on the eve of his twenty-first birthday, and the letter is urbane in its good wishes. Considering Elspeth's legendary meanness, it is credible that the servants might have been planning some kind of strike action, but what are we to make of the white bear? It seems very unlikely that there was a younger child in the house who might have been known by this name, but even if this explanation could be proved, the childishness of Mouse's phraseology is in sharp contrast to the controlled cadences of his letter to Kenneth about the half-crown. Alastair seemed to be making a last-ditch defence against growing up, in a linguistic escape which is uncannily reminiscent of the never-never land which his parents partially inhabited. One wonders whether they used their private, infantile language while speaking to each other in front of their son. Its persistence in their later letters suggests that it may have become an habitual form of communication. If this were so, it is hardly suprising that Mouse found himself split between super-childishness and a resigned acceptance.

This Christmas holiday seems to have seen a crucial battle in Mouse's psyche between super-childishness and a resigned acceptance of the fact that he was, in many ways, more sensible than his childish parents. As a gift for Elspeth's birthday on 3 January, 1914, he made a miniature chest of drawers out of two matchboxes. With it was a short verse:

This thing is a little chest of drawers;
I hope you will think it nice,
For it was made by the little paws
Of one of the Boham's mice.

It was a childish present for a boy of fourteen to give, contrasting a little strangely with Alastair's more usual (and expensive) choice of a vase or jug.

Shopping expeditions may have been difficult in winter-bound Boham's – and yet there are hints that these were difficult weeks in which the balance of power between the boy and his parents was constantly shifting. There is a note of evident relief in the letter which Grahame wrote to Purves on 25 January.

> The holidays are just over, and we are in a state of unnatural peace and calm. The day before yesterday I took Mouse up to town, had him "vetted" by the dentist, filled him up with a solid British Luncheon at Simpson's in the Strand, and fired him off by train along with two carriage-fulls of comrades in misfortune all adorned with a somewhat forced gaiety. Boys don't like going back this term, because it's the dullest of the three, and there is nothing particular to look forward to, and Christmas holidays mean many domestic joys and much home comfort, after which school looks a little bare and bleak.

This is the first reference to any reluctance on Mouse's part to go back to school, and it seems probable that the boy had a subconscious resistance to the premature resolving of his relationship-struggle which the beginning of term imposed. As a senior pupil, he could no longer be childish. When he wrote to Elspeth on the day after his return to school, it was in protective concern:

> . . . I want you to make me a promise. Will you please use the gramo-phone regularly (not less than twice a week) while I am away. I should like you also *not* to shut it up in it's [*sic*] box and put it away unless you are leaving the house. If you will not promise me this, I shall be very unhappy. I want you to play "Bonnie Leezie Lindsay" and all your other favourites.

In mid-February, Elspeth and Kenneth went abroad again. This time, with his new maturity, Mouse was tolerant: ". . . I hope you will both have a very jolly time on the Riviera, but do please keep away from Casinos and such like".

A week later, he hoped that his parents were enjoying themselves and had not "got into trouble yet". There is an odd sense that he and Kenneth had changed places, for his next letter took up a tone of paternal reproof. ". . . you cannot think how pained I was to learn what a pig you made of yourself at Marseilles over the Bouillabaisse. I feel I ought to reprove you severely, but words fail me to describe the sensations of horror and repug-nance with which I read of your bestial gluttony."

This was not Grahame's first encounter with Marseilles and its bouil-labaisse, for he had written to Purves four years previously about "the pleasant city of Marseilles – where I once ate a perfectly whacking and stupendous quantity of *bouillabaisse*".[14] Perhaps Mouse was writing in reminisence of that occasion.

By 1 March, Mouse was writing with mild irony: "I was sorry to hear that you have had a spell of bad weather at Casqueiranne. It seems to me that you might just as well have gone to Stornaway." He preceded this with a message for Elspeth, saying he quite understood that "after all the writing she had at Christmas she must want a complete holiday".

Mouse seems at this point to have moved into a resigned view of his parents as fallible, childish people who needed his care. He sent a little vase for Kenneth's birthday, but even here he was careful to provide a built-in excuse for his father's potential rejection of it: "If you do not like it, you can always leave it on your side of the channel by mistake". He said the same thing in a letter to Elspeth, as if trying to arm himself – or them – against hurt. "If he doesn't like it he can give it away to anyone, and I shan't mind a bit. Perhaps your friend Mademoisellet Lucette would appreciate it."

On 22 March, he is still commiserating with his parents for the bad weather in France, but he then reverts to schoolboyish enthusiasm for his own affairs.

> I and Jennings discovered a ripping cave in the quarry. We are having a ripping game there. The cave is on a desert island and there is buried treasure (doubloons, Louis d'ors, pieces of eight). Also cannibals and a pirate ship. Need I say that Jennings is Rupert of Hentzau and that I am Dick Lawless, the Bloody Buccaneer? On Tuesday I swam over the ledge into the open sea. On Wednesday we played Durleston Court and won by about 100. The Parents were as numerous, as arogant [*sic*] and as overdressed as they always are. On Saturday we went down to the ledge and had a look at the sea. The waves were magnificent. Even on the cliff-top we could feel the spray in our faces. I think a stormy sea is one of the finest sights one can see anywhere. Afterwards we went down to Swanage and I bought a sixpenny edition of George Borrow's *Bible in Spain*. Borrow seems to have been a tireless traveller and as a linguist he was simply extraordinary . . .

Again, the letter is a strange mixture. The artlessly short sentences sound like the work of a much younger child, and yet it touches with great skill on topics which will be well received. Mouse has laid a shrewd finger on Elspeth's prejudices against "dressing-up", and he caters for his father's tastes in his mention of George Borrow and the wilder aspects of nature. Whether consciously or not, Alastair gave his parents what they wanted. Whether he knew what he wanted himself is more doubtful. His letter ends with small verbal gifts to both Kenneth and Elspeth.

Daddy's verses move me to break into song too:
    Once I met a fellow
        Tramping down the road
    A truss of straw, bright yellow,
        Was all that bumpkin's load.
                    The Impressions of a Clodhopper.

                            A. Grahame (Titwillow)

P.S. – I am glad to hear that Uncle Harold had been made Mayor of
Westminster. May his period of office be as prolonged as that of Sir
R. Whittington of feline fame.

This Uncle Harold was the elder of Elspeth's two brothers, and his success
perhaps encouraged her growing sense of high expectation. Everyone in her
family was doing well. Courtauld was on his way to becoming one of the
country's most famous businessmen, Harold was now in high office and her
sister Winifred was becoming increasingly well known, both as a widely
exhibited artist and as a contributor of cookery articles to *The Times*. Such
pieces as "Maids' Bedrooms", "Shopping by Telephone" and "Luncheon
on the Moors" may seem risible today, but Winifred's determined dealings
with editors show a woman of quite forceful character.

In the week which ended on Sunday, 29 June 1914, Mouse sat his common entrance examination, and commented:

the only other person who underwent the torture was Vaughan Jef-
fries, who is destined to be an ornament to Wellington. We were shut
up in Mr Barnes's den, and had a most strenuous time. I felt like some
wretched Chinaman going in for the Mandarin examination, and
afterwards I was as limp as a wet rag. I know I did not do myself
justice, and feel certain I shall not pass. It is simply awful waiting for
the result.

He enclosed the question papers which had caused him "so much agony".
The result was not long in coming. Mouse had scraped through, and was
now destined to become the Tom Brown of the Grahame family, having
earned himself a place at Rugby. On 5 July, he wrote to Elspeth: "It *was*
good of you to telegraph about the exam. I was so thankful to pass at all,
that I did not mind passing so near the bottom. So long as you are satisfied
with the result, I am sure I am."

In the following week, his parents went to Fowey, and on 26 July, Mouse
asked, a little forlornly, "I suppose Inferiority has planted his four hoofs
firmly in the mud and refused to go near Inverary?" It was his last letter
from prep school.

15

No Pity

Alastair's anxiety that his mother should be "satisfied" was well founded. From that time on, no further letters of his are preserved, and there is something chilling about their absence. Elspeth was an obsessive hoarder of letters, keeping even the most trivial scraps of correspondence, and the fact that there is no trace of communication from Mouse at Rugby suggests that she was far from satisfied, and suppressed the evidence of her son's failure.

"I took great pains and trouble to assure myself that that was the best school he could go to,"[1] Kenneth said afterwards, in his own defence – but he had miscalculated badly. Rugby was a tough school, ruthless in its dealings with any boy who put on airs or who seemed in any way odd or less than a "good sport". Alastair, full of airs and debarred by his poor sight from all sports except swimming, had been thrown into a life which was, by his standards, little short of hell.

Elspeth and Kenneth were shocked by their son's unhappiness. In the preceding year, as his letters showed, he had seemed mature for his age, chaffing them as though they were children and he the adult. He must have appeared confident and outgoing. The tragedy lay in the fact that he had learned to be what they wanted, just as his father had learned to be what St Edward's School wanted; as a natural actor and a shrewd observer of parental psychology, Mouse had found out how to manage his parents and keep them happy. At fourteen, he gave them just enough respect to keep their authority seeming intact, but regarded them as a couple of children who played their way through holiday after holiday.

At Rugby, the adults were not children at heart. For the first time, Mouse encountered the Olympian world from which his parents had so lovingly and assiduously protected him. His prep school had been gentle and mildly absurd, but even that institution had begun to seem harsh as the ethic of earnest endeavour began to be established in the final years. Rugby, however, was devoid of imaginative escape. It meant business, both in work and sport, and every trace of childishness was to be expunged.

Mouse obviously wrote in anguish to his parents, for Kenneth went to see the boy's tutor, Roger Raven, who sympathised with the boy's problems and sent him a note which offered support and a refuge.

You know, your Father kindly came on Tuesday to see me and had a long talk with me; so that I more or less understand how things are. I said to him then what I repeat to you, now, that whenever you want somewhere to sit by yourself I hope you will come round here, – mornings, afternoons, &, if you like, after lock up. I do all my work upstairs in the study, so that the dining room below is always at your disposal. I know that invitations to "drop in any time" are difficult to accept in practice, but I hope you will test this one at once; and you will find that you will be welcome and undisturbed. If you feel any delicacy in appearing to make free of someone else's rooms, you have only to put your head round the study door and say "me voici" when you arrive; or if you find me unoccupied, you shall come in and talk to me as long as you like. There are some books here if you haven't enough of your own. – I have written this because I thought that if I came to your study and did not find you alone, it would be difficult to *say*. But in all cases believe me

Your affec. tutor, R. A. Raven[2]

It was a kind and well-meant letter, but Raven could not save Alastair from his fellow pupils and he knew it. The boy was a natural victim, with a combination of physical weakness and defensive bombast which brought out the aggression in his fellows like a flock of sparrows which mob the odd one out. Mouse could not accept his tutor's offer without incurring further contempt and ragging. He was totally without resources, the weakest and newest and least attractive in a rigidly structured society, and the fact that he had a famous father, which might have brought him some respect in the little backwater of The Old Malthouse, stood for nothing at Rugby, where every father was either famous or rich or both. Conversely, to be the son of a man who had written a children's book could well have added to the general impression that Alastair was an affected aesthete.

After six weeks, the Grahames gave in to their son's evident suffering, and removed him from the school. In that short time, Mouse had learned that the outside world was a frightening place, but he had not begun to understand that its hostility might have something to do with his own behaviour; and neither had his parents. They could not for a moment entertain the idea that their exceptionally normal boy might have defects of personality which made him difficult for his schoolfellows to understand, much less like. Kenneth, writing to Purves about the fiasco, shifted the blame as best he could.

So far as I could gather, the pace and pressure were altogether too much for him, and I fancy that the new boys, with whom he naturally had to spend his time, happened to be a roughish lot. Anyhow though he stuck it out for six weeks, he got no better, and in the end I thought it right to take him away.[3]

It became obvious that Q had advised against Rugby from the start. He wrote with a certain crispness in response to Kenneth's appeal for help in the new crisis.

I had my doubts all along and for two reasons. (a) The Public School business has become such a silly specialized system that only the *larger* preparatory school really prepares the poor chap for what he has to undergo ... The smaller private school (with better intentions) quite frequently doesn't. (b) Rugby is the place of all others where you get the system in full blast, with the least pity. Plenty of kindness on the part of X & Y but in the end no pity at all from the system. At Eton, Winchester, Wellington a toad may dodge the harrow: they allow for "eccentricities" (as they call 'em) and a certain understood adoration of the place often carries through a boy who is not of the run. He understands it (after a pathetic struggle often) and it first allows for and finally gets a particular liking for him – or may. But Rugby is ruthless. And it's all system.[4]

Despite the clear warning, Elspeth seized on Q's faint extenuation of Eton, interpreting it as the place which would understand and appreciate her son, even though the letter had gone on to state clearly that Alastair should not be forced to board at any public school. Clifton, Q pointed out, was the only one which accepted day boys as well as boarders, but, as he said, "you will not only have to live there; Mrs Grahame would have to make a vow to yield the boy over to the school while living under the same roof with him".

Evidently he was under no illusion as to the part which Elspeth had played, and continued to play, in encouraging Alastair's eccentricity. The ideal solution, he said firmly, was to provide the boy with a private tutor. He even suggested a candidate for the post – "a thundering good fellow, massive, ex-Rugby blue for Oxford".

The Grahames, however, still could not accept the idea that Mouse was constitutionally unfitted for the hurly-burly of public-school life. Having convinced themselves that his unhappy experience at Rugby was the fault of the school (and Q's letter could be read as a reinforcement of this opinion), they argued that a more liberal regime might succeed where Rugby had failed.

Kenneth's close friend, Graham Robertson, with whom he had barely communicated since leaving Durham Villas, was an Old Etonian, and so his advice was urgently sought. In a long letter, Robertson struggled to be fair to the school and to himself. He found it difficult to separate his feelings about it from the skills he had learned there, but it was clear that he had reservations about Mouse's chances of success in that peculiar society.

> I'm afraid I never discovered the right answer to the question – How to be happy at school. Let me hasten to add that I was not *un*happy at Eton and I do not expect that Mouse will be.
>   But he will be – bored. I was horribly bored, and as I had never been bored before (except at a private school) and have never been bored since, it could not have been merely inherent viciousness.
>   It is useless to conceal that, to persons of the rather indeterminate age of Mouse and myself, boys between 12 and 16 are a little trying as companions. Specially when gathered together.[5]

The point about the "indeterminate age" was perceptive. Robertson himself, with his belief in fairies and his preference for the company of dogs rather than people, had preserved an eternal childhood, and recognised that Mouse, being the son of Kenneth, would be of the same kind. Education has not to this day resolved the problem of the creative, enquiring child-person who is painfully bored by the process of committing facts to memory. Robertson's efforts to offer positive advice were not very hopeful, but he tried hard.

> Quite seriously, any boy can have a passable time at Eton if he has a good temper. There is no fun in worriting a good tempered boy so he doesn't get worried. I dare say, if you had the luck to meet a real friend there, it could be quite larks.
>   But that's not very likely in this case.

Mouse, of course, was not "a good-tempered boy". He was used to giving direct expression to his feelings – and to having that expression listened to and acted on. As a young child, he had been indulged without reservation and, even at fourteen, he was able to be critical of his parents without incurring any protest. He took himself seriously, and expected other people to do the same. He was, in fact, a prime target for "worriting". Towards the end of his letter, Robertson worked himself round to the bleak admission that "I didn't like Eton & there is no use in saying I did". In fact, he hated it so much that he never used the second initial of his name. Although christened Graham Walford Robertson, he "disliked sharing initials with the Great Western Railway which took him away to Eton".[6] He added a faint hope that Mouse would come to like "the queer sad beauty of it", and remembered how he himself spent a lot of time wandering in the "quiet corridors" with imaginary messages for imaginary people, having grasped that the fagging system could be used for one's own ends. The picture he painted was essentially one of isolation and a faintly poetic sadness, but Kenneth did not read the warning signs. He went ahead with his proposal to send his son to Eton.

War had broken out in the summer of 1914, just before Mouse started at Rugby. Thousands of young men had gone off to fight in France, but there was still a feeling that the whole affair was a skirmish that could quickly be settled, provided that a big effort was made. All normal affairs were suspended so that the emergency could be dealt with. Q was released from his university post to travel round the country on a full-time recruiting drive. Parents kept their children at home, alarmed by reports of Zeppelin raids and, as a result, Eton, along with many other prestigious schools, had unfilled vacancies. Kenneth's enquiry on behalf of his son resulted in the immediate offer of a place, and Alastair was launched afresh on his public-school career. He started in January 1915.

It seemed Mouse had fully accepted his parents' view that the Rugby boys had been "a roughish lot" who did not appreciate his finesse, for he brought the same superior attitude to Eton. When urged to join in conversation with his fellows during meals, he said with contempt, "How can I talk to people whose powers of conversation lie only in their elbows?"[7] He perhaps sensed, however, that his parents were desperately anxious that he should succeed at this new school. In the atmosphere of general dismay as the war ground on and the casualty list mounted, it perhaps seemed almost tasteless to point out his small sufferings. But again, his letters were not kept.

Kenneth, meanwhile, was troubled and confused by the war, simultaneously horrified and prompted by his conformity to the standards of "manhood" to regard it as a challenge. His old friend Purves was increasingly unwell and, on 18 February 1915, Grahame wrote him a letter which was to be the last of their long correspondence.

DEAR PURVES, – We have been genuinely distressed at learning from your recent letters of the very poor time you have been having in the matter of health, and can only hope that the slightly more cheerful note in Mrs Purves's postscript is still justified. And then on the top of it you had business troubles and worries – it all seems very hard. Well, one can only remember that troubles mostly pass, sooner or later, and that, when one has sailed into smooth water again, perhaps the pleasant harbour and its sunny shores look more smiling and peaceful on account of the breakers left behind.

We very deeply appreciate all the kind and sympathetic things you say about our position in this appalling war. I was pretty sure about how you both would feel about it, but your kind words made pleasant reading. Your people may feel sure, that their many manifestations of

289

sympathy – and by this I mean both *instinctive* sympathy and *reasoned* sympathy, for there have been many evidences of both – sink deep here, and will not be forgotten. The English are taciturn and ungushing – also their papers often say foolish and tactless things – but they remember all right.

It is strange, isn't it, and also most puzzling, how a great and prosperous nation can pour out its blood and treasure simply for the privilege of being Slaves – and of Enslaving?

Our little village has played up well, sending some seventy men out of a total population of less than 500 souls. I think there has been a certain amount of nonsense talked about the recruiting. From all I have seen I should say that men have come in splendidly – and are still coming in; and good stuff too. We missed getting down to Fowey for a few weeks after Christmas as I had counted on doing, so I'm not in a position to give you any gossip from Town Quay, for though I've heard from Q. once or twice, on business, he was quite silent as to local affairs, except as to recruiting, which had been taking up all his time. So you probably know more about the place than I do, for you see a local paper and I don't. Also I don't go into Oxford as of old. One misses the boys, and it's sad to see the river deserted, and have nobody playing the garden-ass or the giddy-goat. Oxford has played up well and no mistake.

In London, when we run up for the day, things seem to me to be going on very much as usual. Of course we are not there at night, when things may be quieter than of old, but during the day it seems as busy and bustling as ever. I generally go to some sort of afternoon performance, and it is exceedingly difficult to obtain seats.

The "veterans" of Blewbury have started a Volunteer Defence Corps, and we drill, in the evenings, in a beautiful great timber-framed thatched barn – like my own, only three times as big. The rats run in and out of the thatch along the rafters, and the barn cat, who ought to be attending to them, sits on wheat sacks and reviews us with great delight. He is having the time of his life, for he thinks that these drills are specially got up for him, to brighten the monotony of his long dull evenings. The corps have elected me their Commanding Officer – the cat concurring – because they said I was the most martial-looking of the crowd, and there I agree with them; they were careful to add, however, that it wasn't for any other reason whatever, and that also I can fully understand.

E. keeps pretty well.

In normal times we should now run away somewhere where it was dry and sunny, with a cheerful restaurant or two in the foreground; as it is we have to stay at home and talk about the places we would have gone to if we could.

I hope the boys are all flourishing and doing well in their respective pursuits and careers. P.M. will, I suppose, be careering schoolwards daily, and fairy tales are laid aside for facts. We also wish to be warmly remembered to Jerry, who would really weep if he knew how long it was since I saw a lobster, and we are of course anticipating a really better account of yourself, for your case is one that has always responded most hopefully to a complete rest, which is what you talk of trying, and which, after all, is a cure for nine maladies out of ten.

Mrs Purves, I note, keeps up her indomitable spirits, which are worth exactly £1,000,000 a year.

Yours most sincerely,
KENNETH GRAHAME

Austin Purves died shortly after the letter was posted.

For those of us who read it today, the most striking thing about this letter is the absence of any reference to Alastair. It was discussion of schools which had formed the "business" referred to in letters from Q, and the transferring of Mouse to his new school which had made the post-Christmas trip to Fowey impossible, and yet, even after detailed enquiry about the Purves boys and Pierre's schooling, there is silence about the Rugby débâcle. Consummate pretenders as the Grahames were, it may have been that they were at heart ashamed of their awkward, handicapped son, whose refusal to grow up along the anticipated lines was now causing such trouble. Kenneth had at an early age become used to the idea of endurance, and had found within stoicism his own resources of tranquillity; it must have been difficult for him to understand that Mouse could not identify the "little territory" of the private mind which had been known to wise people throughout the ages. Mouse, in fact, was not that kind of person. He had none of Kenneth's introverted centrality, and he had never been thrown on to his own resources and forced to develop a personal security from the irreducible minimum of his own being. He was completely vulnerable to others, and even while he despised them, he needed their recognition.

Graham Robertson worried about the boy, and wrote to Kenneth: "I hope you have good news from Mouse at Eton. For heaven's sake let him be careful how he hangs my pictures upon his walls. They may not be 'the thing', and stamp him as 'odd' . . .".[8]

Mouse, odd or not, survived two terms, and spent the summer holidays at Boham's. He then returned for the Michaelmas term, and was promoted to the Remove. On 11 December, he, together with some 200 other boys, was confirmed by the Bishop of Oxford. His parents attended the ceremony, and Kenneth gave him a bicycle. Elspeth wrote optimistically to her brother that Alastair seemed "to have won very good opinions in the short time that he has been at Eton", but she was closing her eyes to the struggle which was going on in her son's mind. He was sixteen years old, but he had still not managed to overcome his conviction that "the young human boy in the raw", as Kenneth had termed it, was crude and unsympathetic. "Scratch us," he had said, "we are all barbarians but it happens that I prefer curios and they prefer cricket bats."[9] His entire upbringing had encouraged him to be refined in his judgement and contemptuous of the uncivilised, and yet he had been thrown into a Philistine society where the slightest sign of aesthetic pretension marked a boy as an object of derision. Mouse's only friend at Eton seems to have been the maid at his tutor's house, who sent him a Christmas card from "Your faithful maid". Kenneth was immensely tickled by this, and said it sounded like a pastoral poem. His mind was running along poetic lines at the time, for he had only recently finished compiling the entries for *The Cambridge Book of Poetry for Children*. He had filled the obstinate gaps with several contributions from John Masefield, who had for some reason stipulated that they must remain anonymous.

The domestic situation at Boham's was increasingly bleak. One of the first Blewbury volunteers to leave the village had been an ex-sergeant of Marines who, with his wife, had done all the practical work of running Boham's. "For over six months," Kenneth had told Purves, "we had rubbed along somehow with casual help from the village, rough and untrained, and though at last we have secured a couple, they only came two days ago; and meantime the garden of course had gone to pot, and the house was dirty and disordered." Both he and Elspeth had been brought up to depend on servants, and neither of them could cope with the idea that they might have to perform the menial tasks of the house themselves.

Alastair went back to Eton in January, but a few weeks later he entered into a state of overwhelming distress which would in our own time be described as a nervous breakdown. He could no longer face the ragging of his fellow pupils and the no-nonsense discipline of the staff, and collapsed completely. His parents brought him home, and at last had to face the fact that Alastair was hopelessly unsuited to life in a residential boarding school which operated on the traditional British lines of cheerful ruthlessness. According to Green, Mouse began to "drift away" from Elspeth emotionally in his later adolescent years; he may well have started to perceive that her assurances of his wondrous abilities had no foundation except in her own need for esteem. During that Christmas holiday of 1915, in a servantless house surrounded by mud, unhappily reminiscent of Flanders, with a mother growing increasingly querulous and unkempt, the myth of superiority must have been difficult to maintain. On his return to school, it collapsed.

Elspeth's brother, Courtauld, was in the Middle East with the Red Cross, and he was the person to whom she came nearest to telling the truth, even though he was evidently disapproving of his sister's mollycoddling of her son. On 28 March she wrote,

K. and I are very grateful to you for your kind letter and advice &
what is more, agree with all you say as to Eton – but Mouse really
was getting into a settled unhappiness there which was harming body
and mind & the more he got used to the place the less he could endure
it. Probably the very same reasons, or conditions, which made Rugby
unbearable to him did so to a minor extent at Eton – and if we had
fully understood that he could neither be well, work well – nor be
happy in those conditions we should have avoided a year of misery for
him at Eton – but everyone was so eager we should try Eton as
affording the greatest *contrast* to Rugby or *any* of the first class schools
that we did so – thinking it wrong to neglect any chance of his taking
to a Public School.

The result however was that while he found Eton less intolerable
than he found Rugby he was very unhappy indeed there & more so
as time went on. We do not profess *ourselves* to understand exactly why
a Public School life is so uncongenial to him for he is by nature the
most spartan and the most uncomplaining creature possible . . . It is
so great a disappointment to us that it makes me unhappy even to
write about it . . . K. was really splendid in trying to do everything in
his power to buck him up with plenty of pocket & subscription money
& good clothes & orders on the shops & *anything* that cd hearten &
help him – & attach him to the place and life there – but we *cd* do no
more than we have done & it was not of *any* avail as things are.

We hope after the Easter holydays [*sic*] he will go to a very good
Tutor in Surrey . . . He had a younger son of the Hon. A. W. de
Moleyn's sons. He is they say really a gentleman and very particular
in whom he takes.[10]

Even in the face of Alastair's complete collapse, Elspeth was not able to
abandon her insistence on his outstanding qualities. If a tutor was to be
resorted to, he must be a man who would only teach very special boys.
Injured innocence is maintained in a voluble protest of good intentions. In
reality, good clothes and unlimited pocket money must only have served to
increase the contempt and dislike which the other boys felt for Mouse, but
Kenneth, looking back at his own childhood, could only associate unhappiness with deprivation, and Elspeth's main anxiety was to prove that nothing could be held to be her fault. Even the decision to send Mouse to
Eton is represented as the persuasion of "everyone".

It took Alastair a long time to recover from his breakdown. There is little
mention of him in the months following his withdrawal from Eton. Elspeth
was busy, as she told her brother, "with our war work – making crutches
and splints, leg & back rests for base and shop hospitals – in the shed
generally used for repairing agricultural machinery".[11]

It can hardly be imagined that she was out there with chisel and saw, but the presence of the workers gave her a proprietorial interest, and was more rewarding to think about than her mysteriously failed son.

The Cambridge Book of Poetry for Children had appeared in 1916 and possibly added to Alastair's feeling of inadequacy. Kenneth, with habitual modesty, had always played down the fact that his achievements were special and unusual ones; in his efforts to seem un-Olympian and accessible to his son, he had given the tacit impression that anyone of reasonable intelligence could do the same sort of thing. This portraying of his own exceptionally high standard as the norm made Mouse's failure seem all the more abnormal and inexcusable. As the complimentary reviews for the anthology appeared, each one added its own reproach to the bewildered boy who, as the child of a famous father, had assumed that high achievement came automatically.

"If Mr Grahame cannot compile a book of poetry for children," the *Literary World* remarked, "then Lord Kitchener could not compile a book on Army organization!" Most reviewers agreed, though the *Morning Post* objected to the American patriotic poems, and said they were "tosh". Grahame privately agreed. In a letter to Graham Robertson, he confessed that he had only included them "for little boys to spout before their besotted parents on prize day". Robertson went further. "Americans," he said, "though they sing very sweetly about children, are writing wistfully of things they have never seen. Some day a poem may be written about the Being called a child in America – but it won't be pretty reading."[12]

Kenneth's selection of poems reflected his personal tastes, being full of the delights of country life and dominated by the infectious rhythms which had formed part of his earliest memories of childhood. Scott is there, and Blake, and the Assyrian comes down like a wolf on the fold, and Horatius keeps the bridge in his twelve pages of blood-stirring stanzas. The book remains unmatched as a first introduction to the canon of British poetry and, in the preface, Grahame provided a thoughtful statement of his criteria, claiming that his task had been "not to provide simple examples of the whole range of English poetry, but to set up a wicket-gate giving attractive admission to that wide domain . . . to be more fully explored later by those who are tempted on by the first glimpse".

Although his own writing had included the lament for Rollo, and another for a dead bullfinch, plus numerous references to death in *The Golden Age* and *Dream Days*, Grahame jibbed at including the subject in his anthology, and wrote an emphatic paragraph to explain why.

In the output of those writers who have deliberately written for children, it is surprising how largely the subject of *death* is found to bulk. Dead fathers and mothers, dead brothers and sisters, dead uncles and aunts, dead puppies and kittens, dead birds, dead flowers, dead dolls – a compiler of Obituary Verse for the delight of children could make a fine fat volume with little difficulty. I have turned off this mournful tap of tears as far as possible, preferring that children should read of the joy of life, rather than revel in sentimental thrills of imagined bereavement.[13]

Katherine Tynan, writing in *The Observer*, had cogent objections to this policy.

How could one give them heroic poetry without death? And in another mood of all normal children. Death is the playfellow, the funeral the favourite form of pageant. When the two children I know best first found themselves in leafy Sussex, escaped from the London suburbs, they had funerals for each flower as it faded when there was no dead beetle to be had. After all, there is beauty in such funerals. It is our love for the *pompa mortis* that makes human funerals grotesquely dreadful.[14]

Such discriminations did not touch the basis of Grahame's aversion. The casualty lists were coming back from the appalling moonscape of mud where young men were being slaughtered in their thousands, Oxford undergraduates indistinguishable from Blewbury labourers as the remains of them were gathered up, to lie later under the rows of uniform white crosses in the graveyards of Flanders. *Lusisti satis* – an end to playing. Funerals were no longer a game. Atky had died, and Austin Purves, and so had Roland's wife Joan; and in the wake of such deaths, everything changed. Letters came no longer, and houses that had been full of life stood damp and forlorn, and families were riven by dissent. Kenneth had quarrelled with Roland over money, and they no longer spoke to each other – and Helen had removed herself from all friendship with her brother after his marriage to Elspeth at the end of his long convalescence in Fowey. The world seemed to be losing all warmth and colour, leaving only emptiness and bitterness and the mud of the grave, and children, Grahame reasoned, should be protected from that. But there was, too, the shining perfection of Alastair to be upheld. At a time when the cruel world was beginning to erode his confidence, he, the Grahame child who was archetypal of all children, should be wrapped safely in the beauty of life.

Meanwhile, Mouse, now as tall as his father, could not think of life as beautiful. He nursed his shattered nerves and his worsening eyesight as summer came and went, and another Christmas passed, and the year of 1917 arrived.

16

University and Tragedy

A lastair was duly despatched to a Mr A. W. Dall, the "very good tutor in Surrey", where he seemed to settle contentedly enough. In the summer, he went with his parents to Blue Anchor in Somerset. That small hamlet had, as Elspeth said, "no church, post, nor shops, in fact *nothing*".[1] Why they opted for this unknown place rather than their beloved Fowey must remain open to conjecture, but it is at least possible that they did not want to meet the enquiries into Mouse's progress which would be inevitable in their old haunt. It may even have been that Alastair had some say in the choice of location, for he evidently enjoyed the solitude of the place. The empty coves with their clear, deep water afforded him endless opportunity for swimming, and he was at his happiest in the sea. He also realised that his limited eyesight did not prevent him from riding, and quickly developed a passion for this new sport. Elspeth was delighted to find fresh and unexpected evidence of her son's brilliance. "The Trainer told us that he 'never saw anyone take so naturally to a horse'," she said. At home, the Berkshire downs offered Mouse a continued outlet for his new craze, and he pursued it both at Boham's and when he returned to his tutor in Surrey.

At about the same time, he joined the Volunteers. According to his mother, he was "only afraid that the war might end before he gets into the regular army".[2] Bevil Quiller-Couch had joined up as soon as war was declared and was having a characteristically triumphant military career, having won the MC and risen rapidly to become a major in command of a battery, "the Royal Ninth" of the Second Division. He later won the DSO, and remained a glittering role-model for Alastair.

Mouse's readiness to offer himself in the service of his country quickly became the dominating myth of the Grahame household, but the boy's failing eyesight ruled out the possibility of his acceptance in a serving unit. Significantly, when Elspeth wrote to her brother about the situation, she chose to ascribe Alastair's rejection to the traumatic effect of Rugby and Eton rather than to any genetic defect. "Of course," she said, "once a boy *is* overstrained or broken down he is of no use to himself or his country either." It sounded as if she were preparing herself for a lifetime of explaining how the English public-school system had denied her son his rightful role in life.

Kenneth, however, was more positive. Snatching at any chance that Alastair might still make something of himself – or maybe simply hoping, as always, to grant the boy his heart's desire – he went to Oxford and had a long talk with the Colonel of the OTC and Cadet Corps and with Roland's stepson, now Professor Sir Keith Feiling, of Christ Church. Since the Cadet Corps was by definition not a serving unit, it would not matter that Mouse was bound to be rejected for active service at eighteen. He could still come and train for a commission as a Cadet Corps officer. At the close of 1917, the war of attrition had taken its toll, and the Colonel was only too happy to take on an intelligent young man who now stood six foot two in his socks. Whether he could see clearly or not was a secondary consideration.

It looked like a breakthrough. Mouse would have his military career after all, for the Colonel was keen to accept him, and Keith Feiling could pave the way for an immediate entry into Christ Church. Alastair was to go up after Christmas, for the beginning of the Lent Term, 1918.

In his eagerness to bring about a successful solution to Mouse's problems, Kenneth did not stop to wonder if he was, in fact, cruelly calling his son's bluff. For a semi-blind boy to declare a longing to serve his country was a safe enough boast; it gave him the glory of a frustrated hero but did not threaten him with any unpleasant practicalities, for the dream was an impossible one. Now, Mouse's father came back from Oxford glowing with triumph, having made the dream a reality. Joining up was not only possible – it had been arranged. The days of comfortable study with the tutor in Surrey were over. Oxford awaited him, with all its challenges, and its clever, competitive society.

Alastair, like Kenneth, was essentially kind – and a coward about speaking the truth. He perhaps saw his parents' high hopes and appreciated the concern which had driven his father to make huge efforts on his behalf – and yet one senses that he could not respond to their expectations. The prospect of university may well have dismayed him. Apart from his personal difficulties about living in an academic institution, the notion of success was not as central to him as it was to Elspeth on his behalf. To want success is to admit that one is not yet quite successful – and this was a confusing idea to a boy who had been brought up to think himself perfect.

There was another factor which is worth considering. Kenneth's success was associated strongly with *The Wind in the Willows*, and Mouse was of course aware that the Toad stories had been a deeply personal part of his childhood, invented for him as proof of his father's love. Now, they were common property. Mouse had been sent away to school and his father had gone off to foreign countries with Elspeth, on the proceeds of the book which had been Mouse's stories. The boy was interested in money, and could not have failed to realise that Kenneth's relative affluence at this time was connected with handsome royalties. At a subconscious level, he may have felt "sold out". The ambition to succeed may therefore have seemed a suspect thing, a ruthless, love-threatening process, of which he wanted no part. He may very reasonably have felt that a fireside and a friendly tutor were enough, with books and the mind's imaginings, and the wind in the face when on horseback, and the water's close contact with the body when swimming. These things were of his essential being, and until recently they had been enough. But now, his worth was redefined in crudely competitive terms. He was not a marvel after all, and perhaps never had been.

There was no hope of discussing these things. Mouse could not, in any case, fully understand them, and he could see with the logical part of his mind that his father's plans for him were kindly meant, and that it would be monstrously ungrateful to reject them. He duly went up to Christ Church in January.

His tutor was S. G. Owen, Tutor in Classical Literature, and his opinion is unknown, but Keith Feiling, despite his family connection, recalled that Alastair seemed perpetually miserable, often sighing and groaning audibly, and that no encouragement could make him happier.[3] The received mythology has it that the boy's sight was steadily deteriorating, and that it was this which made academic study so difficult, and turned examinations into a nightmare. Previous accounts aver that Mouse was allowed to retake his failed Mods examination by *viva voce*, which resulted in a pass, and that he was offered the use of an amanuensis for all future exams, but a rather different picture emerges from the University's own records.

According to the *Oxford University Gazette*, Alastair Grahame entered and failed Holy Scripture both in Trinity 1918 and Michaelmas 1918. In 1919, he turned his attention to Greek and Latin Literature, but failed again in both Hilary term and Trinity. By this time, servicemen were returning from the war, and there was little time or patience to spare for a clearly substandard undergraduate who had got into the University through parental influence. In Trinity 1919, the tutors' book (a printed list of Christ Church men receiving tuition) bears the annotation, "Pass or go" beside Alastair's name. In other words, he was to go out of residence if he could not get through the exam.

Even in the face of this warning, Mouse could not reach the required standard. In Michaelmas 1919, he attempted the two exams, Holy Scripture and Greek and Latin Literature, and failed them both. The axe fell. There is no board and lodging bill against his name for the remainder of Michaelmas 1919 and Hilary 1920.

This period is shrouded in silence. Many letters must have been destroyed, for there is no record of the agitated debates which must have taken place, although correspondence on trivial matters was carefully preserved. There is, for instance, a bizarre exchange between Elspeth and the firm of Dubarry, perfumers, to whom Elspeth had sent a list of suggested titles for

their fragrances. This had been taken perfectly seriously, and a list of existing titles enclosed with the company's reply, in case she should suspect them
of fraudulent use of her suggestions. They offered to pay 10s 6d for each
title accepted, although even this strange attempt of Elspeth's to publicise
her creative efforts seems to have perished without trace.

Alastair was permitted one last chance to present himself for re-examin-
ation, and took Latin and Greek Literature in Hilary 1920. This time, he
passed – but Holy Scripture remained ahead of him, an insuperable barrier.

Chalmers, under Elspeth's direction, represented this crisis as a religious
dilemma centred on Alastair's lack of faith in Christianity, and there is some
evidence that the boy himself took refuge in this excuse. He was not, after
all, used to the idea of striving to do better. It would have been much more
natural to him simply to hate the subject which so cruelly exposed his
deficiencies, and to find a way in which he could despise it. Throughout his
disastrous Oxford career, he had made no attempt to join in University life.
The glimpses we get of him evoke a young man suffering from a massive
inferiority complex, with all the intolerably contemptuous behaviour which
that condition produces. He never paid the additional subscription which
brought membership of the Amalgamated Athletics Clubs of the College,
together with its social functioning,[4] and he formed no friendly relations
with any other undergraduate.

During the summer of 1918, Kenneth's agent, Curtis Brown, invited
Mouse to attend the coming-out dance given for his daughter Beatrice, in
London. Elspeth despatched her son from Berkshire by train to London,
equipping him with a little American flag with which to identify himself to
those who would be at the terminus to meet him. Beatrice herself recalled
afterwards how oddly the young man had behaved. He made no contact
with any other young person, and never attempted to dance. Instead, he
spent the whole evening at his father's side, talking what she described as
"interminable dullness".[5] He had evidently not got over the loathing of
"Turkey-trotting" which he had expressed at prep school.

Kenneth may have had a hand in the invitation, for he wrote a letter of
personal gratitude to Curtis Brown afterwards.

It was most awfully good of you to give the boy such a splendid time.
He seems to have enjoyed every minute of it. Owing to the War he
has been simply starved on the social side of him and this visit was just
what he wanted and what was best for him. For he is a "social animal"
really. I dare say you discovered what a passion he has for abstract
discussion and first principles as opposed to anything concrete. He
would, for instance, sit up all night discussing the principles that went
to the drawing up of the American Constitution, while being languidly
indifferent to personal details concerning any President.[6]

After his evening with Alastair, Curtis Brown probably knew exactly what Grahame meant.

Compared with the disasters of Rugby and Eton, Mouse seemed to his parents to be coping reasonably well with Oxford. In November 1918 the war ended, and they could relax into the relief of knowing that no more boys would butcher each other in the name of a cause which nobody quite understood any longer. After the strange, spontaneous truce which had arisen at Christmas, when a single voice singing "Stille Nacht" had drifted across No Man's Land to touch the hearts of the young soldiers of both nations, there had been a subtle change. The futility of war outweighed any question of triumph, and people in thousands of little villages like Blewbury ached for it to end.

Bevil Quiller-Couch had survived unharmed, but remained in France as part of the Army of Occupation, to supervise the closing down of his Battery and arrange for the return of its horses to Britain. He had described them and their riders in a letter written to his parents on Armistice Day, as "my children". In February of 1919, when his task was almost completed, he contracted Spanish flu in the epidemic which was sweeping Europe. It turned to pneumonia and, within a few days, he was dead.

The blow was a shattering one. The golden boy was gone, in a cruel, grubby little irony which denied him heroism. Q, who had put so much energy into recruiting, was left to mourn his son and to include in his lectures to a new generation of students the brave conviction that "we must yet carry on somehow, sing a song on the raft we cannot steer, keep a heart of sorts . . .". He was a man of extraordinary wisdom, and it must have saddened him that he could bring so little enlightenment to Kenneth and Elspeth in their treatment of Alastair. As he said in a lecture on the poetry of Thomas Hardy,

> All that *we* can do is to keep our hearts as fresh as we may; to bear ever in mind that a father can guide his son but some distance down the road, and the more wisely he guides the sooner (alas!) must he lose the fair companionship and watch the boy run on. It may sound a hard saying, but we can only keep him admiring the things we admire at the cost of pauperising his mind.[7]

The death of the boy whom Alastair had been encouraged to regard as a model of perfection may well have added to his confusion. If, as seems certain, the idea of God was linked in his mind with the Bible study which he hated so much, then Bevil's death must have taken its place in a loathsome religious mockery. The conventional comfort offered at a funeral service turns on the existence of a caring and all-wise God, and Mouse could see no care or wisdom either in Bevil's death or in his own struggles with the implacable texts of the holy Book. Kenneth was no help. He attended the village church, and sometimes read the lesson, but it was a conventional gesture, in no way connected with his personal faith, which was a thing so deeply tucked away in his mind that Alastair had no access to it. Although the boy was not to know that his father had written to Miss Bradley in 1904 about "the shadow of Scotch-Calvinist devil-worship", which must have clashed so badly with the Catholicism of St Edward's, the underlying attitude of scepticism must have made itself felt, adding to Mouse's suspicion of hypocrisy. His parents probably presented a very different attitude to him during the years of academic disaster. He was no longer their brilliant and admired son, and it must have become evident to him that he never had been.

It was at this point that Kenneth failed his son completely. Had he been able to assure Mouse that success is the effective functioning of the self rather than conformity to some outside standard, something might have been salvaged from the wreckage. But Kenneth himself was not sure of any such thing. His life had, in his own view at least, been blighted by the denial of university education, and he could not see that the object of his heart's desire might be quite inappropriate for his son. Besides, Kenneth was successful. He was by now a famous, much-admired author, and to tell Mouse that he should be contented with something less than that eminence smacked of condescension. Kenneth had not sought fame – he was the most modest and retiring of men – but it had become an element in the family which could not be shrugged off. For Alastair, at the lowest ebb of his self-esteem, there was no contact with his father's outlook, and least of all was there any insight into Kenneth's complex, multi-layered concept of religion.

Grahame, for all his rejection of Calvinism, embraced some of its stoic elements along with the teaching of Marcus Aurelius, but the Catholicism of St Edward's had left him with a strong sense of mysticism and a love of ritual, both religious and secular. He had written of "the acolyte who, greatly privileged, had been permitted to swing a censer at the sacring of the very mass",[8] and of monks whose chapel was "high hushed and faintly scented, beautiful with a strange new beauty born both of what it had and what it had not – that too familiar dowdiness of common places of worship".[9] Overlying all this, however, was his Paganism, which functioned equally on the instinctive and the rational levels.

Previous biographers have tended to dismiss Grahame's pantheism as a faddish picking-up of the Celtic twilight mood which was fashionable in the 1890s, but in fact it sprang from much deeper sources. All his writing makes it clear that God, to him, was self-evidently present in the continuum which is inherent in nature, but a personally experienced spiritual truth is a difficult thing to define. Kenneth, having given it clear expression in his work, culminating in the outright statement of faith made in *The Piper at the Gates of Dawn*, probably assumed, as writers tend to, that he had laid bare his beliefs, and was therefore quite literally "an open book". His son, of all people, he may have felt, must surely have understood the full meaning of the words which had been so painfully and scrupulously selected. Unfortunately, a book needs a positive act of intelligence on the part of the reader before it can act as a free-flowing communication between the originator's mind and that of the receiver. Family-members, familiar with the living presence of the writer, are often the last people to accept the more deeply personal truth which is expressed in his or her writing. For Mouse, who may in any case have had ambivalent feelings about *The Wind in the Willows*, the message was particularly obscure. He was unlikely to turn to a book which was public property for an insight into his father's most private philosophy. Kenneth in any case was a mass of denials. His conventional career as a City man, his military appearance, his Church of England attendance and his unfailing good manners gave little sign of the turbulent mixture of religious and mystic conventions which lay at his centre.

A letter he wrote on 24 September 1919 is light-hearted and relaxed, and yet it reveals Grahame's lack of concern for other people's perception of things and the logic which is conventionally supposed to bind them together. He had received an enquiry from Professor G. T. Hill of London University, who had read *The Wind in the Willows* and wanted to know who cleared up Mole End after Mole himself had flung down the whitewash brush on a spring day and made his bolt for freedom. Rediscovering his home in the depths of the following winter, there was not a trace of stepladder or bucket or hardened brush, and the goldfish were well and happy. Kenneth rose to the challenge with alacrity.[10]

DEAR SIR, – the very natural inquiries contained in your kind letter which reached me this morning are probably best answered by a simple reference to the hopelessly careless and slipshod methods of the author whose work you are criticizing. But it may perhaps be pointed out in his defence, that Mole, though unmarried and evidently in rather poor circumstances, as income goes nowadays, could probably have afforded some outside assistance say twice a week or so, indeed, living as he did, it would be almost a necessity. He probably then had a char-mouse in for a few hours and her dinner on certain days, and the animal would have cleaned up his whitewashing mess in a perfunctory sort of way; then, finding that her weekly pittance was no longer forthcoming, quite naturally and properly would have taken her services elsewhere, though from kindness of heart she might have continued to give an occasional eye to the goldfish.

In support of his theory, I would ask you to observe that our author practices a sort of "character economy" which has the appearance of being deliberate. The presence of certain characters may be indicated in or required by the story, but if the author has no immediate use for them, he simply ignores their existence. Take this very question of domestic service – however narrow poor Mole's means may have been, it is evident that Rat was comfortably off – indeed, I strongly suspect him of a butler-valet and cook-housekeeper. Toad Hall, again, must have been simply crawling with idle servants eating their heads off.

But the author doesn't happen to want them, so for him they simply don't exist. He doesn't say they are *not* there; he just leaves them alone. To take another instance – the wretched fellow, ignorant as he is, must have known perfectly well that the locomotive on which Toad escaped required the services of a stoker as well as an engine-driver, but he didn't happen to *want* a stoker, so he simply ignored him.

I think you will find that this same character-economy runs through all the classic old fairy-tales and our author probably thought he was sinning (if sinning at all) in very good company. The modern method leaves so little to the imagination of the reader that it describes with insistent particularity the appearance of the taxi-driver who did *not* say "Thank you" to the heroine when she gave him 3^d. above the legal fare from South Audley Street to Waterloo. Our author would have treated a taxi exactly as he would treat a magic carpet (which indeed is just what it is) and would not have given the taxi a driver at all. And this is right, for not one passenger in a hundred is ever conscious of the presence of a driver at all. They only see at the end a paw thrust out into which they drop something, and the taxi vanishes with a snort. Probably Magic Carpets had drivers too, but the authors of old saw that they were unessential to their stories, and ignored them.

Grahame may not have been a stranger to Professor Hill, for the type-written letter ends with a post-script: "My best regards to G.R. when you seen him." G.R. was probably Graham Robertson. However, it is a spirited defence, and says more in its few lines about the storyteller's art than ever emerges from the ponderous procedures of analysing plot, setting, character and all the rest of the methodology as commonly adopted by the educational process. But there is also a revealing glimpse into the profoundly subjective world in which Grahame moved. It takes a peculiar intensity of inwardness to be able to think of a taxi-driver simply as a paw (not a hand) into which one drops something. Even the coin or note dropped is external and irrelevant. Nothing matters except the selective awareness of the storyteller. One begins to get an insight into the distance which separated Grahame from other people. Elspeth had been incorporated into a fantasy-hinterland which was not a true intimacy and, although Mouse was theoretically admitted without reserve to the centre of Kenneth's care for him, it was a centre which the boy did not understand and which his father could not explain.

The University relented somewhat after Alastair scraped through his Classics exam, and he resumed his studies, but the bugbear of Holy Scripture remained ahead of him and was compounded by the results of his loathing and disbelief. Mouse did not have the power of intellect which would have allowed him to find his own dilemma interesting. He had never been taught the skill of refining and using his own feelings, and was afloat on a tide of undigested emotion. God as the source of loving kindness seemed impossible to believe in, for Alastair's recent experiences seemed to be a series of cruel mockeries, designed (if, indeed, there were a design) to expose the inadequacy which he had tried for so long to disguise.

As a child, whenever Mouse was confronted by something he did not like, he simply threw a tantrum – and usually got his own way, or at least was rewarded a lot of concerned attention. Now, he was up against a set of circumstances which he hated, but his sighing and grumbling brought him no sympathy. His situation was acutely painful, and it filled him with frustrated anger.

It seems on the face of it that Christ Church, as an essentially ecclesiastical institution, should have been well able to offer advice and guidance to an undergraduate who was suffering a crisis of religious faith; but this is to leave out of the equation Alastair's intense self-obsession. Unless he had changed very radically since his childhood days, he did not want advice on how to adapt himself to a difficult situation. His whole security, precarious though it was, had always rested on the conviction that he could make himself admired, whether he deserved it or not. Oxford did not admire him in the least. That University is tolerant of eccentrics but not of the ineffectual; Oscar Wilde (who also had religious doubts) could get himself rusticated from Magdalen because he went off to Greece and did not trouble to return when required, but he still emerged with a double first. The "Bad Boy", as he, like Mouse, referred to himself, was too brilliant a man not to win recognition. Alastair may have been stupid by Oxford standards, but he was not unintelligent. He was a creative, perceptive boy who, like his father, hated boring, uncongenial work. His inability to fit into the academic conventions raises the interesting question of whether Kenneth himself would have found Oxford as entrancing as he had pictured it. Quite certainly, *The Wind in the Willows* would never have been written without the sense of poignant alienation which illuminates it, and a stream of sub-Quiller-Couch novels and essays would have been a poor substitute.

Although Alastair resembled his father in his basic creativity, they were in other respects very different people. The boy had inherited Elspeth's desperate need to be well thought of by others, which led her to keep up a constant stream of letters and small gifts even to quite slight acquaintances, and which caused Mouse to show off endlessly and sulk when ignored. Any other confused undergraduate would have sought advice, particularly one who had an ally, for Keith Feiling was at Christ Church, and could have been relied on to honour the family connection and give Alastair his attention. If anything, Feiling was inclined to be over-sympathetic to the problems of the young people in his charge, and there is a record that he had problems with the senior historian at Christ Church because the latter thought that Feiling was too easy-going with the undergraduates.[11] For all his kindness, however, Feiling was capable of crisply dismissive judgements. He wrote of Southey, "Few who have held so high a place have had so little intrinsic wisdom",[12] and such impatience with silliness may have given him an aura of forbidding loftiness, specially to a young undergraduate who had begun to suspect that he was himself silly.

Alastair's life had been mythologised from the start, for the inadmissible truth probably was that the Grahames were ashamed of their purblind, less-than-brilliant son. While admiring everything he did which could be called clever, they were seldom physically present in his life, and their pleasures did not include him, as their long periods of foreign travel showed. Brought up in such pretence, the boy had never learned to distinguish subjective impression from objective reasoning. It was all very well for Wilde to defend mythology ("What is true in a man's life is not what he does, but the legend which grows up around him . . ."); Wilde knew the difference. Mouse did not. In February 1920, he wrote to A. W. Dall, who had been his personal tutor in the months between Eton and Oxford, and outlined his problems. If he had hoped for sympathy, he was to be disappointed, for Dall wrote back on 1 March with scant patience.

> Your letter interested me very much. I am not surprised at your Agnosticism. A logical and strongly introspective mind which takes life seriously *always* passes through this phase.
> P.S. I think your writing has improved.[13]

It was a depressing response, indicating as it did that the depth of isolation and suffering which Alastair felt was in no way unusual. A photograph of Alastair taken at about this time shows a young man who has now lost all trace of boyish puppy-fat. The angle at which the head is carried is the same as in the earlier one, but there is a thinness about the face and the sloping shoulders. The cocky smile has gone, replaced by a blankness at the corners of the mouth, and the eyes look out defensively from under level brows like Elspeth's. The dark hair is neatly brushed back from a broad forehead, the ears are set close to the head, the nose, as someone had said of his father's is "short and intelligent". The acne which plagued him for so long is receding, and, given a dash of confidence, he would be strikingly handsome. It is almost as if he refuses to be handsome. Toad, one remembers, was ugly and failed at everything, and yet was loved for the essential sweetness of his nature.

Having struggled through the Greek and Latin exam, Alastair came home for the Easter holidays, to find himself surrounded by well-meaning congratulations and exhortations. Evidently Elspeth had exaggerated his success, for an odd letter came from a Mr Johnson on Palm Sunday.

I hope you are enjoying a holiday, with the consciousness that the bogey of Pass Mods has been settled with for ever. Of course I was not surprised at the news, for we were both determined that nothing else should happen, were it only for the Toad's sake! But now you have satisfied yourself that "will" means "can" you will go on to success in the subject of your choice.[14]

The reference to "the Toad" is strange. Could it have become common knowledge in the family's circle of acquaintances that Alastair had as a child provided a model for his father's bombastic, vulnerable character? If so, the element of self-prophesy deepens.

Elspeth was no help. Her belief in Mouse's brilliance was showing signs of strain. She had written to a schoolboy friend of the family, Kenneth Josling, on 20 March, urging him to work hard. "Your place in form should be just as zealously guarded and as keenly contested as any goal at footer," she said sternly, adding that a boy who did well at school would then have "far more time to devote to getting an Honours Degree the only aim of the true scholar". It would be doubly urgent that her own son should be charged with the same ambition, and yet it was already clear that Alastair would not read for an honours degree. He was attempting Pass Mods, which indicated that he would, at best, achieve only a pass degree, and, as a correspondent to *The Times* had pointed out when the question of compulsory classics in the universities was being debated in 1890, "a very moderate knowledge of Latin and Greek is sufficient to obtain a pass degree".[15] Even so, the required standard was too high for Mouse. As the pressure mounted, he found an opportunity to voice his difficulties to one or other of his parents, but there seems little sign that he managed to convey the horror of his complete inability to cope with Holy Scripture. The problem was passed on to what seemed the appropriate authority. Young Kenneth Josling's father was a clergyman, and he sent Alastair a copy of "Cruden's Concordance" on 4 May, saying it was "By your parents' desire", and adding that he hoped Mouse would find it useful. The letter shows no signs of having understood that the boy was going through anything more than a temporary hitch.

I trust you have settled down comfortably in your new rooms and find everything as you wish. I am wondering what you have decided to go in for. Whatever it is, I wish you all success. In any case, you will have to work jolly hard ... As in a way you're making a new start at Oxford, I hope you are arranging your life on practical lines. You have much to do and time is short.[16]

It was indeed. Three days after Josling wrote his letter, on Friday, 7 May, Alastair walked in the early evening across Port Meadow, where his father had played cricket as a schoolboy at St Edward's. He had dined in Hall, and a fellow undergraduate noticed that he asked for a glass of port at the end of the meal, which, he said, "I had not known him do before".[17] Alastair was not seen alive again. At dawn, railway gangers found his body a little way up the line from the level crossing at the far side of the Meadow. Among other gross injuries, he had been decapitated. His pockets were full of religious tracts.

At the inquest, held the following Thursday, 13 May, a verdict of accidental death was returned. No evidence of financial difficulties had been found, and his family relations were described as "excellent". Medical evidence confirmed his partial-sightedness, and it seemed safe (or at least, kind) to assume that he had been struck by a train while crossing the line.

Dr W. D. Sturrock, who examined the body, would not commit himself to that assumption. His report tells its own story:

> The cause of death was decapitation, and that was compatible with being run over by a train. The right arm was fractured below the shoulder, the left leg four inches above the ankle, and all the toes of the right foot. There were also numerous bruises on the body.
>
> *The Coroner:* Are these injuries compatible with being knocked down by a train and then run over?
>
> *Dr Sturrock:* I could not answer the first part of the question as to being knocked down, but certainly they are compatible with being run over.

But Alastair had not been on the level crossing. Even if he had been, his unimpaired hearing alone would have told him that a steam-train was approaching. The position in which he was found makes it clear that he had lain face down across the rails, a little diagonally, his neck and right shoulder resting across one rail, his left leg and right foot on the other. There is a terrible memory that, as a little boy, he used to lie in the road in front of approaching motor-cars, which, in those days, would always stop for him.

The Dean of Christ Church, Dr T. B. Strong, said that Alastair was "a very quiet and reserved man, and I never got to know him well".[18] Anna

Gregory, the "faithful maid" who had sent Alastair a Christmas card, said "He was always so kind and courteous. He was the only boy in his tutor's house that I ever even *thought* of cutting the bread-and-butter thin for."[19] Keith Feiling, perhaps with regret that he had not been more perceptive when the boy was alive, offered his house in Holywell from which to conduct the funeral, and Alastair was buried in Holywell cemetery. His father scattered lilies of the valley over his coffin on a day of cruelly ironic date. On the headstone he caused to be engraved the words:

> Here was laid to rest on his twentieth birthday, 12th of May 1920, Alastair, only child of Kenneth and Elspeth Grahame, of whose noble ideals, steadfast purposes and rare promise remains only a loved and honoured memory.

Even at the last, the myth of Mouse's brilliance was maintained. Q, for Kenneth's sake, managed to bring himself to believe – at least overtly – that the boy's death had been accidental, for he knew only too well the agony of losing a son. He wrote Alastair's obituary for the *Oxford Chronicle* of 18 June 1920, and dealt gently with the grieving parents.

> He was always an "unusual" boy: not merely one of the boys (far more usual than is commonly supposed) who are unable to view Rugby and Eton save as prisons and look forward to Oxford or Cambridge for the gaol delivery of their souls: but one who, coming to adore Oxford, still saw it as a preparative. School games afflicted his soul, because it was impatient. It could not wait to play with taken-for-granted amusements; it was (I think) a trifle too contemptuous of his fellows so easily accepting themselves as, at the best, "noble playthings of the gods". But he found delight and gaiety and wisdom in the simplest happenings of animals and people.

Much of what Q said was true; but, generous-hearted as he was, even he could not admit that life, for Alastair, had not been "preparative". A boy who has, for reasons obscure to him, been brought up to think that he is perfect cannot regard his existence as preparatory to something better. Suicide is not an act of weakness. It is a massive aggression against the self, and, by implication, against those who have made that self the intolerable thing it has become. It is difficult to disentangle Mouse's educational problems from his religious ones. If his pockets were full of tracts, then his mind had certainly been running on the constant tussle with the tenets of the Christian faith, and one wonders how far the hurdle of exam-passing had affected his general outlook. In that last walk from Christ Church to Port Meadow, which must have taken at least twenty minutes, there may have been many exhortations ringing in his mind. All of them had one thing in common; in the Christian ethic, this life is but a preparation for the next. Alastair's deepest instincts were probably those of his Pagan father, that this life is in fact holy in its own right – but nobody at Christ Church was likely to reinforce that view. Orthodox Christianity tends to suggest that the here-and-now delight in life is sinful, and that redemption lies in an acceptance of the judgement which happens at its end. In its desperate way, Mouse's death could have been a last act of faith. A cruel word-play might have it that he had deliberately "laid his life on the line". It was a demonstration of trust in the unknown power which might not even exist. In destroying his life, he broke through the vicious circle of disbelief and smashed his way out of life's prison.

In his 1959 biography, Peter Green, who had the benefit of talking to many of the people who had known Alastair, alluded to this very image. The Revd K. H. Jocelyn had told him that Mouse once remarked, "This life is a prison". Kenneth and Elspeth had stretched their fantasy-son on the rack of their wish-fulfilment, and had forgotten that he was real.

Such hints as Jocelyn's increase the evidence that the death had indeed been self-inflicted. Keith Feiling told Green he had no doubt of it, and he also confided that Q, for all his sympathy towards Kenneth and Elspeth, regarded the verdict of the inquest as merciful rather than accurate. Q, however, put the living before the dead, and suppressed his suspicions. After listening to Kenneth's version of what happened, he wrote to Elspeth in reassurance: "K's reply and the convincing story lifted for ever a great weight off my heart. I read the evidence carefully; I know the place; it is all as clear as clear to me."[20] For a man normally so fluent and articulate, it is an awkward, stumbling letter which betrays his unease; but Q was as good as his word, and did his best to scotch the rumours which were flying round Oxford. The obituary he wrote for the *Oxford Chronicle* went out of its way to emphasise that the death had been accidental.

Kenneth himself may well have known the truth in his heart, for his customary reticence deepened from this time onwards. He nursed his grief alone, and said nothing. Elspeth, on the other hand, was desperate to construct a new reality which could encompass her son as the innocent victim of a cruel fate. In a process which came close to deification, she recalled (or perhaps invented) how Miss Stott had described Mouse as "a bit of a mystic". After his attack of peritonitis, he saw a picture of Our Lord in a Holland Street shop. "Mouse pointed it out to me. 'That is my Friend,' he said, 'the Carpenter. When I was ill He came to see me and sometimes I go and talk to Him.' On another day he said to me, 'Death is promotion'."[21]

Whatever the self-delusion, there was no avoiding the fact that Alastair had gone, taking with him the anxiety and interest and ambition which his parents had for twenty years felt for him. Now, the emptiness of the days in the old, quiet house in Berkshire were unrelieved by letters from Oxford and by the sense of a continuation (no matter how unsatisfactory) into a future which would run beyond their own life span. Even the desperate effort to summon up a life-picture of Mouse was painful, for Elspeth in particular had hardly known her son except in school holidays. Miss Stott had in effect been the boy's mother throughout his growing years, and it was on her recollections that Elspeth built her card-house of memories. Chalmers had no option but to reinforce it, and Green, though with some doubt, cited Chalmers as his authority, and it is only now, looking at the discrepancies between Miss Stott's actual letters and the long "quotations" from them which Elspeth authorised, that the poverty of the truth emerges, as will be seen.

In August, three months after Alastair's death, the sons of Austin Purves came to Britain. They were diffident about making contact with their father's old friend, knowing of his bereavement, but Kenneth was more than willing to be hospitable. He came up from Blewbury for the best part of a week to be with them and to show them round Oxford. He booked rooms for them, obtained good seats for organ recitals in Christ Church, although he was not himself particularly interested in music, and was solicitous of their every need. "Some of us drew and painted," Austin Jr remembered, "and Grahame suggested various spots such as Iffley where we could sketch some truly romantic English things." Kenneth seemed surprised that the boys could not read Latin, and scrupulously translated every inscription "and was, I am sure, unaware of our lack of interest", Austin said. He added, "This was not, I think, good manners on his part, or bad manners on ours."[22]

There was an air of ceremony about such extreme care. It was quite uncharacteristic of Kenneth, who, although unfailingly courteous, had never been given to putting himself out on behalf of guests. The Purves boys were a little taken aback, and realised that something deeper lay behind his anxious kindness. John Purves perceived him to be "a sensitive, shy, broken man" with whom "we could not establish an entente. Grahame was too reserved, and his suffering must have been intense." The young visitors were, perhaps, not so much real, living young men as symbols of what he had lost. For Kenneth, the risk was doubly poignant, reminding him that these children of his beloved friend were themselves fatherless. They brought out in him a painful paternal instinct, mingled with the knowledge that it had not been enough to keep his own son alive. "We boys," John explained, "had never seen Mouse, but Grahame believed that it was Mouse's earnest wish to show Oxford to us. Back of this was Grahame's deep love for a University and town of which he had never been a part as a student and which he attended vicariously through his son."

It comes as something of a surprise to realise that Alastair and the Purves boys had never met but, of course, Mr and Mrs Purves had been on their own when they visited Boham's, and when the whole family had met Kenneth and Elspeth in Fowey in 1913, Mouse had been away at school. He had visited Fowey only once, during the summer before he went to Rugby. Grahame, for all his love of travel, had never taken the boy abroad. Alastair had spent most of his holidays with his governess in Broadstairs or Littlehampton while his parents stayed at home or went elsewhere. Now that his life was seen in retrospect to have been such a tragically short one, Kenneth must have regretted the time he could have spent with his son and did not. It was perhaps in a spirit of atonement or even penance that he behaved like a conscientious father to the children of his old friend who, like Alastair, had joined that eternity in which all – or nothing – is known.

Elspeth's account of Alastair in *First Whisper of the Wind in the Willows* never wavers in its depiction of her son as perfect. In a macabre way, the verdict of accidental death confirmed his stainless character and at the same time provided the perfect excuse for any shortcomings. Once dead, all dubious potential achievements could be enshrined as a certainty. There were no longer any awkwardly inconsistent realities to be explained. The boy's very gravestone spoke of his "steadfast purposes and rare promise". Mouse was confirmed in a new glory – he was, unalterably, an innocent victim, a martyr to the ruthless outer world which had not understood or appreciated him, but would have come to do so. Elspeth's old friend, Anstey Guthrie, sent her a memoir of her son for publication, and she returned the piece to him for revision, only accepting it when it was satisfactorily fulsome. Meeting Alastair as a child, he said in the final version, "was rather like being presented to a young prince".

The Bishop of Oxford, in whose confirmation class Alastair had been, evidently took no such view of him. Writing to Elspeth after the Chalmers biography had appeared, complete with Guthrie's reverential obituary, he observed that "the account of Alastair is very different from my experience of him".[23]

It did not matter. By then, Alastair Grahame was firmly established as a tragic hero. For Elspeth, it was the role which perfectly suited her concept of him. Despite the shock and grief, his death freed her from the embarrassing reality which his physical presence had imposed on the dream-child she had striven for so long to present. Her writing about Alastair never once mentions his near-blindness, and she did not permit Chalmers to refer to it. In the chapter on Alastair, the biographer is, in fact, at pains to quote Miss Smedley's comment about the boy's "bright calm eyes", and it is only in Q's obituary letter that there is a passing reference to "some defect of eyesight". Very soon after Mouse's death, as if in an urgency to rid herself of a side of her son which she now thought irrelevant, Elspeth packed up all his clothes and belongings and sent them to a local jumble-sale, indifferent to the distress this caused the people of the village. As soon as Kenneth got back from his escorting of the Purves boys round Oxford, he and she together set about discarding all the things that reminded them of the last twenty years. Elspeth took the lead in this. For a recently bereaved mother, her letters are dauntingly businesslike. In a crammed postscript to a list of goods for sale (in which each item was described as "interesting", "delightful" or "really beautiful"), she reminded the auctioneer about a pair of curtains which were quite evidently badly faded:

> 11yds × 11yds made in France from a design by Walter Crane, of wool & silk tapestry in a pattern of grapes & vine leaves. These have toned to a beautiful colouring & are so good & *strong* in texture that they may be well adapted for covering old furniture, chairs, settees &c &c.[24]

Her friends, too, were asked to buy. There is a graceful refusal from Eleanor Gross, with a cheque for the few things she had accepted. "I am afraid these days are very hard on you," she wrote, "but perhaps in a way the work is better than having time to think."[25] She may have been right. After the long years of reclining on sofas, Elspeth was thrown into fevered activity. Eleanor went on: "I will hope that Italy may give you rest of soul, we can only keep on in life by always learning that our souls may grow – your dear boy would like you both to be happy".

Caroline Feiling, writing from Christ Church, Oxford, regretted that the dealers "all say the prices asked are so high they can not possibly touch the things".[26] Judging by the £10 reserve on the faded curtains, she was right.

As a result, everything which had not been privately sold went into the auction, and the house was cleared of all but its most basic furnishing. The Wedgwood china, the Bohemian glass, the lifetime's collection of toys, dolls' tea-sets and "Sailor's Farewell" glass rolling-pins all went, together with the Weber player-piano, the Dutch and Sheraton cupboards and the Welsh dresser "with Nelson's head and motto on the handles". The Grahames were not in need of the money; it was a deliberate abandoning of their previous life, carried out rapidly and with a strong sense of purpose. Nothing was spared. "Many books for children and adults in good condition and beautifully illustrated" were thrown in, and so were the treasures which Kenneth had loved. The catalogue detailed them all, sounding, at times, as affectionate as Grahame's own lament for the lost toys in *A Departure*: "Wonderful miniature Piano (a few inches high) which when lid is opened plays tune and the side candles light up by electricity. When the lid is closed sound and light cease."

There was indeed to be a departure. By October, Boham's, furnished but stripped of all its valuables, had been let for eighteen months to a Mr Davies. On the 28th of that month, Kenneth and Elspeth left the village and went to London, having sent a cabin-trunk ahead to the S.S. *Orvieto*. Two days later, they sailed for Italy.

17

North and South

From this time onward, Kenneth Grahame's life diminished in scale. He lived like a man on the run from his own memories, moving restlessly from place to place as if in constant search of an immediate diversion which would distract his mind and fill his senses. Whatever the inhibition which had prevented Elspeth from travelling with him, it was now swept away. They had been married for twenty-one years, twenty of which had been dominated by Alastair, and now, for the first time, the couple were together in a fulfilment of Kenneth's dream. They had escaped. Evidence of where they went and what they did is scrappy, for they had, in Quiller-Couch's terminology, retreated from "what does" to "what is".[1] They were doing nothing; simply to be was enough. Kenneth had learned at Boham's that reclusiveness can be linked with boredom, and he would not make that mistake again. This time he needed diversion.

The Grahames spent the whole of the following year in Rome. The city had long exercised a special fascination for Kenneth. Even as a child, it had been for him the Golden City, the capital of Italy and the South. In his early story, 'The Roman Road', he depicts the boy-narrator's wonderful meeting with an artist sketching by the wayside, whom he examines in silence. The conversation was then typically laconic.

> After another five minutes or so had passed, he remarked, without looking my way: "Fine afternoon we've having: going far today?"
>
> "No, I'm not going any farther than this," I replied; "I *was* thinking of going on to Rome: but I've put it off."
>
> "Pleasant place, Rome," he murmured: "You'll like it." It was some minutes later that he added: "But I wouldn't go just now, if I were you: too jolly hot."
>
> "You haven't been to Rome, have you?" I inquired.
>
> "Rather," he replied briefly: "I live there."
>
> This was too much, and my jaw dropped as I struggled to grasp the fact that I was sitting there talking to a fellow who lived in Rome.

Kenneth had told Helen Dunham in 1896 that the boy in the story was "more or less myself", and now he settled ecstatically into the city of his dreams. He plunged with greedy enthusiasm into the glories of its architecture and of its cuisine, and devoted himself to a minute investigation of every church, cathedral, classical ruin and trattoria he could find. He developed a passion for Italian ice-cream, and indulged it freely, despite Elspeth's fears that it was bad for him.

There is an odd sense of gradually reversing roles at this time. From being a fretful invalid, too much of a "living skellington" to face the ordeal of a photograph, much less the rigours of Continental travel, Elspeth begins to emerge as the practical one of the pair. It is as if she had reverted to the capable organiser which she had been before a twenty-year trauma robbed her of self-confidence. All her energy was restored. For Kenneth, the years following his son's death are overlaid with a sense of elegy. There is an autumnal, Keatsian feeling about his pleasure in the Italian days which suggests that for him, too, something had been resolved. Dino and Minkie were alone again, twenty years older. They were too damaged by the results of their love to play their childish games any longer, and yet they were perhaps nearer to happiness than they had ever been.

They found new friends among the British and American archeologists who lived and worked in the city. In particular, Frank and Charis Fairbanks, who were on the staff of the American Academy, became very close. They lived in a villa within the grounds of the Academy, and practised an open-handed, casual hospitality, often providing rooms for students, and they were charmed by Kenneth's uninhibited delight in the city. They went with him and Elspeth to see the newly uncovered Pinturicchio frescoes in the little church of San Onofrio, and Charis remembered his "great glorious boyish joy" in showing off his discoveries. She remembered, too, how

sitting on a bench where he could see the cross on the obelisk in the Piazza of St Peter's, he observed in his inimitable way, "They say there used to be a ball on the top of the obelisk where the cross is now; that was said to contain the ashes of Julius Caesar. Probably did – anyhow we haven't any proof that it didn't!"[2]

Grahame loved the numerous fountains, and would sit for hours listening to the music of their running water that rippled the reflection of the deep blue sky and broke up the image of the glinting coins which lay in the basin, thrown by visitors in the hope that their small offering would link them for ever to the magical city, and ensure their return. Kenneth became as much of an expert on the recondite byways of Rome as he had been on the history of Oxford, and he was delighted when two of the Purves boys, Dale and Edmund, both of them now architecture students and touring southern Europe, wrote from Naples asking if he could book rooms for them for a visit to Rome. The obliging Fairbankses put the boys up in their villa, where the current resident student happened to be Thornton Wilder, then about the same age as his young fellow Americans. It was only a year since Kenneth had appeared to be a "broken man" when he had escorted the boys round Oxford, but Edmund Purves found him full of new life.

> Mr Grahame took us under his wing immediately after our arrival in Rome and there seemed to be scarcely a day go by that he did not call for us or send for us and then he, Mrs Grahame and ourselves would walk about Rome – generally stopping at some shop in the morning to buy some bread, cheese, sausage and a bottle of wine for our noon-time meal, which we would eat wherever we happened to be when hunger struck. It was a wonderful experience as Mr Grahame knew every nook and cranny in Rome and seemingly every bit of history. I do not know how any three American students could have had any more enlightening experience for we saw Rome as few others, especially Americans, ever saw it. He was a wonderful and thoughtful companion – always cheerful and kind and gave no evidence of the tragedy that had recently occurred.[3]

The boys also noticed, with some disapproval, that Grahame's passion for good red wine was freely indulged. He was reluctant to pass an attractive-looking tavern without sampling its wares, even though the strictly brought-up Purves boys would not join him. They noticed, too, that there was no question of such frequent tippling when Elspeth was a member of the party. She may have known that her husband already had high blood pressure, or her refusal to condone his drinking may have been simply an extension of her famed parsimony. In Blewbury she had been well known for her skimping on household expenses.

The tenant of Boham's, meanwhile, had written indignantly to complain about the state the house had been left in, with a "good deal of litter and disorder". He was particularly incensed by the presence of mouse-nests in the larder. On 27 May 1921, Kenneth wrote to the Revd K. H. Jocelyn (who had sent Alastair a "Cruden's Concordance" in the last days of his life, and who seems to have been acting as an agent for the house), with a certain amount of bluster. Every farmhouse had mice, he said, and then, as if realising that this merely confirmed his tenant's complaint, took refuge in levity.

> Personally I have not myself seen a mouse inside Boham's for years, though, I am perfectly well aware that every time Mr Lay thrashes out a rick, some non-paying guests of this sort seek admission to the house, and my cat's face begins to wear a strained and haggard appearance suggestive of the need for a rest-cure. But nothing more is seen of mice![4]

315

Grahame must have been an irritating landlord, but he evidently felt, with some reason, that the tenancy of such a house as Boham's must be taken in a large spirit, undisturbed by such minor details as mice. He had moved beyond piffling concerns of that sort. He had, in fact, begun to take up the prominent position which is inevitable when a famous man joins the small "ex-pat" community of fellow nationals. Having chosen to live at the Hotel des Princes in the Piazza di Spagna, which lay at the centre of English and American life in Rome, Grahame quickly became known to its most eminent members. He had lunch with the American Ambassador, Robert Underwood Johnson, who was himself a poet, and as a result, was asked if he would contribute a five-minute tribute to Keats in a celebration of the centenary of the poet's death on 24 February. Grahame agreed, and although the text of his speech has not been preserved, he scored a great success. In turn, the British Ambassador, Sir Rennell Rodd, invited him to address the Keats–Shelley association.

Grahame called his talk "Ideals", and it was later reprinted in the *Fortnightly Review*. From such a title, one might assume that he had, at last, brought himself to tackle an abstract concept, debating the moral principles which underlie all serious thought but, within a few words, it became clear that he had preserved a strictly personal and subjective notion of what constituted an ideal. He opened with an attack on the "morbid craving" as he called it, "for imparting information to other people", and enlarged on "the sullen dislike we all feel for being fed with facts". In a highly revealing phrase, he asserted that "The one thing we do not want, apparently, is truth . . ."

Ideals, Kenneth made clear, are first formulated in childhood day-dreaming. Smith Minor, he said, does not fail to absorb Greek grammar because he is prejudiced against the subject, or because his mind is empty – quite the reverse. His mind is filled to capacity, but its contents are "something far rarer and braver, we may be quite sure, than even the most irregular of verbs". The Socratic process of enquiring what he is *not* thinking about will reveal that he "never wastes the precious hours of class-time in thinking of the obvious . . . his mind is up and away, in a far, far better world than this, a world wherein matters are conducted as they should be, and where he is undoubtedly the best man there, pursuing his ideals, and his mind is fully occupied with them".

Some of Grahame's audience may have begun to shift uneasily in their seats by this time, and he moved in to a vigorous defence of his standpoint.

But now I seem to hear the objection, that I have deceived you, that I have let you down. At the mention of ideals, you looked for me to trace and follow some of those rare and passionate visions which have taken our great ones by the hand and led them from crag to crag, from

316

height on to further height, till they have reached Olympus itself and brought back to level earth some of its sacred fire. And instead I am offering you, it would seem, the wayward, self-indulgent daydreams of an unconcentrated and purposeless boy – dreams he will grow out of or will shake off when the time for action is at hand – dreams which are no help to his self-development, but a real hindrance. Ah, but can we, dare we, attempt to draw a strict dividing line between the wayward dream and the high purposeful ideal, to pronounce exactly where one leaves off and the other begins? Is it not indeed of the essence of both, that we are carried away by them into an intenser, finer, clearer atmosphere than this earth can possibly offer? Most of such visions, it is true, come to nothing; only a very, very few achieve actual concrete results. But this is only because actual artists, shapers, makers, are scarce, while dreamers are many. It is no disparagement of the dreams themselves that only a very few of the dreamers have the power, or rather the gift, to harness their dreams with mastery and bend them to their imperious will.

He went on to hammer the point home, with all the conviction of a man whose childhood is still alive in him, and still acts, as Graham Greene put it many years later, as "the bank-balance of the writer".

And when we are tempted to speak somewhat contemptuously of the wayward fancies of a boy, let us ask ourselves seriously whether we ever entirely lay aside this habit of mind; whether we do not all of us, to the last, take refuge at times from the rubs and disappointments of a life where things go eternally askew, in our imaginary world where at any rate we have things for the time exactly as we want them? I hope to persuade you that this is really so – that in each and all of us the real and ideal places, so to speak are co-existing and functioning side by side.

Detailing the imaginary picture which a child will build up of a thing not yet known – the sea, for instance, or a grandparent he has never met, or the present to be revealed on a birthday morning – Grahame points out with inexorable logic that adults retain the same facility. It is in this lecture that he makes the observation quoted in Chapter 5, that one's first experience of Rome, however delectable, does not quite live up to the imagined ideal which vanishes under the impact of the reality. One wonders whether he realised that the same thing had been true of his son.

He develops this theme of the privately conceived ideal in a comparison of North and South which explains much of his passion for the Mediterranean.

The Greeks, who were in a way greater idealists than we, were also idealists of a more practical sort. By this I mean that, having arrived at their ideals, they were satisfied with them and thereupon proceeded to set them forth, to display them, nay more, to perpetuate them as the final ideal in bronze, marble, and so on. In their theology and their literature, again, still satisfied with the ideal they had arrived at, they produced the demi-god – the man made perfect as they saw perfection, very flesh of our flesh, always essential man and yet a god too, or at least a *divus*, one whom, while hailing him at times as brother, you were also free to worship as a god – if you wanted to. Now we Northerners would never have done all these things, even if we had the particular genius or technical skill; because *we* are never satisfied with our ideals, never reach even a temporary finality, must always be breaking our moulds, re-fusing our metal, entreating our public – which is of course the world itself – to wait a little bit longer, till we can give them the real thing at last. And meantime we give them nothing – or at least so very little!

It is an immensely shrewd and perceptive argument. Grahame pushed it to the crux of the question which he had pursued so often in his writing, most notably through Rat's attack of wander-lust in *Wayfarers All.*[5]

Which is the method of idealism of most benefit for the race? That of the South, which arrives, attains, achieves, and then – well, remains there satisfied, advancing no more, but yet bequeathing so great a legacy? Or that of the North, which never arrives, achieves but little, yet knows no limit to its flight?

Dreams, he ended by saying, are an essential part of living.

For your hill-top may disappoint you, and your sea-coast be too stuffy or too expensive, but the mountain air of dreamland is always recuperating, and there Apollo and all the Muses, or at least Pan and his attendant Fauna, await you.

What then, is the conclusion of the whole matter? Is it not that we are all idealists, whether we would or no? And that we are all idealists, chiefly by virtue of our waking dreams, those very imaginings which we are so ashamed of, and so reluctant to speak about, which we sternly discourage in others, but which all the same we secretly cherish to the very end? For in these dreams we are always better than ourselves, and the world is always better than it is, and surely it is by seeing things as better than they are that one arrives at making them better. This indeed is what "vision" means, and one knows that "without vision the people perish". Not – stay as they are; not even – go backwards. But – perish, from the anaemia of no ideals.

For a man so commonly accused by later generations of indifference to the welfare of others and lack of interest in the general good, it is an eloquent defence.

The Grahames had been long enough in Rome to regard it now as their home, and to feel the need for a holiday from it. In August, as if in renewed escape, they went to the Dolomites and stayed in Cortina d'Ampezzo, where Kenneth at once went off on long mountain walks, glad, perhaps, of the change from the city which, for all its seven hills, lacked the herby fragrance and the clean upland air of high places. A Miss J. L. G. Crookston, reminiscing to Green in 1957, said she had seen Grahame there. Her memories, as a complete stranger to him, have a trace of the presumption which people feel about the famous. He was, she said,

a remarkable looking man, striding across hill and dale, his Inverness cape swirling around him, his hair all swept up by the wind. On and on he went, solitary, absorbed in his own thoughts, until he vanished in the distance. I think he was deeply grieved over the loss of his son and I hesitated to intrude on his self-imposed isolation.

Miss Crookston's hesitation was well founded. Whether or not he was troubled by memories of Alastair, Kenneth was becoming increasingly disinclined to bother with strangers. Visiting cards piled up in the Hotel des Princes, and Elspeth would occasionally draw his attention to them, asking if they should return the compliment. This would trigger a small charade as he patted his pockets and remarked that he had no cards with him – did she? Elspeth would shake her untidy white head, and the pair of them would agree that the courtesies could wait until another, unspecified time. A few friends were enough. Kenneth was far more interested in the eccentric characters of Rome, such as the exiled Russian princess who ran a restaurant with her archduke husband, and wore diamond earrings while she cooked omelettes.

In the autumn following the Cortina trip, Grahame received a letter from Curtis Brown, suggesting that he might consider an abridged version of *The Wind in the Willows* for use in schools. The idea was to cut the book down by four complete chapters, or by piecemeal reduction to the same extent, on the grounds that this smaller version would be affordable by elementary schools. Kenneth was emphatic in his refusal, fulminating at length about "the indifferent hash of the grade 'Reader' ...". He went on:

I do not care to have a form or version of the story in print which has been cut down – not for literary reasons, such as redundancy or verbosity or parts being not quite so suited to children, or too much over their heads, and so on and so on, but for the purely arbitrary and "trade" reason of getting it within 192 pages. I can't abridge satisfactorily without a loss of quality, and that's the long and short of it. I know that School Committees will only have books on their own terms, more or less, but that's not my fault.[6]

By Grahame's standards of courtesy, it was a stiff letter, and his judgement was accepted without question. Quiller-Couch wrote at about the same time with a far more acceptable proposal. He wanted to include two long passages, one of them an extract from "Wayfarers All" in the *Oxford Book of English Prose*, which he was currently editing. This, far from seeking to cut down Grahame's rich writing to a simplified version, would confirm it as an example of the best the English language has to offer, and Kenneth was happy to give his permission. Restlessness, however, was afflicting him again and, after Christmas, he and Elspeth travelled slowly northward, with many overnight stops in places he found interesting, until, in February 1922, they reached Rapallo. They spent the spring in a village by Lake Garda – but by now Mr Davies's tenancy of Boham's had expired, and the problem of re-letting or selling the Blewbury house had to be faced. Were they to abandon a British base completely and reconcile themselves to a wandering life until infirmity overtook them? Even for such addicted travellers, the prospect was a little too frightening to contemplate. Travel, after all, owes much of its charm to the sense of being away from home and, without a home, one cannot relish the strangeness of being abroad. Kenneth and Elspeth went back to England to tackle the problem, arriving at Blewbury in June.

On 1 September, Grahame wrote to A. A. Milne, having heard that he was in search of a country house, and offered him the tenancy of Boham's.[7] The two men had never met, but Milne had suggested a sequel to *The Golden Age* many years ago and, in 1918 had written a congratulatory letter to Grahame, having just read *The Wind in the Willows*; they had kept up an intermittent correspondence ever since. Milne, however, wanted a permanent home, and was not interested in rented accommodation, so the Boham's proposal got no further. Eventually the Grahames gave up the effort to find a tenant and decided to put the house on the market. With this decision made, they went back to Rome.

It was a momentous time. Mussolini had marched on the city, and was about to form his Fascist government. Europe was beginning to shake itself to pieces. By the following year, all non-Fascist Italian political parties would have been outlawed, and Hitler's "Beer Hall Putsch" in Munich would have failed, even though the signs of dangerous instability were still clear, with the German mark standing at four million to a single US dollar. The Grahames were unconcerned. They were contained, as ever, within their own world. Elspeth alluded to the events later in a laconic letter to her brother, in which she said, "we used to hear the Fascists cracking the skulls of the Socialists at street corners, with cannons at both ends of the bridges and snipers shooting over the high wall surrounding the courtyard of the GPO".[8]

Ignoring bullets and political events, Kenneth continued to enjoy the restaurants and the archaeology, impervious to the outside world. It was hardly surprising that he had chosen animals to represent the varying aspects of his own being when he wrote his classic book, for his awareness was very close to the essentially sensate animal world. "The smells of Italy are more characteristic than those of the South of France,"[9] he had noted years ago, after his first journey south, and the delights of that fragrant country, with its olives and rosemary, its garlic and great, red tomatoes, its wine and peppers and roasted rabbit, never failed to excite him. The Grahames returned again and again to Rome from their various wanderings; as Elspeth put it, "we wintered in Rome, and summered there, and Eastered, and Christmas'd and knew every one of the 490 old churches".[10] Nevertheless, they left it for a while after they had "Christmas'd" there in 1922, migrating south to Capri, where they stayed, not in a hotel, but in the Pensione Faraglioni. During that winter, Kenneth had an attack of bronchitis, for the first time for several years. Since leaving the Bank, his health had been much better, and on this occasion he recovered quickly, and was soon on familiar terms with the old women who acted as porters and who would obligingly "remember back", dredging up tales of the past which went far beyond their own lifetime in order to please the white-haired Englishman who seemed so interested.

The Grahames were back in Rome for the spring, and Elspeth dealt with the pile of mail which awaited them. Kenneth had ceased all pretence of being interested in correspondence from strangers, and even an inquiry from a young fan who wanted to know the details of Otter's story about the lock-keeper failed to rouse his interest. He left it to Elspeth to write a plausible answer. Readers unfamiliar with the circumstances might like to be reminded that Otter, who had hauled himself out of the water to join Rat and Mole, shared their amusement at the sight of Toad "splashing badly and rolling a good deal" as he rowed inexpertly down the river. Rat remarked that he would "be out of the boat in a minute if he rolls like that".

"Of course he will," chuckled the Otter. "Did I ever tell you that good story about Toad and the lock-keeper? It happened this way. Toad . . ."

An errant May-fly swerved unsteadily athwart the current in the intoxicated fashion affected by young bloods of May-flies seeing life. A swirl of water and a "cloop!" and the May-fly was visible no more.

Neither was the Otter.[11]

Elspeth supplied a slightly lame response to the questioner: "I am afraid I must not tell you. The fact is, they both lost their tempers, and said things they much regretted afterwards. They are now friends again, so we have all agreed to let the matter drop."[12]

Kenneth signed the letter.

The Grahames went on travelling throughout the restless year of 1923, moving up to Florence for a while, and on through the fragrant joys of Tuscany, where Kenneth found a village fair which far outdid Blewbury in its colour and flavour. The chickens roasting on spits above the wayside fires put out an aroma which was irresistible – and he was never inclined to resist such indulgences. On one occasion, torn between visiting a cathedral and sampling fresh sardines with sweet potatoes and a salad of "green and purple and red and gold" leaves, the sardines won hands down. As he said, "Cathedrals know how to wait."[13]

In Bologna, he commented that the little pigs which he saw running after their stately mothers were like the pink-sugar mice which "one used to buy in Torquay". That they were destined to appear on the table, roasted whole and stuffed with rosemary, did not worry him. As we have seen before, he had long adopted a professional farming attitude towards pigs. In Perugia, the full-grown hog was roasted whole for saints' days, and Grahame would stop in his perambulations and peer down into the bake-houses where these gargantuan culinary operations were taking place, sniffing appreciatively.

Elspeth, too, was enjoying herself in her own way. There are some faded "box-Brownie" photographs of nuns in fly-away white coifs holding small Italian children, and these seem to relate to a visit to what she simply called "A Lace Village". She wrote about this, not in a letter, but apparently with some thought of publication, for occasional words are crossed-out and replaced. She described how the babies and young children were looked after by the nuns so that their mothers might work at the lace-making.[14]

> ... the good sisters seem the very soul of patience and kindness – but the children of that countryside great and small are fond of play-time and of the handful of chesnuts [sic] and torn pieces of bread eaten in the doorway – the glass of sour-wine when thirsty, the slice of melon when hot. Even the lace mothers and the lace grandmothers too for that matter, play like great girls on feast days when they put their bobbins by ...

She went on to explain how the agent came to buy lace, driving hard bargains for it which the women were in no position to refuse.

> For even bread and chesnuts [sic] cost money, nets cannot be mended for ever, and the husband wants wine when he comes from the sea.

Then coffee is dear, and the Priest expects something, and on feast days one must at least have a handkerchief with flowers round the shoulders. So the bargain for that time is struck, and the Lace-mothers patiently begin again the long lengths of cobweb trimmings that shall travel far from the quay side and the shadow of the tall dim houses, where each window flutters with gay coloured rags, washed when needs must be, and hung there to dry, for each family has but one floor to harbour itself and its lace children in. In Northern countries the laces will lie in shop windows with never a hint in their folds of the patient fingers that have wrought them, nor of the fishermen husbands, and the tiny round-eyed children. And people will say they are dear, not knowing how little of the price goes to the women who sit in the street far off there between the bright sea and the gloomy olive woods, working, working all the day light, while the children stay with the good sisters so that the lace may be made.

It is, of course, a sentimental piece, and yet it is not without perception.

By 16 August, the Grahames had arrived in Siena on a date deliberately chosen so that they would be there for the *palio*. This spectacular event was well explained by Chalmers ten years later.

The *Palio delle Contrade* are famous feasts. They are held in the public square, the Piazza del Campo, in July and August annually. They date from the Middle Ages and they commemorate victories and the Virgin. They were initiated as bull-fights. But in the sixteenth century, races on mounted buffaloes were instituted and the bull-fighting ceased. Since 1650 the festivities have centred round a pageant and a fancy-dress horse race, three times round the stony and precipitous square, to win a *palio*, or banner.

Siena is divided into *contrade*, or wards, each one having a distinct title – The Giraffe, the Goose, the Wave and so on – each one with a chapel and flag of its own.

There are seventeen *contrade* and yearly, ten of them, chosen by lot, may enter one horse to compete for the *palio* and be galloped lame on the pavement of the Piazza.

The Grahames had arranged to make a party of it for this event. They met up with Anstey Guthrie, and several others, one of whom recorded the details of halberdiers, drummers and men-at-arms, all of them in thirteenth-century costume.

The dresses were as rich as stained glass windows – green and white, blue and scarlet, black and yellow. The banners were stiff with bullion

323

and slashed with flaming colours. The processions saluted the Arch-
bishop's balcony and moved to their stone seats above the Palace
steps. There they broke like kaleidoscopes and sat down glowing like
a garden of flowers.

Marching eight abreast in gala, the children followed linked up by
garlands of laurel. Lastly came a four-horse wagon. Its postilions wore
green livery and the tall caps of the Middle Ages. In the wagon was
the *Palio* itself – great and old and splendid, guarded by mounted men
in helmets and bronze armour. The belfries clash and are silent. There
is an interval for refreshment.[15]

It sounds like the sort of thing Grahame would have adored. When the
races began, hooves clattered "as if Cheapside were mad". Riders fell and
horses ran loose, one of them being declared the winner on this occasion
until the decision was fiercely contested by the jockeys and overthrown. It
was a wild scene and a strictly local affair, for these were the days before
organised tourism had turned every traditional custom into an international
event. Foreigners, and particularly six-foot Scotsmen, were a rarity. The
narrator goes on:

Mr Grahame was a noticeable-looking man anywhere and here,
among that Southern crowd, he seemed remarkably so. Heads turned
his way and a courtly priest approached him and, bowing, paid him
the compliment of begging that he and his party would eventually
accept the hospitality of his house which overlooked the street where
the winning *Contrada* was later to celebrate victory with a dinner.

Kenneth Grahame was as pleased as a boy and named himself "the
man who found the key in the horse's ear". "And who might he be?"
I asked. He told me a French fairy tale about a seeker who sought "a
golden key on a green silken cord" which unlocked all doors. It was
to be found in a far city, in a secret stable, and hidden in a horse's ear.

Elspeth remembered that

late on the night of the race-day we were returning to Florence by car,
not being able to get accommodation in Siena itself, and as it was just
at the time when the Socialists held sway, we were warned that by
driving such a long distance after midnight we should in all probability
be shot at sight, and at our first hold-up on the way we thought this
prophecy was about to be fulfilled. But all the crowds wanted was the
information as to which *contrada* [region] of Siena had won the Palio,
and when we told them it was Onda they let us proceed. This question
was asked us at least twenty times in towns and villages on our way,

but after the first alarm we knew it was only their sporting instincts that made them arrest us in order to hear the earliest possible news of so great an event.[16]

The priest's invitation for the following week was to witness the open-air banquet rather than to participate in it but, even so, the spectacle was well worth watching.

> Tables were set, so as to form one continuous switchback table in the centre of the narrow, hilly street. It was spread with white cloths and embellished with flowers and regiments of wine flasks. At one interminable end sat Melone, the winning jockey. At the other stood Lola, the winning mare. She wore a necklace of green apples and seemed, on the whole, to be enjoying herself. The illumination made the warm night as bright as day. Great moths fluttered and swooped, a hundred bands played, the fun was noisy and grew noisier . . .[17]

Their host regaled them, Guthrie said, "on biscuits from china bowls and delicious golden wine in blue Venetian glasses", and they got back to Florence "nearer five than four in the morning".

Grahame, very naturally, loved the idea of "the key in the horse's ear".[18] Every traveller takes a particular pride in boasting how he or she has gained access to the privacy of another culture, normally closed to inquisitive eyes, and sometimes there is a hint of commercial benefit to the issuer of such invitations; but Kenneth seems to have had an openness which endeared him to people of all kinds. There was an unguarded, ever-boyish quality about him which countless witnesses have commented on, and it was perhaps this lack of defence which made him so irresistible. In Italy, he was clearly regarded with amused affection. The French had dubbed him "colonel" but the Italians – or, more precisely, the Sicilians, in the taverns of Palermo – referred to him as "*il barone*", and Chalmers averred that ten years later, the cask of marsala from which he had filled his glass on many occasions was still known as "the baron's favourite".[19]

The visit to Palermo, however, would not take place until the following year. They spent the winter in Ospedaletti and, on 14 March 1924, Courtauld wrote to Elspeth about the death of their brother, Harold, detailing the last stages of his illness and the care which Courtauld had taken of him. "He gave his life for others," he said, "and I fear had not very much enjoyment for himself except the satisfaction which I hope he had in knowing what splendid public-spirited work he had done. I know Kenneth will feel it very much and I do realize from the bottom of my heart that it is almost worse for you being so far away than it is for us. Goodby dearest E & love to you both."[20] The letter reached them at the Hotel d'Italia, Ospedaletti, Ligure.

Courtauld's career had been meteoric. He had moved into a series of lucrative directorships, having sold his carriage business at the peak of its success on perceiving that the motor car was about to supersede horse traffic. He had invested in building, and had been responsible for the first block of flats to go up in Mayfair, and, with his taste for doing things on a big scale, had replaced the Old Bailey with a new building, the Central Criminal Court. He was knighted in 1912, and went with Winifred to India to attend the Durbar of 1913. On return, he had become a partner in an antiques reproduction business, and was soon the Chairman of the Goldsmiths and Silversmiths Company.

For all his fame in the City, he was a compassionate man, and during the 1914–18 war, he had as Commissioner of the Red Cross been personally involved in working with wounded and dying men, and wrote movingly of his experiences. He said of a boy who had been shot through both eyes, "I saw his hand moving about trying to find something. I asked him what he wanted. He said simply, 'I want your hand.' When he had taken it he held it a minute and then went on: 'Please tell me your name, you have been very kind to me.' It was really a minute or two before I could answer . . ."[21]

Within three weeks of the Armistice, Courtauld had written to Winifred to tell her he was going to buy the lease of Dorney House, as it was then called, an historic mansion in Burnham, near Slough, which had been partially destroyed by fire in 1910. By the time of Harold's death, he had bought the freehold of the house and its surrounding farmland and cottages, and was living there with Winifred, steadily improving and decorating the place, and filling it with the pictures and tapestries and *objets d'art* which can be seen there to this day. He moved in high circles and was immensely popular. His friends, in a cheerful abbreviation of "Sir Courtauld", called him "Scorts".

The Grahames did not come home for Harold's funeral. Later in the spring, however, news reached them that a buyer had at last been found for Boham's. If they were to retain a foothold in Britain, a new home would have to be found. They returned to Berkshire, and began to house-hunt. Kenneth's lifelong passion for running water drew them to Thames-side locations, and within a few weeks they had bought Church Cottage in Pangbourne.

They went to the dispersal sale of the contents, and the catalogue is meticulously annotated with the price of each item in Kenneth's neat handwriting. He himself bought a chair, perhaps to sit on there and then. By the time the bidding reached the pantry, Elspeth had arrived, for he handed the task over to her, as the fly-away figures show.

Apart from the fact that they were both in Berkshire, Pangbourne and Blewbury could not have been more different. Blewbury was an archaic place, hidden away from public eyes, and continuing a slow, virtually medieval lifestyle which was unaffected by the outside world. Pangbourne, on the other hand, *was* the outside world. Grahame had referred in *Pagan Papers* to a collective figure which he called "Mercury" – a symbol of the gilded youth of his time, out on the reaches of the Thames in a steam-launch hired for the day. His innocence of sexual innuendo is enchanting.

> The flower-gemmed banks crumble and slide down under the wash of his rampant screw; his wake is marked by a line of lobster-claws, gold-necked bottles, and fragments of veal-pie. Resplendent in blazer, he may even be seen to embrace the slim-waisted nymph, haunter of green (room) shades, in the full gaze of the shocked and scandalised sun.[22]

Kenneth had compared Mercury unfavourably with Pan, the true god of the countryside, and yet, as the end of his life approached, he abandoned the dreaming rural depths of Berkshire and set himself in the middle of the most fashionable and bustling riverside resort of its day, where Mercury was inescapable. The change could not have been more dramatic. It continued the revolt against seclusion which had been so marked since Alastair's death. While remaining intensely private, the Grahames had seemed to need constant change and stimulation and gratification of the senses, as if unwilling to hear the "still, small voice" which waited for silence and solitude in which to make itself heard. Their home – if home it was – had been in the centre of one of Europe's busiest, noisiest and most colourful cities. And now, they bought Church Cottage, three minutes from the water's edge, but not far from what was then the main Oxford road, with its roar of traffic. It seemed that they would not risk isolation. The memory of Alastair was bound up with the ten sleepy years in Blewbury, and, too, with Kenneth's growing impatience with the smallness of outlook there, and the boredom – and the mud. He did not want any repetition of that ultimately unbearable combination.

For all its modishness, Church Cottage was not without tranquillity. Its tile-hung gable-end came right down to the top of the ground-floor windows and the roof extended to a supporting pillar in a Swiss-chalet style. A vast old ship's bell from the *Rosarian* hung by the front door, and the building used as a tool shed had once been the village lock-up, "a squat, circular building with a pepper-pot roof and a grille window".[23] But its main attraction was the garden. Any British person who has lived abroad for a long time must, on return, be struck afresh by the wonderful greenness of these islands, and Kenneth was enchanted by the sweep of the lawn and the banks of scarlet Oriental poppies, the fruit trees and the sunny terrace, just right for the leisurely perusal of the morning paper. The garden had one other quite irresistible feature. At its far end was a grassy amphitheatre circled by high banks like a miniature circus ring. There ought, Kenneth said, "to be Shetland ponies galloping round, ridden by monkeys".[24]

Inevitably, it took some time for the Grahames to move in and settle their possessions – such as they were – into their new place. Although Boham's had been stripped of all that was valuable rather than practical, it had been a big house, and the Grahames were getting older, taking longer over their decisions and plans. Kenneth was now sixty-five. Elspeth was three years younger, but she was gaunt and white-haired, a strange mixture of kindness and meanness, hospitality and intolerance and loquacity, with an inexhaustible fund of anecdotes about the famous figures she had known in her youth, and a tendency to retail them to anyone who would listen. Pangbourne soon recognised its new residents as full-blown eccentrics. Kenneth wore bright chestnut-coloured Harris tweeds and a flowing black-and-white checked scarf, and refused to have either a telephone or any form of domestic help in the house – a curious change of outlook from the dependence on paid staff which had been so marked at Boham's. Possibly the Grahames had become so unconventional in their personal habits that they did not want anyone from the village to see inside the house; or it may simply have been part of Elspeth's obsessive reluctance to spend money, causing her to regard the employment of staff or the installation of a telephone as wildly extravagant. He did permit a gardener to take care of the extensive lawns and flowerbeds, but gave him strict orders that he was not to come near the terrace during those specific times when the master required to be undisturbed. Elspeth explained that "Mr Grahame wanted to be free to sit there and think". The gardener quite understood. "And what likelier place could he want?" he said.[25] For a while, the restless urge to travel seemed to have died down.

Elspeth could not abandon the Continental habit of haggling over purchases, and approached the village store as if it were an Italian market stall, arguing fiercely over the price of two ounces of ham. The Grahames continued to feed themselves as they had done in Rome, buying bread and cheese, sausage and wine, and eating it in the open air whenever they could, often on their doorstep, out of the paper bags from the shop, much to the astonishment of their neighbours. In the absence of the cheap and delectable Italian restaurants, Kenneth would sometimes concoct an elaborate curry, but the pair of them had never been domesticated, and their expenditure on food was minimal. According to two village ladies talking to Green later, however, they bought an incredible quantity of champagne and port – hardly the best thing for a man whose blood-pressure was mounting.

The Grahames stayed in Pangbourne for over a year, and Elspeth acquired a carefully selected circle of friends despite her jumble-sale clothes and her garrulousness. She could, on occasion, dress up in a somewhat ferocious *grande dame* style, but perceptive people saw beneath it the insecurity which drove her to try to impress. One who did not was Malcolm Elwin, who gave a dispassionate account of the Grahames as he knew them.

> He was a biggish, broad-shouldered man, inclined to portliness as all of his generation over sixty tended to be, grey of hair and grey of face, his shoulders bent so that he stooped slightly, his general appearance giving the immediate impression that he suffered from ill-health. I suspect that he also suffered from the wearing personality of his wife, a chinny woman of leathery countenance, who wore well-cut tailor-made tweeds and talked stridently and interminably, laying down the law about her preferences in literature and art, and never taking much heed of what anybody else had to say. I gathered that Mr Grahame had long since learned that it was a waste of time and energy to attempt to express an opinion in his wife's company.[26]

Elspeth, it seems, had now stepped into the leading role – or perhaps she simply tried too hard to keep up with her famous husband when the occasion demanded. Some of her friends were less condemnatory than Hartley. Mabel Heinemann wrote later that she knew how entirely Kenneth depended on "dear, Dear Elsie" – and yet, her reminiscences make it clear that Elspeth's old image of the poetic, suffering woman was still being maintained. "I think of dear Mr Kenneth Grahame in that glorious copper-coloured suit (smelling so deliciously of peat!) & his fine, splendid face crowned with beautiful white hair. And I think of you, as you lay on your couch, as a second Elizabeth Barrett Browning." Elspeth must have found that a gratifying letter.[27] Many people did not share Mabel Heinemann's opinion. Dale Purves called Elspeth "a superficial and twilight woman",[28] which was a more compassionate opinion than that expressed by Elwin, who had clearly found Elspeth intolerable.[29] Her inferiority complex feasted on her new-found ascendancy.

Whether dependent on his wife or not, however, it was Kenneth who continued to excite the public imagination. Word had gone round that he had returned to the country, and he was receiving requests to address various assemblages. It was in this year that he went back to his old school, to tell the boys his memories of being there, and to advise them, with gentle cynicism, to take full advantage of the Old Boy network, a system "almost as good as the general's way of dodging education altogether". And then he added, "But I perceive by the pained expression on the Headmaster's countenance that I am becoming rather – shall we say – morbid. I am talking the sort of stuff that during the War was called, I think, defeatism. So I will now ask you to try and forget everything I have said as speedily as possible . . ."[30]

In a letter to A. J. A. Symons in July 1925, Grahame said, "I very rarely go up to town nowadays", which was no doubt true. Even during the increasingly tedious days at Boham's, he had shown little inclination to return to the city except for an occasional trip to the theatre. There were exceptions, however, and Malcolm Elwin, according to Chalmers, found himself at one point in the same railway carriage with Kenneth and Harold Hartley, though (no doubt to the latter's relief) without Elspeth. Elwin remembered Grahame "sitting in his corner seat with his back to the engine, elegant in pepper-and-salt trousers, short black coat, and neat cuffs, a handsome and dignified figure of an elderly city man". Evidently Kenneth, for all his Bohemianism, could still present a formal appearance when the occasiion demanded.

Curtis Brown had not given up hopes of persuading Grahame to begin writing again, and scored a small success when Kenneth agreed to provide a preface for *Seventy Years a Showman*, the memoirs of "Lord" George Sanger, of circus fame. It is a long piece, and the bulk of it constitutes a defence of the travelling showman's way of life. They are, he insists, "a quiet and reserved people, subdued in manner, clannish, living a life apart; scrupulously neat and tidy, as indeed anyone must be who lives in a caravan; self-reliant, asking little from anyone except some tolerance from officials and freedom to come and go . . .". He discourses on the changing styles in "rides" which had introduced the child-sized car rather than his beloved wooden horses, and then goes on to talk about freaks and Fat Ladies, the Pipe-smoking Oyster and other examples of "joyous fake", and turns finally to the cinema, which at that time had been shrewdly incorporated into the travelling attractions provided by the showmen. This was a great new enthusiasm of Kenneth's. "We like it," he said, "because it is not exactly the sort of life we daily lead; and as we stroll homeward across the starlit common towards our farmhouse, vicarage, or simple thatched cottage, we think 'I wish – oh, *how* I wish – I had married an Indian half-breed!' " With her dew-draggled dress and her necklace of daisies, that was, perhaps, what poor Elspeth had tried to be, all those years ago, on her wedding day.

Within a few weeks, the Grahames went back to Italy, and resumed the trek from place to place. Palermo delighted Kenneth with its puppet shows, where audiences of children greeted *The Damnation of Judas* with ecstatic screams. "Mr Punch will have to take a back seat," he said admiringly, as the anti-hero was first hanged and then, as Chalmers put it, "engulfed in an inferno of flames".[31] It was there, too, that he managed to get into the Court of Appeal to hear the notorious brigand, Paolo, argue against a sentence of one hundred years' imprisonment for crimes which included thirteen murders. It was a theatrical event with a ludicrous number of "extras" in the form of guards, ten of them (with fixed bayonets) surrounding the judge and five to each advocate. The well of the court was filled with soldiers, and Grahame, as the sole member of the public present, was allocated a single rather undersized bodyguard, it being considered that a man so much larger than the Sicilian average could probably look after himself in the unlikely event of the brigand's escape. Paolo, as the star of the show, put up a performance of high comedy despite his manacled wrists, cracking jokes which totally undermined the solemnity of the occasion. When he was finally led away, the sentence having been reduced from a hundred to ninety years, even his guards were laughing.

The Grahames kept moving, although they returned constantly to Rome and occasionally to Florence. Venice, too, became a favourite place, and Kenneth was astonished to see that gondoliers disposed of old oar-blades by pushing them through the ilex hedge which surrounded that rare Venetian thing, a garden. Three enormous mastiffs lived there, and they would crunch up the blades like biscuits. Staring down at this spectacle from his hotel window which overlooked the garden, Kenneth accidentally dropped his wallet which was full of banknotes, and waited in horror for it to be wolfed down along with the splintered wood. One of the dogs, however, picked up the titbit, carried it to a corner of the garden and carefully buried it, and Kenneth, with permission from the owner, subsequently dug it up again, unharmed.

In Taormina, he went to the house and its surrounding orange-groves which had been given to Lord Nelson. He browsed through the old manuscripts and was regaled with a white wine which had been kept in the cellars for forty years. It was, he said, "like molten sunshine". As the goblets were raised, someone appropriately quoted *The Golden Age* – " 'It's Trafalgar Day,' said Selina." Grahame smiled, and completed the quotation before he drank. "And nobody cares," he said,[32] if Elspeth's memory is to be trusted.

He was always pleased by the fitting-together of place and legend. In Syracuse, as he stood gazing at the Fountain of Arethusa, he overheard two girls asking their mother who Arethusa was and, when the woman confessed that she did not know, Kenneth told them how a frightened nymph turned herself into a spring of running water which crept secretly below the sea and emerged as the very fountain at which they were looking.

The Grahames went to Genoa, to Perugia, and to the lava-fields of Etna, and in 1926 they stayed for some while in Amalfi, where they made friends with an American girl called June Mussey. Kenneth's liking for Americans is interesting. Members of that nation had for years formed a very large proportion of his acquaintance, and it may be that he liked their directness. The layers of subtlety and of unspoken but rigid expectation which form such a notable part of the English upper-middle-class attitude had always baffled him, partly because he was a Scot and partly because he had retained his boyhood conviction that the "Olympians" were an inscrutable lot; but Americans were more open. June Mussey, like the Purves boys, found herself taken under his wing.

Mr Grahame's white hair and moustache seemed to light up the room; and the first impression he made was always one of distinction ... It was not long before he was guiding us round Amalfi. Although he walked leaning on a cane, he took us up and down through the labyrinth of passages and stairs that pass for streets there; he seemed to know every odd corner of the ancient town. His knowledge of the history of Amalfi, and of almost everything else, was encyclopèdic. I remember his saying, "The strongest human instinct is the desire to impart information, and the second strongest the desire to resist such teaching"; but it was not true of him ... Mr Grahame always seemed interested in any new fact or idea, even from somebody like me, who had few of either. His modesty was such that he had to be drawn out before one found out how much he knew, or, indeed, who he was ... It all wound up in a grand party to which we invited everyone in town, native or foreign. Mr Grahame sat in a corner, as he had when we first saw him, and enjoyed it all in silence.[33]

The ever-optimistic Curtis Brown wrote to him during this year, suggesting that he should start work on an autobiography. Kenneth turned over the idea, but was clearly disinclined to undertake such a massive task. On 29 April, he wrote making his excuses.

My chief trouble is that I have kept no diaries or memoranda at all and since the war my memory seems to have gone all to pot. I doubt much if I could ever get as much as a book together; but I will, as I said, consider if I can get out an article or two on a line of my own, which should be reminiscent in character.[34]

For the next two years, Curtis Brown waited in vain; not a word arrived. In November 1928, he tried again. It would be, he suggested, very interesting to read Grahame's reminiscences of the Bank of England. He added, with disarming honesty,

Of course, there is deep craft and guile in this scheme, for I figured it out that if you were to do the article you would find it so interesting that you could be tempted to do another later on, and then another, until the first you knew there would be most of that volume of Memoirs I have been yearning for.

Kenneth did not rise to the bait. His reply was prompt and emphatic: "Many thanks for your would-be provocative letter. But Nothin' Doin' about B. of E. Much too dull a subject."[35]

Since he was still trying to make up for the years of commitment to an occupation which had prevented him from gypsying his way round the South as he had wanted to, it is hardly surprising that the idea did not attract him. He was, however, not without an ex-banker's interest in the progress of his financial affairs and, a few months later, on 21 January 1929, he wrote a beady-eyed letter to his agent about his foreign rights. Curtis Brown explained that an increase in commission was necessary in order to pay the continental managers their ten per cent, and that "our small extra charge on translation transactions was as nothing compared with the 50 per cent commission most publishers then charged on similar transactions". Kenneth's highly entertaining reply is delicately poised between addressing his oldest friend and the man who was also his business manager.

My dear C.B. Before I received your kind letter of the 18th, I had frankly suspected – & no doubt you suspected that I had suspected – that the account that had so shocked me had been a piece of quite laudable if mistaken departmental overzeal, which had somehow escaped the eye of the Capitoline Jove. But when I read your classic periods, so firm yet so tender, I wilted, I sagged, I crumpled, I shed bitter tears. I finally collapsed on the floor, a sodden heap of misery. As I lay there, however, I found myself murmuring something, but very soft and low, so that it could not reach your ears. Something like this: "alas, yes, how true it is, and how well I knew it, that there are publishers who claim 50 per cent on Foreign rights, and others who ask 100, and many who will demand 150, & then ask for a little bit more for 'all their trouble';

but –

but –

(here I become almost inaudible)

since when – (I was now only whispering) –

since when have ...... Ltd. based their practice on the tenets of Messrs B-r-b-b-s & Co?"

Then I shed a few more tears.

Then I rose to my feet & washed and had some light refreshment – the first for days.

So now that is all over, & I will try and be good, and I will try and not do it any more. And I am ever so glad that you couldn't have heard a word of those awful sentiments I murmured to myself as I lay crying on the floor. But ...

(No I won't begin again. I have sworn it.) All the same ...

No; the end of the page is in sight, and I am not going to get on to a new one. At least I will turn over a new leaf, of course, for I have said so already. But not a new leaf of this letter.

~~BECAUSE IF I DID~~ O this unruly typewriter! It all comes of using a Blick. Common little beasts, Blicks. I ought to get something high class and toney and expensive. "~~But how can you if~~" ... There he goes again. He must be stopped.

Yours finally and very truly,

KENNETH GRAHAME

For the first time, we get a clear glimpse of the Mr Toad element which lay deeply buried in the personality of Kenneth himself. If he had gently mocked Alastair's tantrums in his depicting of the character, it now becomes evident that his son had inherited a streak of fury which had been sternly suppressed in the father. Only now, towards the end of his life and in the confidence that Curtis Brown would understand and smile, did Kenneth permit himself to express his hatred of that outside world which tried to thwart him and, even then, he did it with self-disguising humour.

In October of the same year, 1929, Roland Grahame died. Kenneth had not been in contact with his brother since Joan's death and their subsequent quarrel seventeen years ago, and the funeral had taken place before Kenneth heard of his brother's death, the news having reached him by means of a letter from his equally estranged sister, Helen. The family feeling which had bound the children together in their golden age had not survived the test of growing up. Anthony Hope, who had been Kenneth's best man, was at the funeral, and so, of course, were Roland's stepsons, Anthony and Keith Feiling. It is ironic to recall that it was from Keith's house near Oxford that another funeral cortège had left, taking Alastair to his tragically early resting place. Suddenly it is starkly obvious how complete Kenneth's severing of himself from his family had been, and again, there is the feeling that, from complex, uncomprehending motives, he and Elspeth had fled from anything which linked them with the memory of their son. Even the conventional communication between one family member and another may have had a painful significance.

But the days of restless travel were almost over. Perhaps the Grahames were beginning to feel old and tired, or the wander-lust had finally burned itself out – or maybe Roland's death had put a chill finger on their enjoyment of life. *Et in Arcadia ego.* Even in Arcady, death is present. By the end of the year, Kenneth and Elspeth were back in the Pangbourne cottage they had bought in 1924 and had hardly lived in. They had been on the move for nearly ten years.

18

Going Home

When the Grahames came back to Church Cottage in 1930, Kenneth found himself busy again, though mostly through the medium of other people's activity. His infrequent returns to Britain always triggered off interest, to which he responded, one senses, with reluctance. A Marian Ryan had managed to interview him in 1927, and the Poetry Society asked him to chair a meeting on modern poetry for children, at which Eleanor Farjeon and Rose Fyleman were to read from their work. This letter is marked "answered", but there is no record that he attended the meeting. A lot of people sent him stories and drawings and adaptations of *The Wind in the Willows* for use in the schools where they taught, and these letters were always courteously answered, though mostly by Elspeth.

Kenneth himself dealt with an enquiry from John Wilstach of New York, who thought that Grahame had not only written the introduction to "Lord" George Sanger's book, *Seventy Years a Showman*, but had ghosted the whole thing. He pointed out that Sanger's work first came out as a serial in a London Sunday newspaper "and it is not unlikely," he went on, "that one of the staff may have been told off to take the matter down from dictation and lick it into shape. This would be natural enough, wouldn't it? But this is only guesswork as I really know nothing about its genesis." His reasonable response did not silence the questioner, who then sent some of his own stories to be looked at.[1]

Some of the enquiries, however, were more businesslike – and more fruitful. A new edition of *The Wind in the Willows* was planned, this one to be illustrated by E. H. Shepard. Both the artist and the author had misgivings about it. Three illustrated editions had already appeared, none of them completely satisfactory. In 1913 Paul Branson produced naturalistic representations of the animals which failed to suggest the very human characteristics embodied by them, and the same could be said for Nancy Barnhart in 1922. Wyndham Payne, trying to get to grips with the problem in 1927, used an almost comic-book approach, with a slickness of line totally unsuited to the underlying lyricism of the book. It was hardly surprising that Grahame viewed the latest project with some caution. As Shepard himself remembered:

Not sure about this new illustrator of his book, he listened patiently while I told him what I hoped to do. Then he said, "I love these little people, be kind to them." Just that; but sitting forward in his chair, resting upon the arms, his fine handsome head turned aside, looking like some ancient Viking, warming, he told me of the river nearby, of the meadow where Mole broke ground that spring morning, of the banks where Rat had his house, of the pools where Otter hid, and of the Wild Wood way up on the hill above the river . . . He would like, he said, to go with me to show me the river bank that he knew so well, ". . . but now I cannot walk so far and you must find your way alone."[2]

Shepard's style was, of course, a perfect match for Grahame's writing. Kenneth's simple request that the illustrator should "be kind" to his characters triggered exactly the right mixture of humour and delicate sympathy, coupled with a matchless sense of landscape. In the same year, Shepard produced drawings for a new edition of *Dream Days*, but his representations of real children have a touch of sentimentality which is quite absent from his conjuring-up of the River Bankers. He obviously understood that the animals, for all their smallness of literal scale, were adult beings, going about the business of their lives with as much common sense and blamelessness as they could manage, and so he invested them with immense plausibility.

1930 was also the year when Curtis Brown realised one of his most cherished ambitions. He had for a long time been trying to interest theatrical managers in the idea of a dramatisation of *The Wind in the Willows*, but with no success. As he records in his book, *Contacts*, the usual response was that the story was "too whimsical, and the characters quite impossible to represent in believable costumes". Grahame had been increasingly disappointed by these refusals, for, with his love of all things theatrical, he had set his heart on the idea of his book taking on a new life as a stage play. Curtis Brown must have realised that it was not practical to expect theatrical managers to work from a complex and wordy novel; what they needed was a ready-made script, prepared by a professional writer. A. A. Milne had begun his literary career as a playwright, and had turned to writing for children only in recent years, although it was this field which was already making him famous. His books of verse, *When We Were Very Young* and *Now We Are Six*, had appeared when the Grahames were in Italy, as had *Winnie-the-Pooh* and *The House at Pooh Corner*, so it was only now, on Kenneth's return to Britain, that A. A. Milne seemed such an obvious choice as the dramatist to work on *The Wind in the Willows*. When asked, Milne was delighted by the idea. "I think it should be a children's play," he wrote, "with a little incidental music." Harold Fraser Simson agreed to write the score, and the play came together quickly. Inevitably, it dealt only with the action of the book, treating Toad's adventures in a broad, pantomimic style

336

which, while a gross simplification of Grahame's original concept, was triumphantly theatrical. *Toad of Toad Hall* became a classic in its own right, but it never attempted to touch the mystic lyricism which lies at the heart of *The Wind in the Willows*.

Milne himself was acutely aware that he was carrying out major surgery on the book. In his preface to the play, he wrote down some of his scruples and anxieties. "There are both beauty and comedy in the book," he remarked, "but the beauty must be left to blossom there, for I, anyhow, shall not attempt to transplant it." His respect for Grahame's original work remained undimmed, and he wrote a stern injunction to the reader in an introduction to a later edition of *The Wind in the Willows*: "When you sit down to it, don't be so ridiculous as to suppose that you are sitting in judgement on my taste, or on the art of Kenneth Grahame. You are merely sitting in judgement on yourself. You may be worthy; I don't know. But it is you who are on trial."

The practicalities of interpreting Grahame's book with the literality which a stage performance demands were daunting. As Milne wrote:

In reading the book, it is necessary to think of Mole, for instance, sometimes as an actual mole, sometimes as such a mole in human clothes, sometimes as a mole grown to human size, sometimes as walking on two legs, sometimes on four. He is a mole, he isn't a mole. What is he? I don't know. And, not being a matter-of-fact person, I don't mind. At least, I do know, and still I don't mind. He is a fairy, like so many immortal characters in fiction; and, as a fairy, he can do, or be anything.[3]

This view helps to account for the sweetness with which the play proved to be overlaid. Milne even felt that "Mole might well be played by some boyish young actress". And yet, if his definition of a fairy is a being with a life unconfined by the tiresome restrictions of normal physical presence, he was right. The private reader solves the problem of scale without even realising it exists, simply by becoming in imagination Mole-sized, so that the discrepancy vanishes. Within the mind, magic occurs quite freely.

Milne, having dealt with the question in his own brisk (if pixillated) way, was unapologetic about the results. "Of course," he said, "I have left out all the best parts of the book; and for that, if he has any knowledge of the theatre, Mr Grahame will thank me."

The critics were not entirely in agreement. *Punch* muttered that Milne "perhaps has had his eye too exclusively fixed upon the children and averted from the less important grown-ups . . . [he] has jettisoned, perhaps perforce or for policy's sake, all that makes the enchantment of *The Wind in the Willows* for the mature mind". It is interesting that *Punch*, for all its

337

disillusion and worldly wisdom, accepted completely that Grahame's book was a classic in the full sense of the word, with value to people of all ages. It was not until 1991 that an attempt was made to convey the real magic of *The Wind in the Willows* in dramatic form, but then Alan Bennett's stage play of the same name brought in big audiences, and established an enchantment of its own. There were, however, some odd quirks about his interpretation. Badger appears as a gently homosexual housemaster, and Bennett says in his introduction to the published script of the play "it seemed to me that Grahame meant Toad to be Jewish . . . he must have been thinking of characters like Sir Ernest Cassel and the Sassoons . . .". Bearing in mind that *The Wind in the Willows* was written in 1908, it is of course impossible for any such influence to have been felt. More likely is the late-Victorian prejudice against Jews which crops up so casually in writers like Trollope, equating Jewishness with vulgarity. This interpretation of Toad, however, was manifest only in Bennett's reading of *The Wind in the Willows* for the BBC. In the first production of his stage play, rather more alarmingly, it was the stoats and weasels who had the ripely Jewish accents of the street trader, and there is no basis in Grahame for any such characterisation.

The many layers of personal psychology in Grahame's book allow the reader to reach a wide variety of conclusions as to what it all meant. For Humphrey Carpenter, whose analysis of the book in *Secret Gardens* is very detailed, the Wild Wood stood for the dark depths of the mind, "the tangle of rich and dangerous symbolism which threatens the mental life of even the most sober of artists". His is a rational, strictly non-intuitive approach, dismissing Grahame's description of Pan as "a ghastly error in taste"; but such objectivity is, alas, Olympian, and misses the direct intensity of experience which gives the book simplicity. Although, as Carpenter rightly points out, the language is adult throughout, the viewpoint is that of a child seeing the world for the first time.

A very different response to Grahame's book was Jan Needle's 1981 *Wild Wood*, a fantasy novel in which the underprivileged ferrets, stoats and weasels are viewed as the heroes of the Toad Hall takeover. The satire is amusing in a mild way, with its hero, Boddington, called after a North-country beer, "peculiarly yellow, a little lacking in body, extremely bitter, but one of the best", acting as revolutionary leader; but even the Wild Wooders as triumphant partisans are unable to resolve the dilemma which Grahame had articulated a hundred years previously in his musings over the galley-slaves of society. The "sinking of differences" which he saw as essential to the efficient running of a democracy proved as elusive to the stoats and weasels as it had been to Grahame's underpaid clerks and shop-workers and, at the end of the day, Needle's revolutionaries founder on the same rocks, with Boddington attacking the Chief Weasel for his whole-hearted enjoyment of the facilities provided by the captured "Brotherhood Hall".

"Right from the start it's been the same," he ranted. "You said you'd come into it on account of Toad & Co. needed taking down, on account of their vicious and criminal misuse of other animals' wealth. But you never meant it. As soon as we got here you was just like him, only worse."

The ending of the book would have caused Grahame a wry smile.

Some of the Wild Wooders got even more humble and kowtowish after Toad & Co. recaptured the big house, while others like the Chief Weasel, say, became almost as posh as they were.

There was nothing facile about Grahame's political thinking. The paradox which he saw in the circle of democracy, freedom, greed and the greedy abuse of democracy is still unresolved, and he would not have been surprised to see that, a century later, it begins to threaten the political process itself. He would, however, have been utterly astonished to find that his own concepts had passed into the national consciousness. In March 1967, for instance, Martin Sharpe designed a calendar in the form of a fold-out poster which was issued as a supplement to *Oz*, depicting Harold Wilson as a power-crazed Mr Toad, monstrously in charge of a car with a Union Jack on its bonnet. *Oz* itself, whose editors were brought to trial because the publication "tended to deprave and corrupt", was inescapably reminiscent of *The Yellow Book*. More recently, the *Guardian*'s weekly strip cartoon called *Claws* (1993 on) by Tony Wilkinson, is clearly based on *The Wind in the Willows*. It is a hard-hitting commentary on the social divisions which are no less marked in contemporary life than they were in Grahame's time. Additional animals have been invented, but much of the action centres round the Wildwood Comprehensive School. We also see the plucky efforts of the working-class Stoat family to preserve its own traditions and outlook in the face of the snobbish values and bureaucratic hypocrises thrust on it by barking terriers and – alas – by the deeply Conservative Badger.

In the last years of his life, however, Grahame, at over seventy, had ceased to concern himself with political matters – or, indeed, with anything much beyond his garden and his walks and his beloved river. Curtis Brown's repeated requests for autobiographical material prodded him into a slightly reluctant activity, and he noted down some recollections which he called *Oxford Through a Boy's Eyes*.[4] The jottings were rambling and discursive, but immensely valuable to biographers in search of material about his early life. It was this piece which provided most of the information on which the early part of the present book is based, with its recollections of the fairs and markets, of the university town, and of the dark, high-gated colleges, ever closed to him. With final, obstinate stoicism, he wrote:

As to the exclusiveness, I have nothing to complain of personally. The only things I wanted to get at were certain gardens, and I never remember being refused entry, though this might very well have happened to a small boy, always such an object of suspicion. It was really better than at home, where, of course, one had friends with beautiful gardens, but they usually meant formal calls and company manners, and perhaps tedious talk of delphiniums and green fly and such. Here, one strolled in when one was in the mood, and strolled out when one had had enough, and no one took the slightest notice of you. It was an abiding pleasure, and to those who made it possible for me I here tender, *ex voto*, my belated thanks.

On 16 January 1931, a letter arrived which was to tug at memories of the past. It was from a cousin, Marjorie Ingles, who had been staying with Kenneth's sister Helen at the Lizard. Together, they had been to see a local production of *Toad of Toad Hall*. Helen, Marjorie said with regret, "seems so far away from us all. She has some kind friends but otherwise it is lonely & bleak altho' I love it being hale & hearty . . . I have not seen you since I was a child at Witham . . . I hear you go abroad on Monday to the sun".

Marjorie was still living at Witham, with Bessie Luard, Uncle John's daughter. Marjorie herself was the daughter of David, Grannie Ingles' curate son, and the Witham of which she spoke was at Locksheath, near Southampton.

To be so aware of the Grahames' intentions must indicate that the family connections had been re-established. As Marjorie had been out of contact for so long, it is obvious that knowledge of Kenneth's movements must have come through Helen. Roland's death had perhaps healed the rift; certainly, in a late letter to Elspeth, Helen refers to having visited her and Kenneth at Pangbourne.

Evidently the Grahames did go abroad "on Monday", for there is no more correspondence until later that year. The annual pilgrimage to the South was more important to them than anything else. On 21 September 1931, Kenneth received a request from King's College, London to give a lecture to their Literary Society, but he turned it down unhesitatingly: "For reasons of health I always go south for the latter part of the winter – roughly from Christmas to Easter – so that I should not be within reach during the Lent term".

Consistent with this is an exchange of letters shortly before Christmas 1931. Margaret Stewart Somerville had written "distractedly" to complain that Shepard's illustrations to *The Wind in the Willows* showed Rat rowing, although the text stated that Mole "took the sculls". "What am I to say to my grandchildren?" she demanded.

Grahame was clean bowled, having not spotted the discrepancy. His response is barely adequate in logical terms, but he had not lost his charm.

Dear Lady,

Yes – it is exasperating. These artists are very tiresome fellows – and they all do it.

I hardly know what to suggest that you should tell the children. You might perhaps say that the animals had evidently "changed over" for just a minute while in full view of the windows of Toad Hall, in case Toad, looking out, should say afterwards to Rat, "Who's your crab-catching friend?" For poor Mole couldn't row *very* well yet. But I admit it sounds lame. Let us hope that they may not notice it. (But they will!)

Kenneth Grahame[5]

A letter written to a schoolboy, though undated, is on paper supplied by the Hotel Augusta, rue de Canada (Croisette), Cannes, and it is in the same collection as others written in 1930 and 1931. In it, he said,

... it is a great pleasure to me to think that you have found a new world in the company of Toad and his friends, into which you can retire when bored with outside things. Of course, it is useless for me to tell you that you should not read fiction during Prep, for people have always done so, and always do so, and always will.

At heart, nothing had changed. Grahame still recognised the "little territory" which lies at the centre of people like himself, for whom existing is more fascinating than any exercise of thought or reason.

When spring was safely established, Kenneth and Elspeth again came home to Pangbourne. The garden was an "abiding pleasure", but the village, too, had much to offer. It was an active place, acutely aware of the famous occupant of Church Cottage. It had a very positive interest in literary affairs, and called upon Kenneth as its resident celebrity to introduce speakers and open fêtes and, on occasion, to address meetings of the Literary, Dramatic and Musical Guild in the local village hall. It was in this unpretentious place that he gave his last public speech, and, characteristically, he cut no corners but gave a full-blown academic lecture, which he called "A Dark Star". People had come from many miles away to hear him, filling the little hall to overflowing, and among them was Patrick Chalmers, who was to write down his account of Grahame's life only two years later. Kenneth was, on that occasion, he said, "as upright as a man half his age and his voice was musical, far-reaching and young".

Grahame spoke about criticism, and about the shifting standards which result in constant reinterpretation of established masterpieces, even though, as he said, "sheer quality, as such, remains the same through all the ages". That being so, there must, he argued, be "some missing element" in criticism which, like the recently discovered "dark stars", exerts an influence

341

without being identifiable. It is not inherent in the quality of the writer, otherwise the problem of fluctuating public esteem would not exist; it is, he contended, rather some element inherent in people's regard for each other: something close to actual living awareness. For the first time – and the last – Grahame seemed to be trying to evaluate himself in terms of how other people saw him. As always, his scrupulous sense of decency prevented him from any overt reference to his own work, and yet there is in his musings an implied confession of need. He had throughout his life rejected the conventional status-seeking which lesser men use as their yardstick; he had been honest in striving to put down only the truth which he genuinely perceived, but, as the end drew near, he wanted the reassurance of knowing that his work had connected with those who read it. He had never courted popularity, and even now, he alluded to it only in the most dispassionate of terms.

What is usually missing, I think, in criticism or estimates of past writers, is a proper recognition of the special contemporary appeal which almost every good writer has for his own actual contemporaries, the subtle *liaison*, the bond between themselves and their actual contemporaries only, and never between the writer and later generations. Other bonds there are, of course, and plenty, between them and posterity; never this particular one.

It was in trying to define what he meant by the "incommunicable thrill" of newly produced work that Grahame cited the case of his grandmother who, as a girl, lay on the hearthrug all night to read the newly arrived volume of *Waverley*. What entranced her so much, he argued, was that the book came hot from the press. No later generation could feel quite like that about Scott.

The lecture follows its own logic into a reluctant discarding of Gibbon and Goldsmith, Fielding and Johnson as writers for all time, and comes to a conclusion which Grahame may have begun to suspect would predict the death of his own earlier books, and perhaps, eventually, of *The Wind in the Willows* itself.

I suppose the explanation is that, as compared with colloquial talk, all writing has a touch of artificiality about it, and the essayists of the Eighteenth Century deliberately pushed this artifice to an extreme . . . Really, at times, with Johnson you are not quite sure when you are reading English and when you are reading Latin . . . It is strange too to consider that it was at this very period of arid Latinity that the passionate and romantic Ballads of the North Country – what we speak of as "The Border Ballads" – were beginning, for the first time, to assume literary shape and form.

From a man whose own prose had emerged from an indigestible soup of Latin tags and convoluted structures, this is a startling statement in favour of the living voice. Grahame had spent his life learning hard lessons, and it was perhaps the last decade spent in Italy which had taught him to look at his work from outside, so to speak, as a completed *oeuvre*, an ideal settled-for and achieved, in accordance with his own definition of the spirit of the South.

Green contends that Grahame wrote only as a response to imaginative deprivation, citing the six years of intense production when he was in mid-career at the Bank of England and the writing of *The Wind in the Willows* when under pressure from the Governor, but this is to ignore the facilitating effect of such men as Furnivall, Henley and the *Yellow Book* set, not to mention Mouse. Grahame, as a profoundly isolated person, had in fact a tremendous need to be listened to and encouraged. This is the "dark star" which he groped to define, and which for a while shone on him with its invisible light in the approbation and enthusiasm of his contemporaries. Curtis Brown's exhortations did not contribute to it, for he was a professional agent, and his opinions could not be dissociated from ideas of success and financial advantage. Grahame, in fact, wrote for love, both of the work itself and of the unknown reader who would confirm that a communication had been made. In this last lecture, he recalled Swinburne, who, for all his faults, had the power to inspire wild enthusiasm in his contemporaries. What should the modern poet know, he asked,

> of the wonderful thrill that shook the reading world when the "Ballad of Dolores" made its appearance in the sixties?
>
> How undergraduates of *both* universities, even Cambridge, rushed to each other's rooms to shout it and declaim it, how they whooped and chortled over it, or dreamed and moaned it, in their sleep, how they parodied it and how, alas, they tried to write similar poetry with very indifferent success. "Thou wert fair," this new poet sang,
>
> > Thou wert fair in the fearless old fashion,
> > And thy limbs are as melodies yet.
>
> Limbs, if you please; in the sixties; up to then, there had been no limbs in England. Not a single limb. Now we have very little else, but it doesn't really seem to make much difference, at least, not the difference we thought it would make in the sixties, when poor Swinburne got all the blame for it.

Grahame's most endearing quality was his honesty, and, during the course of his talk, he worked his way to the conclusion that popularity was a transient thing. Some writers achieved it in their lifetime and others, perhaps greater, did not. Keats "just missed his market by thirty years", and there were some who tried to avoid public adulation at all costs. George Eliot, for instance, had been unenthusiastic when someone tried to introduce her to " 'a very interesting person, whom you will be glad to include in the number of your friends.' George Eliot ... merely observed plaintively, 'Don't you think that we have most of us got *enough* friends?' "

Samuel Butler ("cold-blooded and very perverse") had said firmly that he wrote for the next generation, not for the current one and, as it turned out, he spoke the truth.

We should recognise, Grahame concluded, that the dark star of popularity, although "no solid body but rather a will-o'-the-wisp" still acts to influence judgement, and should be allowed for in our efforts to evaluate worth.

For all its detached, analytical quality, the lecture had been charged with the brooding inwardness of a man who knows that his life's work is over. At the end, a writer can only ask, in Kipling's single word of enquiry, "*Kun?*", "Is this right?", hoping that the Eldest Magician will answer, "*Payah kun*" − "Quite right."

"As we went out into an October evening," Patrick Chalmers recalled, "some of us looked back. The lecturer stood, white head and shoulders high, among those who congratulated. He seemed as one who heard with a polite indifference."

By the beginning of 1932, the Grahame household had settled, a little reluctantly, into the restrictions imposed by Kenneth's failing health. Dr Bourdillon, concerned about his patient's high blood-pressure and worsening arteriosclerosis, forbade long walks and did his best to restrict his diet. Fatty degeneration of the heart had set in, and a liking for rich food and ample quantities of good wine did not help. It was an irksome discipline, and the doctor knew that each time he called, he would receive the entreaty, "Do let me have something to eat, Bourdillon!"[6] With Toad-like naughtiness, Kenneth would slip out and eat forbidden ice-creams in the village, if Elspeth's memories are to be relied on.

Throughout the research for this book, there has been the difficulty of deciding how far Elspeth could be trusted as a witness. Her accounts sound so vivid and so plausible that it seems needlessly cynical to doubt them, and yet, again and again, factual evidence reveals that she could never resist a good story. In some cases, this has led to a knock-on effect which has preserved myth, not only through the easily impressed Chalmers, whose biography she virtually dictated, but through the much more vigilant and academic Green. The adroit side-step by which Elspeth ascribed her own memories to someone else is the technique of a storyteller, and one might say, charitably, that Kenneth's wife, with an unfulfilled longing to be recognised as a writer herself, created fiction out of the raw material of her life. It is impossible to know whether she was consciously aware of doing this − but if she were, it is likely that she regarded it as a virtue. The trauma of her early married life may have taught her to make every effort to find pleasure and reassurance wherever she could.

Chalmers's book avers that Kenneth had a small friend in Pangbourne, a little girl called Anabel who had expressed enthusiasm for the picnic basket packed by Rat in *The Wind in the Willows*. The account continues:

> Before she went to school she had made Kenneth vow to her that he would, when the holidays came, lecture to the Pangbourne children on animals. But Anabel died during her first term. And her friend, without Anabel to listen to it, never gave his lecture at all.

This tale has the characteristically Elspethian ring of sweet completeness. There may well have been a child called Anabel, and a child who died. There certainly was a child who wrote about the picnic basket, but that was many years earlier. The idea of Grahame lecturing to the village children on animals has the same unlikely quality as his telling of stories to spellbound Breton children who did not even understand his words.

In these early summer days, life continued to have its small interests, with trips to fairs and markets and an occasional day's outing to Oxford, the beloved, elusive city, where Kenneth indulged his personal tastes in private shopping forays. "A man's tie and a man's tobacco are what he alone can choose," he had said. Such things were a small continuing indulgence in the exotic, keeping him in touch with the conviction that life was colourful and varied, offering him a wealth of its richnesses, from which he could choose.

On 25 June 1932, Grahame went to London, to attend the Lewis Carroll centenary held at Bumpus's bookshop. After his long absence from the country, he must have seemed a legendary figure, white-haired and distinguished, the author of a book as famous as *Alice*, a man who already lived within immortality.

Ten days later, on 5 July, he had a very normal day. He sat on the terrace in the morning with *The Times*, filling in the crossword clues and complaining that completing it did not take long enough. After lunch he walked down to the river and spent most of the afternoon there, returning for dinner in the evening. He mixed the salad in accordance with his long-established ritual of combining fresh leaves and herbs, tarragon and chervil, olive oil and vinegar, and enjoyed his meal, even if it did observe Dr Bourdillon's restrictions. Not unusually, he retired to bed early for the pleasure of a long read, and took Scott's *The Talisman* with him. As he had said only a few months earlier, "Scott was perhaps the only one who was really 'popular' in the widest sense. He was read by high and low, educated and ignorant alike."

At about one in the morning, Elspeth heard a sound from his room and came in to investigate. She found the light still on and *The Talisman* lying on the floor. Kenneth lay very still. He was alive, but in a deep coma following a brain haemorrhage. He died a little before six o'clock that morning, without regaining consciousness.

The funeral was held the following Saturday, 9 July, at the church of St James the Less, Pangbourne. Curtis Brown, remembering the event in his book, allows the words of his secretary, Miss Barnes, to evoke the scene.

The church was a marvellous sight – a blaze of glorious colour and sunshine – with masses and masses of flowers, delphiniums and roses (and willows gathered from the river that very morning) and all the things that grow in a cottage garden. And perhaps the most touching thing of all were the flowers sent by children from all over the country, with cards attached in a childish scrawl, saying how much they loved him. The grave was lined with thousands of sweet peas and the scent was unforgettable.[7]

That grave, however, was not to be Grahame's last resting place. Perhaps at the suggestion of the Feilings or of Elspeth, remembering that Alastair lay buried at Oxford, Kenneth's body was later transferred to the same churchyard of Holywell. The inscription which was carved on his headstone was composed by Anthony Hope. It read:

To the beautiful memory of Kenneth Grahame, husband of Elspeth and father of Alastair, who passed the River on 6th July 1932, leaving childhood and literature through him the more blest for all time.

Hundreds of letters came, but Elspeth selected only a few to be included in Chalmers' account of her husband's life. One of the ones she chose was from a neighbouring child, making no mention of Kenneth.

Pangbourne Lodge
Dear Mrs Grahame – I hope these flowers will comfort you as I am sorry you are unhappy.
Love from
Penelope.

Another came from Ann Spencer Watts, who had been the Grahames' maid for many years, back in the London days. She wrote, "I've so often compared other people with Mr Grahame and wondered why there were so few real gentlemen in the world".

Helen wrote from the Lizard in genuine distress, though her letter did not appear in Chalmers's book, nor was there any reference to a reconciliation.

My dear Elspeth,
I am so dreadfully grieved & shocked but bless you for *writing* [her italics].
I have just had your letter and can hardly believe yet that he is gone.
how much I feel for you I need not say.
You will let me know what you wd like about my coming up.
With love and deepest sympathy,
Yours ever affectionately,
Helen Grahame

She did not, in the event, attend the funeral, although Annie had offered to drive her back. At seventy-six, three years older than Kenneth, she had become frail, and said, "I am hardly equal to the journey and might collapse after my arrival". She went on, "How I shall think of you & my dear Kenneth and that he will lie close to his own loved garden. I am so glad that I was that little time with you & so can picture it."

She sent "a scarlet wreath", ordered by wire from a flower shop, and asked Elspeth to affix a card to it. "Dear Kenneth," her letter ended, "I can't believe it is for him."

Helen could never become quite whole-hearted in her liking for Elspeth, but she tried hard. She sent her sister-in-law a little purse made of string which Kenneth had given her as a schoolboy. He had made it, she said, in his early years at St Edward's.

Patrick Chalmers, who had been present at Kenneth's last lecture in Pangbourne, offered the most substantial tribute of all. He wrote to Elspeth, suggesting a biography of her late husband, and Elspeth agreed, not only with alacrity, but with considerable business acumen. On the grounds that she would gather the material from friends and relatives, she demanded a half-share in the book's royalties. Chalmers wriggled a little, but he had no choice. If the book was to be written, he needed Elspeth's co-operation. He gave in like a gentleman, stressing that he wanted to write in admiration of Kenneth Grahame, not for money.

Elspeth plunged into the composing of countless letters, soliciting information on her husband's early life, and it suddenly becomes evident that he had told her very little. Her approach to Helen must have been oblique, for the letter which came back was crisp in tone: "Do you mind telling me if you are compiling a Life of Kenneth? & with whom you are collaborating as you speak of 'we' and 'us'? I am naturally very interested."

It was only after this that Helen revealed the family secret about Cunningham's "failing wh. he shared with many other clever men". She was clearly not happy about doing so, and added, "I wish that you had asked Kenneth about it all for I feel great reluctance to recount anything that he withheld." What she had said was "for your private information and I have burnt your letter".[8]

Helen remained suspicious about the book and, after its publication, sent Elspeth a list of inaccuracies, remarking, "I think it was a pity he did not let you see the typescript nor give you time to correct the proofs". This may have been Elspeth's excuse, or perhaps more probably, Chalmers wearied of her constant interference and simply sent the book in as it was.

Elspeth, true to the lifelong insecurity which made her so desperate for love and admiration, bombarded people with letters. When replied to, she often sent them back for revision, dissatisfied with anything less than the fulsomely laudatory. Her old friend, Anstey Guthrie, had a particularly bad time. His allotted task was to supply memories of Alastair, but he was uneasy about it, writing that

> although my recollection of Mouse is still vivid, it is as you say, many years since I saw him & I don't think I saw him more often than three times . . .
>
> All you write & all the governess writes strengthens the picture of a very noble & beautiful nature & deepens the tragedy of the frustration of so much promise.
>
> But I feel I could add nothing by retelling it in my own words – I could only do so at second hand & it would necessarily lose its effect.[9]

He returned the enclosures, but Elspeth did not give up. Again, Guthrie refused to "copy out your & Miss Stott's notes".

Elspeth continued to push him, and at last he caved in. Of the seven paragraphs of breathless admiration which appeared in the 1933 biography, some reminiscences have the ring of truth – the miniature piano for instance is cited, with its "faint and tiny sound" – but others are sadly dishonest. The "starchy with perambulators" phrase has been accepted as Guthrie's own memory, and the last paragraph is virtually as Elspeth had dictated it.

> Even then I realized that, in addition to a charming and lovable nature, Mouse had ability and originality that in all probability would develop into genius. *I know now* [my italics] that as he grew up, he never lost his charm, and as a boy and a young man, was fearless, generous, kindly and gracious to all he met, while there were already indications that he would leave Literature the richer for their existence. I myself believe that he would have been a very great writer.

At least he managed to resist a suggestion that he should authenticate a favourite piece of Elspeth's Mouse-mythology, which she offered him at this time. He would not remember Alastair as saying, "If there was a Daddy-Tree & all the Daddies in the whole world were hanging on that tree, I would cut down *my* Daddy from the tree & keep him for my very own always because he would be the very best Daddy on the whole tree".

One begins to realise the weight of expectation which Elspeth's son had carried throughout his short life, and the intensity of emotional demand which had bedevilled the marriage.

Elspeth was satisfied with the new draft, but Guthrie obviously felt uneasy about what he had done. There is even a hint in his letter that he feared she might alter his text further.

> Dear Mrs Kenneth,
>
> I am relieved to find that you approve of my second version. It is very far from what I should have liked it to be, but I'm afraid it's the best I can do ... When the time comes for the book to be printed I should like to see a proof of my own contribution.

Judging by Helen's comment about the non-availability of proofs, this request is unlikely to have been granted.

Guthrie's uneasiness was well justified, for eyebrows were raised when the book came out. It was at this point that the Bishop of Oxford, as if to dissociate himself from anything less than honourable, wrote to Elspeth to point out that "the account of Alastair is very different from my experience of him".

Elspeth vetoed contributions from other correspondents ruthlessly, and the curious thing about these deletions is that they usually refer to just the kind of quirky behaviour which (at least, in her early days) she most claimed to admire. Miss Stott, who knew far more about Alastair than his mother did, wrote in affectionate reminiscence of "the boy's nursery days", but the passage which followed was suppressed, even though the governess remembered Mouse, as "he skipped along a field path saying 'I am covered with joy' ". It was more likely the next words which incurred disapproval: "He was aware of the sense of freedom, that he did not feel in Kensington Gardens. Once there he watched some street arabs doing gymnastics on some railings, his remark was, 'I wish I was like that not a gentleman!' "

Even if her memories had been severely edited, Miss Stott was deeply touched to be sent a copy of Chalmers's book: "Naturally women will weep at times! & I am rather in that condition this minute ... But I write to thank you, & you know how I shall value the book ..."[10]

Evelyn Sharp courteously refused to lend letters, pointing out that she had already used them in her autobiography which was due out in May, but in fact she alluded to them in that book only glancingly, and obviously regarded them as private. Elspeth, a little morbidly, wanted to know more from this woman who had been a close friend of Kenneth's, particularly about the two Christmas holidays in Brussels and Boulogne: "I would greatly like to know if he were exhilerated [sic] by the change to other lands, if he spoke more & was more animated through it?"

There is a sense of growing obsession and of reconstructed reality. Elspeth's own memories are untidily written in a small, fat notebook, and their illegibility elicits pity, for her sight was beginning to fail. There is an entry on Mouse being shown the neighbour's cat, with the explanation that it was not well bred but had good manners. "I see – one of Nature's Pussy-Cats," Elspeth had written – but she could find nobody to confirm that the child himself had uttered this quip. It did not deter her from recording it in *The First Whisper of The Wind in the Willows*.

Remembering the ruthless stripping of Boham's, one feels a kind of anguish on reading Elspeth's words after her husband's death.

> Looking through his most secret hoardings was like examining the Treasure Trove of some darling child – tiny shells picked up from some Cornish beaches, miniature fishing nets from Brittany, blue the Filets bleus that matched the water so as to be disguised to the Fish.
>
> Little gew-gaws from foreign and English fairs of which he was a lover . . .[11]

Suddenly, one has a sense of how alone Kenneth was.

Annie Grahame was a little stiff at first, remarking only that she thought Chalmers would be "very competent" as a biographer, but she duly contributed her memories of Kenneth at Draycott Lodge and in Italy. A little wistfully, she said of the Della Robbia plaque, ". . . when the house was sold last year I tried to rescue that medallion & wrote to the landlord & to Kenneth about it, but I don't know what became of it".

She added that her brother, contemplating taking a job in Persia, was much encouraged by Kenneth, who had advised him: "any experience is worth having, and I would think it worth while to go to Hell for the sake of the experience".

It is the true credo of the lover of life.

Constance Smedley wrote unguardedly to Elspeth: "You have no idea of the diffidence with which I approached you & Mr Grahame – and yet I felt – & feel more than ever – the most curious understanding . . .". In a further letter, twitching with over-sensitivity, she added:

> I felt I knew you both so well – but I never dreamed of being a real friend. It was only when I read Mr Grahame's last sentence a little time ago, about "having a greater & more real share" – it dawned on me, we *might have* been real friends Mr G & I, – & both of you. [her italics.]

She did not get away with such rashness. In Elspeth's writing there is a paraphrase which begins: "I do not think I was ever afraid of anyone in my life but I was terribly afraid of Mr Grahame. Though it was not exactly fear, but a kind of awe."

Constance must have argued, for a further draft follows, much of it pencilled out. The disagreement seems not to have been resolved for her offering remained for the most part unpublished, and there is no evidence of any further correspondence beween them. What she wrote about Kenneth, however, deserves to be heard.

> He had an unerring sense of values. He found in folklore better standards than obtain in ordinary life. In the world of Grimm and Andersen the battle is almost invariably to the poor, the simple, the childlike & despised, animals mingled with humans on equal terms shewing equal intelligence & power; it was also a world of good craftsmanship where the hand is more valuable than the machine & man lives in friendly & intimate relationship with the soil & its produce.
>
> To Kenneth Grahame each creature had its own life as important to it as his own, but he was not curious about its habits; that would have been ungentlemanly. He respected its private life.
>
> He lived, worked & wrote simply and with dignity; and he saw the dignity & wonder of its intricate relationships; he never seemed very interested in himself nor his writing but he was passionately interested in everything about riverlife & the outdoor world: in noble literature: in "all things lovely & of good report".

Elspeth failed to recognise the quotation from Philippians, and marked the word "report" with a query that it should be "repute". Unbelievably, this substitution went through to take its place in the bowdlerised version of Constance's words which appeared in the Chalmers biography.[12] The original continued:

> Beneath the delight in the Earth & the fruits thereof, was a great reverence. When he dressed a salad, the oil meant the olive trees of Italy & France, the herbs, chervil from the sunbaked sand, tarragon from watered soil, mere creatures of the elements, the lettuce was the green leaf, wet with dew & strong with rain & sun – the occasion, a lovely intimate ceremony.
>
> He understood so fully the things that other people only half understood that he could interpret them to others; & those others felt more than love for an author. His books are sacred. He comprehended instinctively the great verities & Principles concerning this existence, and knew that beyond what he saw now, lie wider revelations of the wonder-world he knew.[13]

Graham Robertson was Kenneth's oldest friend, and the long tribute which he wrote began with a salute to him as a writer, pointing out that he wrote what he wished when he wished and he wrote no more than he wished, and this very fastidiousness will probably win him an enduring name.

The pictures of Leonardo da Vinci are less prized for their beauty than because only about five of them exist; if the lost poems of Sappho were found it would be a serious blow to that lady's reputation; in fact nothing can obscure an artist's merit like over-production. In Kenneth Grahame's work there is no need to winnow the wheat from the chaff; he has left us nothing but the purest golden grain, and his mere handful of writings have swept round the world on a gathering wave of love and admiration for the man who would give nothing short of his best, and whose best is, perhaps, about as near perfection as may be compassed by our poor mortality.

Elspeth accepted this for inclusion in the Chalmers book, but the next paragraph was a very different matter. Robertson probably understood Kenneth better than any other living person and, like Constance Smedley, he wrote a passionate requiem for the man with whom he had shared his most intimate thoughts.

Now he has gone from the riverside that he so much loved to seek the source of that River that "came out of Eden", and I only hope that it will prove to be a nice, ordinary river, a happy river, laughing as it runs between banks and loosestrife and meadow sweet, past furrow and fallow and cool, shadowy woods. And there should be a boat or two, when wanted, and friendly animals, and cheery rustics giving him "Goodnight" as they tramp home at curfew bell – there really was a curfew at Blewbury. Yes, I very much hope that all these things may be there, for if not – though politeness will restrain him from mentioning it – I don't believe that he will care about the place one bit.

Elspeth permitted Chalmers to use the first two lines and discarded the rest. There is no sign that she suggested any re-writing; she knew when she had met her match. Robertson had been Kenneth's friend, not hers, and it had been to Robertson's company that he had fled in the early days of the marriage, leaving Elspeth to write her bleak verses and nurse her jealousy. The dust-jacket for the Chalmers book, however, looks like Robertson's work, with its rapturous, classically draped figure, holding its arms to the billowy sky on an open hillside.

The book brought a criticism from Arthur Symons, written in a curious diagonal block of calligraphy which announced that he was himself about to write a biography of his friend Oscar Wilde and his circle. Arthur, who had known Kenneth well in the *Yellow Book* days, was in sympathy with the pantheism which Constance Smedley and Graham Robertson recognised in Grahame, and which his wife had so sternly suppressed in the biography. Of Chalmers, he wrote,

> He had a difficult task, and one I should not, myself, have courted. But I feel that, if I had attempted it, I should have emphasised the Pagan side of Kenneth's mind, which I seem to see not only in his Hellenic personification, but in all sorts of side hints that glint from all his work.[14]

Elspeth would have found this difficult to understand. She had managed to remain uneducated, despite her contact with literary people, and wrote to Quiller-Couch shortly after Kenneth's death to ask him the origin of the phrase "the plaything of the gods". He wrote to her from the riverside house in Fowey where he still fished "on the whiting grounds", and where he and Kenneth together had so much enjoyed the wind and the sun and the sea, advising the gaunt, ever-girlish woman to read Plato. An academic to his finger-tips, he could not imagine that she might fail eternally to enter the world of the classics which meant so much to him, and recalled how he had been so overcome with emotion when reading of the last hours of Socrates "with my boys at Cambridge" that he had been forced to turn away to the window to hide his tears.

Elspeth's enquiry had been prompted by the letter which Q had written to the editor of *The Times*, to say about his old friend the things which the official notices had left unsaid.

> In the obituaries of Kenneth Grahame one misses (though friendship may be exacting) full recognition of his personal charm and the beauty – there is no other word – of his character. This, of course, could be divined in his books, few, yet in their way, surely, classical; but he avoided publicity always, in later years kept deeper retirement under a great sorrow; and so, perhaps, as these books must by their nature have attracted many readers towards a further intimacy of which he was shy, a word or two about him may be acceptable to them and pardonable by his spirit. One does not, anyhow, wish to go out of this world without acknowledging one of the best things found in it.
>
> He came to these parts and to this house (from which he was afterwards married) a little more than thirty years ago; convalescent from a severe illness. Lazy afternoons at sea completed his recovery and made me acquainted with a man who combined all enviable gifts and yet so perfectly as to soften all envy away in affection. Noble in looks, yet modest in bearing; with flashes of wit that played at call around any subject, lambent as summer lightning, never hurting, and with silences that half-revealed things beyond reach of words, he seemed at

once a child and a king. Withal he was eminently a "man's man" and keen on all manly sports; a man, too, who – as Secretary of the Bank of England – knew much of practical affairs and could judge them incisively if with amusement, while his own mind kept its loyalty to sweet thoughts, great manners, and a quiet disdain of anything meaner than these. I must remember him as a "classical" man, perfectly aware of himself as "at best a noble plaything of the gods", whose will he seemed to understand through his gift of interpreting childhood.[15]

Patiently, Q explained to Grahame's widow the phrases which, to him, were so self-evident.

What I meant by "a classical man" was a man who exemplified the Hellenic ideal of perfect adjustment between his intellect, with its speculations on life, & his behaviour towards his fellow men; a harmonious blending of high thoughts with social graces – the power to see far in things, & at the same time to filter it all through a sort of tender chastity.[16]

Even then, his meaning may have remained obscure to Elspeth. She and Kenneth never spoke the same language. He had from an early age moved into the Graeco-Latinate English which is common to educated people, whereas Elspeth had continued to speak basic Anglo-Saxon. The baby-lispings of their written correspondence provided them with a common means of expression, but in speech, there must have been a gulf of non-comprehension which was ultimately too wide to span.

Elspeth lived on for fourteen years after Kenneth's death, sending out a constant stream of letters and small gifts to friends and acquaintances, who dutifully wrote in thanks. Her need to be noticed remained obsessive, and her leanings toward spiritualism increased. At one point she sent a photograph of Mouse to "May", a medium who wrote back in green ink to say that the boy did not know where he was at the time of the accident, that he was under-nourished and over-worked and "still sorry he failed in his high ambition".[17] It ended by advising Elspeth to eat parsley. There must have been some protest from her rationally minded friends and relations – one cannot imagine that Courtauld would have approved – and Elspeth wrote for confirmation of her beliefs to Harry Price at the University of London's Council for Psychic Investigation. Her hopes were dashed, for he sent her a debunking letter to warn her against fraudulent mediums, and was firm that she should not believe what she was told.[18]

The Poetry Society invited Elspeth to address its members about her memories of Kenneth, and one must suspect that she took the opportunity to read them some of her own verse. Courteously, they invited her to become their Vice President, which she accepted.

Despite her tenuous grasp on reality, Elspeth's business acumen remained sharp. When the Chalmers biography went out of print in 1937, she wrote furious letters of protest to Methuen and badgered her friends to support her demands for a reprint. She mentions a "very nice note" from Hugh Walpole. Methuen eventually reprinted the book in their 5/– Devereux series. Although she cannot have been badly off, Elspeth's impulse to make money continued unchecked, and a slightly shocked cutting from the *Daily Telegraph*[19] reveals that she put up for sale one of Kenneth's favourite pieces of furniture, a bookcase which had been in Apsley House. This, the *Telegraph* claimed, no doubt from Elspeth's information, "had association with the 'Iron duke', and through it runs a black line, thought to be a mark of mourning for Nelson. Mr Kenneth Grahame was very proud of it, and his friends knew it as the Wellington bookcase. He kept his first editions and other literary treasures in it, and on an escritoire forming part of it he wrote most of his books."

Unabashed, Elspeth sent this cutting to the auctioneer in Reading to encourage the bidding. She had put a reserve of fifty guineas on the bookcase, and her letter was understamped.

Although her sight was failing, Elspeth remained ferocious in her efforts to keep the Grahame name before the public. She wrote to HMV in 1934, suggesting they should record the songs from *Toad of Toad Hall*, but they were not enthusiastic. At eighty-two years of age, she made her last great effort to cement the myth of her perfect, talented, happily united family. In 1944, two years before her death, she published *First Whisper of The Wind in the Willows*. It reads like a remembered dream, its facts hopelessly jumbled, its dates confused, a kaleidoscope of mixed rememberings through which Elspeth herself glides, seen in her own eyes as the creative genius who brought order and tranquillity to a mad world, and without whom a book of lasting wonder would never have been written. In a tragic sense, she was right, for had he not married her, Kenneth's life would have been very different.

Elspeth asked Graham Robertson to design a jacket for the book, but he declined, pleading that he was too old and feeble and poor-sighted. He could not resist adding a small dig at his old enemy's lack of taste. "And if I *could* do it," he said, "I fear that I cannot see weeping willows – or weeping anythings – in connection with Kenneth."[20] He had not forgotten that the words which he wrote for his beloved friend had not been allowed to appear in print.

Another war came, and Courtauld, now Director of the Red Cross, threw open Dorneywood, as his big house in Burnham was now called, as a leisure retreat for officers, he and Winifred acting as capable and ever-welcoming hosts. Elspeth went there for frequent weekends, and was fervently supportive, sending her meagre tea and sugar ration to supplement the provisions. Letters were exchanged constantly, and Elspeth's yearning for success was perhaps partially assuaged by her brother's growing fame. The house was visited by statesmen and by the crowded heads of Europe as the good work continued unabated. Winifred wrote of the constant fund-raising in her usual matter-of-fact manner, mentioning to Elspeth that "one of my letters from T. Hardy fetched £7 at a small Red Cross sale. I can't think why they fetch so much. I'm rather afraid it's my last, but I'm going to have another poke round."[21]

Queen Mary came to look at a century-old dolls' house which had been given for sale, and Winifred commented wryly on the old lady's stamina, quoting a friend who had said, "Royal legs must be made of something different from ours". Winifred herself, however, was ceaselessly active and busy. Always more intellectual than her sister, she was in the habit of finishing the *Times* crossword over breakfast, but when visiting officers expressed disappointment at finding the grid completed, she obligingly did it merely in her head, leaving the diagram untouched for the use of others.

In a letter to Elspeth in 1942, Courtauld announced his intention of leaving Dorneywood to the nation as a country retreat for the Prime Minister or one of the Secretaries of State. He carried out this intention, and was rewarded with a peerage, but Elspeth seems to have been more excited about the fact that her brother's name had been mentioned on the radio as a questioner to the popular *Brains Trust*. He had asked, perhaps significantly, whether a biography or autobiography presented the best picture of a subject.

Elspeth herself at that time was working on further memoirs of herself, Kenneth and Alastair, and an interesting letter from a Canadian serviceman, John Ward, dated Christmas 1945, mentions "working with you, and noting the care and patience you took in looking for the exact word to express your meaning". She was probably using him as a scribe during a Dorneywood visit, for her later letters tend to be dictated, and those in her own writing have large, uncertain spaces between the characters which make up the words.

Time was running out. Winifred had died in the summer of 1944, a few months before her brother took his seat in the House of Lords as Lord Courtauld-Thomson and, although he himself was as vigorous as ever, still working a twelve-hour day at over eighty, the days were becoming precious. Elspeth still sought outlets for the creativity which had never found full expression, and found occasional unexpected ways in which she could use it. One of these came into my hands quite recently.

By coincidence, it turned out during the writing of this book that a friend of mine was in possession of a letter written to her parents by Elspeth on 12 April 1945, and dictated to a young airman at Dorneywood. It is an extraordinary document. My friend's parents, knowing Elspeth to be a good storyteller, had asked her to contribute a pen-portrait of Rebecca, the family's Anglo-Indian ayah, as a contribution to the family archive. Elspeth did as she was asked, and did it with an empathy which has all the assurance of first-hand knowledge. Although the recipients noted that it was "incorrect in certain facts", Elspeth had let herself go in describing the ayah's plans to provide "tiny swings so low as to be safe for tiny swingers and sand-heaps and little deck chairs and dolls and other toys, and wholesome food and everything that Rebecca could devise . . .".[22] It is hard to believe that the writer had never met her.

Elspeth herself, in the letter which accompanies the piece, says, "it was a work of love, in some measure, to preserve the memory of the dark face illuminated by the white soul . . .". The phraseology is, by today's racially sensitive standards, outrageous, but it was all part of her attempt to make things as lovely as possible. She had always found reality alarming.

Elspeth died on 19 December 1946, after a stroke, and left everthing she possessed to the Dorneywood Endowment Trust. Her obituary appeared in *The Times* on Christmas Eve, written by her brother, Courtauld, and it is curiously guarded. He wrote of the blindness which had for many years "prevented her from reading or writing" and added a cautious tribute, if such it was. "Although largely generous and intensely interested in the well-being of others, she cared nothing for her own comfort." It is a dry summing up of a life. Courtauld himself died at the age of 89, on 1 November 1954.

Elspeth's tragedy was that she had never managed to break a lifetime's habit of selecting what she found acceptable from the rich muddle of life, and discarding the rest. Clutching her treasures, she had still not managed to possess happiness. One can only hope that her substitute dream of it was, at the end, enough to sustain her.

As to Kenneth, the opposite had been true. He gazed at life with the unselective stare of a child, and the awareness which brought him intense delight brought also its pain, which, being unresisted, was no threat. He never allowed the mechanics of human organisation to interfere with the essence of his own being. He was what Kenneth White, a fine poet of our own time, has called "a real man without situation".[23]

When all is said, it is Grahame himself, in *The Piper at the Gates of Dawn*, who finds the words which state his own truth.

All this he saw, for one moment breathless and intense, vivid on the morning sky; and still, as he looked, he lived; and still, as he lived, he wondered.

Alison Prince
Isle of Arran
1991–1994

357

Notes and References

Abbreviations:

BL – Bodleian Library, Oxford
CTC – Courtauld Thomson Collection, Dorneywood
WW – *The Wind in the Willows*
PP – *Pagan Papers*
GA – *The Golden Age*
DD – *Dream Days*
KG – Kenneth Grahame
EG – Elspeth Grahame
AG – Alastair Grahame
PG – Peter Green, biography
PCh – Patrick Chalmers, biography
Q – Sir Arthur Quiller-Couch

See Bibliography for details

1: Edinburgh and the Wild West

1. Letter, 18.4.1933, quoted PG p. 8.
2. PCh p. 1
3. Letter, Helen Grahame to EG, undated (1932), BL
4. PCh p. 4
5. Letter in Argyll archive, 1.3.1862
6. Letter, Helen Grahame to EG, undated (1932 or 3), BL
7. "The River Bank", WW
8. "Loafing", PP
9. "The Triton's Conch", *National Observer* 16.12.1893
10. "Romance of the Rail", PP
11. Letter, Bessie Grahame to Mary Ingles, now lost, PCh p. 7
12. *A Dark Star*, lecture given in Pangbourne shortly before Grahame's death in 1932, reprinted posthumously in *The Cornhill* Vol. 74 (June 1933), pp. 649–67 PCh 286–310.
13. Letter, Helen Grahame to EG, undated (1933), BL
14. As note 12

2: All on Fire

1. Maurice Collis, *Stanley Spencer* pp. 25–6
2. "The Olympians", GA
3. Letter, Helen Grahame to EG (1933), BL
4. op. cit.
5. "The Olympians", GA
6. "The Roman Road", GA
7. "A Holiday", GA
8. Constance Smedley, *Crusaders* (1929) p. 150, PG p. 17
9. "The Olympians", GA
10. op. cit.
11. "Alarms and Excursions", GA
12. "The Blue Room", GA
13. Letter, Helen Grahame to EG (1933), BL
14. as above
15. "A Harvesting", GA
16. "A Departure", DD
17. "Romance of the Rail", PP
18. op. cit.
19. Letter, Helen Grahame to EG (1933), BL
20. PG p. 28, personal communication Maxfield Parrish to Peter Green
21. op. cit.

3: Schooling and Learning

1. KG, address to St Edward's boys, reprinted PCh p. 14
2. Revd Irton Smith, R. D. Hill, *A History of St Edward's School* p. 10
3. op. cit. p. 14
4. "The Fairy Wicket", PP
5. "Oxford Through a Boy's Eyes", reprinted *Country Life*, 23.12.1932 and by PCh, pp. 17–25
6. op. cit.
7. op. cit.
8. op. cit.
9. Robert Louis Stevenson, *Virginibus Puerisque* (1881)
10. R. D. Hill, *A History of St Edward's School*, p. 12
11. "Oxford Through a Boy's Eyes", as note 5
12. op. cit.
13. op. cit.
14. "Saturnia Regna", *New Review* vol. 14, no. 82, March 1896, quoted PCh pp. 103–9
15. "Orion", PP
16. "The Twenty-First of October", DD
17. "Orion", PP

18. "Oxford Through a Boy's Eyes", as note 5
19. "Lusisti Satis", GA

4: Dreams Demolished
1. Letter, Bessie Luard (*née* Grahame) to EG (1933), BL
2. Helen Grahame to EG (1933) BL
3. Letter, Bessie Luard to EG, as above
4. "Justifiable Homicide", PP
5. "Oxford Through a Boy's Eyes", *Country Life* 23.12.1932, PCh p. 25
6. Letter, Annie Grahame to EG (1932), BL
7. Letter, Evelyn Lidderdale to EG (1932), BL
8. "Saturnia Regna", *New Review* vol. 14, no. 82, March 1896, PCh pp. 103–9
9. op. cit.
10. "Pastels", *National Observer* 17.2.1894, PCh pp. 52–4.
11. Letter, Helen Thorp (*née* Syrett) to EG, BL
12. Letter, Reginald Ingles to EG, 16.3.1933, BL, PG p. 85
13. *Transactions*, The New Shakespere [*sic*] Society, PG p. 66
14. Letter from EG to Chalmers 4.9.1933, quoting Miss Richardson, BL
15. P. B. Shelley, *Essays and Letters* 1886
16. Oral statement, Annie Grahame, quoted PG p. 55
17. Annie Grahame, letter to EG (1933), BL

5: The Solitude of the Roaring Street
1. Allan Fea, *Recollections of Sixty Years* (1927) pp. 142ff quoted PG p. 77
2. "To Rollo, Untimely Taken", *Yellow Book* Jan 1897
3. Sidney Ward, letter to EG 1.3.1933 BL, PG pp. 92–3
4. KG, letter to Helen Dunham, BL, 28.7.1896
5. "The Roman Road", GA
6. "The Iniquity of Oblivion", *Yellow Book* October 1895, PCh p. 131
7. "Cheap Knowledge", PP
8. "The Rural Pan", PP
9. *Quarterly Review*, January 1891
10. Letter, Reginald Ingles to EG 16.3.1933, part quoted PG p. 85
11. Letter, KG to Helen Dunham 28.7.1896, BL
12. Letter, Annie Grahame to EG (1933), BL
13. "Loafing", PP
14. Letter, Mrs M. E. Squibb to EG (1933), BL
15. Letter, Helen Grahame to EG (1933), BL
16. Letter, Mary Richardson to EG (1933), BL

6: Long John Silver and the Great God Pan
1. Letter, Sir Gordon Nairn to EG, quoted PCh pp. 109–10
2. Robert Louis Stevenson, *Memoirs of Himself*, Philadelphia 1912

3. PCh p. 63
4. W. B. Yeats, *Autobiographies* (1955) p. 129, quoted PG p. 115
5. Letter, KG to Mr Traill, quoted PCh p. 42.
6. R. H. Tawney, *Religion and the Rise of Capitalism* (1926)
7. W. B. Yeats, *Autobiographies* (1955) pp. 124ff, PG pp. 113–14
8. C. L. Hinds, *Authors and I* (1921) pp. 103–4. Chalmers, however, quotes on p. 50 from a reprint in the *Christian Science Monitor*, Boston
9. Letter, Mary Richardson to EG (1933), BL, quoted PG p. 94
10. PCh, p. 48
11. C. L. Hinds, *Authors and I* (1921) pp. 103–4, PG 114
12. "Long Odds", *Yellow Book* July 1895
13. op. cit.
14. "The Rural Pan", PP
15. op. cit.
16. James Joyce, *Portrait of the Artist as a Young Man* (1916)
17. Richard Le Gallienne, *Attitudes and Avowals* (1910) pp. 19–20, PG p. 142

7: Golden Days
1. Annie Grahame to EG, letter undated, but 1933, BL
2. PCh p. 48
3. Robert Louis Stevenson, *Virginibus Puerisque* (1881)
4. J. W. Lambert, *The Bodley Head* (1987) p. 10
5. op. cit., p. 119
6. op. cit., p. 44
7. Baron Corvo (Frederick Rolfe) *Nicholas Crabbe* (1969) p. 27
8. Letter, Helen Thorp (*née* Syrett) to EG (1933), BL
9. Evelyn Sharp, *Unfinished Adventure* (1933) p. 62
10. *op. cit.*, p. 64, and letter from KG in undated series, BL
11. Letter, Evelyn Sharp to John Lane, 27.12.1911, BL
12. Letter, Evelyn Sharp to John Lane, 22.10.1911, BL
13. KG to Evelyn Sharp, letter dated 23.7.1896, BL
14. Evelyn Sharp, *op. cit.*, p. 65
15. Jean White, *née* Cage, letter to EG (1933), BL. Chalmers, perhaps thanks to misinformation from Elspeth Grahame, wrongly attributes Jean White's letter to Netta Syrett, in a long "quotation", pp. 65–7, of which the last sentence was in fact written by Evelyn Sharp, see note 26
16. Evelyn Sharp, op. cit., pp. 61–2. Again, misrepresentation has been at work, causing Chalmers to aver on p. 65 that "it was Kenneth Grahame's practised hand that broke the eggs that made the omelet . . ."
17. PCh p. 55
18. PCh p. 84
19. Letter, Annie Grahame to EG, 10.3.1933, BL
20. J. W. Lambert, *The Bodley Head* (1987) pp. 60–1

21. Evelyn Sharp, op. cit., pp. 59–60
22. Letter, Sidney Ward to EG (1933), BL
23. J. L. May, *John Lane and the Nineties* (1936), quoted by Cecil Woolf in his introduction to Baron Corvo's *Nicholas Crabbe*
24. Baron Corvo (Frederick Rolfe) *Nicholas Crabbe* (1969) p. 31
25. Richard Le Gallienne, "Tree Worship", *The Yellow Book*, Vol. 1, April 1894
26. Letter, Evelyn Sharp (as Mrs Henry Nevinson) to EG 16.4.1933. (See note 15, above)

8: An End to Childhood

1. J. W. Lambert, *The Bodley Head* (1987) p. 105
2. op. cit., p. 65
3. op. cit., p. 106
4. op. cit., p. 107
5. Helen Holmes Spicer (*née* Dunham) to EG, letter dated 18.3.1933, BL
6. Letter, Evelyn Sharp to EG 16.4.1933, BL
7. L. A. G. Strong, *Courtauld-Thomson: A Memoir* (1958) p. 15, PG p. 202
8. Valentine m/s, BL
9. Pre-trial document signed by Courtauld Thomson, CTC
10. The Hon. Hugh Fletcher Moulton, *Life of Lord Moulton* (1922) p. 147, PG p. 203
11. as in note no. 9
12. m/s of EG's Ronsard translation in BL, with letter from André Maurois, to whom she had evidently sent it, hoping that they would meet, and politely describing the translation as "charming"
13. J. N. P. Watson, *Dorneywood* (1992) p. 23
14. t/s of EG's poems, BL, comments pencilled in margin, unsigned
15. m/s of poem CTC
16. L. A. G. Strong, *op. cit.* (note 7) p. 14, PG pp. 203–4
17. Personal information to Green from A. W. Dascombe, then himself Secretary of the Bank of England, PG pp. 168–9
18. "Deus Terminus", PP
19. Letter, Sidney Ward to EG, 1.3.1933, BL
20. Letter, Bessie Luard to EG, undated, but 1933, BL. Green, quoting this on p. 52, adds a note (p. 356) in which he states, wrongly, that Bessie was the daughter of David Ingles. Bessie Luard was the daughter of John Grahame
21. Letter, KG to Grace Dunham, 10.3.1898, BL. Partially quoted PCh pp. 112–13

9: Dino and Minkie

1. St Edward's School Chronicle, Vol. 12, no. 321, quoted in entirety PG pp. 4–6

2. Miss R. M. Bradley, PG p. 205. No source given, but Chalmers on p. 95 uses same words, followed by "and her gift of imagination and intelligent sympathy enabled her to follow her husband's mind and give him, throughout his life, an ideal companionship". He gives no source for this, although the statement is immediately followed by a letter from KG to Miss Bradley; one must therefore suspect that it originated from Elspeth herself

3. m/s BL, first item in a bound volume of letters which are otherwise Alastair's

4. m/s BL

5. KG, letter to EG (then Thomson), 2.4.1899. PG p. 207. Chalmers made no reference to this long series of letters.

6. Letter, KG to John Fletcher Moulton, 21.5.1899, BL

7. Personal information to Green from Dr Anthony Feiling p. 207

8. Letter, KG to EG(T) 25.5.1899, BL

9. Letter, Miss R. M. Bradley to EG, 11.4.1933, BL

10. Letter, KG to Miss R. M. Bradley, 25.5.1899, BL, PG p. 209

11. Letter, KG to John Fletcher Moulton 29.5.1899 BL, PG p. 209

12. Letter, as above, 4.6.1899, BL

13. Letter, KG to EG(T) 26.5.1899, BL, PG p. 209

14. Letter, KG to EG(T) 8.6.1899, BL, PG p. 211

15. Letter, KG to EG(T) undated, "Mundy", BL

16. Pre-trial document signed by Courtauld Thomson, CTC

17. Personal information to Green from Miss Barbara Euphan Todd, PG p. 215

18. Letter, KG to EG(T) 7.7.1899, BL

10: Durham Villas

1. Letter, Mrs Emma Hardy to EG, 20.8.1899 BL, PG (part), pp. 220–1

2. Poem m/s, BL, PG p. 223

3. Letter, Helen Thorp (née Syrett) to EG, undated, but 1933, BL. Quoted by Chalmers in the long compilation attributed to Netta Syrett (PCh p. 66), though in fact Helen was the writer. This mistake, like those referred to in Chapter 7 (notes 15, 16), was no doubt thanks to misinformation supplied to Chalmers by Elspeth, to whom all the letters were addressed

4. "The Magic Ring", DD

5. "A White-washed Uncle", GA

6. Graham Robertson, tribute sent to EG in letter, 11.4.1933, BL, PG pp. 225–6

7. Graham Robertson, *Letters* (1953) p. 284. The correspondents in this volume are unnamed, but the context suggests that this letter was to Curtis Brown, as the writer ends, "It's nice of you to want a novel from me and I wish I could write one, but I cannot invent plots . . ."

8. op. cit., pp. 288–9, correspondent unknown
9. op. cit.
10. op. cit.
11. Personal communication to Green from Mr H. A. Siepmann, PG pp. 224–5
12. Frederick Rolfe, letter to KG 16.8.1900 BL PG pp. 224–5
13. as note 6
14. op. cit.
15. op. cit.
16. m/s poem, BL
17. as above

11: Mouse

1. m/s poem, CTC
2. Letter, undated, Muriel Bure to EG, BL
3. Courtauld Thomson, document, pre Moulton trial, CTC
4. PCh p. 150
5. PCh p. 152
6. Letter, Naomi Stott to EG, undated, 1933, BL
7. Letter, AG to his parents, from long, mostly undated series, BL
8. PCh p. 116, but source not identified. Reports, *The Times*, 25 and 26 Nov. 1903
9. Letter, John Fletcher Moulton to EG 24.11.1903, BL, PG p. 230
10. *Quarterly Review*, April 1981, but also in previous issue, Jan. 1891, under heading "The Autumn Season of Parliament"
11. *Deus Terminus*, PP
12. Draft pencilled on back of Miss Hoveed's letter, BL, PG p. 233
13. Eleanor Graham, *Kenneth Grahame*, The Bodley Head (1963); Elspeth Grahame, *First Whisper of The Wind in the Willows*, Methuen (1944), p. 2
14. Letter, KG to EG, from undated series, BL
15. J. N. P. Watson, *Dorneywood*, p. 27
16. Pre-trial document, Courtauld Thomson, CTC
17. J. N. P. Watson, op. cit. p. 24
18. as 16
19. Letter, KG to EG, undated, but Sept. 1904
20. m/s poem, BL
21. L. A. G. Strong, *Courtauld-Thomson: A Memoir*, pp. 45–53, also the Hon. Hugh Fletcher Moulton, *Life of Lord Moulton*, both quoted by Green, p. 231ff
22. Figures of Final Adjustment, CTC
23. BL
24. Letter, Naomi Stott to EG 12.3.1933, BL

25. Letter, Reginald Ingles to EG (1933), BL
26. *First Whisper of The Wind in the Willows*, Elspeth Grahame, p. 17
27. Letter, Graham Robertson to EG, undated (1933), BL
28. W. B. Hillkirk, writing in *The Old Lady*, magazine of the Bank of England, Vol. 26, no. 117, March 1950 quoted by Chalmers, p. 117, and Green, p. 288

12: The Wind in the Reeds

1. PCh p. 112, personal communication from the then Secretary
2. Question paper and answers m/ss, BL
3. *First Whisper of The Wind in the Willows*, EG p. 41, original m/s BL
4. "The Wild Wood", WW
5. Letter, KG to AG 10.5.1907, BL
6. Series of "Toad" letters, BL, reprinted *First Whisper of The Wind in the Willows*
7. Personal communication, Edmund R. Purves to Green, PG p. 267
8. Letter, KG to Ann Channer, 22.2.1931, BL
9. Letter, KG to Austin Purves, PG 298
10. *First Whisper*, EG p. 2
11. op. cit., p. 10
12. op. cit., p. 3
13. PG pp. 269–70
14. PG p. 224
15. Letter, Theodore Roosevelt to KG 20.6.1907, BL
16. Curtis Brown, *Contacts*, PG p. 291
17. Letter, KG to "Miss Joy" 8.1.1909
18. Letter, KG from unnamed correspondent, PCh pp. 92–3
19. Letter, Graham Robertson to KG, undated, BL
20. op. cit.
21. op. cit.
22. Valentine m/s BL
23. Constance Smedley, *Crusaders*, p. 152, PG p. 292
24. op. cit., pp. 180–3, PG pp. 292–3
25. W. B. Hillkirk, *The Old Lady*, magazine of the Bank of England, Vol. 26, no. 117

13: A Difficult Freedom

1. Letter, Trant Chambers to KG, 1.2.1910, BL
2. Letter, KG to Constance Smedley, 3.1.1909, BL
3. PG p. 299
4. Letter, KG to Q, 10.1.1910, PG p. 300
5. PG pp. 300–301
6. Letter, KG to A. W. Lidderdale, 28.5.1910, PG 301

7. Letter, KG to R. E. Moody, 2.6.1914, PG p. 304
8. Letter, KG to AG, undated, BL
9. Letter AG to EG 15.6.1910, BL
10. *Frater Ave Atque Vale*: *Bookman* Vol. 76, pp. 69–74, Jan. 1933, reprinted *First Whisper* pp. 22–32
11. *First Whisper of The Wind in the Willows* (1944), p. 24
12. Letter, KG to Graham Robertson, undated, BL
13. "Lusisti Satis", GA
14. "Exit Tyrannus", GA
15. Letter, KG to Austin Purves 12.1.1911, PCh 231
16. Personal communication, Austin Purves Jnr to Green, PG p. 304 quoting letter 4.4.1957
17. Letter, 27.7.1910 A & C Black to KG, PG 305
18. Letter, KG to Austin Purves, 2.8.1910, PCh p. 226
19. Letter, AG to EG, undated, BL
20. Letter, KG to Austin Purves, 15.5.1911, PCh p. 235

14: Alastair at School

1. Letter, AG to EG, with pencilled note, BL
2. Curtis Brown, *Contacts* p. 65, PG p. 307
3. *First Whisper*, EG, pp. 19–20
4. Letter, KG to Austin Purves, 8.2.1912, PCh p. 238
5. PCh p. 183
6. Letter, KG to Austin Purves, 12.12.1913, PCh p. 242
7. as above, 8.7.1912 PCh 239
8. Curtis Brown, *Contacts*, pp. 58–9, PG p. 310
9. Letter, KG to Q, 26.12.1911, PG p. 308
10. Personal communication Austin Purves Jnr to Green, PG 4.4.1957
11. Letter, KG to Graham Robertson, 4.12.1913, PG p. 312
12. Letter 26.3, year unstated, AG to EG, BL
13. Letter, AG to "Alan", undated, BL
14. Letter, KG to Austin Purves, 24.8.1910, PCh pp. 227–8

15: No Pity

1. PG p. 313
2. Letter, Roger Raven to AG, 22.10.1914, BL, PG pp. 312–14
3. Letter, KG to Austin Purves, PG 314
4. Letter, Q to KG, 27.11.1914, PG pp. 314–15
5. Letter, Graham Robertson to KG, undated, BL
6. Kerrison Preston, editor, Graham Robertson's *Letters* 1953 Introduction p. ix
7. PCh p. 153
8. Letter, Graham Robertson to KG, undated, BL

9. Letter, Naomi Stott to EG, 12.3.1933, BL, PCh p. 151
10. PG p. 316
11. op. cit., p. 318
12. Letter, Graham Robertson to KG, undated, BL
13. *Cambridge Book of Poetry for Children*, KG's preface to the first edition, Oct. 1916, p. xiv
14. *The Observer*, 17.5.1916

16: University and Tragedy
1. Letter, EG to Courtauld Thomson, 16.8.1917, PG p. 322
2. op. cit. quoted in PG p. 322
3. PG, p. 323
4. Letter to the present author, 29.6.1993 from Mark Curthoys, archivist, Christ Church, Oxford, to whom I am much indebted for information about Alastair Grahame as an undergraduate
5. Personal information to Green from Beatrice Horton (*née* Curtis Brown) PG p. 323
6. PCh p. 167
7. Qiller-Couch, *Cambridge Lectures* (1934) Everyman Edition p. 276, also in *The Art of Reading*, Cambridge University Press (1920)
8. "The Twenty-first of October", DD
9. "Dies Irae", DD
10. Letter, KG to Professor G. T. Hill, 24.9.1919, BL
11. *Dictionary of National Biography*, *Obituaries*
12. Keith Feiling, *Sketches in Nineteenth Century Biography* (1930) p. 73
13. PG p. 325
14. Letter B. Johnson to AG, Palm Sunday. 1920, BL PG p. 326
15. Letter quoted in the *Quarterly Review* no. 343, January 1891, Report of Head Masters' Conference, Oxford 23.12.1890
16. Letter, Ernest Josling to AG 4.5.1920, PG pp. 326–7
17. PG p. 327
18. Testimony at inquest, PG p. 327
19. PCh p. 168
20. Letter, Q to EG, 19.5.1920 (Miss Foy Quiller-Couch) PG p. 328
21. PCh p. 151
22. Personal communication to Green, PG p. 332
23. PG p. 318
24. EG letter to auctioneers, 22.9.1920, BL
25. Letter, Eleanor Gross to EG, 22.10.1920
26. Letter, Caroline Feiling to EG, undated, BL

17: North and South
1. Q, *The Art of Reading*, Cambridge University Press (1920)

2. Letter, Charis Fairbanks to EG, 10.4.1933, BL
3. PG p. 336, personal information
4. Letter, KG to Ernest Josling, 27.4.1921, PG p. 336
5. "Wayfarers All", WW
6. Letter, KG to Curtis Brown, PCh, quoted at length, pp. 145–7
7. Letter, KG to A. A. Milne, 1.9.1922, PG p. 338
8. Letter, EG to Courtauld Thomson, 10.6.1944, CTC. PCh p. 256
9. Entry in ledger-diary, lost after 1933, PCh p. 276
10. PG pp. 338–9
11. "The River Bank", WW
12. Letter, EG to Thomas Woodman, 10.7.1923, PG p. 339
13. PCh p. 277
14. m/s, undated, BL
15. Unidentified informant to Chalmers – possibly Elspeth herself. PCh pp. 278–81
16. *First Whisper of The Wind in The Willows*, EG p. 33
17. see note 15
18. The "horse's ear" story may originate with Elspeth, as it is told in rather more detail in *First Whisper of the Wind in the Willows*, pp. 33–4
19. PCh p. 281. Chalmers provides the only evidence of where the Grahames went and what they did during these years of wandering, and Green clearly distrusts it, giving only the barest account, probably feeling that Elspeth was not a reliable witness. In my own view, this was the period at which she was most clearly in charge of things, and have used her memories as the basis for this chapter, while discarding the most obvious romanticisms
20. Letter, Courtauld Thomson to EG, 14.3.1924 CTC
21. J. N. P. Watson, *Dorneywood*, p. 30
22. "The Rural Pan", PP
23. PCh, p. 312
24. Personal information to Green from Mrs Margery Newnham Davis, PG p. 340
25. PCh p. 312
26. Personal information to Green, PG pp. 341–2
27. Mabel Heinemann, letter to EG, undated, BL
28. PG p. 205
29. as above
30. Lecture to St Edward's pupils, 1925, PCH p. 17
31. PCh p. 281
32. *op. cit.*, p. 282
33. PG pp. 342–3
34. Letter, KG to Curtis Brown, 29.3.1926 PG p. 343
35. Letter, KG to Curtis Brown, 11.11.1928 PG p. 343

18: Going Home

1. Letters from John Wilstach to KG, BL
2. "Illustrating 'The Wind in the Willows' ", *The Horn Book*, April 1954, pp. 83–8, PG 346
3. A. A. Milne, introduction to *Toad of Toad Hall*
4. PCh pp. 17–26
5. Letter KG to Margaret Stewart Somerville, 20.12.1931, BL
6. PG p. 348
7. Curtis Brown, *Contacts*, p. 61, PG p. 349
8. Letter, Helen Grahame to EG, undated, BL
9. Letter, Anstey Guthrie to EG, from an undated series, BL
10. Letter, Naomi Stott to EG (1933) BL
11. m/s, BL
12. PCh p. 196
13. Letter from Constance Smedley to EG, undated, BL
14. Letter, Arthur Symons to EG, undated, BL
15. Q letter to *The Times*, PCh p. 317
16. Letter, Q to EG, 21.7.1932, BL
17. Letter, "May" to EG, undated, BL
18. Letter, Harry Price to EG, undated, BL
19. *Daily Telegraph*, undated cutting, BL
20. Letter, Graham Robertson to EG, undated, BL
21. Letter, Winifred Thomson to EG, undated, CTC
22. m/s kindly lent by Mrs Jane Williams and her sister, Mrs Ann Tomlinson
23. 'Out of Asia 8', from *The Bird Path*, Kenneth White (1989)

Bibliography of the Works of Kenneth Grahame

Initials in parentheses after an item indicate its subsequent inclusion in one of Grahame's books. PP – *Pagan Papers*, GA – *The Golden Age*, DD – *Dream Days*. FW – Elspeth Grahame's *The First Whisper of "The Wind in the Willows"*. An asterisk indicates that original publication was anonymous.

Aboard The Galley *National Observer* 3.9.1892 * (PP)
Alarums and Excursions *National Observer* 10.2.1894 (GA)
Argonauts, The, *National Observer* 10.3.1894 (GA)
As You Like It (poem) *National Observer* 30.5.1891
Atumn Encounter, An, *National Observer* 11.2.1893 * (PP)
Barn Door, The, *National Observer* 28.10.1893 *
Bertie's Escapade 1907, first printed by Chalmers (FW)
Blue Room, The, *Phil May's Illustrated Winter Annual* Dec 1894 (GA)
Bohemian in Exile *St James's Gazette* 27.9.1890 * (PP)
Burglars, The, *National Observer* 24.6.1893 (PP, GA)
By a Northern Furrow *St James's Gazette* 26.12.1888 *
Cambridge Book of Poetry for Children, preface and ed. 1916
Cheap Knowledge *National Observer* 11.4.1891 * (PP)
Christmas (poem) published by Chalmers only
Concerning Ghosts *National Observer* 5.11.1892 *
Cradle Song *National Observer* 8.10.1892
Dark Star, A (lecture) *The Cornhill* Vol. 74 June 1933
Departure, A, *Dream Days* 1898
Deus Terminus *National Observer* 1.10.1892 * (PP)
Dies Irae *The Yellow Book* Jan 1896 (DD)
Dream Days The Bodley Head Dec 1898 (date on fly-leaf 1899)
Eternal Whither, The, *National Observer* 9.7.1892 * (PP)
Exit Tyrannus, *National Observer* 28.4.1894 (GA)
Fabric of the Fairy Tale (review of children's books) *Daily Mail* 16.12.1899
Fairy Wicket, The, *National Observer* 20.2.1892 * (PP)
Falling Out, A, *The Yellow Book* Jan 1895 (GA)
Felowe That Goes Alone *St Edward's School Chronicle* Vol. 12, no. 321 July 1913
Finding of the Princess, The, *National Observer* 20.5.1893 (PP, GA)
Funeral, A, set up in proof for the *National Observer*, but never published (FW)

Golden Age, The, London, John Lane Feb/March 1895

Good and Bad Effects of Rivalry *St Edward's School Chronicle* No. 5, Oct 1873

Harvesting, A, *National Observer* 13.1.1894 (GA)

Headswoman, The, *The Yellow Book* Oct 1894, and reprinted by John Lane as No. 5, *Bodley Booklets*

Holiday, A, *New Review* Vol. 12, no. 70, March 1895 (GA), but originally published with "Lusisti Satis" under the joint title of "In Arcady".

Hundred Fables of Aesop, A, introduction to P. J. Billinghurst's book (translated by Sir Roger l'Estrange) John Lane 1899

Ideals (lecture) *The Fortnightly Review* Dec 1922

Iniquity of Oblivion *The Yellow Book* Oct 1895

Inner Ear, The, *The Yellow Book* April 1895

Invention of Fairyland, The (review of Evelyn Sharp's *All The Way to Fairyland*) *Academy* 18.12.1897

Its Walls Were as of Jasper *Scribner's Magazine* Aug 1897 (DD)

Justifiable Homicide *National Observer* 10.10.1891 * (PP)

Letters to his son, later forming chapters of *The Wind in the Willows*, 1907 (FW)

Lizard Lights (poem) Chalmers, 1933

Loafing *National Observer* 24.1.1891 * (PP)

Long Odds *The Yellow Book* July 1895

Lost Centaur, The, *National Observer* 26.11.1892 * (PP)

Love's Reveille (poem) *National Observer* 27.2.1892

Lullaby-Land, preface to Eugene Field's book, John Lane 1898

Lusisti Satis *New Review* Vol. 12, no. 70 (March 1895) (GA) Originally published with "A Holiday", q.v., without the two final paragraphs which appear in The Golden Age, and titled "Satis Diu Lusisti".

Magic Ring, The, *Scribner's Magazine* Dec 1896 (DD)

Marginalia *National Observer* 26.3.1892 * (PP)

Mountain Stream, The (poem) *Hull Weekly News* 15.4.1905

Mutabile Semper *New Review* Vol. 14, no. 83 (April 1896) (DD)

Non Libri Sed Liberi *National Observer* 28.2.1891 * (PP)

Of Smoking *Scots Observer* 18.10.1890 * (PP)

Old Master, An, *National Observer* 24.3.1894 *

Olympians, The, *National Observer* 19.9.1891 * (PP, GA)

Orion *National Observer* 13.11.1892 * (PP)

Oxford Through a Boy's Eyes *Country Life* 3.12.1932

Pagan Papers, London, Elkin Matthews and John Lane Oct 1893

Parable, A, Overheard and Communicated by our own Cat, *St James's Gazette* 19.11.1890

Pastels *National Observer* 17.2.1894

Plate-Smashing and the Conjuror, inaccurately transcribed by Chalmers from m/s (Bodleian Library)

Quis Desiderio? (poem) *National Observer* 19.9.1891
Reluctant Dragon, The, *Dream Days* 1898
Roman Road, The, *The Yellow Book* July 1894 (GA)
Romance of the Rail, The, *National Observer* 8.8.1891 * (PP)
Romance of the Road, The, *National Observer* 14.2.1891 * (PP)
Rural Pan, The, *National Observer* 25.4.1891 * (PP)
Saga of the Seas *Scribner's Magazine* Aug 1898 (DD)
Saturnia Regna *New Review* Vol. 14, no. 82, March 1896
Sawdust and Sin *National Observer* 25.8.1894 (GA)
Secret Drawer, A, *The Chapbook* (Chicago) 15.1.1895 (GA)
Seventy Years a Showman, preface to "Lord" George Sanger's book, Dent, 1926
Snowbound *National Observer* 23.9.1893 (PP, GA)
To Rollo, Untimely Taken (poem) *The Yellow Book* Jan 1897
Triton's Conch, The, *National Observer* 23.12.1893 *
Twenty-first of October, The, *New Review* Vol. 13, no. 77, Oct 1895 (DD)
What They Talked About *National Observer* 16.12.1893 (GA)
White Poppy, The, *National Observer* 5.9.1891 * (PP)
Whitewashed Uncle, A, *National Observer* 25.3.1893 * (PP, GA)
Wind in the Willows, The, London, Methuen, Sept 1908
Young Adam Cupid *National Observer* 20.5.1893 (PP, GA)

Secondary Bibliography

Unless otherwise stated, the books listed were published in London. The editions cited are those used in the preparation of this biography, but, where known, the dates of first publication are given in brackets.

Anstey, F. *Humour and Fantasy* John Murray, 1931
   Vice Versa: A Lesson to Fathers John Murray, 1882
Atkinson, Tom. *The Lonely Lands: A Guidebook to Argyll* Argyll, Luath Press, 1985
Bennett, Alan. *The Wind in the Willows* (play) Faber, 1991
Bennett, Arnold. See Hepburn, James
Blake, William. *Complete Writings* Oxford University Press, Oxford, 1991
Booth, General. *In Darkest England* Salvation Army, 1890
Borrow, George. *Lavengro* Harrap, 1947 (1851)
   The Romany Rye Dent, n/d (1857)
Brontë, Charlotte. *Shirley* Penguin Classics, 1985 (1849)
Browne, Sir Thomas. *Religio Medici* Walter Scott, 1886 (1642)
Carlyle, Thomas. *Sartor Resartus* and *Hero Worship* (one vol.) Dent, 1926 (1834, 1841)
Cambridge Guide to Literature Guild, 1988
Carpenter, Humphrey. *Secret Gardens* Houghton Mifflin, Boston, 1985
Chalmers, Patrick. *Kenneth Grahame: Life, Letters and Unpublished Work* Methuen, 1933
Chambers Biographical Dictionary Edinburgh, 1990
Chesterton, G. K. *Heretics* John Lane, The Bodley Head, 1919 (1905)
Conrad, Joseph. *The Nigger of the Narcissus* and *The Shadow Line* (one vol.) Dent, 1945 (1897, 1917)
   Youth Blackwood, 1922 (1902)
Courtney, Jane. *Recollected in Tranquillity* Heinemann, 1926
Crane, Walter. *The Decorative Illustration of Books* Bracken, 1984 (1896)
Curtis Brown, A. *Contacts* Cassell, 1935
Davies, W. H. *The Autobiography of a Super-Tramp* Cape, 1929 (1908)
Desmond, A. and Moore, J. *Darwin* Michael Joseph, 1991
du Maurier, Daphne. *The Infernal World of Branwell Brontë* Gollancz, 1960
Ellman, Richard. *Oscar Wilde* Hamish Hamilton, 1987
Elwin, Malcolm. *Old Gods Falling* Collins, 1939

Emerson, R. W. *The Conduct of Life and other Essays* Dent, 1908 (1860)
Encyclopaedia Britannica, Fourteenth Edition, 1932 (1768)
Fea, Allan. *Recollections of Sixty Years* Richard Press, 1927
Feiling, Keith. *Sketches in 19th Century Biography* Longman's Green, 1930
Forster, Margaret. *Lady's Maid* Chatto and Windus, 1990
Frazer, Sir James. *The Golden Bough* Abridged edition, Macmillan 1922 (2 vols. 1890, 3 vols. 1900, 12 vols. 1911–15)
Gaskell, Elizabeth. *Life of Charlotte Brontë, The* Penguin Classics, 1985 (1857)
 Mary Barton Penguin Classics, 1985 (1848)
 North and South Penguin Classics, 1985 (1855)
Godwin, William. *Caleb Williams* Penguin Classics, 1988 (1794)
 Enquiry Concerning Political Justice Penguin Classics, 1985 (1793)
Graham, Eleanor. *Kenneth Grahame; A Bodley Head Monograph* Bodley Head, London 1963.
 The Story of The Wind in the Willows: How It Came To Be Written Methuen, 1944
Green, Peter. *Kenneth Grahame* John Murray, 1959
Grossmith, George and Weedon. *The Diary of a Nobody* Bristol, Arrowsmith, 1905 (1892)
Hepburn, James. (ed.) *Letters of Arnold Bennett*, Vol. 4, Oxford University Press, 1986
Hill, R. D. *A History of St. Edward's* St. Edward's School Society, Oxford, 1962
Hilton, Timothy. *The Pre-Raphaelites* Thames & Hudson, 1974 (1970)
Hinds, C. L. *Authors and I* John Lane, 1921
Hope, Anthony. *The Prisoner of Zenda* Arrowsmith, Bristol, 1945 (1894)
Housman, Laurence. *The Unexpected Years* Cape, 1937
Hudson, W. H. *Afoot in England* Hutchinson, 1911 (1909)
 Far Away and Long Ago Dent, 1935 (1918)
Hughes, Thomas. *Tom Brown's Schooldays* Puffin, 1971 (1856)
Jackson, Holbrook. *The Eighteen Nineties* Grant Richards, 1913
Jefferies, Richard. *After London* Cassell, 1885
 Bevis Cape, 1943 (1891)
 The Story of My Heart Staples Press, 1946 (1883)
Kingsley, Charles. *Alton Locke* Walter Scott, New York, n/d (1850)
Lambert, J. W. *The Bodley Head, 1887–1987* Bodley Head, 1987
Lancelyn Green, Roger. *Andrew Lang* Edmund Ward, Leicester, 1946
Lang, Andrew. *Letters to Dead Authors* Longman's, 1886
Le Gallienne, Richard. *Attitudes and Avowals* John Lane, 1910
 The Romantic '90s Robin Clark, 1993 (1925)
Lucas, E. V. (ed.) *The Open Road* Methuen, 1905
Lurie, Alison. *Not In Front of the Grown-ups: Subversive Children's Literature* Bloomsbury, 1990

Marcus Aurelius. *Meditations* (trans. George Long) Collins n/d

Marshall, Peter. *William Blake, Visionary Anarchist* Freedom Press, 1988

May, J. L. *John Lane and the Nineties* John Lane, 1936

Mill, John Stuart. *On Liberty and Utilitarianism* (one vol.) Dent, 1972 (1859, 1861)

Milne, A. A. *Toad of Toad Hall* (play) Methuen, 1929

Moore, George. *A Story-Teller's Holiday* Heinemann, 1928
Esther Waters Dent, 1977 (1894)

Morris, William. *Socialist Diary* Journeyman Press, 1982

Needle, Jan. *Wild Wood* John Murray, 1981

Oxford Companion to English Literature Fourth Edition, Oxford, Clarendon, 1967

Paine, Thomas. *Rights of Man* Penguin Classics, 1985 (1791, 1792, published in two parts)

Pearsall, Ronald. *The Worm in the Bud: A Study of Victorian Sexuality* Penguin, 1969

Pennell, Elizabeth and Joseph. *The Life of James McNeill Whistler* (2 volumes) Heinemann, 1908

Piaget, Jean. *The Language and Thought of the Child* (Trans. Marjorie and Ruth Gabain) Routledge, 1978 (1926)

Quiller-Couch, Arthur. *Charles Dickens and Other Victorians* Cambridge University Press, Cambridge, 1925
On the Art of Reading Cambridge University Press, Cambridge, 1933 (1920)
Oxford Book of English Verse (ed.) Clarendon Press, Oxford, 1942 (1900)
The Poet As Citizen Cambridge University Press, Cambridge, 1934
Studies in Literature Cambridge University Press, Cambridge, 1927

Robertson, Graham. *Letters* Hamish Hamilton, 1953
Time Was Hamish Hamilton, 1931

Rolfe, Frederick (Baron Corvo). *Nicholas Crabbe* Chatto & Windus, 1958

Ruskin, John. *The King of the Golden River* George, Allen and Unwin, 1938, first edition, though this children's story was written in 1841.
The Political Economy of Art Routledge, n/d (1857)
Sesame and Lilies Nelson, n/d (1865)

Russell, Bertrand. *A History of Western Philosophy* George, Allen and Unwin, 1983 (1945)

Sassoon, Siegfried. *Meredith* Constable, 1948

Seymour-Jones, Carole. *Beatrice Webb, Woman of Conflict* Allison and Busby, 1992

Sharp, Evelyn. *The Making of a Schoolgirl* Oxford University Press, Oxford, 1989 (1897)
Unfinished Adventure John Lane, The Bodley Head, 1933

Shelley, Percy Bysshe. *Essays and Letters* Walter Scott, 1866

Smedley, Constance. *Crusaders*, Duckworth, 1929

Smith, Gipsy. *By Himself* Evangelical Free Churches, 1906

St John Adcock, A. *Gods of Modern Grub Street* Sampson Low, Marston, 1905

Stevenson, Robert Louis. *The Art of Writing* Chatto & Windus, 1905 (essays written in the early 1880s)

The Strange Case of Dr Jekyll and Mr Hyde (1886)

Travels with a Donkey in the Cévennes Macmillan, New York, 1929 (1879)

Virginibus Pueresque Chatto, 1912 (1881)

Strachey, Lytton. *Eminent Victorians* Chatto, 1948 (1918)

Strong, L. A. G. *Courtauld-Thomson: A Memoir* privately printed, 1958

Syrett, Netta. *The Sheltering Tree* Geoffrey Bles, 1939

Tawney, R. H. *Religion and the Rise of Capitalism* Penguin, 1990 (1926)

Thackeray, William. *Vanity Fair* Penguin Classics, 1985 (1847–8)

Thoreau, Henry David. *Walden* and *Civil Disobedience* (one vol.) Penguin Classics, 1986 (U.S.A. 1854, 1849)

Tomalin, Claire. *The Invisible Woman* Viking, 1990

Traherne, Thomas. *Centuries of Meditations* Clarendon Press, Oxford, 1960 (1908, though written about 1660)

Trevelyan, G. M. *English Social History* Longman, 1944

Trollope, Anthony. *The Way We Live Now* Oxford University Press, Oxford, 1941 (1874–5)

Watson, J. N. P. *Dorneywood* Robert Hale, 1992

Webb, Beatrice. *My Apprenticeship* Pelican, 1938 (2 vols.) (1926)

Our Partnership Longman, 1948

Webb, Mary. *Gone to Earth* Constable, 1917

White, Kenneth. *The Bird Path* Mainstream, Edinburgh, 1989

Travels in the Drifting Dawn Mainstream, Edinburgh, 1989

Whitman, Walt. *Leaves of Grass* Anthony Treherne, 1904 (1855)

Wilde, Oscar. *De Profundis* Methuen, 1919 (1905)

The Happy Prince Methuen, 1883

Wingfield-Stratford, Esmé. *The Victorian Aftermath* Routledge, 1933

Wollstonecraft, Mary. *Vindication of the Rights of Woman* Penguin Classics, 1985 (1792)

Yeats, W. B. *Autobiographies* Macmillan, 1955

Poems T. Fisher Unwin, 1912

The Yellow Book 13 Vols., quarterly, April 1894–April 1897

Index

377

Busk, Mrs 39, 40
Butler, Samuel 344
By a Northern Furrow 76
Byron, Lord Alfred 5–6, 31

Cage, Jean 117
Calvinism 3, 5, 36, 40, 73, 106, 162, 205, 301
Cambridge Book of Poetry for Children 277, 292
  published 1916, 294
Campbell, Alexander 7
Cannes 341
Capri 321
Carlyle, Thomas 19
Carpenter, Humphrey 37, 338
Carroll, Lewis 209, 220, 345
Catholicism 27–30, 64, 109, 169, 203, 236, 301
Celtic Revival, The 93, 192, 301
Cenci, The 52
Chalmers, Patrick 6, 44–5, 51, 55, 59, 74, 85,
    102, 159, 162, 169, 178, 179, 188, 200,
    211, 213–14, 215, 220, 223, 235, 242, 243,
    246, 265, 266, 276, 299, 310, 311, 323,
    325, 330, 341, 344, 346, 348, 350–3, 355
Chamberlain, Joseph 66–7
Chamberlain, Neville 67
Chamberlain, Thomas 28–30
Chambers, Trant 243–4
Chapbook, Chicago 128
Cheap Knowledge 64, 87
Cheatham, Kitty 275
Chesterton, G. K. 237
Christ Church, Oxford 28, 29, 297, 298, 304–5,
    307, 308, 309, 310, 312
Church Cottage, Pangbourne 326–8, 335, 341
Colburn-Mayne, Ethel 122
Collins, Wilkie 154
Collins, Sir William 187
Condon, Charles 124
Conrad, Joseph 131, 209
Conservatism 62, 65, 79, 80, 96, 158, 191
Contraception 185–7, 220
Conway, Martin 168
Cookham Dene 14, 16, 17, 213–14, 215–16,
    223, 225, 236, 241, 252
Cornhill, The 84
Courtauld, Samuel 198
Courtney, Jane 56
Crackanthorpe, Hubert 122, 123
Crane, Walter 118, 312
Crookston, Miss J. L. G. 319
Curzon, Lord 253

Daily Chronicle 125
Daily Mail 131
Daily Telegraph 354–5
Dall, A. W. 293, 296, 297, 298, 305
d'Arcy, Ella 67, 122–3
Dark Star, A 341–4
Darwin, Charles 128
Dascombe, A. W. 57, 146
Davidson, John 123
Davies, Mr (tenant of Boham's) 312, 315, 320
Deakin, the Hon Alfred 244–5
Departure, A 148–50, 176, 312
Deus Terminus 93, 146
Devey, George 8
Dickens, Charles 20, 65, 67, 154, 168
Dicksee, Sir Frank 135, 138
Dies Irae 67, 130
Dobson, Austin 59–60
Dorneywood 326, 355, 356, 357
Douglas, Lord Alfred 129
Dowson, Ernest 123
Draycott Lodge, Fulham 43, 46, 350
Dream Days 14, 20, 24–5, 143, 148
  published 1898 154, 178, 227, 228, 232, 244,
    254, 256, 294, 335
Dubarry, perfumers 298–9
Dunham, Grace 149
Dunham, Helen 69–70, 71, 133, 134, 149, 313
Durham Villas, no. 16 171, 174, 178, 179, 202,
    205, 207, 209, 213, 220, 223, 227, 279, 287
"Dutchy" (Nanny to Alastair Grahame) 188,
    194–6, 201, 209

Edward VII, King 209, 251
Elgar, Sir Edward 122
Eliot, George 201, 344
Elwin, Malcolm 329, 330
Eternal Whither, The 59
Eton School 50, 181, 198, 287–9, 291–3, 296,
    300, 305, 308
Everybody's 225, 235

Fabian Society 80
Fairbanks, Frank and Charis 314–15
Farjeon, Eleanor 335
Fascism 320–1
Falmouth 220, 221
Fea, Allan 56
Feiling, Anthony 132, 150, 334, 346
Feiling, Caroline 312, 346
Feiling, Joan, *see* Grahame

INDEX

INDEX

INDEX

Rolfe, Frederick ("Baron Corvo") 102–3, 106, 114, 123, 181

Romance of the Rail, The 120

Romance of the Road, The 36, 87, 120, 249

Roman Road, The 111, 275, 313

Rome 53–4, 313–21, 327, 328, 331

Ronsard, Pierre de 139

Roosevelt, Theodore 228–9, 232, 239–40, 253

Rosebery, Lord 247

Rossetti, Dante Gabriel 50, 72

Rostand, Edmund 131, 209

Rothenstein, Will 108, 109

Rugby School 34, 279, 284, 285, 287, 289, 293, 296, 300, 308, 311

Rural Pan, The 90, 100

Ruskin, John 42, 50, 54, 80, 209

Ryan, Marian 335

Saga of the Seas, A 143, 145–6, 175

St Edward's Chronicle 32, 33, 35, 51, 54, 151–2, 243, 276

St Edward's School 25, 26–39, 41, 43, 49, 50, 69, 79, 243, 272, 276, 277, 285, 301, 307, 329, 347

St James's Gazette 76, 77, 78, 84, 101, 119

Saintsbury, George 122

Sanger, "Lord" George 330, 335

Saturday Evening Post 253

Saturday Review of Literature 237

Saturnia Regna 46, 131, 133

Saunders, Farmer 259–60

Savoy, The 116

Sawdust and Sin 111, 125–6, 131, 132

Scotsman 103

Scots Observer 77, 79, 81, 86

Scott, Sir Walter 1, 2, 11, 12, 294, 342, 345

Scribner's Magazine 131, 145, 240

Secret Drawer, The 72

Shakespeare, William 23, 248

Sharp, Evelyn 102, 110, 112–18, 121, 124, 133, 135, 136, 144, 145, 149, 192, 217, 237
marriage to H. W. Nevinson 349

Sharp, William 93

Sharpe, Martin 339

Shaw, George Bernard 79, 80, 131, 209

Sheldonian Theatre 253

Shelley, Percy Bysshe (*see* Keats–Shelley Society) 52, 243

Shepard, E. H. 335–6, 340

Sickert, Walter 108

Siena 323–4

Siepmann, H. A. 181

Simeon, Algernon Barrington 29–30, 244

Simpson, Dr James 4, 78

Simson, Harold Fraser, 336

Smedley, Miss, governess to Grahame children 177, 225, 311

Smedley, Constance 17, 225–7, 230, 231, 234–5, 244, 249, 252, 350–1, 352, 353

Smith, Gregory 119

Socialism 35, 50, 51, 66–7, 79, 80, 190, 213, 233, 247, 321, 324

Socrates 47, 67, 316, 353

Somerville, Margaret Stewart 340

Southey, Robert 305

Spencer, Stanley 14

Spiritualism 206, 354

Squibb, Mrs Mary Ellen 74

Star, The 125

Stevenson, Robert Louis 2, 20, 33, 68, 71, 78, 100–1, 104, 133, 253

Stoicism 26, 36, 42, 64, 69, 96, 106, 291, 301, 302, 339

Stott, Naomi 188, 209–11, 216, 220, 221, 223, 260, 270, 309, 348, 349

Strong, L. A. G. 135–6

Strong, Dr T. B. 307

Sturrock, Dr. W. D. 307

Sully, Professor 125–7, 132, 134

Swinburne, Charles 50, 51, 59, 72, 96, 120, 123, 125, 138, 343

Symons A. J. A. 330

Symons, Arthur 116, 122, 123–4, 352

Syrett, Helen, *see* Thorp

Syrett, Netta 109, 111, 112, 122, 176

T.P.'s Weekly 237

Tawney, R. H. 80

Tenniel, Sir John 136–7, 138, 211

Tennyson, Alfred Lord 23, 50, 136

Terry, Ellen 212

Thomson, Clara, *see* Moulton

Thomson, Courtauld 137, 138, 139, 153, 165, 167, 187, 197–200, 205, 207–9, 213, 227, 284, 291–3, 296, 325, 326, 354, 355, 356, 357

Thomson, Elspeth, *see* Grahame

Thomson, Harold 138, 187, 284, 325, 326

Thomson, Robert William 135, 137, 139, 197

Thomson, Winifred 138, 139, 140, 165, 187, 192–3, 197–8, 208–9, 284, 326, 355, 356

Thoreau, Henry David 257